Interdisciplinary
High School
Teaching

Interdisciplinary High School Teaching

Strategies for Integrated Learning

John H. Clarke

Russell M. Agne
University of Vermont

Foreword by James A. Beane

Allyn and Bacon

Boston   London   Toronto   Sydney   Tokyo   Singapore

Library of Congress Cataloging-in-Publication Data

Interdisciplinary high school teaching : strategies for integrated
    learning / [edited by] John H. Clarke, Russell M. Agne.
        p.   cm.
    Includes bibliographical references and index.
    ISBN 0-205-15710-6
    1. High school teaching—United States.   2. Interdisciplinary
approach in education—United States.   3. Education, Secondary—
United States—Curricula.   I. Clarke, John H., Date–
II. Agne, Russell M.
LB1737.U6158   1997
373.11′02--dc20   96-7009
                                                                   CIP

Printed in the United States of America
10 9 8 7 6 5 4 3   00 99 98

We dedicate this book to our families:
John Clarke to Nancy Cornell, his wife,
and to Cindy, Jesse, and Ethan;
Russell Agne to Susan, his wife,
and to Rob and Jon

CONTENTS

FOREWORD
Perhaps This Time

In the early 1970s several commissions released reports recommending sweeping changes in the U.S. high school. One after another proclaimed that the high school had undergone significant change in the late 1960s and was now ready for deep reform in everything from the compulsory leaving age to longstanding organizational structures to its rigid curriculum. I found this assumption puzzling since the high schools I was in touch with at the time looked very much like those of my own school days and showed little sign of interest in change. So, along with some graduate students, I undertook a series of studies of the high school curriculum including two large-scale surveys of nearly 250 high schools around the country, first in 1974 and then again in 1979 (Beane, 1975; Tubbs & Beane, 1981).

The principals who responded to those surveys reported, among other things, that almost 99% of their schools were organized exclusively around a separate subject approach and vertical departmentalization and, conversely, that almost no interdisciplinary arrangements were used. Moreover, nearly 90% reported exclusive use of Carnegie scheduling and other features of the standardized high school structure. Given such data, where could the reform panels possibly have gotten the idea that high schools stood teetering on the brink of sweeping change?

Dismayed by the results of the surveys, I also wrote several papers calling for change in the high school curriculum (e.g., Beane, 1977, 1980). The emphasis for at least part of the overall program, I demanded, should be on addressing the self-concerns of adolescents and large social issues through an integrated approach, with knowledge organized in the context of those concerns and problems rather than into separate subjects. And, I suggested that the problems and issues that organized the curriculum should be identified cooperatively by teachers *and* students who would be organized in heterogeneous groups. This, I proclaimed would promote democracy, honor "pluralism," and respect student dignity. I am not kidding about this—it really happened.

Alas, however, I must confess that the reaction was deafening silence. As for how the recommendations of the reform commissions fared, about the only changes made in the high school curriculum were, as we all know by now, more specialization and fragmentation than before. In honor of our studies of the high school curriculum, one graduate student presented me with a copy of the *Golden Book of Dinosaurs*. The metaphor was obvious. What could I possibly have been thinking of?

I relate this small anecdote not as a matter of waxing nostalgic or to whine about good ideas ignored, but rather to raise an important question. It is this: Why, when the high school has historically been so resistant to change, so thoroughly intransigent, would we believe that it would now, in this time, be open to the possibility of interdisciplinary and integrated curriculum arrangements?

Currents of Hope

It is true that we are living in the midst of a great Conservative Restoration when progressive curriculum ideas are under attack (Apple, 1993). The demands of conservative critics and the drive for national standards and tests, both clearly drawn along separate subject lines, would seem to preclude any attempts at interdisciplinary and integrated curriculum approaches. Without underestimating the strength of these movements for a moment, I also believe that they are not necessarily the contemporary currents that will most powerfully influence the shape of the high school curriculum. Think about what else is going on in the midst of the loud politics of the conservative restoration.

As we close out the twentieth century, important new ways of thinking about knowledge are taking hold. The perennialist notion of fixed truth, independent of time and place, is collapsing under the scrutiny of poststructural and postmodern theories of multiple meanings dependent on context and historical conditions. Put simply, the theory of knowledge undergirding the separate subject, discipline-centered organization of the curriculum is in serious trouble. And it is being replaced almost everywhere other than in the schools with organizations and uses of knowledge that are more fluid, dynamic, and flexible. Think for a moment about the impact of quantum physics on our understanding of the world. Think about the emergence of fields like biomechanics and biophysics. Think about the mix of participants in almost any large-scale project these days.

One of the great ironies of this shift in the understandings of knowledge is that while high schools seek desperately to look like universities, their continuing allegiance to a strict separate subject curriculum organization makes them less and less like universities. The interdisciplinary and integrated fields just mentioned did not come from some supernatural force; they are the result of collaborative efforts among scholars. This is why college majors, such as environmental studies and integrated liberal studies, are appearing with increasing frequency (Klein, 1993). Meanwhile, as I write this, several state-level projects are underway to create college admissions procedures that will be available to graduates of high schools that engage students in interdisciplinary and integrated approaches.

But new ways of thinking about knowledge and its organization are not the only relevant developments we should pay attention to. The separate subject approach has always depended on the idea that the best knowledge is available to young people through the resources provided by the school—teachers, textbooks, and so on. The subsequent role of "knowledge disseminator" insulated both teachers and texts from demands for change. Today, new technology makes available to almost anyone knowledge that is broader, deeper, and more up-to-date than that which any one high school faculty or library could possess. And it is often accompanied by visual and other aids that make it more understandable, more accessible, and more easily reorganized by issues or problems of interest.

This new technology does two things. First, it opens to question the claim of the school as knowledge disseminator and the excuses for intransigence that go with that claim. Second, it begins to solve the historical problem of access to information that has plagued many teachers who have tried to use interdisciplinary and integrated approaches only to find that few if any resources are available in any form other than separate subjects.

I would claim that taken together, these developments and others like them are more likely to affect the substance and organization of the high school curriculum than the Conservative Restoration. I am not saying that the latter is insignificant— indeed, it is incredibly powerful—or that advocates of a strict separate subject, discipline-centered approach will not persist. Rather I believe that the developments I named open the door for advocates of interdisciplinary and integrated approaches to make a stronger case than they ever have and to sustain their work beyond the stage of novelty.

My claim is at least partially supported by the fact that there is a growing movement in this direction and that it is stronger for its contemporary context. The fact is that Sizer's Coalition of Essential Schools, regardless of some criticism, has made many high school educators take notice of the need for change and has affirmed those who have been pointing to that need for a long time. Moreover, more and more high schools, partly supported by middle school efforts, have organized interdisciplinary teams (although such teaming does not guarantee interdisciplinary or integrated teaching). More and more high school teachers are showing up at conferences on curriculum integration. And, educators in the midwest have organized a network for those interested in interdisciplinary and integrated curriculum in high schools. Why are these organizational efforts more likely to succeed than similar ones in the past? The answer is partly this: airplanes, telephones, fax machines, and e-mail. Teachers who use those approaches no longer need to feel that they are alone.

Even as these possibilities develop, though, it is important that those who use and advocate interdisciplinary and integrated approaches pay attention to their roots. This begins by acknowledging that the present projects are part of a long stream of work stretching back over most of this century. Indeed there is a great deal to be learned from work on the Project Approach in the 1920s, from the interdisciplinary and integrated arrangements of the high schools in the Eight Year Study of the 1930s and 1940s, from the problem-centered core curriculum of the 1940s and 1950s, and, yes, even from some of the bold experiments of the 1960s—a time when some current advocates began their teaching careers.

There is also a rich literature over these decades reporting fascinating classroom and school accounts of progressive curriculum work and the theoretical frameworks with which they were related. Among those that are especially instructive for high school consideration are Aiken's *The Story of the Eight Year Study* (1941), Hopkins's *Interaction: The Democratic Process* (1941), Lurry and Alberty's *Developing a High School Core Program* (1957), Zapf's *Democratic Processes in the Secondary Classroom* (1959), Leonard's *Developing the Secondary School Curriculum* (1960), and Alberty and Alberty's *Reorganizing the High School Curriculum* (1962). Those who consult these sources will find responses to most of the questions being raised today about interdisciplinary and integrated curriculum approaches as well as a sense of historical context.

And Now This Work

Now, with the publication of Clarke and Agne's *Interdisciplinary High School Teaching: Strategies for Integrated Learning,* we have a book in our own times to add to the decades' long list of references on high school curriculum beyond the separate subject approach. Large in its scope, this volume offers us several important things. First, for those who are seeking some reasons to undertake interdisciplinary and integrated work, the authors offer many openings to walk through including the disadvantages of compartmentalizing knowledge, the advantages of project learning, research on thinking and learning, the need to take on serious issues and problems, and more. Although I do not believe that when fully analyzed all of the support sources named are necessarily supportive of interdisciplinary and integrated curriculum, it is important to see how some aspects of even the most problematic still suggest the need for this kind of work.

Another important aspect of this book is the tour it takes us on of current events in the high school curriculum. So much attention has been paid to developments at the elementary and middle school levels as well as the high rhetoric of curriculum traditionalists and national standards advocates, that one could miss the fact that creative and progressive teaching persists, albeit without much publicity, in many high schools. In this sense, the book brings us up-to-speed and sets the stage for what will hopefully be a new momentum.

Perhaps most important, the authors have gathered here a wonderful collection of interdisciplinary and integrated curriculum examples written by teachers from a variety of schools. It is here that the case for optimism is made. I am not so naive as to think that these stories represent a rampant movement among the overwhelming majority of high schools, but I do believe they serve as an organized set that illustrate the arguments I made before regarding new views of knowledge, emerging networks of progressive educators, helpful uses of information technology, the growing understanding that individual disciplines are not sufficient to approach significant issues, and the expanding recognition of the advantages of project-centered work. One other thing these stories do is to remind us that interdisciplinary and integrated approaches offer more engaging *and* challenging content and processes than the separate subject approach.

Finally, the book gives us an opportunity to raise several questions regarding interdisciplinary and integrated curriculum in high schools. For example, what portion of the overall program will be organized this way? What portion of the content now taught in high schools is likely to surface in these designs? Are some organizing centers—problems, issues, topics, concerns—preferable to others? In what ways will students be involved in the selection of organizing centers and other aspects of curriculum development? How do locally created projects make use of external curriculum content mandates? As we begin to hear such questions more frequently, we will know that interdisciplinary and integrated approaches are taking hold.

But, as Clarke and Agne are careful to point out, this is not easy work and no one should think otherwise. Teachers who undertake this work almost always face difficulties in putting together nonseparate subject resources, criticisms from colleagues who are reluctant to take on the work or the visibility of interdisciplinary and integrated programs, parents whose fears for their children are fed by conservative critics in the media and politics, and the chilling movement for national tests and curriculum drawn along strict separate subject lines.

Given these caveats and problems, why would any high school teacher want to take on the design and use of interdisciplinary and integrated approaches? A strong answer lies in the pages of this book—the arguments of the main authors and the stories told by teachers of their work. Here are cases of more learning, of knowledge made more accessible, of young people constructing meanings and generating their own ideas, of active engagement in real-life issues, of contributions to community life and well-being. And frequently lurking in the background, if not named explicitly, is the idea of helping young people to learn the instrumental uses of knowledge that are the intellectual aspect of the democratic way of life.

Interdisciplinary High School Teaching, then, is not only about what interdisciplinary and integrated curriculum arrangements might look like in the high school but also about why they ought to be there. This is a curriculum of greater significance, of more likely engagement, of more powerful value than the strict separate subject curriculum that has held a stranglehold on the high schools for too long. We are lucky to have this book. We will be lucky if there are more like it to follow.

James A. Beane
National College of Education
National-Louis University

References

Aiken, Wilford J. (1941). *The story of the Eight Year Study.* New York: Harper & Brothers.
Alberty, Harold B. and Alberty, Elsie J. (1962). *Reorganizing the high school curriculum,* 3d ed. New York: Macmillan.
Apple, Michael W. (1993). *Official knowledge: Democratic education in a conservative age.* New York: Routledge.
Beane, James A. (1975). Curriculum trends and practices in high schools. *Educational Leadership, 33*(2):129–133.

Beane, James A. (1977). The high school: Time for reform. *Educational Leadership, 35*(2):128–133.

Beane, James A. (1980). The general education we need. *Educational Leadership, 37*(4):307–308.

Hopkins, L. Thomas. (1941). *Interaction: The democratic process.* Boston: D. C. Heath.

Klein, Julie. (1993). *Interdisciplinarity: History, theory, and practice.* Detroit, MI: Wayne State University Press.

Leonard, J. Paul. (1960). *Developing the secondary school curriculum,* rev. ed. New York: Holt, Rinehart, & Winston.

Lurry, Lucille L. and Alberty, Elsie J. (1957). *Developing a high school core program.* New York: Macmillan.

Tubbs, Mary P. and Beane, James A. (1981). Curricular trends and practices in high schools: A second look. *The High School Journal, 65*(5):103–208.

Zapf, Rosalind M. (1959). *Democratic processes in the secondary school.* Englewood Cliffs, NJ: Prentice-Hall.

PREFACE

In a culture dazzled by the speed of change, the high school remains one institution noted for stability. Empires may rise and fall, body organs may prove absolutely interchangeable, and an electronic network may slowly gather us all into one organic system, but the high school experience persists—classes, passing periods, lunch, and school-sponsored activities—a standing monument to predictable order. When new ways of teaching emerged, they were often dismissed as fads and left to wither. Some deserved that fate; others have lingered quietly in the background, adapting to their circumstances and growing more elaborate with research and extended practice.

For many years, the durable structure of high school education has sheltered pockets of innovation—small, experimental programs in which students and teachers develop new ways to learn in an increasingly challenging environment. We believe we can see the shape of an emerging high school curriculum in the current practice of creative teachers who have responded to the challenge of making education work in a changing culture. This book is a collection of their efforts, organized to illustrate some basic strategies for linking learning to life. To the extent that new strategies for teaching high school are proving powerful, they also represent avenues for further development.

We believe that a shift that has begun in high school teaching will gradually replace a subject-based curriculum with a curriculum organized around questions students recognize as important. The emerging high school curriculum emphasizes making connections between bits of knowledge and skills from different realms, organized around focusing questions students can ask and answer in their own way:

- How does a civilization come into being?
- What does it take to solve a major environmental problem?
- What do I need to know to thrive in a technological society?

Good answers to questions like these require students to connect facts and ideas from different disciplines, to explore the expanse of their intelligence, and to apply abstract ideas to real problems in real situations. The shared aim of recent innovations in high school teaching is to help students learn to manage the process of their own lives, and to continue learning until the world stops changing—to learn forever, in other words.

The subject-based curriculum that aimed for content acquisition is slowly giving way to a process-based curriculum that emphasizes information management and problem solving in the real world. The emerging high school:

1. Aims to empower students to learn and use what they learn to manage their minds and direct their lives.
2. Supports students as they survey and practice adult roles in the community.
3. Engages students in understanding how their world works so they can exert influence over their quality of life in that world.

In the emerging high school curriculum, the student is learning to become an information worker. The teacher is becoming a guide and mentor. Contracts, portfolios, flexible schedules, and learning and teaching teams are transforming the eight-period day into a fluid and far-ranging quest for answers to questions that matter. All these ideas imply active and purposeful learning. Active and purposeful learning requires a different structure from the one we have relied on for the past hundred years. Adapting to small innovations is leading us toward a major transformation in the high school as a place of learning.

Integration is the key idea linking all the ideas in this book. Integrated learning requires an integration of the mechanisms teachers have worked so hard to separate to create a stable system. Conventionally, we have separated teaching from testing. The current reform aims to integrate learning performances with appropriate measures of achievement. Conventionally, we have separated school from adult responsibility in the community and the world. The current effort aims to link learning to adult work and service, posing the questions all young people need to ask and answer as they take their place as responsible citizens. Conventionally, we have separated each discipline from all others, hoping to focus learning on purified versions of subject-based knowledge. The current reform reaches across the disciplines, aiming to connect facts and ideas that students can use to solve real-world problems. *Integration* is the principle that brings some order to the proliferation of new ideas in high school teaching, curriculum design, and assessment.

If there were no connection among the innovative teaching strategies that are being developed separately in different high schools, we would not assert so boldly that high schools have begun a general process of transformation. High school teachers are transforming their profession in three basic ways:

1. *Making Connections:* They are connecting subject-area knowledge from the disciplines to persistent themes, trends, ideas, or questions in the human experience.
2. *Focusing on Processes:* They are shifting attention from discrete subject-area knowledge toward the processes that make the content meaningful or useful.
3. *Solving Problems:* They are showing students how to put knowledge to work in a world where our survival and theirs hangs in the balance.

In each part of this book, three chapters describe specific ways to integrate high school teaching. Each chapter includes illustrations from high school classrooms and a "Curriculum Showcase" that describes one approach in detail. We have represented these three strategies as a cycle because we have noticed that teachers who succeed with one kind of innovation quickly move on to experiment with other strategies that promise to extend their successes (see Figure P.1). As the cycle suggests, teachers are discovering how to use information from content areas to teach processes of information management that are useful in solving real-world problems. Scattered innovations are beginning to assume a shape that fits their shared purpose.

Our experience with the teachers who created the illustrations, however, suggests that these approaches are rarely found isolated from each other. Once integration has begun, change appears to generate its own momentum. For the sake of convenience, we describe the ten approaches to integration separately, even though they are not separate in the "natural state" of high school teaching. We hope the organization of chapters into three parts will provoke teachers to use one experiment as the basis for another, beginning a cycle of transformation that we see as essentially creative. Despite our specialties, we are all one profession, dedicated to helping young people learn to control the work of their minds and thereby gain some greater control over the world in which they live. In the continuing cycle on renewal, we should draw on each other, fashioning from the best examples of "what works" to a general approach to teaching that adapts steadily to the changing context of our world.

There are examples in each chapter from teachers who still differ widely in motive and method. Differences in purpose and process are essential to continued experimentation. Despite major differences in orientation, the teachers whose work is represented here all share one attribute, a passion for a vision of learning more humane and more empowering than the kind of education we associate with the standard high school. It is the passion for progress among the teachers who fill these pages with

FIGURE P.1   Overview of Integrated Learning

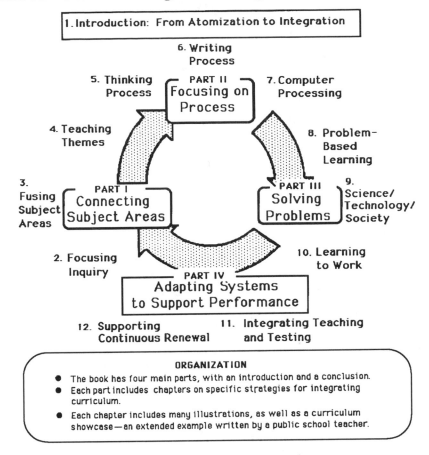

their work, rather than for a single new model, that we find inspiring. We wish we could have found all the innovations and all the teachers attempting to make changes, but we are satisfied with the hope that this book might help bring them to the forefront where they can share what they have learned.

ACKNOWLEDGMENTS

To compile the examples of fine teaching that fill this book, we traced our way into regional networks of teachers and administrators who are experimenting with new ways to engage high school students in learning. With faith that good teaching would find local recognition and leave clear traces, we read widely, looking for names and ideas. We used the telephone much of the time, but also found our way to conferences and schools at every opportunity. Wherever we went and whomever we called, we found understanding, support, and gracious hospitality. We did not find all the great teachers, not by any means. We are convinced they are everywhere. We found enough examples to illustrate the ten basic integrating strategies in this book, then stopped looking, persuaded that pursuing contacts through the network of fine high school teachers and administrators could consume a lifetime.

Although we wish it were possible to recognize all great high school teachers, we can only hope that they find their reflections among these illustrations and make contact with each other. We want to acknowledge here those who helped us gather information and understand its importance.

Chris Stevenson, our good colleague in the middle school movement, kept his eyes open for great projects at the high school level and kept a steady stream of good leads coming our way. Dennis Littke gave us encouragement and hospitality, opening his fine school to our curious questions. Bill Stepien welcomed us to the Illinois Mathematics and Science Academy and was good enough to read initial drafts and to guide us toward examples of problem-based learning. Joyce Conkling, Staff Assistant at Harvard's Project Zero, fed us readings and many leads. Jay McTighe led us into the network of assessment projects, starting in Maryland and extending widely. Kim Cannon at the Foxfire Foundation in Rabun Gap, Georgia, guided us toward writing-based projects throughout the country.

Grant Wiggins asked us to look again for assessment ideas among the schools in the Coalition for Essential Schools. We found much more than assessment. Ted McEnroe at Coalition for Essential Schools in Providence, Rhode Island, helped us find great teachers doing great projects. Reeve Love at the Hispanic Culture Foundation in Albuquerque, New Mexico, led us toward a network of teachers working on linking local events to Hispanic history. Emily Robin and Mae Miller at the Center for Collaborative Education in the Bronx, New York, helped us understand graduation by portfolio and shared the *Motion Curriculum* from International High School and LaGuardia Community College.

Leslie Colis gave us early connection to the movement in work-based learning. Julie Ayers at the Maryland Student Service Alliance gave us information and access to remarkable projects in the area of service learning in Maryland. Rick Larson at REAL Enterprises in Chapel Hill, North Carolina, helped us find examples of entrepreneurial teaching in Washington State. In Boston and Cambridge, Barbara Roche and Doug Zimmerman at Jobs for the Future gave us a lot of materials and access to the conferees at the Institute on Work-Based Learning plus other written materials on the Work/Learning Connection. Trudy Volk at Southern Illinois University, Carbondale, Illinois, used her understanding of the National Diffusion Network to help us find examples of fine Science/Technology/Society units.

Clearly, our schools in Vermont, where we have worked with teachers for many years, provided many useful illustrations and ideas. Casey Murrow in Brattleboro,

Nancy Cornell at Otter Valley High School in Brandon, Jan Willey and Peter Ryersbach at Middlebury High School in Middlebury, Amy Mellancamp at Mt. Abraham High School in Bristol, Jim Warnock at Burlington Votec Center in Burlington, Martha Ozturk at Champlain Valley Union High School in Hinesburg, and the whole faculty at the Cabot School in Cabot, provided counsel and access to their work. We owe particular thanks to Marge Sable, David Book, Darlene Johns, and Helen Morrison at the Cabot School for giving us a vision of a school in transformation.

The Essex Junction Educational Center, where one of us helps manage a Professional Development School, provided us with a steady stream of examples. Brian Nelligan, Nancy Smith, Carol Lacy, Mike Hornus, Brian Walsh, Kevin Martell, Carol Willey, Jane Goodman, Steve Dowd, and Marilee Taft have included part of their work in this book. Steve Sanborn, Director of Curriculum for Chittenden Central Supervisory Union, has read several chapters, offered comments, and provided ongoing support. Colchester High School, where another of us has a long association, showed us the proliferation of inquiry-based projects at their school.

Sue Hutchinson at Allyn and Bacon got us very helpful reviews of early chapters. Thanks to Frances Kochan and Jay McTighe at the Maryland Department of Higher Education, and Dennis Littke, Principal of the Thayer Junior-Senior High School in Winchester, New Hampshire, for carefully reading and reviewing our first drafts and helping to encourage us on our way. In addition, David Eckhard, Heather Garson, and Armando Vilaseca read and helped us refine several chapters.

If we had pursued each lead to its ending point, we would have made contact with thousands of teachers within a short period of time. Because we were looking for good examples—and good examples were everywhere to be found—we foreshortened our search as soon as we had something great in hand, and missed meeting many people who should have a place in this book.

CHAPTER *1*

Introduction

From Atomization to Integration

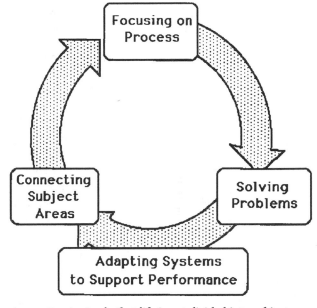

The master argument for curricular integration is simply that life is not divided into subjects.
James Moffett (1992, p. 83)

Focus on Learning

Integrated teaching is a movement in secondary schools that lets questioning and problem solving, rather than the structure of the academic disciplines, direct the process of acquiring knowledge and skills. Integrated teaching empowers students to use knowledge and techniques derived from the academic disciplines to devise answers for themselves. Integrated teaching forces students to learn enough to answer the questions they recognize as important in their daily lives, questions that defy easy answers.

- What does it mean to be free?
- How did democracy come into being?
- What are the costs and benefits of supermalls?
- How should we manage health care, gene splicing, transportation, housing, energy production and conservation, religious differences, racial strife, and world starvation?

Integrated teaching promises to be more compelling than subject-based teaching because it is infused with the challenge of meaningful questions, inviting all students to create sensible, workable answers based on their own assessment of the facts and alternative ideas. Each of the subject areas or disciplines can provide knowledge and methods relevant to essential questions, but integrated teaching shifts the focus of high school instruction from the discrete subject areas toward issues in the world outside the classroom, where complex issues demand carefully constructed response.

The basic secondary curriculum has retained the same general structure for a hundred years, gathering bulk and losing coherence as each generation adds to the existing store of aggregated wisdom and essential skills. The high school curriculum currently consists of a proliferation of teachable "pieces" that have obscured the larger purpose from which they were derived. We can add no more, not without sacrifice. High school learning becomes meaningless when separated from contexts where it really makes a difference to know something—and know how to use what one knows to solve complex problems. Conventional curriculum design has atomized learning, reducing general goals to specific outcomes that prove susceptible to reliable testing. Integrated teaching puts knowledge and skills to work in the world high school students are preparing to enter.

Sue Berryman (1993) points out that traditional high school teaching does not prepare students to work in a world that demands the flexible application of knowledge to problems that constantly evolve toward greater complexity. Traditional classroom teaching treats students as passive vessels to be filled, and knowledge as a quantity to be poured. It also rewards "responses" that correspond precisely to a given "stimulus." High school learning has tended to be "right answer learning," acquired in preparation for tests rather than in responding to an actual challenge—a question or problem for which no set answer exists. To be useful in life, knowledge should be acquired in the context of a meaningful challenge that students recognize as familiar in their own experience. "What do I need to know to understand and solve this problem?" Answering this kind of question usually requires the flexible application of higher-level thinking and the willingness to refine answers with new questions.

The movement toward integration is promising because it aims to multiply the effects of high school study by focusing on a relatively few important questions, then subtracting elements of the established curriculum that do not appear to help students get reliable answers. As Sizer (1992, p. 109) argues,

> the process of creating a simpler program—the politics of subtraction—can restore a necessary set of priorities for the resources of schools, focusing on that which is the most important function of schooling, the development of intellectual habits, even as legitimate student interests and diversity are respected.

Integrated teaching requires us to emphasize the habit of asking important questions and searching for workable answers.

Learning as Knowledge Construction

Integrated learning is based on a constructivist view of how we assemble knowledge of ourselves and the world that lets us manage both our minds and our world effectively. From a constructivist perspective, the bits of knowledge that make up high school courses can be learned only to the extent that they extend what the learner already knows and provide a platform for further elaboration. With its roots in Piagetian psychology, a *constructivist* approach to teaching emphasizes that learners need to be actively involved, to reflect on their learning, and to experience cognitive conflict as they struggle to reconcile alternative perspectives. Fosnot (1989, pp. 19–20) lists the following four principles to define constructivism:

1) Knowledge consists of past constructions (i.e., we can only know something through our existing logical framework, which transforms, organizes, and interprets our perceptions).

2) Constructions come about through assimilation and accommodation—our attempts to integrate new information with what we already understand.

3) Learning is an organic process of invention rather than a mechanical process of accumulation; we create a coherent worldview from disjunctive pieces.

4) Meaningful learning occurs through reflection and resolution of cognitive conflict and thus serves to negate earlier, incomplete levels of understanding.

What are the implications for such a psychological framework when we employ it to analyze the conventional high school curriculum? Fosnot (1989, p. 20) offers this explanation:

> A constructivist takes the position that the learner must have experiences with hypothesizing and predicting, manipulating objects, posing questions, researching answers, imagining, investigating, and invention in order for new constructions to be developed. From this perspective, the teacher cannot ensure that learners acquire knowledge just by having the teacher dispense it; a learner-centered, active instructional model is mandated. The learner must construct the knowledge; the teacher serves as a creative mediator in the process.

In a constructivist classroom, students spend the greatest amount of time making explicit what they already know, working with others to make new knowledge fit an expanding sense of how things work, and projecting their new conceptions into the world around them where those conceptions are tested against new experience.

As Figure 1.1 suggests, the process of constructing knowledge is a circular process (Clarke & Biddle, 1993). We begin learning with what we already know. Our prior knowledge creates an expectation for how things will work, but it also provokes questions about how to make things work better—how things should be. We act largely on the basis of our expectation. Prior knowledge and all our expectations collide with experience—life in the streets as well as all the information we encounter in school learning. When some of that experience fits what we expect, we assimilate it, fusing it with similar kinds of experience. When other parts of experience do not fit what we expect, however, we have to accommodate what we know to make it fit. As we resolve the differences between expectation and actuality, we reconstruct our "mental models" to explain larger swaths of experience. From a constructivist perspective, effective learning is a process of gradual elaboration in which we expand our mental models to fit increasingly complex and inconsistent experience (Brooks & Brooks, 1993).

Reconstruction of prior knowledge, however, does not occur automatically as a result of experience. As every high school teacher knows, students may be just as

FIGURE 1.1   A Constructivist View of Learning

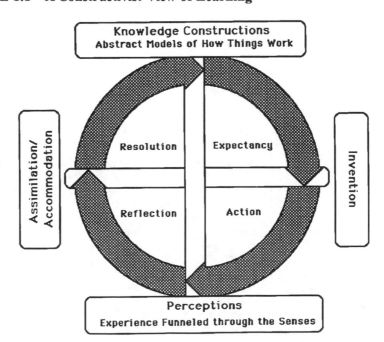

happy without struggling to reconcile new information with their existing knowledge. Teachers have to act intentionally to engage the learning process. They have to develop curriculum and teach in ways that activate the cycle. Each chapter in this book represents a variation on the constructivist view of learning and explains techniques teachers have developed to keep the wheel turning. We have organized the chapters into sections—connecting subject areas, focusing on process, and solving problems—to show how many ways there are to help students better manage aspects of knowledge construction. Focusing on knowledge construction, instead of knowledge structures represented by the academic disciplines, has led us to integrated learning as a way to improve the effectiveness of high school learning.

Crossing the Boundaries of the Disciplines

The questions students ask in integrated learning quickly escape the neat confines we have arranged to manage academic subject areas (see Figure 1.2). Integration forces us to leave the comfort of a known body of knowledge acquired through familiar procedures to take on issues that are far less predictable. We did not develop a subject-based curriculum by mistake or through ill-intention. We devised the subject-based curriculum by analyzing what is known to discover more about the unknown. An intellectual process with indisputable academic credentials, *analysis* is the process of breaking things down into small parts so the relations of those parts to the whole can be better understood. Analysis is the one central skill in all the subject areas. Literary analysis, scientific analysis, historical analysis, mathematical analysis—all are central both to discovery and to education. Analysis is central even to creative fields such as art, where analysis of different media may reveal new avenues

FIGURE 1.2   Comparison of Subject-Based and Integrated Instruction

	Subject-Based Teaching	Integrated Teaching
Purpose: Acquisition vs. Application	**Acquiring Knowledge**—To expose students to established knowledge in the subject areas and prepare them for further subject-based learning.	**Applying Knowledge**—To help students fulfill a mission, help ideas and techniques from the subject areas and from other sources.
Process: Passive. vs. Active	**Memorization**—Passive accumulation of facts, concepts, rules, and theories, conveyed in symbolic form—letters, numbers.	**Higher-Order Skills**—Learning process organized around questions, themes, or problems.
Organization: Focus on subject vs. Focus on learning	**Analysis of Subjects**—Parts to whole, first step to last, simple to complex procedures, based on integrity of the subject area.	**Analysis of Learning**—Instruction organized around steps in inquiry, aspects of a theme, or phases of problem solving.
Schedule: Time-based vs. Task-based	**Built-to-Cover**—Parts arranged in logical order until the whole subject is covered.	**Built-to-Produce**—Steps of learning arranged to produce a product.
Outcomes: Qualities vs. Quantities	**Test Scores**—Tests of knowledge acquisition and skills application, referenced to norms for a large group.	**Production**—Product of learning judged on its utility, ingenuity, coherence, and completeness.

for expression, and design, where analysis of needs begins the process of planning. Analysis is central to student learning as well, but as the guiding force for high school learning, it guarantees hopeless diffusion in the curriculum and frustration among students and teachers alike.

In the spirit of the parable in Figure 1.3, let us imagine for a moment that *theology,* the study of God's Word and Works, was the first discipline in medieval cathedral schools during the eleventh-century (Baldwin, 1971). "What's true?" the scholars asked, as they are wont to do. They looked to the Bible and other ancient works. By analysis, they discovered that grammar, rhetoric, and logic *(The Trivium)* may hold the key to the truth of God's Word and that arithmetic, astronomy, geometry, and music *(The Quadrivium)* give them insight into God's Works. As they stared at the skies or at the written page, they soon discovered that these new vehicles for truth themselves prove susceptible to analysis. By analyzing God's Word, they inadvertently invent the "humanities." By analyzing God's Works, they invent the sciences. Soon they and their students are analyzing language rather than scripture, music rather

FIGURE 1.3   Two Sisters: A Parable

In the early days, two sisters made ready to inherit the realm. The first, named True, stood perfect in symmetry, graceful beyond dreaming. The second, named Works, stood great both in strength and in courage. If True feigned helpless in matters of state, she yet won favor in the form of her discourse. If Works hung back, hulking readiness by hearth pit, she yet proved willing against all distress. When time came to divide the domain, True spoke fair and won first choice.

"I'll take schools and all students, thereof," pallid True affirmed. And so it passed. "What would you prefer?" she asked her stout sister.

Works thought long and said, "I'll take all else, perchance." And so it passed.

True lay out her desks in neat rows and let in the children. Works looked out the window and wrung her fingers, then passed into the fetid streets.

Beauty is fecund, ywis, and True bore children. She begat triplets—Grammar, Rhetoric & Logic. She then bore quadruplets, Arithmetic, Astronomy, Geometry and Music. All seven stood perfect in symmetry, all beautiful to behold. And True brought forth as many languages as peoples of the earth. Then Physics, Calculus, Algebra I and Algebra II, and many more came forth in the same cast. To each at birth, True awarded full classrooms. Each received from Proud True a classroom full to o'ertaxing.

In the meantime, Works toiled the streets. Four horsemen brought scourge—she failed. The scurilous palace guard rebelled—she fell. The masses huddled in misery—she folded. Resolute, Works rose again and faltered not, indefatigable.

In her time Works bore children, too, Charity, Honor and Obedience, and other virtues in their turn. They and their many children joined Works in the almshouse, the jailhouse and the charnal house.

And then the morning sun from Work's poor dooryard framed the sudden form of Sister True, weeping in pathos. "Come in," implored Sister Works. How fare you and all your family?"

"A pox called boredom afflicts the realm, I fear!" wailed Sister True. "My students lie o'ercome in lassitude, lax with lethargy, tending not their figures, rhymes, script—nor any basic competency, withal."

"We know not boredom here, dear Sister. "Look out this window!"

"True looked out upon the streets. Not boredom but human pain assailed her sight.

"How can this be?" asked Sister True, aghast.

"Perhaps you will help?" Sister Works implored. And that is how it all began. Works joined True in the classroom. True joined Works in the street. As one family again, they found, if not joy, high purpose.

than harmony, and earth rather than heaven. As God divided light from dark and ocean from land, scholarly analysis divides subject from subject. The disciplines have been dividing and knowledge has been exploding in each field ever since.

Let the begats begin! In the fertile crucible of analysis, how long does it take astronomy to beget physics or alchemy to breed chemistry? How long before biology springs from the study of Genesis? Does history spring from the study of Corinthians? Greek and Latin breed Spanish, English, French, German, and Russian. History shall beget in its time anthropology, archaeology, economics, sociology, psychology (with biology), and political science. Physics and geometry shall bring forth astrophysics and small particle physics, plasma physics, and cosmology—and the fields shall multiply. Particle physics meets cosmic physics; string theory is born: quarks, leptons, neutrinos in all their colors, with all their charms.

Each discipline adds to its own store of knowledge; each brings forth new fields of study. The factual base of each discipline may expand at a fairly regular pace, but the paradigms through which we view those facts shift inexorably. As we understand the universe differently, facts that once seemed central become secondary or irrelevant (Kuhn, 1970). In a high school curriculum students face not only an expanding universe of purported facts, but a constantly changing set of "isms" (Darwinism, Marxism, Post-deconstructionism) that bring different kinds of meaning to the facts. Which of these boisterous progenitors and progeny have we managed to evict from high school? Only theology, mother of them all. There may be nothing new under the sun, but in the modern high school, there is neither time nor season long enough to cover the constantly expanding universe of what is being known.

As the curriculum has grown by multiplication in all subject areas, we have resorted to division as a way to manage the school day. Eight periods of study, 35 to 40 minutes in length, divide the day into discrete bits, each with its own content, language, and expectations for learners. During three-minute passing periods, high school students cross borders dividing warring realms—math, English, social studies, physical education, chorus—staying long enough to observe the rituals but not long enough to absorb (or to challenge) the experience. Inadvertently, we have trained students to be experts in transportation but not in travel. They ask, "When do I have to be there?" They watch the clock, asking, "When do I get to leave?" By the time they reach high school, they can fly most of the route on autopilot, asking few questions and making little effort to adjust what they know. What are they learning along the way? National test scores trends do not provide encouraging answers to this question.

Analysis of subject areas as a way to define the high school curriculum is surely a self-limiting exercise. As most high school teachers recognize, no more room remains in the schoolday for additional subjects and no gain seems possible by further dividing the schedule into smaller and smaller pieces. Yet we try to wedge it all in. Sometimes we are stopped by World War I. Sometimes we make it through World War II. Sometimes we read *Hamlet*; sometimes we just see the movie. Some of us pass through graph theory on our way to trigonometry; some get stopped by polynomials. Some leave high school fluent in French; others leave with only three years of English grammar. By focusing high school teaching on quantities of knowledge rather than on qualities of intellectual work, we have guaranteed failure for ourselves and a large proportion of our students.

In a subject-based curriculum, predetermined right answers align themselves nicely with a series of formalized questions. Through long exposure to discipline-based knowledge, students come to see each subject area as a huge system of immutable answers. Six (or five or two) causes of the French revolution? "A" squared plus "B" squared equals "C" squared. "Man versus nature" is the theme of *Moby Dick*. Integrated teaching focuses on questions with many answers, all of them as uncertain as the world that forces them to surface. Integrated teaching shows students how to gather information that will help them solve problems in the world at large. Integrated teaching empowers students to construct a worldview in which problems can be identified, understood, and solved through a variety of means.

Predictable Results

We should not be surprised that our effects are spotty if our effort is scattered. "Subject fields," James Moffett points out, "are not of themselves learning fields. They are expedient and logical classifications of content that do not take into account how individuals learn, as is shown in one way by the very fact of their being conceived and purveyed essentially in isolation from each other (Moffett, 1992, pp. 75–76). In a rush to cover the subjects, we risk making all learning either futile (if most students get left behind) or meaningless (if willing students try to memorize it all).

Few of us still aspire to be Renaissance learners, but we do not hesitate to require a curriculum for most high school students that holds encyclopedic knowledge as its ostensible purpose. We require a four-year exercise in memorization of all students, though few teachers would attempt to acquire knowledge so broad. As a group, high school students seem increasingly unwilling to respond to the purely abstract, symbol-based, subject-area curriculum we have derived from the academic disciplines. As James Moffett (1992, p. 85) again observes,

> To sacrifice the psychology of the learner to the logic of the subject is to jeopardize not only the meaning the subject may have for the student but the meaning the subject may have for the specialist as well.

Track by track, we teach as much as they can take. The high school graduate who wrote the survey response in Figure 1.4 had surely learned enough to recognize the source of frustration he felt, but not enough at the time to recognize useful alternatives.

FIGURE 1.4 Response to the Last Five Items on the Class of 1987 Survey

To begin with, I am compelled to tell you that five and half years after my graduation, I continue to be surprised by the depth of anger and frustration I feel in relation to my high school experience. I am surprised because as I reflect on my time at Central, there are not a large number of specific negative incidents that I can point to and say," *That* is why I have these feelings." The immediately observable data, I tell myself, do not seem to warrant the intensity of the response. Nevertheless, the feelings are there. Although I am focusing on my experience in high school, these feelings are related to my entire twelve years in public school.

To the best of my understanding, the anger and frustration I feel stem from underlying, less obvious elements of my schooling experience. I have asked myself, What are the fundamental messages I acquired and took with me from high school? The "messages" were mixed, but the ones that dominate my attention are the negative ones. Let me give you a sample of some of these:

Don't trust your own thinking!
Your interests and desires are not important.
School is not the "real world" and therefore your life is not a real life.
Learning is hard work and generally not fun.
What you learn doesn't count as learning if it can't be measured by a test or grade.
As a young person, you have little to offer.

Though my experience at Central was not wholly negative, the powerlessness I felt as a student is one of the most intense and persistent memories I carry with me. I say this as a person who was largely successful by the criteria laid out by

(Continued)

FIGURE 1.4   *(Continued)*

school: I attended "honors" courses and graduated with a grade point average in the top twenty of my class.

As I have gained distance and perspective on my experience at Central, I have shifted from blaming my specific school, teachers, and social dynamics for my frustrations, to recognizing the larger context in which my experiences took place . . . One thing is clear from my perspective: small, superficial changes in schools will not address the basic elements that largely created my negative experience—radical, fundamental change is required in how we conceive of and act upon education.

It is with this perspective that I address your survey.

I am happy to report that I have greatly re-awakened my passion for learning. This has involved, in part, the difficult work of confronting and changing basic negative messages I acquired in school. Though far from complete, I would consider this work of re-awakening to be one of my "extraordinary experiences" since graduation.

*   *   *

You have asked for my feedback regarding courses, activities, etc. that I found most useful in high school, and ones I would recommend for current and future students. Let me share three examples of educational activities that worked for me. The first was an Architectural Drawing class in which I was allowed (after gaining skills in previous courses) to design and create plans for a house. The teacher, Mr. _____ , gave me the freedom to follow my own interests while being available for consultation. The second example was my participation in the Mock Trial team. This was mostly an after school activity in which I learned a great deal about law, group dynamics, and commitment. The third experience occurred in the Humanities course offered to seniors. Occasionally the teachers would set aside the required agenda and let us discuss and debate issues of real importance to us.

*   *   *

To begin with, two major obstacles must be overcome: 1) student conditioning that has taught them to ignore their own interests and distrust their own thinking, and 2) adult training which makes adults distrustful and fearful of giving students more control of students' learning. I suggest group activities that assist students in identifying and articulating their immediate interests and needs while locating the obstacles (internal and external) that keep them from addressing these at school. I imagine students asking such questions as: If we are supposed to be preparing to live in a democratic society, why isn't school democratic? I suggest that all adults in the school meet and undertake similar activities; learning to listen to each other. Questions might arise such as: Why do so many students seem to resist learning? Why does it seem to be "us" against "them"? Adults and students could then come together and listen to each other, entering into the messy and difficult and fantastic process of democratic, real-life education.

By Brian Sherwin, class of 1987, Central High School. Used with permission.

Two unintended ill-effects follow our reliance on subject areas as a basis for a high school curriculum, bad teaching and inequitable learning. Bad teaching results from trying to teach too much. Inequitable learning results from trying to learn subjects that do not fit what the students need to know. As Mark Tucker (1993) points out,

> By the end of the seventies, our high schools had become warehouses for young people in the general track everywhere. They had neither hope nor expectation for going to a selective college and knew that they could go to any community college or get a job with only a diploma. It was pointless to take a tough course or to study hard, because it would not change the outcome for them in any way. . . . The high school diploma, only a few decades ago a shining symbol of real accomplishment, had become now merely a certificate of attendance.

Pointlessness breeds pointlessness. Teachers in the subject areas sought out for non-college students virtually any content that might fill the required days of school.

Tracking in high school subjects results in part from an attempt to hold the subject areas constant but to vary the requirements to fit varying degrees of commitment and ability among students. Tracking does not increase student achievement, but it seems to make more feasible the task of "covering" required topics in a subject-based curriculum (Slavin, 1990; Gamoran, 1992). Teachers in high-tracked classes feel justified in pushing more content knowledge at their students; in low-tracked classes they push less knowledge or "dumb it down." Higher-tracked students are said not to gain as much in this transaction as lower-tracked students are said to lose. If the purpose of education is to help students apply what they know to the problems and opportunities they face, however, it is hard to see how tracking does anything but reinforce the concept of learning as rote memorization, favoring the few who want to qualify for a competitive college at the expense of many others.

In the constrained 40-minute class period, teachers force-feed isolated bits of their subject area, deprived of meaning by their separation from the whole subject and from application in the world outside the classroom. High school students wait and listen to see if they are "good" students. How can they prevail against the enormous historical momentum of five core subjects and some electives? As Moffett (1992, p. 82) states,

> It is schooling [that] is running on a lot of dead assumptions about the subjects based on historical fallout, governmental pressure, bureaucratic distortion and . . . the absence of a learner advocacy to put the subject advocacies in their places within the total learning enterprise.

Because not all students can learn well when most learning is atomized to fit 40-minute blocks and taught largely as a language exercise, the results of conventional secondary teaching are distributed unevenly in patterns reflecting initial differences in race, ethnicity, gender, class, and family wealth.

Forty-minute periods favor one teaching method over all others, a lecture/recitation approach that is consistent with an atomized view of subject-area learning. Teachers talk; students listen. Biology, the study of life itself, decays into a recitation of taxonomies. Shakespeare becomes a translation exercise, two or three scenes per day. History degenerates into a litany of names, dates, wars, and locations, deprived of connection to each other or the present day. Mathematics becomes mindlessly mechanical, a series of operations without purpose. With two- to three-minute breaks, students move from one 40-minute exposure to the next, seven or eight periods in a row. "What happened in school today?" we ask. "Nothing" is the predictable answer. We blame the bland response on adolescent recalcitrance.

Integrating Subject-Area Knowledge

Integrated teaching is often organized around projects in which students try to develop reliable answers to questions that have no predetermined answers. To answer an open-ended question, students need to devise a strategy and gather reliable information from all possible sources. Asking and answering questions lie at the core of learning projects for high school students. If the questions are large, the sources will have to be interdisciplinary. "In the reemergence of interdisciplinary teaching, the role of mission-oriented projects cannot be overstated" (Klein, 1990, p. 33). From Lewis and Clark to the Manhattan project, worldchanging discoveries have resulted from highly focused, multidisciplinary investigations—"How can I answer the questions?" In integrated teaching and learning, the learning project becomes a vehicle for discovering answers and for testing methods for finding answers. The learning project, conducted by individual students or learning teams, allows the teacher to shape the process of inquiry to fit challenges typical of adult experience. Interdisciplinary projects become authentic when they are focused on problems palpable to students and teachers as well.

The recent movement toward integration is most visible, perhaps, in Theodore Sizer's Coalition of Essential Schools, where nine common principles organize curriculum innovation with many varieties.

1. The school should focus on helping adolescents learn to use their minds well.
2. Each student should master a limited number of essential skills and areas of knowledge—"less is more."
3. The school's goals should apply to all students.
4. Teaching and learning should be personalized.
5. The governing practical metaphor for the school should be student-as-worker and teacher-as-coach.
6. The diploma should be awarded on a successful final demonstration of mastery—an exhibition.
7. The tone of the school should stress values of unanxious expectation.
8. The teachers and principals should conceive of themselves as generalists first and disciplinary specialists second.
9. Student loads should not exceed 80 per teacher and costs should not exceed 10 percent more than traditional schools.

In short, these principles help put the student at the center of school activity, facing challenges of a high order and then creating a response worthy of celebration (Sizer, 1992).

The Essential Schools goals reduce the volume of subject matter to be learned and emphasize creative and critical skill. They shift emphasis from tracking groups to helping individuals create "demonstrations of mastery" in student projects. They propose that teachers act as generalist coaches rather than subject experts. A school following principles such as these might grow to resemble a work setting more than it resembles a conventional high school. Such a school aims for high productivity among all its members. The results it would seek are not uniformity of product, but "fit" between a learning product and its unique purpose. They measure their success in terms of quality more than quantity (Schlechty, 1991). They aim to prepare students for a world that most needs new solutions for a bewildering array of real problems.

What can the subject areas provide to an integrated curriculum? As Klein (1990) points out, early efforts at interdisciplinary teaching abstracted three aspects of disciplinary study for use in solving practical problems:

- *Methods of Investigation*—The disciplines had developed research methods that could be applied to many situations.
- *Kinds of Discourse*—The disciplines had adopted forms of argument or proof that could also be applied in educational settings.
- *Levels of Abstracting*—The disciplines had assembled hierarchical structures for knowledge tying related facts and ideas into large systems.

Reliable methods for investigating systemic patterns produce useful arguments in science—or in classrooms. Integrated teaching helps students search existing knowledge for useful information, plan a strategy for organizing and interpreting what they learn, and present their discoveries in a way that is useful to others.

Klein (1990) organized the subject fields into four layers, which most subject areas fit (see Figure 1.5). At the empirical level, the sciences analyze physical phenomena to identify patterns of organization. At the pragmatic level, the technologies describe the general systems that drive physical experience. At the normative level, physical and social engineers create modifications for those systems hoping to solve problems. At the purposive level, philosophers and anthropologists struggle with questions of value—what's worth doing? Integrated teaching engages students in all four

FIGURE 1.5   Contribution of the Disciplines to Interdisciplinary Study

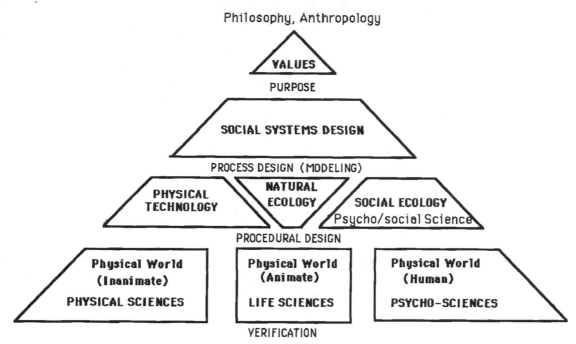

Adapted from *Interdisciplinarity: History, theory and practice* by J. T. Klein (1990, p. 67), with permission of the Wayne State University Press.

levels of inquiry, using material and methods from many subject areas to answer questions and crossing as many disciplinary bounds as necessary to find defensible answers. Klein's conception of the relationships between the disciplines also calls to mind the constructivist view of learning in which students use what they know   to ask questions and then use new information to reconstruct their mental models.

Focusing Questions

Integrated learning occurs when the discovery of new facts and ideas is connected to the search for answers to important questions that have no ready answers. Answering "real" or authentic questions always involves a degree of uncertainty, challenging the principle that all important learning must be measurably right or wrong (Clarke & Biddle, 1993).

- Will it rain during Saturday's shuttle launch?
- Are there intelligent creatures on other planets?
- To what form of government should we aspire?
- How can we reduce the greenhouse effect?
- Can I live on $200.00 per week?

These questions may require knowledge from the subject areas, earth science, biology, history, chemistry, and mathematics, but they also force students to reason and make connections across subject areas. Questions like these help students design "projects," organize attempts to assess a group of facts, and make tentative conclusions. Integrated learning has a mission in the world—to discover and communicate a usable version of truth. To prepare students to lead successful lives, secondary teaching will have to bring knowledge to bear on important but ill-defined questions.

Research suggests that teachers use too many questions at procedural and factual levels, with 60% of classroom questions aimed at recall, 20% aimed at procedure, and only the remaining 20% for inferential and higher-order thinking (Gall, 1984). We believe, in contrast, that these proportions may not be inappropriate if the questions that guide learning are organized to guide students through a comprehensive examination of one issue. If a lesson or unit is guided by the cycle shown in Figure 1.6, a teacher might use one focusing question at the abstract level, 4 or 5 questions to help students plan, and any number of questions to help them gather information and make sense of it. Level of question is not the issue. Purposeful organization is the *heart* of integrated teaching. To what use will we put this information? A teacher might return to a focusing question several times over one class period to remind students of the purpose.

To answer questions about authentic situations, students may have to explore several fields, proposing answers based on the connections they can make. As Figure 1.6 suggests, the four levels suggest four kinds of questions that students can ask when pursuing a project that integrates subject areas:

1. *Value Questions:* Why? What's worth doing? What's wrong now? What's the best we can hope for?
2. *Process Questions:* How can we make this better? How can we figure this out? How can we make a difference in how things work?

FIGURE 1.6   A General Framework for Integrated Learning

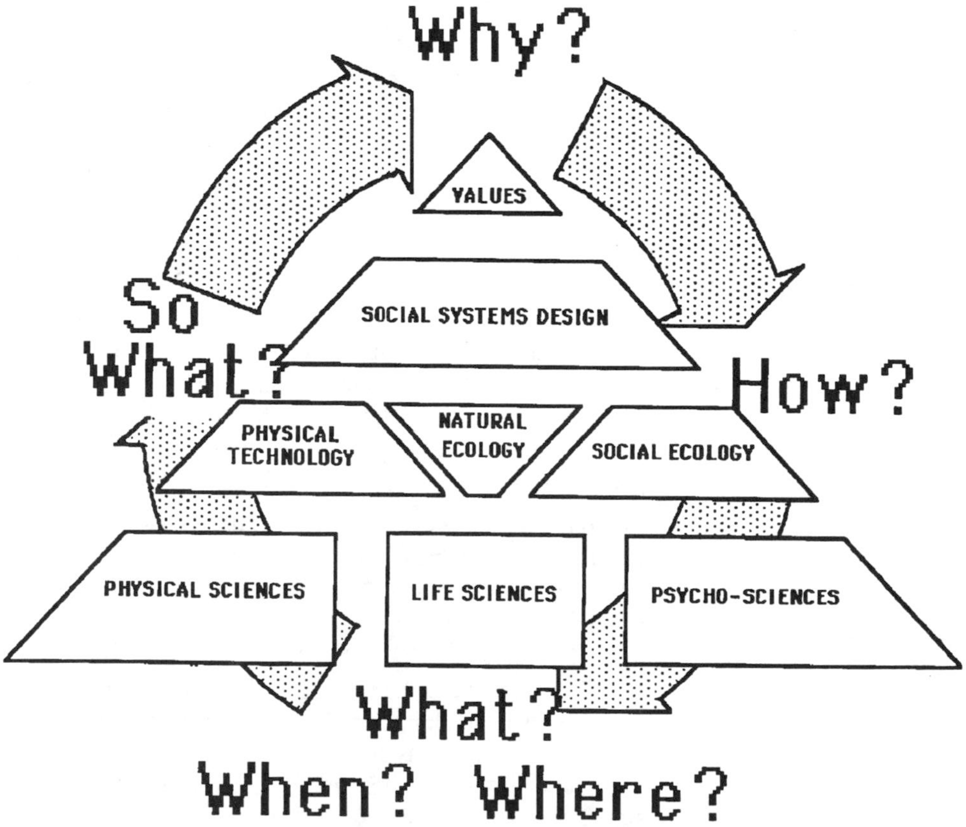

Adapted from *Interdisciplinarity: History, theory and practice* by J. T. Klein (1990, p. 67), with permission of the Wayne State University Press.

3. *Procedural Questions:* How do things happen now? How can we find out what's going on? What steps will we take?
4. *Empirical Questions:* What's happening? What happened? How can we explain the facts as we find them?

Working across the levels of Klein's hierarchy, students are forced to use different kinds of thinking. At the level of value, they have to decide between alternative courses of action, assessing costs and benefits for each. At the social systems level, they have to create models or plans that they hope will have some affect. At the level of technology, they will have to develop procedures for finding things out. At the empirical level, they will have to locate facts and organize them so they contribute to finding answers.

Integration of learning and life is hardly new. The aspiration toward integration characterized most of the moral education of early U.S. schools. Merging learning and work was a theme in John Dewey's writings and in the emergence of the U.S. high school (1965). Interdisciplinary teaching reemerged in the United States during the thirties and forties as it became clear that students faced problems larger in scope than any of the disciplines—war, labor disputes, propaganda, population shifts, shortage of housing, social welfare, and crime (Klein, 1990, p. 24). Then, as now, it became clear to some educators that a classical education did not automatically prepare students to thrive in modern society.

If the subject-based curriculum aims to help students climb a very long ladder from facts to abstractions, the question-based high school curriculum follows a circular path of inquiry driven by questions that matter to them (see Figure 1.7). Students pose higher-level questions: How or why does stuff happen? They figure out a way to find answers: How can I find out about this question? They search as large a base of information as they can manage: What are the most relevant facts? Who assembled them? What can I rely on? Finally, they interpret the facts and develop a new perspective—a usable answer or a solution to a problem they have identified (Clarke & Biddle, 1993). The constructivist cycle is self-adjusting and perpetual. When a situation represents an authentic problem, the cycle raises more questions than it answers. The learning cycle subordinates particular parts of content to the process of finding answers that work.

Crossing subject areas to find answers to real questions requires many kinds of thinking. Making sense of the facts and developing organizational models for experience requires inductive thinking. Developing a plan based on values and goals and then carrying it through requires deductive thinking. Thinking at the concrete level requires students to interpret information from their hands, eyes, ears, and feelings or to plan out steps of a process to gain some outcome. Thinking at the abstract level requires students to work with their minds, organizing what they have seen into "models" that let them understand how things work and plan how to make new things happen.

Though relationships between the content areas are complex, the questions guiding integrated learning are simple. In many variations, the questions—Why? How? What? and So what?—can be found in each of the examples we have assembled to make this book. Some of the unit plans and lesson plans emphasize inductive thinking. Others emphasize deductive thinking and problem solving. Some focus on the power of ideas; others aim to explain specific phenomena. As a whole collection, the integrated teaching strategies included in this book aim to help all students control the processes of their own minds so they can enter the world with practice in finding information and applying it to problems in the world at large.

Teaching students to generate important questions and answer them is the simple principle at the heart of the movement toward integration. How can we find questions so compelling that they provoke students to learn independently? Lauren Resnick (1987) has proposed that we design school learning on what we understand about

FIGURE 1.7   Focusing Questions for Integrated Teaching

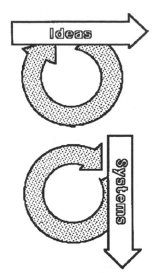

Questions of Purpose: Why?

Value: Why should we care?
Beliefs: What should we stand for?
Futures: What are we aiming for?
Policy: What are our priorities?
Choices: How shall we decide?

Questions of Process: How?

Models: How do things happen?
Theory: How can we explain events?
Systems: How does this work?
Forces: What factors make a difference?
Plans: How can we manage events?
Contingencies: What will we do if...?

Questions of Fact: What? Who? When?

Relationships: What facts are relevant?
Connections: What parts are linked?
Procedures: What is the order of events?
Steps: What is the path?
Components: What parts make up the whole?
Evidence: How reliable are the facts?

Questions of Meaning: So What?

Categories: What ideas organize these facts?
Interpretations: How can we explain the facts?
Generalizations: What must be true?
Inferences: What do the facts mean?
Trends: Where are things headed?
Implications: What are other possible meanings?

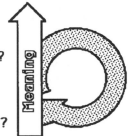

learning in the real world. In a school classroom, students are expected to learn the subjects; in life, they are expected to use their learning to do something well. In school, knowledge has been distilled into symbols; in life, knowledge must be brought to bear on unruly circumstance. We have built schools to protect students from the intrusion of reality—bricks and cinder block walls seal the subjects from each other and from the streets outside. Students complain that school learning is meaningless because they have become perhaps too familiar with life beyond the walls, where questions of life and death are all too pressing. By focusing high school study on problems and ideas that come from the "real" world, we can teach students to use what they learn to manage the work of their minds and the lives they will lead as adults.

Assessing Integrated Teaching

Integrated teaching has begun to produce assessment technologies that measure qualities of a product rather than quantities of information acquired. If we persist in measuring school learning through norm-referenced tests that emphasize recollection of facts, procedures, and concepts, we are sure to miss the value of integrated teaching. Newmann and Wehlage (1993) have proposed five standards we can use to judge authentic instruction, standards that pertain as well to integrated teaching. These standards put the student at the center of classroom work, using reason and knowledge to solve real-world problems and working together as they will when they enter the world of work and start a family.

Five Standards of Authentic Instruction

Higher-Order Thinking: Do students use higher-order thinking as they work with ideas and concepts in the classroom?

Depth of Knowledge: Do students explore complex relationships and important concepts in the subject matter?

Connectedness to the World: Does the class have value or meaning in life beyond the classroom?

Substantive Conversion: Does the process of teaching build on student ideas, revealing connections between ideas, processes, and facts in a coherent process of exploration?

Social Support for Achievement: Does the class encourage high expectations, respect, and inclusion of all students?

In this set of standards, knowledge and methods from the subject areas may provide the equipment students use to work with their minds. The game itself is played on a larger field.

Throughout this book, there are examples of assessment developed by teachers to evaluate the products their students create, and the process they use to create them. We have also dedicated Chapter 11 to assessment projects from many sources—standards, project portfolios, performances, and assessment rubrics—that help students better understand the work they have done. Assessment techniques include grading scales with set criteria, assessment rubrics for content and process, and portfolio systems. Still, we are not at a point where we should try to attach these assessment techniques to a great, overarching scheme of "new, higher outcomes" (O'Neil, 1994; Spady, 1994). To fully explore the power of integrated teaching, we have to let the student work stand for itself. Measurement of quantities learned will not suffice. To assess integrated learning, we have to look for quality in the best work students do as they ask and answer questions.

Quality is a difficult term to use as a beginning point in defining assessment. Quality takes its shape from the beliefs of the viewer (Clarke & Cornell, 1993). In a high school classroom, the most important audience is the individual student, who must develop a sense of quality while also assembling instances of improving quality. The idea of quality develops incrementally as the conception in Figure 1.8 shows. As Al Mamary points out, even in an outcomes driven curriculum, conceptions of quality should be developed by students and teachers working together (Brandt, 1994, p. 26). In a high school curriculum, students should be led to develop an increasingly sophisticated view of quality that they can apply to their work and the work of others. The ability to define and recognize quality may prove to be the most significant outcome of the emerging high school curriculum.

In a general sense, assessment of integrated learning is just one more way to fuse learning and life. David Casterson, Charlene McKaren, and Tim Willis (1993), an integrated teaching team at Soquel High School in California, have developed six criteria they use to measure the success of integrated teaching. While engaged in an authentic learning activity, all students:

1. Are able to articulate the purpose of the activity;
2. Practice and analyze what they do know;

FIGURE 1.8   Ninth Graders Define Quality to Guide Their Learning

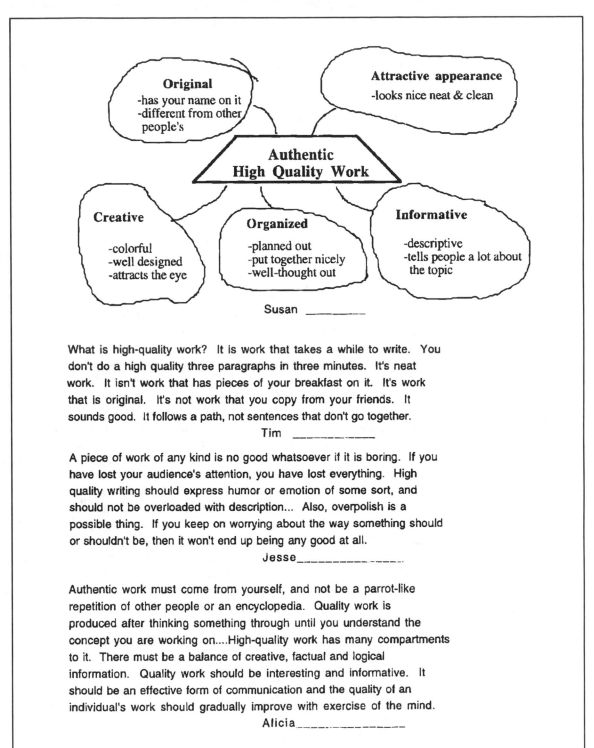

Susan _____

What is high-quality work? It is work that takes a while to write. You
don't do a high quality three paragraphs in three minutes. It's neat
work. It isn't work that has pieces of your breakfast on it. It's work
that is original. It's not work that you copy from your friends. It
sounds good. It follows a path, not sentences that don't go together.

Tim   _____

A piece of work of any kind is no good whatsoever if it is boring. If you
have lost your audience's attention, you have lost everything. High
quality writing should express humor or emotion of some sort, and
should not be overloaded with description... Also, overpolish is a
possible thing. If you keep on worrying about the way something should
or shouldn't be, then it won't end up being any good at all.

Jesse_____

Authentic work must come from yourself, and not be a parrot-like
repetition of other people or an encyclopedia. Quality work is
produced after thinking something through until you understand the
concept you are working on....High-quality work has many compartments
to it. There must be a balance of creative, factual and logical
information. Quality work should be interesting and informative. It
should be an effective form of communication and the quality of an
individual's work should gradually improve with exercise of the mind.

Alicia_____

Student work by Sarah Harford and Kate Fink, Champlain Valley Union High School. Used with permisssion from
Martha Ozturk.

3. Acknowledge what they do not know;
4. Formulate questions that lead to further knowledge;
5. Synthesize connections between knowledge and life experience now and in the future;
6. Evaluate what was learned, and how it could be more effectively learned as a formal part of the assignment.

As Figure 1.9 suggests, these assessment questions constitute a process guide for assessment, following the pattern of the cycle which organizes much of this book. We believe simply that assessment criteria must be developed with plans for integrated teaching and that those criteria must be shared with students before they begin an integrated unit. Rather than dedicating a whole chapter to assessment, we have included the assessment techniques developed by teachers with the examples they have contributed to this book. Setting high standards for product and process helps students recognize their purpose as distinct from memorization and encourages them to exploit the freedom they gain by pursuing important questions in a large and complex world.

Challenges

Integrated teaching does put new pressure on teachers. Where once they might serve well enough as repositories for subject-based knowledge, now they must have open access to far greater supplies of information than they have acquired themselves. When once they could manage a classroom using a few "classroom management" strategies and a set of rules, now they must manage the work of teams and individuals who are working on different tasks. Where once they could close the door and keep out confusion, now they must open the door and help students explain and manage confusion in the outside world—the tumult of life itself. High school teachers, as majors in an academic discipline, have not been prepared to guide the process of open-ended questioning.

FIGURE 1.9   Assessing the Process of Integrated Teaching

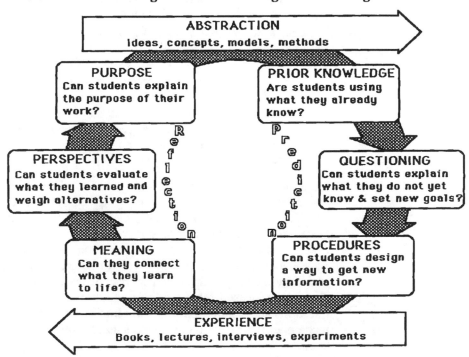

Integrated teaching also throws into question much of the machinery of high school teaching—bells, schedules, roles, duties, texts, tests, and timetables—all the paraphernalia that brings order to a regular day in school. Moving toward integrated teaching forces us to look for new answers to questions we settled long ago:

- Who is in charge here?
- How long will this take?
- What are we going to do today?
- Why are we doing this?

In the top-down management system that typifies most high school classrooms, teachers have taken responsibility for answering these questions. Integrated teaching puts the problem into the hands of students, creating management issues new to schools, but old to most adult work settings. Creating processes that let students manage their own learning is the main challenge in integrated teaching. We have dedicated Chapter 12 to the complex challenge of restructuring high schools to support integrated teaching and learning.

More specific problems emerge as soon as a school explores integrated teaching. The sequentially ordered subjects—math, science, and language—are harder to integrate than the conceptual subjects—English, social studies, and health. Block scheduling can make it very hard to schedule equal time to all teachers. Grading through criteria and rubrics makes reporting student achievement to colleges and employers a more complex enterprise than a transcript can accomplish. We believe that integrated teaching will produce many responses to these problems, rather than one response, as the examples in these chapters show. Still, we have reserved the final chapter for solutions to the systemic problems that come up when teachers attempt change of this magnitude.

Somewhat paradoxically, freeing teachers to define a curriculum that meets the learning needs of their students has not closed out the larger community. On the contrary, integrated teaching is linked with the opening of doors and the engagement of whole school communities.

Projects: Integrated teaching often aims toward student projects.

Team Teaching: To answer big questions, teachers have engaged other teachers whose knowledge can be brought to bear.

Cooperative Learning: To find good answers, students have learned to use one large purpose to organize smaller tasks, trust others to contribute, and to make the whole effect somewhat greater than its constituent parts.

Active Learning: The search for good answers has led students outside the classroom, to the community at large and to electronic networks where the amount of useful information is enormous.

Community Involvement: As the questions asked are large, there is no limit to the number of people—parents, workers, and citizens on the street—who can be involved in the process of learning.

Integrated learning is a process designed and managed by individual teachers, but it also becomes a group enterprise in which teamwork is essential.

Experimentation with a single method of integration appears to lead inexorably toward wider experimentation requiring teamwork. In the parts of this book that follow, we describe three methods for crossing the boundaries of academic discipline. Each depends on a few focusing questions. Each asks students to make connections and draw meaning from varied sources of information. Each helps students explore or develop ideas or themes that explain how events transpire in this world. Asking questions and finding answers will remain as basic components of all the integrated techniques described in the chapters that follow.

PART *I*

Connecting Subject Areas

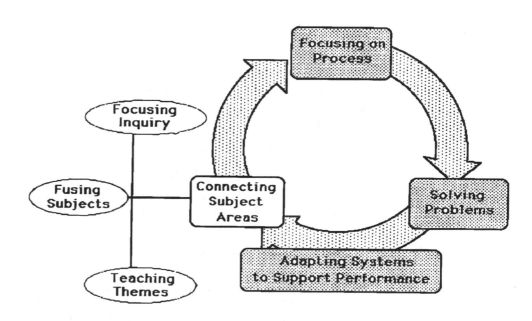

This part of the book focuses on making connections between *disciplines* or *subjects,* perhaps the first and still the most prevalent way to integrate the curriculum. The high school curriculum has been defined by subject area divisions since the days of Colonial America. At grades 9 to 12, the disciplines have become thoroughly entrenched and teachers have come to see themselves as subject-area specialists (ASCD, 1992). Indeed, certification or licensure for secondary school teaching has placed primacy on academic preparation in a discipline. Consequently, high school students, who often have no precise sense of why they are in school at all, find few connections between their classes or any relationship to the world they recognize outside the door.

We have arranged the chapters in this first part first to reflect the motive for integration (inquiry), then to show how teachers merge curriculum by focusing on a time or place (fusion), and finally to show how themes have emerged as the organizing basis for much integrated teaching (thematic teaching).

Chapter 2, Focusing Inquiry—Using Questions to Organize Learning, shows how teachers or teams of teachers can help students generate questions that lead them across subject area lines toward answers that satisfy their need to know. When books like *Teaching as a Subversive Activity* (Postman & Weingartner, 1968) challenged subject-based learning during the sixties, inquiry education began its recent history in U.S. high schools. Contemporary inquiry teaching organizes students as investigators of important local or regional issues. Questioning becomes the organizing process in the classroom, student projects become the medium in which knowledge is gathered or developed, and the student presentation forms the basis for evaluation. Inquiry process has generated the most promising new approaches to high school learning: navigating computer processing (Chapter 7), problem-based learning (Chapter 8), issues analysis education (STS) (Chapter 9), and learning from work or community experience (Chapter 10).

Inquiry Showcase: Human Impact of the Lake Champlain Basin
    Michael Long, Colchester High School, Colchester, Vermont

Chapter 3, Fusing Subject Areas—Linking Subject to Subject, explains how teachers use concepts and facts from more than one discipline to help students find answers to the questions they ask. Possibly the easiest and oldest way to integrate curriculum, the fusion curriculum exploits parallels between subjects that are effects of history (time) or geography (place). For example: Why did humans develop civilization so many times in so many places? Why do some cultures thrive while others fail? How does technology drive change? How do class differences affect civilization? Questions of this magnitude can lead students to explore connections between history, sociology, science, literature, religion, and art, among other subjects. Accessing multiple sources allows different students to learn differently but contribute something substantial to the learning of the whole group.

Fusion Showcase: Humanities Program: Richard Rorty and Postmodernism
    Nina Gifford, Ray Linn, Neil Anstead, and Chris Biron, Grover Cleveland Magnet High School, Los Angeles, California

Chapter 4, Teaching Themes, shows how individual teachers, or teachers working with colleagues, can honor the intellectual content of their field (discipline), yet employ instructional strategies that are more consistent with the learning styles of students today. Themes, such as "power," "communication," "groups and institutions," "ecology," or "body physics," can serve as the organizing basis for affiliating content. This content ordinarily might have been taught *in vacuo* by one teacher, with related content taught at a different time and place by another teacher from a different field. We offer here a straightforward approach for a teacher, working alone or with colleagues, to develop and successfully use a *thematic unit,* often of a week or more in length. Although such units are available off-the-shelf, our contention is that they work best when teachers design them for their own students. Locally developed thematic units ensure close fit between student interests and academic learning.

Thematic Teaching Showcase: Team Zenith: Integrating Teams, Themes, and Projects
    Tom McGuire, Thayer High School, Winchester, New Hampshire

CHAPTER 2

Focusing Inquiry

Using Questions to Organize Learning

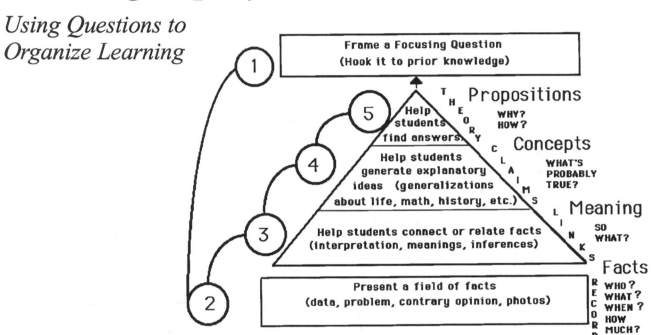

Inquiry teaching places a mass of information before students, arms them with questioning and analytic skills, and then asks them to locate, organize, and analyze pertinent information so they can answer the questions they have asked. Activities are planned to make students see that they can learn on their own (Collette & Chiappetta, 1989, p. 1). In an inquiry classroom, students have the opportunity, with teacher help, to decide *what* is going to be studied. Further, they then proceed to choose *how* to find pertinent information, go about the data gathering, and analyze it for themselves. Whether or not their conclusions are consistent with established knowledge, the inquiry process produces more questions and continuing refinement of perspectives.

Is there a polar opposite to learning by inquiry? Surely, it is *reception learning,* based on "traditional, chalk and talk" lecture/recitation. In reception learning, the student remains in a passive role and simply receives knowledge that *others* have gathered and organized. There are times when it is appropriate to use reception learning techniques and expository or lecture teaching. With a huge expanse of content to "cover," reception learning may seem an efficient use of instructional time, if transmittal of a finite amount of information is a measure of the desired outcome. The rub, of course, is that lecture/recitation may not be best for students who are not predisposed to listen. While seeming efficient, lecture/recitation may not be very effective.

Inquiry and Interdisciplinary Learning

The notions of group inquiry, discovery learning, and interdisciplinary study are related, but we need to make clear the differences between the terms. Curriculum designers have created a taxonomy consisting of subsets of "disciplinary"—inter-, cross-, multi-, pluri-, trans- —to describe all kinds of teaching that crosses conventional boundaries. Without making any fine-grain distinctions, we will adopt the generic interdisciplinary definition offered by Jacobs (1989, p. 8):

> *Interdisciplinary:* A knowledge view and curriculum approach that consciously applies methodology and language from more than one discipline to examine a central theme, issue, problem, topic, or experience.

When the term "interdisciplinary" is used, the intent is to highlight content and conceptual *linkages* between disciplines, and not necessarily the *process* of investigation. Inquiry teaching demands attentiveness to the processes and procedures of the disciplines and most often is conducted in an interdisciplinary manner. However, much inquiry has been done *within a single discipline* and without an interdisciplinary orientation. For example, a biology teacher can develop an *inquiry* unit on insect metamorphosis that incorporates the recognized science *process skills,* yet never moves beyond the realm of invertebrate zoology. On the other hand, a social studies teacher could develop a group inquiry unit on the War in the Persian Gulf/Operation Desert Storm that was also interdisciplinary. Here, students might recover pertinent information from many sources on one historical event. The teacher would help them to see the nature of the event in terms of politics, geography, economics, technology/science, communication, and psychology. Our point is that inquiry instruction can mute the interdisciplinary emphasis, or it can consciously strive to combine *inquiry* and *interdisciplinary* approaches.

To complicate the definitional picture, one often encounters the term *discovery* learning. While a much discussed topic by learning theorists, who promulgate competing and confusing definitions to be found in education psychology textbooks, we settle here on the view of Jerome Bruner as being both respectable and useful for what we are arguing for in this chapter. Bruner did not restrict discovery to the act of finding out something that was unknown to humankind before, but rather included all forms of obtaining knowledge for oneself by using one's mind. For him, discovery was "... in its essence a matter of rearranging or transforming evidence in such a way that one is enabled to go beyond the evidence so reassembled to additional new insights" (Bruner, 1961, p. 22).

In a classic paper, which buttressed the psychological roots of many nationally developed inquiry curriculum projects of the 1960s and 1970s, he went on to suggest the benefits that could occur from the experience of learning through discoveries that one makes for oneself. These were: (1) the increase in intellectual potency, (2) the shift from extrinsic to intrinsic rewards, (3) learning the heuristics of discovering, and (4) the aid to memory processing (Bruner, 1961, p. 23). Because we are focusing on teaching, we want to describe inquiry teaching as the process of guiding students to discover answers to questions whether or not preexisting answers exist.

Why Inquire?

In 1990, Ken Bergstrom, one of our colleagues, conducted a study to determine why teachers become involved in interdisciplinary study. He was especially interested in discovering why teachers who were *successfully teaching* in this manner chose to begin developing an inquiry approach. Bergstrom's study was based on careful listening to many teachers from many disciplines who had firsthand experience with interdisciplinary teaching—*voices* from inside the school (see Figure 2.1). For a further insight into the perceptions, complaints, satisfactions, fears, and hopes of students, teachers, parents, administrators, and staff inside four California schools, we recommend *Voices from the Inside* (Clarement Graduate School, 1993).

Inspiration for inquiry teaching at the secondary school level has come from the writing of Joseph J. Schwab, a biologist at The University of Chicago. His *Biology*

FIGURE 2.1   Why Try Interdisciplinary Teaching?

1. To Ensure Developmental Appropriateness: Through interdisciplinary teaching, there are opportunities for richer kinds of learning. More students can become involved at their own level with more chances for successful growth. Hands-on, creative, learning activities help students build abstract concepts. Learning is more sound and retained longer. The learning activities in an interdisciplinary study also promote problem-solving skills and critical thinking skills while exploring a topic in depth.

2. To Promote Collaboration: Many teachers are seeking the opportunity to collaborate with others. Many teachers also value the chance to collaborate with their students and to get to know them better through a joint endeavor. Teachers are also searching for ways to get kids working with each other in healthy, cooperative learning in order to build social skills and class morale.

3. To Reflect the Real World: Because an interdisciplinary study is a reflection of the real world, students become more interested and motivated in their learning. This kind of learning involves and engages students positively. They understand the need to learn a skill and to apply it. Thus students can readily develop a life-long love of learning.

4. To Try an Exciting Approach: Many teachers responded that teaching in a new and different way is exciting. Teaching an open-ended unit is not only very interesting for them, but also very engaging for their students. Besides, one teacher mentioned, it shakes things up and keeps us all moving.

5. To Connect School Subjects: Making connections between a school's often artificial categories or disciplines makes sense to teachers and students. This "whole" topic approach can actually cover more in greater depth as well as fill in the gaps between subjects. The flow of study also provides meaningful continuity through an unlimited number of ongoing activities.

6. To Have Fun: Some teachers noted that a good motivator for an interdisciplinary study is simply to have fun. This kind of unit can regenerate enthusiasm for learning. Teachers and students can enjoy their unit activities, and celebrate learning. Having fun is a great motivator for all involved.

7. To Motivate Self: Just teaching an interdisciplinary study can be its own motivation. The challenge of developing something new can be an intensely rewarding experience. Improving oneself as a teacher is the goal.

8. To Involve the Community: The opportunity to garner community support also encourages some teachers to pursue an interdisciplinary study. By involving community resources with the school in a special project, positive public relations can result for both.

9. To Respond to Collegial and Administrative Support: A very few respondents indicated that their teaching situations already offered collegial support for teaching an interdisciplinary unit. To take advantage of that encouragement was a worthy reason to pursue this approach.

By Ken Bergstrom, Goddard College, Plainfield, VT. Used with permission.

Teachers' Handbook (1963) was written in support of one of the most successful and longlasting science curriculum projects in U.S. history—the Biological Sciences Curriculum Project (BSCS). Schwab introduced what he termed "Invitations to Enquiry" (emphasis ours on the letter "e" rather than "i"), an instructional strategy in which teachers confront students with *actual data* from wide-ranging scientific contexts, and help them unveil phenomena that are inherent in that data. In a classic example, students would look at the numbers of animal pelts turned in annually over many years by trappers to the Hudson Bay Company in Canada. By making graphs, investigating the life cycles of the animals involved, researching predator and prey relationships, finding out about the economies of the fur industry, and trying to explain the changes in the ecosystems involved, students were placed in the role of investigators.

In an inquiry classroom, students become creators of knowledge rather than recipients. Concepts remain important but are subordinate to the experience of active participation. In an Inquiry classroom, students learn *how to conduct a scientific investigation.* According to Schwab (1963, p. 46), the benefits that accrue from this inquiry confrontation include the propositions that:

1. Students see how knowledge arises from data.
2. Students see how data and the quest for that data proceeds on the basis of concepts and assumptions that change as knowledge grows.
3. Students learn that knowledge changes when the facts, principals, and concepts change.
4. Students learn that though knowledge changes, it changes for good reason—because we know better and know more than we knew before.

With inquiry as the governing process, the *content* and *concepts* learned are less important than the *process* of conducting an investigation and communicating what was learned to others. Inquiry teaching focuses on a topic that is both sufficiently *broad* and *discrete* to permit individual students to pursue a significant study of particular interest to them. As students pursue questions about content, distinctions tend to blur between traditional disciplines of social studies, English, science, and mathematics. Stated somewhat differently, in inquiry teaching, the process of inquiry is featured as the organizer for the instructional design, and "content" is relegated to an ancillary place.

Focusing and Following Questions

With many variations and adaptations, inquiry learning can be viewed as a self-renewing cycle of questions and answers (see Figure 2.2). The learning cycle is a simplification of the scientific method (Clarke & Biddle, 1993; Clarke, Martell, & Willey, 1994). Using what they already knew as a beginning point, students generate questions about the things they do not yet know. For these questions, they design a method of investigation that will get them information. They gather information on their own, sifting for pertinent data and grouping facts that point toward answers. As they interpret the information and generate answers, they also discover the limitations of their answers. New questions emerge. The quest goes on. Skill in inquiry depends on posing focusing (or essential) questions, supported by following questions that bring answers to light.

Focusing questions that begin with "how," "why," or "what if" tend to lead students to more abstract thinking. "What," "where," and "when" questions generate more concrete thinking. Student effort focuses on specific information from the content areas. From their analysis of the facts, the students infer general answers from the specific information they have gathered. The following focusing questions are examples of what one might generate for the concept "culture" in a unit on China:

FIGURE 2.2   A Four-Step Inquiry Process Guiding Student Teams

Focusing Questions: How do things happen? Why? What predictions are most defensible? What if . . . ?

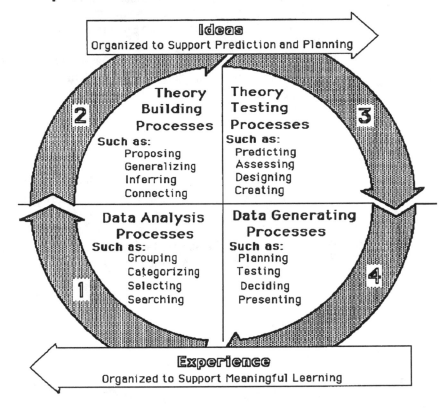

Adapted from Clarke and Biddle (1993), from Costa (1985). Used with permission of Prentice-Hall, Upper Saddle River, NJ.

- Why does a culture (flourish, die, or change)?
- How is (technology, tradition, or geographical setting) important for a culture?
- How do cultures evolve as a consequence of (books, improved technology, or conflict)?
- How is (religion, family, or money) important in Chinese culture?
- How has (war, overpopulation, education) affected Chinese culture?
- What characteristics do all cultures have?

General questions force students to search the data carefully. More specific questions should force them toward general answers based on the data. The cycle is continuous.

The "key words" listed below may be helpful in writing focusing questions. Some of these words will evoke questions that lead students to think more concretely (Shoemaker & Lewin, 1993). Others will evoke questions that generate more abstract thinking.

Key Words

kinds	characteristics	purpose
significance	evolution	value
time	function	style
importance	cause and effect	similarities and
use	types	differences
conditions	relationship	

Terms such as these shift student attention from the facts to the meaning of facts.

If focusing questions play the central organizing role in the development of an inquiry unit, following questions drive students deeper into the available data (see Figure 2.3). In daily work, questioning serves in its traditional role as an important strategy to be used with students to foster thinking and learning. Questions also serve as a planning tool to help drive decisions about which activities to choose and how to develop assessment criteria. Such questions can be posted in the classroom for the duration of the unit to provide structure for the unit and create clear linkages between the day-to-day activities and the major concepts. Further, in requiring students to pursue answers, the questions require students to produce rather than just consume knowledge.

Student as Scientist

In January of 1988, the School District of Philadelphia (The PATHS/PRISM Project) gathered 80 teachers and scholars to redesign its history courses for grades 9 and 10 to improve instruction and meet the needs of an increasingly diverse student population. The project developed an inquiry format when, according to James Culbertson (1993, p. 54), the Social Studies department head at Benjamin Franklin High School, participating teachers came to realize:

FIGURE 2.3   How Focusing Questions Lead to Following Questions

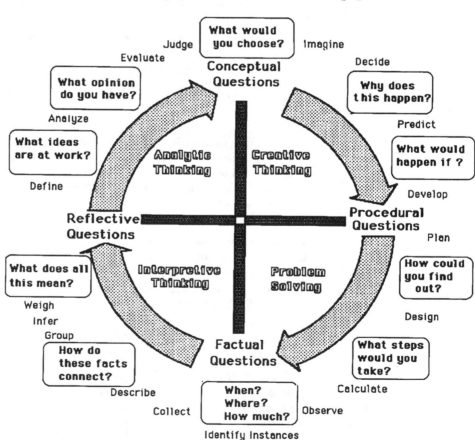

What we wanted students to be able to do was to investigate the role of continuity and change over time. Instead of imparting information to students, our new curriculum centered on getting students to formulate questions about the past and to seek answers to them. In the process of planning how to do this, we discovered that less could be more.

What emerged after five years of development is included in three volumes of teacher resources—guides, activities, experiments, primary data, handouts, and overheads—that show students how to ask and answer questions. Beginning with simple analytical questions for historical artifacts, the guides for Philadelphia's World History Project quickly move toward highly sophisticated investigations of ancient and modern civilizations.

Historical chronology provides the superstructure for these volumes, but inquiry ranges from anthropology (artifacts) to zoology (animal and human bones). The exercises in the books are designed to help students practice hypothesis generation and evaluation based on Dewey's "How We Think" (School District of Philadelphia, 1993, p. 13):

How We Think

- A question is generated
- A hypothesis is generated
- A proof strategy is determined
- A conclusion is reached

Conclusions are always tentative. Tentative conclusions produce more questions.

Although the general structure of Philadelphia's history curriculum follows the pattern of scientific inquiry, the questions themselves come from the humanities:

- Who are we as a people?
- Who are we as a nation?
- Who are we as a religious group?
- Who are we as a political group?
- Who are we as an artistic group?
- Who are we as an occupational group?
- Who are we as a city?
- Who are we as upholders of important values?

Descriptive answers to these questions may be found in the present. Their antecedents and origins come from the past. How did we come into being? is the focusing question. Students search widely for answers: Africa, Asia, Europe, and the Americas produce different answers at different times.

When we called Benjamin Franklin High School, Gloria Barnes, a social studies teacher, had just finished an exercise that shows students how hard it is to develop inferences about a culture from any isolated artifact found from an earlier age (see Figure 2.4). Working in small groups her students were developing hypotheses about a lost culture for which the only remaining remnant is one penny. Her students recorded fragments of data they derived from the penny and then tried to postulate aspects of the culture that must have created it. How do scientists gain confidence in the conclusions they draw from such information? In their discussion, her students gained respect for the amount of "data" found on one artifact, as well as for the number of conclusions that can be drawn from the data.

In Philadelphia, the history inquiry curriculum helps students practice their inferential skills on simple data before they begin struggling with complex sources. The inquiry process becomes more challenging when students read about excavations of early human sites, receive a kit full of artifacts including pictures of skull structures, chipped stones, animal bones, and descriptions of an ash-filled hole (see Figure 2.5). What can we learn about early humans from these remnants? What con-

FIGURE 2.4   Developing Inferences about Cultures

Lesson 2: The Penny

Active teacher direction is needed for this exercise to succeed. Students should be told that they have been sent to Earth from another planet to gather information about its inhabitants. However, when the students land, they find that everything has been destroyed except for an object which the teacher holds up or distributes (a penny—but it's not identified as a penny).

Give the students a few minutes to record any data they find (In God We Trust, 1909, etc.). Then have them draw conclusions about earthlings. Then draw your own conclusions, as follows:

- These were a very religious people (Motto)
- The figure on the object must be a God (Lincoln)
- If you turn the object over, you see a temple with God sitting on a throne between pillars. Obviously, these people worshipped God on a daily basis and their whole society revolved around worship.

At this point, discuss with the students what may have gone wrong with your thinking (assumptions, bias, omissions of data, unwarranted conclusions, etc.).

Lesson 3: Archaeology

Active teacher direction is needed for this exercise to succeed. Tell students that they are archaeologists and that in order to become the leading expert in the world, they will have to solve a problem. They will be placed in the middle of a wilderness where very few artifacts are intact. The only thing they can find is a list of words inscribed on a rock, as follows:

cotton	cattle	ghost	aunt	Bible
ivory	tent	furnace	tax	market
goat	onion	mule	silk	God
Sabbath	money	cheap	banana	walll
slave	owe	town	music	son
house	lamb	trade	cold	rainy season
desert	yams	horse	daughter	law
rust	cheese	prophet	devil	temple
bargain	war	teacher	herd	school
brass	salt	spider	elephant	farm
family	harvest	witch	camel	grandfather
umbrella	debtor	gold	canoe	blacksmith
dry season	barber	road	mountain	cemetery

Students will begin to generate answers to what they have seen on the rock. Make them back up their thinking and realize that they are creating categories to group the words before they hypothesize. Then have them generate numerous hypotheses concerning the nature of the inhabitants. Have them make an hypothesis about who these people were, where and when they lived, and how similar or how different they are from us. Add some of your own ideas such as why two sets of apparent belief are present (superstition/religion).

From The World History Project, School District of Philadelphia, © 1992. Used with permission.

clusions can we draw from the evidence and what explanations of human culture can we derive from our conclusions.

As students gain skill and confidence in asking and answering questions from artifacts, they can begin to struggle with comparing and contrasting cultures, using more complex data. What can we learn about a people from the cities they build? For this question, the students receive a map of modern Jerusalem and a map of Princeton University (School District of Philadelphia, 1993, Vol. 3, p. 30):

FIGURE 2.5   Matrix Guiding the Analysis of Early Human Artifacts

THE SEARCH FOR EARLY HUMANS—AN EXCAVATION

Names _____   _____   _____

_____   _____   _____

ITEMS FOUND	CONCLUSIONS	EXPLANATIONS	DATING PROCEDURE
SKULL			
CHIPPED STONES			
ANIMAL BONES (some charred)			
ASH-FILLED HOLE (surrounded by rocks)			

From The World History Project, School District of Philadelphia, © 1992. Used with permission.

- Locate the three biggest buildings. What were they used for? What does this tell us about the priorities of this culture?
- Locate two other large buildings. What do these structures tell us about the culture?
- Why is there a lack of housing? Farms? Power sources?
- Is this a city? Or a village? If not, what is needed for this site to become a city?

As they struggle to differentiate a city from a university (see Figure 2.6), they discover attributes of both that let them understand the larger concept of civilization.

Fosnot (1989) nicely summarizes what is taking place in guides such as those created by the Philadelphia history project:

> On the surface, the integration may appear to be a "rehash" of the old "core" curriculum notion, but when looked at with more scrutiny it has a distinct contemporary flavor. Students are involved in project work that integrates the traditional disciplines of language arts and mathematics, but in so doing they are learning not only to *solve* problems but to *pose* problems. Rather than teachers deciding on themes of study, students choose areas they would like to research, refine their questions into researchable issues, then spend time accessing information and organizing it for communication to others.

For teaching such as this, Fosnot concludes that, "In a sense, the process, rather than the product, becomes the curriculum" (1989, p. 123). Teacher willingness to explore integrated curriculum approaches is in response to their belief that what worked poorly in the past is working even worse today. They have begun to design schools that can do better.

FIGURE 2.6   What Is a "City?"—Comparing Two Maps

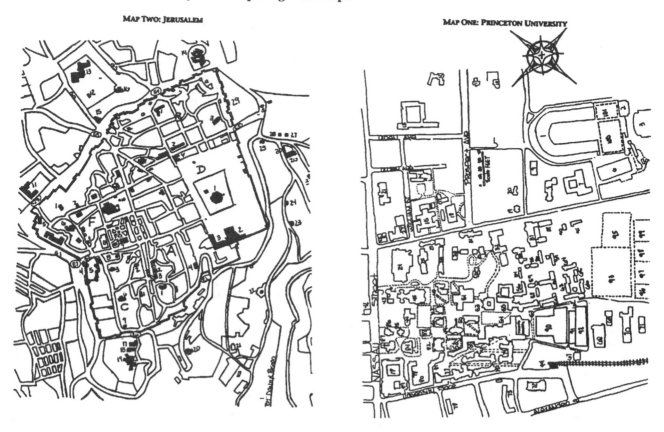

MAP TWO: JERUSALEM   MAP ONE: PRINCETON UNIVERSITY

From The World History Project, School District of Philadelphia, © 1992. Used with permission.

Student as Researcher

Inquiry teaching puts students in the position of researchers, asking and answering questions about information that may range far beyond the boundaries of a single discipline. Many teachers find this focus on *research* skills compelling, and they are the ones most likely to embrace it. While the group inquiry instructional strategy advocated in this chapter can be followed for a unit-length or quarter-course basis, our Showcase example presents what can be seen as the penultimate expression of inquiry teaching—a year-long course for legitimate Carnegie unit credit in either English, science, social studies, or mathematics.

Inquiry may start with a personal question: "How do I fit into the stream of history?" With twenty-five or thirty students in one room asking this kind of question, personal answers can be assembled into general answers that reflect general rules, trends or theories. At Soquel High School in California, students ask the same question in a linked biology/history/English class. For the history and biology portion of the project in Figure 2.7, they collect genetic information from their families. For the history and English portion, they collect personal narratives from older relatives. The answers different students assemble give them a fair sample for testing Mendel's law and for creating a timeline for 500 years of immigration from Africa, Asia, Europe, and the Americas. Each student contributes something different to the general pattern of American history; from a personal standpoint, the whole effort of tracing history becomes somewhat larger than the sum of the parts.

FIGURE 2.7   Immigration and Geneology: A Biology/History/English Project

Purpose:

- To learn about the inheritance of specific genetic traits in your family
- To learn more about your own family's immigration experience
- To increase your awareness and tolerance for unrelated, present-day immigrants

History and Biology Section

To complete the genetics exercises, you will need as much of the following information as possible:

- Names and relation to you of as many family members as possible
- Birthdates and places
- Dates, causes, and locations of deaths
- Nationalities (indicate fractions if possible)
- Genetic family traits: Select two from the following list that you can trace through three generations. Only select traits that some members have and others do not.

DOMINANT TRAITS		RECESSIVE TRAITS
Dark eyes B__		light eyes bb
Curl tongue T__		Can't curl tongue tt
Normal hair HH	Wavey hair Hh	Straight hair
Right handed R__		Left handed rr
Type A-B-AB blood I		Type O blood ii
Near or far sighted E__		Normal vision ee
Free earlobes L__		Attached earlobes ll
Normal hearing D__		Deafness from birth dd
Normal color vision XF		Color blind Xf

History and English Section

You will interview a member of your family who is most knowledgeable and/or charming regarding your family's arrival in the United States . . . Remember, ask good follow-up questions.

In addition to three optional questions, you must find out:

WHEN: When the first member of your family arrived in the United States
WHO: Names, ages, relations to each other; name changes on arrival
WHERE: From where they came, where they settled initially, and then later
WHY: Motivation for leaving native country
HOW: Method of travel and how hard the journey was
EXPECTATIONS V. REALITY: Differences encountered between preconception and reality

Option #1:   Based on the information given in your interview, create a fictionalized account of the original immigration experience of your family. Humor, style, and creativity are encouraged.

Option #2:   Make your interview an observational experience. This means you must record your interview, because your note-taking will largely consist of observational strategies: complete character description focusing on physical traits, body language, tone of voice, language used, personality quirks; complete description of surrounding environment; your own feelings (apprehension, excitement, curiosity) before, during, and after interview.

By David Casterson, Soquel High School, Soquel, CA. Used with permission from David Casterson, Charlene McGowon, and Tom Willis.

Student as Reporter

In an inquiry curriculum, scientific research involves more than finding the truth. It requires representing what has been discovered so others can benefit as well. Students must demonstrate their *conceptual and factual* understanding by constructing personally meaningful yet plausible answers to the key focusing questions. Their answers may be expressed (and assessed) in a variety of forms, including personal interviews, creation of graphic representations (such as models and concept maps), generation of metaphorical images, and, of course, written essay tests.

Reporting back to the class gives students a chance to practice speaking and writing, and also expands the base of content to which all students are exposed. In a well-organized inquiry unit, individual students may ask different questions and still contribute to a broad understanding of a topic. As individuals discover answers from the information they dig up, they present their findings to the whole class. The class then becomes responsible not only for the information they have found themselves, but for the questions and answers gathered by the whole group.

In Martha Ozturk's ninth grade social studies class at Champlain Valley Union High School in Vermont, student investigations often end with formal exhibitions, tied to locally developed graduation proficiencies for which each student is responsible. Martha Ozturk bases most of her rainforest unit on individual inquiry projects developed by her students. Martha's students choose a medium of communication as carefully as they conduct their studies. In reporting back on exhibition day, her students employ virtually all the media, including:

models	cartoons	essays	graphs
narratives	charts	music	art
recipes	collections	costumes	skits
poetry	multimedia		

Students make their presentations on exhibit day and class discussion ranges far as students make connections between many different kinds of presentations (see Figure 2.8).

Interdisciplinary Research as Real Life

What goes on in an inquiry classroom? Some advocates for inquiry instruction have identified the types of activities that should be going on when students take from teachers the task of generating questions and answers. When they manage a broad investigation of a topic, as Collette and Chiappeta (1989, pp. 76–77) state, inquiry teachers are:

> (1) Giving students many opportunities to find out for themselves; (2) asking and answering questions should predominate classroom instruction; (3) making laboratory and library work common activities; (4) encouraging students to gather information, classify, predict events, construct hypotheses, experiment, solve problems, and make decisions; (5) balancing "hands-on" experiences with thought-provoking activities; (6) putting *students in charge* of digging up information and determining cause-and-effect relationships.

Although the context for this listing was the world of science teaching, in our view it has general application for curriculumwide inquiry teaching.

Fosnot (1989) looked at the traditional disciplines in a new light and urged education to emphasize interdisciplinary thinking so as to favor *breadth* rather than *depth*. This change in emphasis is taking place because of our focus on real-world problems, a rise in technology, and the increase of abstract methodologies within disciplines

FIGURE 2.8   Rainforest Project and Exhibit

Types of Projects:

Cartoons, models, graphs, essays, narratives, charts, musical performances and/or composition, artwork, oral participation in "Speak Out," recipes, treasure chests, artifact collections, costumes, skits, poetry, multimedia displays.

Assessment:

Each student must show evidence of:

- a viable plan
- a processfolio, containing plans, notes, changes, record of work, record of human and print resources, drafts of work
- project completed on time
- authentic work
- successful roles (see below)
- project presentation on Exhibit day
- thinking about their own learning (recorded in learning log)

Roles Students Play (as they produce multiple outcomes):

- Critical and creative thinker: Discovering meanings of the ecosystem and the part of the rainforest in the ecosystem; analyzing the effects of human actions on the rainforests; problem solving and decision making on what needs to be done
- Investigator: Research one topic of your choice: access resources, detect assumptions, take careful notes around a theme, idea, problem-solving or decision-making strategy
- Composer: Produce a composition (in any medium) which shows deep understanding of your topic
- Major performer during "Speak Out" on Exhibition day
- Communicator: Participate in oral discourse, listening, and speaking
- Self-Directed Learner: Make a plan and revise as needed, embrace high standards, and keep a Processfolio and reflect on learning in "Making Connections" log

Rainforests

Panama	Indonesia	Japan
Philippines	Thailand	Camaroon
Malasia	Costa Rica	Rwanda
Madagascar	Cote D'Ivorie	Tanzania

Some Student Choices

Stats on Amazonia	Women's roles	Mining/logging/dams
Native Amazonians	The journey of a Brazil nut	Sustainable development
Forest gatherers	Indiginous people and the	Oral traditions
Colonists	land	Earth Summit
Support groups	Human rights	Climate change
(Rainforest crunch)	World map of rainforests	Extinction
Chico Mendes	Biodiversity issue	Tropical timber
Yanomami Indians	Burger King	World Bank
Refugees	Global warming	

From Martha Ozturk's ninth grade class at Champlain Valley Union High School, Hinesburg, VT. Work by students Sarah Harford and Kate Fink. Used with permission.

(p. 119). Few would argue with her contention that "real-world problems" fit into the jurisdiction of single disciplines alone. For example, AIDS research involves epidemiologists, molecular biologists (a field combining physics and biology), chemists, lawyers, politicians, and human rights activists.

Teachers who move into inquiry teaching report that it is the most satisfying and at the same time the most demanding teaching they have ever done. (It is not unlike the reflection of one of the dude-ranch buddies, in the film *City Slickers,* who related a childhood memory that when his abusive father left home it was both the happiest and saddest day of his life.) Outstanding results will not result from casual planning for group inquiry. The design can work with a lone teacher in any of the traditional disciplines, or with instructional teams of two or more teachers.

Predictable Pitfalls

Because group inquiry, or discovery learning, is not a miracle cure, it has its detractors. Savy educators are wary of zealots who offer one-size-fits-all approaches to instruction. While we encourage more teachers to use this special approach to integrated teaching, its demands on both teachers and resources make its optimum implementation problematic in some schools today. Collette and Chiappetta have been advocates for the inquiry approach to teaching but also summarize (1989, pp. 79–80) where the problems can arise:

> (1) Many teachers are inadequately trained to handle the many and diverse questions that students ask during inquiry sessions; (2) pressure on preparing students for the next grade, standard examinations, and college, result in information being stressed and inquiry skills deemphasized; (3) there can be difficulty in getting materials, supplies, equipment; (4) some teachers found that the approach does not work for most students—it seemed to cause confusion and difficulty for all but the very brightest students; (5) the inquiry approach can lead to management problems in classrooms where discipline was a problem; (6) students who are left to discover ideas for themselves usually make mistakes in their thinking; (7) discovery learning takes more time than reception learning.

We share these concerns not to discourage those who want to attempt inquiry teaching, but rather to suggest the assemblage of factors that *can* discourage the otherwise motivated teacher. Even the most partisan backers of inquiry teaching do not suggest that this method be used exclusively. However, it is certainly true that if a teacher has been "converted" to teaching in an inquiry manner for a particular course, those inquiry teaching strategies that have proven effective often begin to transform other courses in his or her schedule.

What does it take to succeed in inquiry teaching? Our list of factors that make the difference between success and failure imply that a mixture of goodwill and good luck form the basis for a successful experiment with inquiry teaching (see Figure 2.9). We will make reference to these factors as we explore the establishment of the "Human Impact on the Lake Champlain Basin."

The Inquiry Showcase at the end of this chapter takes you to a rural, suburban community in northern Vermont about 50 miles from the Canadian border. Here, a group of dedicated teachers developed and implemented a course that exemplifies some of the best practices in integrated teaching. It is a course that recognizes that students are capable of conducting inquiry but must be prepared adequately and supported in the endeavor. We can benefit from the fact that this program has a developmental history of success of more than ten years. Having evolved and overcome a series of implementation challenges, it continues developing today. Inquiry teaching affirms that "state-of-the-art" schooling can occur when committed teachers, supported by their school administrations, are willing to invest their best thinking and psychic energy to create something to serve students well.

FIGURE 2.9   Factors Associated with Success in Inquiry Teaching

1. *Internal motivation* to try the approach on the part of the classroom teacher or teachers
2. *Political savvy and gumption* of the teacher to "work the system" to accomplish something worthwhile
3. *Teacher expertise* in the area of the planned curriculum
4. *Appeal of the product*—students see the curriculum as having value
5. *Relevance* to contemporary lives of students and the community
6. *Priority on inclusiveness*—serving a wide range of academic abilities, not just the high flyers
7. *The absence of prerequisites* and exclusionary enrollment policies
8. The personality and *perceived quality of the teacher* or teachers to be the instructors
9. *Scheduling and administrative* adaptation and accommodation
10. *Altruism*—despite financial and other dilemmas, the teacher and school "know" that this type of schooling is better for students

INQUIRY SHOWCASE

Human Impact on the Lake Champlain Basin

Michael Long
Colchester High School, Colchester, VT

The Lake Champlain Class is a multidisciplinary, team-taught, project-oriented program for high school students of various abilities. Three teachers, twenty-five to thirty-five students, two computer labs, and a wealth of community resources come together in this class to provide learning experiences of a measure and intensity not common in the single-discipline, one-teacher classroom. Because this class focuses on individual student research and presentations, its subject matter is fluid and in significant measure student-selected.

The classroom is one that insistently connects students with the world beyond it through the multidisciplinary teaching team, guest speakers, telephones, modems, and a classroom database listing printed sources and personal contacts. On a random visit you might see lecture and discussion, but you would more likely see some brief announcements made as the class begins, followed by a surge of activity as students head for the computers, the library, the telephone, meetings with teachers, or trips to The University of Vermont's (UVM) Special Collections. What distinguishes this classroom from many is that students often need to be told to stop working as the end of the period approaches.

Guest speakers are one of the community resources regularly utilized. Geologists and journalists, folklorists and engineers, park planners, ornithologists, psychologists, and many others come not to enrich a preordained curriculum but to create a new one. By informing students about their areas of expertise, speakers stimulate students to develop research projects and expertise of their own. Students who have never before felt remotely like experts in anything, design, pursue, and ultimately present their research out in the community with flair and satisfaction, despite some inevitable trepidation. This community presentation, or "roadshow," is the centerpoint of the class and its culmination. In a tangible public way, it embodies the course's ultimate goal: to produce independent learners and thinkers who can find, organize, analyze, and present information and ideas of special importance to them. To achieve this we use a format stark in its simplicity but, like all successful teaching, subtle and varied in its implementation.

In a nutshell, we:

1. Introduce students to a variety of Basin topics from AIDS to zebra mussels and encourage them to contribute to the list of endless possibilities;
2. Help students develop research, computer, and communications skills as tools in finding, analyzing, and presenting ideas and information; and
3. Assist students in completing a series of three increasingly complex and self-directed research projects, the last of which is presented out in the community in lieu of a final exam.

The Lake Champlain Class meets for two periods daily and students earn two credits which they choose from three disciplines: English, social studies, and science.

Central Concept: Exploring Basin Issues

The title of the course, "Human Impact on the Lake Champlain Basin," suggests the context in which students develop from receivers to presenters of information and ideas. The Lake Champlain Basin, together with the idea of humans having an impact on it, is a sprawling and inclusive organizing principle which paradoxically contains and liberates the curriculum. What it means is that students and teachers are free to study anything that humans have done, are doing, or might do in the future that could have a cultural or environmental impact here. This includes creating or exploring art, science, literature, history, technology, public affairs, or combinations of these. Indeed, a presiding notion in the class is that disciplinary lines can be blurred and broken so that information and ideas can be pursued and problems explored and solved through a real-world blend of intellectual and practical capabilities.

Students often choose topics that are intrinsically interdisciplinary (like the economic value of a healthy environment) or so current and local (like the role a financially strapped teen center plays in the cultural life of local teens and in the community at large) that print sources are few and elusive (see Figure 2.10). There is no road map, so students are compelled to use various avenues they discover themselves—phone calls, letters, interviews, personal contacts, databases of periodicals and newspapers, and library special collections. They are sleuths discovering a new path, not grunts trudging down a well-worn one. Paths that fade into bushes and brambles are part of the learning experience. As one student recognized:

> At the beginning of the year I was not very skilled in research. My idea of research was a few notes from the encyclopedia. This class taught me how to do effective research by getting information from the source itself.

As teachers we provide guidance along the way. We are resources ourselves, and we point them toward other resources, making educated guesses about the most fruitful way, but we don't necessarily know ourselves where the path will lead.

Although we aim to develop independent and self-directed learners, we also require a modicum of independence even before the course begins and we emphasize this by requiring students who would register for the course to have a faculty member attest to their ability to work independently. What this means essentially is that students in this course need to be especially trustworthy because we cannot watch all of them all the time. Eventually they will be engaged in research at various locations in and out of the building, and we will be engaged working with individuals and small groups on their projects. Students need to tend to their work even when unattended.

The Beginning: Basin Issues and Software Instruction

As the course begins, we work in various ways to develop interest in and understanding of a wide range of topics and issues both for their intrinsic value and to provide a large number of potential research project topics for later consideration. We take field trips to the Lake and the mountains, which are the center and perimeter of the Basin, respectively. We involve students in readings, activities, and presentations connected with the history, literature, and science of the Basin. Finally, through news and reading reviews, we give students the responsibility to design an independent reading program for themselves and to write and talk about their reading on a regular basis (see Figure 2.11).

Simultaneous and integrated with this introduction of topics and issues comes instruction and practice in using computer software and in research skills like interviewing, outlining, and utilizing various library references. In software instruction, we teach word processing, desktop publishing, spreadsheets, databases, and graphics. Our approach is to provide basic information about a program and then give

FIGURE 2.10   Topics Students Often Choose to Research

TO: Colchester Teachers
FROM: Lake Champlain Class teachers (Mike Long, Ken Perrotte, Bill Romond)
RE: Annual Class Presentations
DATE: May 17, 1994

The students in the course, "Human Impact on the Lake Champlain Basin," are now completing their research projects. The last phase of the course involves what we like to call "The Road Show."

Each student must present his or her project to at least one group outside the high school. We are also requiring each student to develop a presentation suitable to some other class in the school district. If you feel that one of our students has a topic that might be of interest to you (please circle up to three), complete the information and return the form to **Bill Romond** at the high school.

Unfortunately, each year we get well over 100 requests, so there is a chance that you may not get your first choice. Completion of this form merely indicates that you would like more information. Our students *will get in touch with you* if they want to go to your class. Please return this form by *May 25.* Thank You.

NAME: _____   **SCHOOL:** _____

GRADE: _____   **PHONE:** _____

Project Topics

AIDS in Vermont
AIDS: A Vermont/U.S. comparison
Comic book, reflecting the conflict over water and water conservation ("Scorched Earth")
Comparison of Champ with Nessie (of Loch Ness fame)
Disciplinary systems in Vermont high schools
Economics and environmental policy relating to the value of Lake Champlain
Fictional short story based on the archaeological history of Vermont ("The Thunder Rolls")
Fictional story based on the Green Mountain Boys (untitled)
Gun control: Is it worth the fight?
Health care: A comparison between the United States and Sweden
History of the Burlington, VT Police Department
History of covered bridges in Vermont
History of the Long Trail (VT's portion of the Appalachian Trail)
How the first year of college Affects the health of students
Poetry compilation of the people in Vermont
Public opinion concerning sex education and condom availability at Colchester High School
Snowboarding injuries—Is it a dangerous sport?
Technical aspects of snowboarding
The local rock 'n roll music scene in Burlington
The Colchester mooring law and its impacts
Vermont artists who make a difference (Jon Gailmor, Jim DeFilippi, Joe Citro)— A video

FIGURE 2.11   Checklist for Major Projects

One of these papers is to be completed for **EACH POTENTIAL TOPIC** that you have identified.

Topic: _____

Print Resources: Specific sources found:

Type: _____   _____

Type: _____   _____

Type: _____   _____

Non-Print Resources: Specific sources found:

Type: _____   _____

Type: _____   _____

Type: _____   _____

Government Agency Resources: Specific sources found:

Type: _____   _____

Type: _____   _____

Type: _____   _____

Reference Resources: Specific sources found:

Type: _____   _____

Type: _____   _____

Type: _____   _____

Vertical File Resources: Specific sources found:

Type: _____   _____

Type: _____   _____

Type: _____   _____

Electronic Resources: Specific sources found:

Type: _____   _____

Type: _____   _____

Type: _____   _____

students a task to complete or a problem to solve using it. For word processing and desktop publishing, this might involve developing a newsletter on a selected Basin issue or interviewing a classmate, developing an outline based on the interview notes, and writing a biographical sketch on the basis of the outline. This avoids isolating software instruction from overall course content and prepares students to see and use the potential for computer applications later in their own research.

Public Presentations from the Outset

Because a public presentation will be the culmination of each student's work in this class, opportunities to make and criticize presentations are woven into the study of Basin issues and software from the beginning, well before independent research begins. Early presentations may be as simple as introducing a classmate or telling about a book, or they may be more elaborate group presentations using graphs and other visuals to explain the group's proposal for controlling phosphorous levels in Lake Champlain. However simple or elaborate, the essential elements remain the same: gathering information, organizing it within an appropriate format, and presenting it to an audience. Thus in some sense students learn the same thing over and over again from the beginning to the end of this course, but the intensity and significance of the result progresses geometrically as the volume of information and the depth of analysis increase and as the audience evolves beyond classmates and course teachers to adult community members who usually are unaffiliated with the school or the course.

The Micro-Project

When the introductory phase of the course concludes, students have considerable information about the Basin as well as tools for acquiring, understanding, and presenting information. The balance of the course, roughly the last three quarters of it, allows students to pursue a series of increasingly challenging and increasingly independent research efforts called the micro-project, the mini-project, and the major project. In the first of these, we select the topics and groups for the students. Our aim is to guide them through the process from initial research to final written and oral presentations under conditions controlled to increase the chances of success. We choose, as best we can, group members who will support rather than distract or sabotage one another. We choose topics for interest and variety, but especially for the ready availability of resources. In subsequent projects, many students will learn and grow from the frustration of finding little or nothing at first and the subsequent necessity of taking another tack; for now, we try to keep the sailing smoother.

When the micro-projects begin, students are divided into mentor groups, each teacher taking primary responsibility for one-third of the projects. This arrangement allows for close supervision and good communication, and it remains in place for the balance of the course, though the groups are reconfigured for each project. At this time, we also institute a daily log requiring students to write about what they accomplished the day before at the beginning of each class and what their work plans for the present day involve (see Figure 2.12). This helps students focus, improves communication within groups, and provides us with an informative, written record of their progress. When the micro-project is finished and students have made their presentations to the class or to subgroups within the class, we ask them what has gone well or badly to help plan for the future and make adjustments in the projects to follow (see Figure 2.13). Inevitably some students cite the time crunch at the end as a misery they hope to avoid the next time by minimizing procrastination. Many recognize too that daily communication and coordination among group members makes for a smoother process and a better product. A few learn this the hard way by not communicating as

FIGURE 2.12   Sample of a Student's Daily Log

```
Jamie Weiner
Lake Champlain
Log 8

5/15/94--
   Well finally after all the hard work and endless amounts
of hours put into this project I can finally put it to a
close. This was all amazingly done last Friday. All I have
left to do is put the beginning music into my video and
annotate my bibliography. Today I will try to make my road
show contact for this report.

5/17/94--
   Yesterday I did the final edit on my video. Now it is
for real, all done. I might have to do some more editing on
my paper, but that will only make it better. After that I
want to sit down and plan out what I am going to say when I
do my presentation. Although my video will be taking up
about ten minutes, I still want to talk about other things
in my own words.

5/18/94--
   Yesterday I did some corrections on my paper and other
things dealing with the paper. I also was able to put to-
gether a database with the time allowed yesterday. Today I
want to make a transparency and make some contacts for my
final road show.

5/19/94--
   Today is the day when the guest speaker is coming to
talk about phos.

5/20/94--
   Yesterday of course was the guest speaker. The other day
I managed to sit down and write out my outline. I still need
to get a transparency and bring in my annotated bibliogra-
phy. After that it will be a few thousand pounds of stress
off my shoulders. Still the road show contact and that
should get me off my feet. Wow!! I can start to feel that it
is finally coming to a screeching halt.
```

Used with permission of log author.

well or often as they should with other members of their group because they are not necessarily working with their favorite classmates.

The Mini-Project

In the next project, the mini-project, the time for research, writing, and presentation preparation is extended to develop greater depth and more polish in the final product

FIGURE 2.13   Micro- and Mini-Project Review Form

Name: _____	Date: _____		
List important things you have learned about the following issues from your Mini-Project work:			
TOPIC	What went well?	Problems?	Improvements?
Working well in groups			
Finding information			
Organizing and analyzing information			
Using time wisely			
Phone use and interviews			
Preparing and making presentations			
Working on assigned topics			

(see Figure 2.14). For this project we merely coordinate group formation and leave topic selection open to students offering and soliciting dozens of topic possibilities (see Figure 2.15). This gives students considerable influence not only on what they work on, but also on who they work with, since expressing interest in the same topic will likely land friends or conspirators in the same group. Those who take advantage of this opportunity also face the attendant challenges and risks. Some friends support and inspire one another academically; for others, the chemistry of their relationships may diminish the project if not the friendships too. One or two students typically complete the mini-project determined to work alone on the major project. Many others learn that a healthy social relationship is not always equivalent to a productive working relationship. These are subtle but profound lessons only to be learned by living through them. As one student wrote:

> I would have to say that the best learning experience I've had this year has been how I've learned to make my own schedule for getting work accomplished. Even though I was

FIGURE 2.14   Mini-Projects Presentation Information and Grading Sheet

Parameter	Description	Possible	Total
Content	Specific facts, figures, and sources		
	Logical arguments		
	Recognition and/or rebuttal of contrary views		
	Basin connections and relevance		
Organization	Introduction–Body–Conclusion		
	Coordination and transitions		
	Time		
Delivery	Eye contact		
	Body language and demeanor		
	Enthusiasm		
	Response to questions		
	Integration of appropriate visuals		

Total _____ / _____

aware that this class was based on independent work, it isn't the same when you are actually posed with the assignment in front of you to accomplish. This has given me a very good lead in how I will do next year in college. If nothing else, I have learned to depend on only myself to get my part of the deal done and to be prepared if someone else falls through.

The incremental increases in independence, responsibility, scale, and risk from one project to the next position students to make discoveries like these that will become part of the backdrop for the academic and work careers before them.

The Major Project

When the major project begins in the third quarter, it seems enough like more-of-the-same to give comfort and enough like a large and overwhelming task to give fright. This is an ideal paradoxical balance; it allows students who were uncomfortable and tentative just making phone calls for their earlier projects, to proceed and persevere to the point of presenting their work to adult and professional audiences. Requiring such an audience, one beyond the classroom and the school community, sets the major project apart from its predecessors. Students' research is no longer an insular, in-house matter, but ultimately a public one because the final exam in a "road show" out in the community. This is intimidating, but also motivating and in the end, almost without exception, gratifying. Knowing that the road show looms ahead, even a re-calcitrant student will push himself or herself. Such a student may not be grade-conscious and may be perfectly comfortable presenting shoddy work to peers, but still wants to make a favorable impression on the town council, the historical society, or the entrepreneur down the block. This leads many students to make a greater commitment to this project than they have to any previous academic requirement. This commitment often yields dramatic results, even though, objectively measured, the quality of projects varies widely.

What many, if not most, Lake Champlain students experience for the first time in this class is the sense of being respected as virtual equals by the adults in their

FIGURE 2.15   Possible Topics to Research

```
File:     topics 95
Report:   TOPIC brainstorm
Topic
```

AIDS in VT	foliage in VT	overdevelopment of lakefront
architectural styles in VT	frog population decline	PCBs and other pollutants
automobiles	gene research	pesticides
Basin humor, art, poetry, writing	government gifts to the people	Pine Street Barge canal
Bill Hauke's influence on Colchester	health care—U.S.–Sweden comparison	pollutants in the Bay
Burlington Free Press history	health education	promoting Vermont
Burlington waterfront development	health care	property tax and education funding
censorship in Basin	hiking trails	racism in VT
Champ & Loch Ness	historical architecture	railroads and culture/economics
child abuse	historical families in VT	Rutland Railroad
children and families under stress	hockey stars from VT/athletes	school systems
cliff jumping/recreation	hotels	sex discrimination in cyberspace
climate changes	human impact on wildlife	Shelburne Museum
Coates Island history	hunting	ski resorts
Colchester Bog	Hydro Quebec	smoking teenagers
Colchester development	IBM history	snowboarding injuries
condoms in schools	important battles	snowfall in VT
covered bridges	junk mail	solid waste/recycling problems
criminal justice system in VT	Lake Champlain & Great Lakes— similar problems	sports history VT
criminology	Lake Champlain history	tax burden/will the rich go to Florida
cyberliteracy	Lake Iroquois/Phosphorous	tobacco ad ban
Daisy Turner/slave narratives	lake pollution	tourism
development	lamprey	TV stations in VT
discovery of Lake Champlain	library budgets—will there be books?	underground railroad
discrimination in schools	long trail history	unemployment
downhill skiing history	Malletts Bay history	Vermont accents, economy, history
early ski areas/their failure	maple sugaring	Vermont in Civil War
endangered plants	Marble Island history	Vermont schools, colleges
erosion in Burlington	mooring law	villages
erroneous theories/what the future will reveal	moose hunting	VT health care
ethnic groups	mosquito spraying	water quality
farming in Vermont	movie	weather in VT/historical storms
fatalities on Lake Champlain	native–flatlander cultural conflict	Webb estate
fisheries—changes in	neo-Naziism	wildlife
	old Vermont farmhouses	world markets for maple products
	organic farming	zebra mussels

audience. This perceived respect, which students highlight again and again when they return from presentations out in the community, is part common courtesy and part acknowledgment of effort and expertise. The most important thing is that students are buoyed by it to the point of believing more powerfully than heretofore in their own talent and intelligence. They realize they have things to communicate and contribute to the community and the world at large. As a school experience, this is at least an order of magnitude beyond doing well on a test or assignment designed simply to show understanding of some material presented by a teacher or a text.

The Results

The effectiveness of the Lake Champlain Class is evident in observing and listening to students who have completed it. In fact, almost every year one or two take the class for a second time. One student, who had been particularly insecure about speaking in public, was so transformed after presenting his research to ferryboat company executives that he requested an opportunity to speak to the class the following year about his earlier anxiety and the growth in self-assurance he had experienced. A similarly anxious student, after nearly abandoning her scheduled public presentation in a panic ("I can't do it; I can't do it. I've never felt so terrible and frightened in my life."), later sought out opportunities to present her findings and recommendations on the problem of homelessness.

Another student's presentation on biotechnology and its ethical implications became the springboard initiating discussion among the university faculty researchers in attendance. One of the researchers explained that he and his colleagues were so caught up in their own projects that they rarely took time to discuss the broader ramifications of their work among themselves. He expressed appreciation that this student's work had provided the opportunity and the impetus for such discussions and hoped they would continue.

Possibly he was going out of his way to encourage a student, but in some sense she may have opened his eyes, not so much with her expertise as with her perspective. And it is the eye opening—the insight, the surprise and delight of learning that comes only from seeing a variety of perspectives—that is at the philosophical center of this program. It is this that makes the "multidisciplinary" element not a catch word or a gimmick, but a bona fide difference with visible results.

In this case, a high school student had taught something of value to a group of Ph.D.'s, as well as to herself, her classmates, and her teachers. In another case, a very different kind of student, not particularly motivated academically, had a potentially momentous learning experience because he was allowed to discover and analyze a variety of perspectives on the conflict between environmental values and ski area development (see Figure 2.16).

The student began the project as an avid skier, annoyed at the state for interfering with Killington Ski Area's expansion plans. However, as his research proceeded, he came to see the partisan nature of Killington's view and gained respect for the state's role in protecting the environment for the general public good. Though his enthusiasm for skiing never waned, his assessment of this conflict between development and the environment turned around completely as he absorbed and analyzed the available information. Ultimately, he presented his findings to Governor Kunin, but more important, he learned the difference between opinions based on thoughtful consideration of the evidence and those based on emotional gut reactions. This is the discovery we aspire to for all the Lake course students, a discovery of their own reasoning ability and of the responsibility and consequences of using it.

Lake Champlain students choose their own research areas; they independently gather information from printed and electronic sources, phone calls, interviews, lectures, and surveys, and in the end, they are the experts presenting information and analysis to the public, their classmates, their parents, and teachers. This is not a common experience for high school students, but it is one we have observed repeatedly in the Lake Class. (See Figure 2.17 for some "tricks of the trade.") High school students of varied abilities, given the freedom, the resources, and the guidance necessary for them to think independently, can grapple with and grasp issues in the same way, if not necessarily on the same level, as much more highly educated and trained people in many fields. With little opportunity to be passive receivers of information, they become active participants in locating, organizing, synthesizing, and analyzing it, and in generating products and presentations that put them on a similar footing with more professional researchers, managers, businesspeople, and politicians in the real-world situations.

FIGURE 2.16   Ski Research Project Data

Spreadsheet Problem: How to Solve the State's Financial Crisis

As Vermont's Chief Financial Advisor, you have been given the assignment to solve Vermont's current financial deficit. As an avid skier, you look toward that industry to solve the problem.

Following are some skiing statistics taken from *The Vermont Almanac (1989–90)*. Use those statistics by building them into a spreadsheet, and then use that spreadsheet to develop a plan to raise more money. The specific assignment follows the tables.

Skiing in Vermont: Table includes expenditures and number of skier days

Season	Estimated Annual Skier Expenditures	Estimated Skier Days
1985–86	1985–86	1985–86
Vermonters	15,000,000	710,000
Out-of-staters	235,000,000	3,750,000
1986–87	1986–87	1986–87
Vermonters	20,000,000	850,000
Out-of-staters	310,000,000	4,350,000
1987–88	1987–88	1987–88
Vermonters	16,000,000	780,000
Out-of-staters	274,000,000	4,070,000

Daily expenditure per capita for out-of-state skiers:

Expense	1985–86	1986–87	1987–88
Skiing	$17.10	$18.70	$17.20
Lodging	20.10	21.80	17.20
Food	16.20	20.30	20.60
Gasoline	2.20	2.80	2.10
Other	6.60	7.70	10.10

FIGURE 2.17   Developing an Inquiry Course

Maintaining a Diverse Student Body: A research-based course will very quickly attract the college-bound students who have a variety of interests. A question that must be asked is, "Are the cream of the crop the students who will benefit most from a multidisciplinary course such as this?" Our answer was to design a program that can benefit most students, from the college bound to the slow learners. Our "Lake Champlain" Class has had students on Individualized Education Plans (IEPs) working along side the class valedictorians. Our procedure is then to sit down with selected students individually and explain our reasons for recommending that they take the class.

Negotiating a Flexible Schedule: It is the viewpoint of those responsible for scheduling at Colchester High School that the *programs* should "drive the schedule" and not the other way around. For example, giving the four teachers the same "prep" period for planning purposes was a must. In fact, on most occasions and in particular during the project phase, we felt the need to meet on a daily basis. Also, because during the project phase the teachers worked closely with only a small handful of students, meeting daily with the other teachers allowed at least some indirect contact with the progress of all.

Expanding Class Time and Setting Dates: Having taught the course in years with expanded classtime and years with no extra time, we strongly recommended expanding the class time to at least one hour per day, preferably more. Another area where clarity is needed is in due dates. Teachers post at the beginning of each month a calendar of upcoming dates. It includes days in which students cannot expect class time for research, as guest presenters or field trips are scheduled. Most important, however, are the days on which various parts of the project are due: thesis statement, outline, database of resources to date, letters sent to officials, proposed format of presentation, and final presentation dates.

Requiring Four Course Credit: With a philosophy that there are in fact links between "disciplines," students are required to take one-half credit in each of two different subject areas. Then, on completion of their major project, they are judged to some degree on their illustration of accomplishment in both of their selected curriculum areas. This has created some headaches for the schedulers because our computerized scheduling program does not allow for the recording of split credit in any one class. Therefore, the grades for the class must be recorded by hand on the transcripts of those students who complete the course.

Teaming to Evaluate Student Performances: Establishing a truly team-based system of evaluation when the class has little formal testing after the first quarter and relatively independent expectations for each student takes planning. Having one grade book and four teachers creates some logistical maneuvering. We have rotated the grade book each quarter so that each teacher takes attendance, calculates averages, and deals with student questions and concerns about their grades. At the beginning of the year, the teacher assigning work is responsible for grading it and recording marks in the grade book.

CHAPTER 3

Fusing Subject Areas

Linking Subject to Subject

Although any teacher can reach across the discipline lines to seize material from other subject areas, a more powerful *fused curriculum* develops when two teachers from different subject areas get together to exploit the connections that exist between their related areas. Some connections are obvious and ready for exploitation: English and social studies, math and physics, art and music, or physical education and health. American Studies, World Perspectives and Integrated Humanities are instances of natural affinity. When teachers can recruit the same students for their classes and arrange the schedule so they teach "back-to-back" periods, they gain a block of time to focus on linkages. From there, it is a short step to fusing classes, putting two or more teachers in charge of a large group of students. The advantages of teaming with others and blocking time have proven so alluring that some schools now fuse three or four subject areas, creating a large team with a lot of time held in common.

The end point of the fusion impulse is the "school-within-a-school" structure in which as many as five teachers share 100 to 120 students and manage the schedule for a whole school day (see Chapter 12). The examples in this chapter are meant to illustrate the remarkable variety that can be attained by juxtaposing and fusing different subject areas, even by individual teachers in conventional classrooms. The examples also reveal simple techniques that make possible a fusion curriculum.

Fusing two or more areas usually shifts focus away from the content of what is known toward the process of knowing. When subjects are taught in isolation, the subject matter itself tends to become the focus of learning. Students infer from a presentation of content as a "subject" that their role in the classroom is to absorb the material—to acquire the body of knowledge that constitutes the substance of the discipline. In history, students come to believe they are memorizing dates, warriors, and wars. In literature, they come to believe they are memorizing characters, plots, and possibly authors. Fusing literature, history, and other subjects gives teachers a way to focus student attention on the meaning of human events, as well as the events themselves. Juxtaposing two or more subject areas forces meaning to the front. "What does Wilfred Owen's poem say about how people felt about fighting in World War I?" The question aims at meaning. "Can you find evidence in the paintings of Brach, Picasso, and Duchampe suggesting some problems with the industrial age?" Bringing together evidence from two related disciplines helps students ask the questions that are the heart of the learning process in all the disciplines.

Working cooperatively to develop and carry out a plan is common in most professional settings—in medicine, law and social services—but cooperation in high school teaching has a spotty record. As an ideal, fusing subject areas requires teachers from different disciplines to cooperate in the development of a curriculum that helps stu-

FIGURE 3.1　Levels of Intensity in a Fused Curriculum

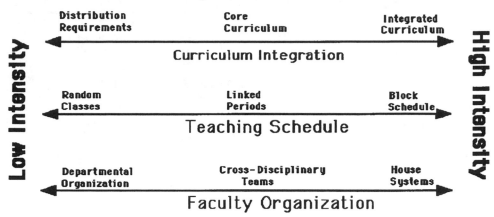

dents focus on important questions as they learn. In fact, the degree of integration or fusion varies widely, depending largely on the extent to which teachers from different disciplines can agree on the focus for curriculum reorganization, can change the teaching schedule so their students are in the same room at the same time, and can meld their personalities into a teaching team with greater power than any teacher could generate separately. As an experienced team member will attest, team planning is absolutely necessary to team teaching, and planning takes time. Increased planning time and some reduction of personal freedom in deciding what will happen in the classroom are the most obvious costs in team teaching.

Curriculum, schedule, and teacher personality influence the extent to which students can see the disciplines coming together to serve a single purpose. Figure 3.1 represents these three factors as three parallel choices, ranging from loosely linked associations between teachers to an intensively structured team approach. In its loosest form, a fused curriculum can consist of distribution requirements teachers establish once—and never speak of again (Roberts & Cawelti, 1984). At its most intensive, an integrated curriculum brings five or six different teachers from different disciplines into one group with a hundred or more students who then make connections across the subject areas. Team teaching is like a professional marriage, and it is subject to the same fluctuations of passion and purpose that married people experience. At the optimal level of fusion, five or six teachers representing different disciplines meet to create a single curriculum framework that they teach together over a whole school day, a whole schoolyear, or throughout a whole high school program. As intensity increases, more team time is needed.

Fusion Reactor versus Post and Rail

In developing a fusion curriculum, teachers have tended to rely on one of two basic structures:

1. A *Fusion Reactor* uses the idea of culture or geographic regions to show the interplay of history, art, technology, and social activity in human events.
2. A *Post and Rail* uses the historical chain of events to show how change occurs.

As Figure 3.2 suggests, studies of civilization use basic chronology to form an organizing structure, letting history guide the curriculum. (The chain of events organizes inquiry, subordinating ideas.) In a cultures curriculum, basic ideas or geographic

FIGURE 3.2   Basic Structures for a Fusion Curriculum

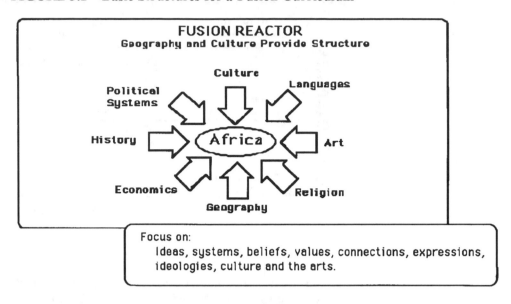

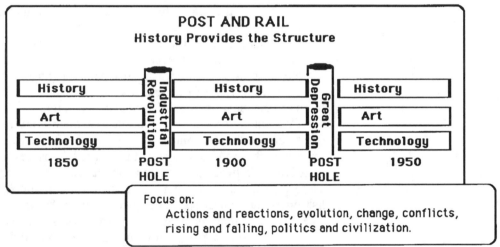

areas focus the curriculum and philosophy, arts, languages, sociology, anthropology, and political science usually form the intellectual basis. (Overarching ideas subordinate the story of how things happen.) As both "fusion reactor" and "post and rail" curricula emphasize coherence, both sacrifice coverage of facts for the search for meaning in connections between facts.

Both approaches to fusion tend to reduce the spread of material students confront in class; "less is more," as Sizer (1992) said. The "fusion reactor" focuses lots of information on a few concepts. The "post and rail" curriculum digs a few deep holes at intervals along the track of history. Still, the two structures also have distinct advantages. A cultures curriculum develops energy like a fusion reactor, thrusting subjects together so similarities and differences become clear. Focusing on one culture, area, or people promotes understanding of how elements of human culture interact to form a coherent whole. On the other hand, focusing on historical periods allows students to see how things change and evolve so the forces that promote and restrict change can become visible. "Post and rail" develops energy by moving from causes to effects. As cultural studies favor the languages, period studies make it easier to integrate science, math, and technology, each with its own history and evolutionary track.

As Figure 3.3 shows, organizing by chronology or by ideas can produce simple curricula or highly complex investigations. This chapter describes area studies (fusion reactor) and period studies (post and rail) as the two most venerable methods for organizing an integrated curriculum. Thematic curricula, which use large ideas to organize inquiry, have become a powerful force in high school teaching and are described fully in the next chapter. Chapter 12 presents examples of school structure, team organizations, and block schedules that increase the intensity of an integrated learning experience in either method.

FIGURE 3.3 From Simple to Complex Structures

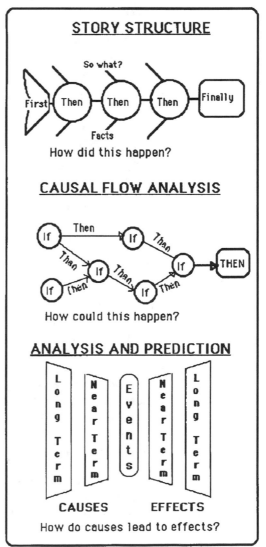

Fusion Reactor

FOCUS: Part to whole, specific to general, concrete to abstract, facts to meaning.

DESCRIPTION/DEFINITION

AFRICA

What does this mean?

DIFFERENCES & SIMILARITIES

ASIA   AFRICA

How do they compare?

THEORY BUILDING

EXPLANATION

Theory
Interpretation
Facts

ILLUSTRATION
What do the facts tell us?

S I M P L E

C O M P L E X

Post and Rail

FOCUS: Beginnings to endings, steps in the process, causes to effects, explanations to predictions.

STORY STRUCTURE

So what?

First Then Then Then Finally

Facts

How did this happen?

CAUSAL FLOW ANALYSIS

If Then If Then
Then   Then
If Then If Then THEN

How could this happen?

ANALYSIS AND PREDICTION

Long Term | Near Term | Events | Near Term | Long Term

CAUSES   EFFECTS

How do causes lead to effects?

Connecting Content to Questions

Focusing on the intellectual skills needed to manage facts and ideas from the subject areas has been a guiding purpose for integrated curriculum since the beginning (Relan & Kimpson, 1991). In fusing two or more subject areas, higher-level questions usually become the organizing force in the classroom. In creating a fusion curriculum, teachers tend to rely on either concepts (ideas) or process (chain of events) to organize the questioning process. Because both "fusion reactor" and "post and rail" emphasize different kinds of purpose for learning, they emphasize different kinds of questions. Although many taxonomies of questions exist, in a fusion curriculum there are two major families of questions:

Process Questions

- *Questions of Process: Focused on Causes and Effects*
    How did this happen? (Description/Story)
    What made this occur? (Explanation)
    What causes this kind of thing to happen? (Analysis)
    What will happen next? (Prediction)

Concept Questions

- *Questions of Interpretation: Focused on Ideas*
    What does this mean? (Definition)
    What inferences can I draw? (Interpretation)
    How do these ideas connect? (Comparison)
    What is the relationship between these ideas? (Synthesis)

In any complex intellectual process, both kinds of questions interplay to create a comprehensible and useful perspective of the past, present, and future (Clarke & Biddle, 1993). Still, in a fusion curriculum, one of these families of questions tends to prevail over the other, providing general structure and purpose to the whole enterprise.

With regard to basic purpose, it is possible to view most fusion curricula as either examinations of cultural perspective (area studies) or examinations of change over time (period studies). As Figure 3.4 suggests, area and period studies in high schools tend to differ in focus. Cultural perspectives tend to focus on geography and emphasize ideas while period studies tend to emphasize events in historical sequence. In practice, both area studies and period studies rely heavily on themes, ideas important to culture, or ideas that explain historical periods. Often, a curriculum plan quickly moves toward a fully thematic orientation, which is why the next chapter is dedicated to thematic curriculum. Still, areas and periods have provided a useful starting point for teachers in the past and continue to provide good models for fusing curriculum and teaching today.

Both chronological periods (growth of civilization) and geographic areas (cultures) provide useful focus for a fusion curriculum. Perhaps because World History and American History found an early place in the high school curriculum, Global Perspectives and American Studies have become the most common fused courses in high schools. Both create a context in which art, artifacts, historical events, philosophical positions, political trends, and beliefs can be questioned and meanings can be discovered. In general, social studies teachers have taken a leadership role in developing integrated studies, allowing history, rather than humanities (art, philosophy, literature), to dominate the organization of most interdisciplinary curricula (Cakmak, 1990). To prove truly inclusive and become fully comprehensive, social studies, particularly history, may have to relax its grip on curriculum structure.

FIGURE 3.4   Differences in Emphasis in Four Fusion Curricula

	Cultures *Fusion Reactor:* *Focus on Geography (Place)*	*Civilizations* *Post and Rail:* *Focus on History (Time)*
	Global Perspectives	World Civilizations
Global Studies	Multicultural education Human interdependence World economy Cultural awareness Geographical adaptation Community and family Ecology Regional history Philosophies and culture Aesthetics	Human origins Social structures Political systems Technological development Migration and conquest Wealth and power Law and society Women and power Development of knowledge
	American Culture	American Civilization
American Studies	Ethnicity Regionalism Cultural differences Communication Heritage Women Black literature Urban and rural values Arts	Colonialism Federalism Democratic systems Capitalism Industrialization Black history Population expansion Regional conflict International relations

Taking on the World: World Civilizations and Global Perspectives

As the world has grown smaller, global perspectives and world civilizations have become increasingly important to integrated high school teaching. Increasingly, the stated purpose of global studies is to promote a vision of interdependence and cooperation among the groups that make up this world (Jennings, 1993). Global studies usually have a humanistic flavor, focusing on ethnicity, cultural patterns and differences, the expressions of different cultural groups, values, philosophies, arts, and communication. Students in global studies gather information that lets them gain multiple perspectives on their own lives and the lives of those with whom they live. In contrast, civilization studies focus more on institutions than on ideas, aiming to illuminate the processes that drive human events. The purpose of world civilizations is to help students understand how things come into being so they can recognize the forces that influence their own lives. Systems of government, economics, technology, and conflict between different groups focus the curriculum. If global studies tend to focus on cultures and geographic areas, world civilizations tends to focus on historical change and the mechanics that make society work.

World Civilizations: The Chain of Events

Period studies, with a focus on civilization, provides a simple and effective structure for integrated teaching. Since human history flows in a linear sequence, the history of human events creates a natural sequence to follow in planning curriculum. The history of art, science, literature, sociology, and economics of any period often provide useful perspectives on how things evolve in human affairs. Why not design curriculum that helps students see human development from multiple perspectives? In fact, world civilization curricula have been developed for the full K through 12 curriculum (Alabama, 1983). One major focusing question organizes most period studies: How do things change? By looking at patterns in the process of change, students become aware of the forces that drive change in the present as well as the past.

How did we get here? The relentless march of time becomes mindless plodding after a millennium or two and this question is easily lost in conventional studies of world civilizations. Interdisciplinary world civilization courses rely on broad themes to make great leaps across time. In Mike Hornus's global civilizations course, students read *Lord of the Flies,* Hamurrabi's code and other ancient texts, and Howard Gardner's theory of multiple intelligences—while they also try to develop a city of their own in a computerized simulation called *Sim City.* The computer game, ancient code of laws, modern allegorical novel, and theory of intelligence may seem disjointed, but they all help students focus on one question: What does it take to make up and maintain any civilization?—What laws? What structure? What human capabilities appear essential? As Figure 3.5 suggests, different students make different kinds of connections between these four sources.

What does it take to build a civilization? Because history tells and retells the story in different ways at different times, the question defies easy answers. Beginning their civilizations course with *Lord of the Flies,* Deb Taft and Mike Hornus at Essex Junction High School, ask their ninth grade students to work through a desert island exercise during the first weeks of the year: "You are stranded together on a desert island with little to sustain you. Using this list of supplies, we want you to decide together what you are going to do?"

The chaos is immediate. The class has no rules, no roles, no procedures, and no decorum. Conflict is endemic. The strong try to rule by fiat; the meek resist passively or overtly. Over the two-period block, they have to invent enough civilization to allow them to make decisions about their welfare. A modest constitution, some division of labor, parliamentary rules, a way to keep records—all these must be in place before the group has the power to manage its own decisions. In eighty-four minutes, the class develops rules for interaction that they will use to manage their own classroom throughout the year. They also gain insights about *Lord of the Flies* and a solid introduction to the purpose of the course they are taking: World Civilization from Prehistory to the Present (see Figure 3.6).

History is a matter of imaginative reconstruction. Assigning students to use their imaginations to recreate history forces them to make connections among the facts, artifacts, and texts left by our forerunners. Kevin Martell and Carol Willey, also team teaching World Perspectives at Essex Junction High School, asked their students to take a journey in the medieval world: "Where would they choose to go? With whom would they travel? How would they travel? What would they need? What dangers might they face?" (see Figure 3.7). The task appears simple, but it asks students to confront social history, geography, economics, and philosophy in one creative leap. (One team of four women chose to travel to Jerusalem, seeking a benevolent Saint and some redress from the depredations of medieval men.)

Math and technology often fit well in a "civilizations" course, because math and science have driven a great deal of history. Looking at technology gives students a view of a historical period that they could not obtain simply by reading. Teachers at University Heights High School in Bronx, New York, developed a project on navigation in the sixteenth century to show students how math created the opportunity to explore the new world and to give students a chance to practice mathematics, history, and English all in one unified exercise. Students may choose to end the challenge described in Figure 3.8 after making some basic calculation on a world globe, or they may extend the challenge to begin imagining travel at that time and in the society that supported such travel.

FIGURE 3.5 **Student Summaries of an Early Civilization Unit (Grade 10)**

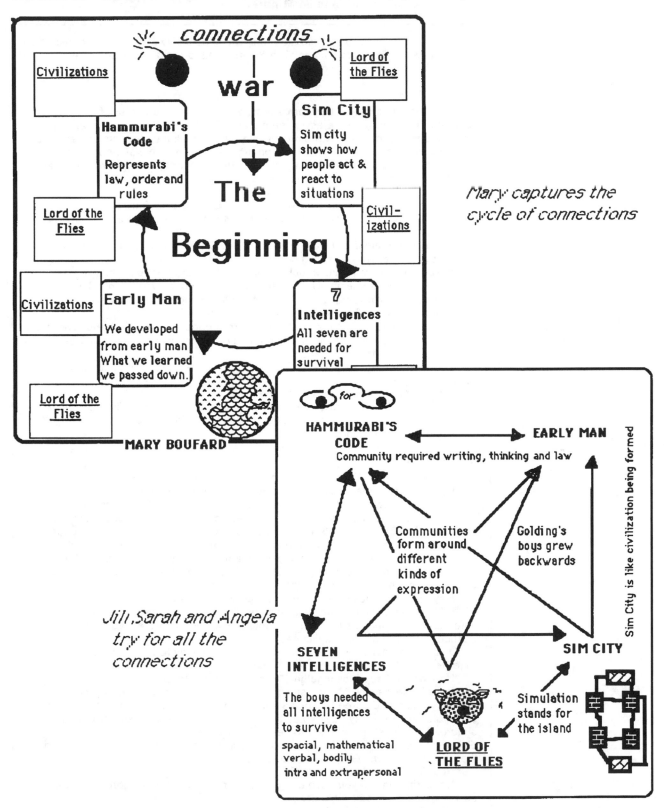

Used with permission from Mary Bouffard.

FIGURE 3.6   The Shipwreck Island Simulation: Intro to Western Civilization in 84 Minutes

Deb Taft and Mike Hornus distribute a shipwreck scenario early in their fused ninth grade English/history class. Can the students organize themselves well enough to escape the island?

Chaos: 7:50 A.M.

The students arrange themselves in free-form array in a corner of the classroom and begin to read the assignment sheet. Soon, two students are talking about the situation. Then, two more. Within a minute all the students are engaged in some conversation with one or two others. The noise level rises and falls in waves. What to carry, what to eat, how to float, whether to eat right now—all are questions floating like foam on the chaos. A few early attempts to gather the whole group are washed away in the rolling tumult.

"Why don't we try to get everyone's input?" a voice calls from the edge of the storm. The wind dies momentarily as students look around for a way to focus but soon rises again.

"Raise your hand if you want to speak!" The same voice. Silence falls. Five or six hands rise above the settling sea.

"Break open a crate, one shouts. "And distribute the goods to the group!"

Chaos ensues immediately. "Which crate? How much? To whom?" The group had discovered how to raise a question, but not how to get an answer.

"Raise your hand!" someone remembers.

Two hands rise. Two separate groups form around each raised hand. The two groups begin supplying answers to the question of opening crates. Other questions diffuse the effort.

"You guys are not participating!" a member of one rump group shouts to the other rump group.

"Who's not participating?" comes the reply.

Still, the whole group manages to reassemble itself, with a visible tendency remaining to split in half at the slightest provocation. Still, a leader has emerged, the voice calling for hands.

Leader of the Globe: 8:05 A.M.

"Everyone quiet!" Whoever wants to talk must raise her hand."

"Can you please talk up?" They want the leader to be heard.

A young woman has detached a plastic, blow-up world globe from its plastic stand. She and a small group around her decide that the globe conveys the right to speak. One globe; one voice. Conversation should follow the globe. The globe begins traversing space among the students, dragging conversation after it.

"That's a good idea," says a voice from a neighboring group, creating the first instance of affirmation of one group idea. A boy on the periphery has started to describe a method of escape to three classmates.

"Hey, you don't have the globe," another voice warns.

"I think we should go with Jessica's idea," the leader asserts. "All in favor?" No vote follows. Tumult ensues. The students are worried that they won't get a chance to talk. The leader shifts gears.

"Jessica, repeat your idea!" Jessica describes a way to tie some palm trees together.

"How do we keep it all together?" a student asks Jessica.

"Belts!" "Necilasses!" "Shoe strings!" For a minute, the whole group has worked as one and agreed on one solution. The leader calls the question and a brief vote ensues. They have voted to sail the palms. Jessica has earned new stature. The globe moves often to her call. Still, the group becomes unruly and dissatisfied again. The globe carried too much power, the power to speak—and the power to determine who else can speak.

"Hold it. We need some order!"

"No talking unless you have the globe!" Hands shoot up in vigorous pleading for the globe in Jessica's hands.

"Hold it. We need a leader."

(Continued)

FIGURE 3.6   *(Continued)*

"We need a Gilligan."

"We need a Jack." Jack was the character in *Flies* who won leadership through the promise of violence.

"No we need a government."

Government: 8:20 A.M.

"Who wants a formal government?" the leader begins.

"I like anarchy!" Laughter all around.

"I don't think we need a government. We just need one person to kind of organize."

"What's wrong with anarchy?"

"It's bad."

"You don't need government. You just need people to listen to each other."

"Yes! Yes!" Chaos is immediate, an orgy of agreement.

"Guys, we're not getting anything done here."

"Let's vote on whether to have a government." No vote ensues.

"Key. That kid has not talked yet!" The globe, now mostly deflated by the pressure of hands, flies across the room to a boy who has been watching from the side. "Tell us what you think!"

"I think we should store water in the big balloons." Heads nod in agreement.

"Can everyone here swim?" A delightful but divisive question. The wind is soon howling once again.

"We're not getting off this island unless we start talking about it." This observation immediately depresses the storm. Many students have slumped into resignation. The globe, no longer a sphere, lies on a desk, flat and unattended.

"Let's set up an agenda!" Samantha has introduced the idea of constitution, but none recognize it. As the bell rings for the four-minute break, notably weariness pervades the group.

Constitution: 8:30 A.M.

During break, while others discuss their plight, Samantha has walked to the blackgoard and begun to organize the questions:

1. How can we make a raft? (She has drawn the raft the group designed next to that question.)
2. How do we fit everyone on?
3. How can we transport water?
4. How can we transport food?

Mr. Hornus opens the second period with a warning: "You have only ten minutes," he says.

Possessing both the chalk and the courage to stand, Samantha has seized leadership. She leads the group quickly through the first question.

"Everyone focus on the board." The group arranges itself in a neat semicircle around the four questions.

"OK. Danny. You got the conch. Go for the next one." Rather than consolidate her dictatorship, however, Samantha hands the chalk to another student and returns to her own chair. Leadership passes from hand to hand with the dented globe and stump of chalk.

The next question gets a 12–6 vote. The pace of progress is quick but the minutes are passing quickly too.

Dissent: 8:45 A.M.

As Deb Taft and Mike Hornus call the whole class together again to process their experience, a dissenting group has decided to stay on Shipwreck Island and die rather than subject themselves to the will of the majority. The group has not yet created a mechanism for managing dissent.

Used with permission.

FIGURE 3.7   World Perspectives: Medieval Period Journey Project

We have spent the last few weeks discussing the way in which people lived during the Middle Ages. Through your research, you have discovered many interesting aspects of medieval life, including castles, clothing, weaponry, and belief systems.

As you watch the group presentations over the next few weeks, you will be able to see how people lived, worked, and celebrated in various parts of the world: France, England, Germany, Scotland, and Japan. What would it be like to visit one of these areas or castles? From reading the *Canterbury* you have gained some idea of what it is like to travel during this time period. How would you make a journey to a far off place? What would you need to bring? How would you prepare for your trip? What would you hope to see and experience?

Your task, as a group, is to make a journey to "somewhere" during the middle ages. You might wish to visit someone's castle. You might go on a pilgrimage, as did the characters in Chaucer's book. You might be fearless explorers seeking wealth and fame in far off lands. You might be a group of pious crusaders going to fit the infidel in the Middle East. It's up to you!!

Wherever you decide to travel, you will have to take certain things into consideration. Who are you and why are you taking the journey? How will you travel and how will you be able to afford your journey? What will you need to bring? Once you have decided on your destination and you have made your preparations, you will embark on your journey. What will you experience? Who will you meet and what will happen?

Be creative and have fun!!!!! This is a group effort, so make sure that everyone is involved and plays a key role. Be creative with your presentations.

*   *   *

Your Project Must Include:

1) a detailed itinerary that explains your travel plans
2) maps
3) anything that might enhance our understanding of your experience and the sights you encounter on your trip

From Kevin Martell's team teaching course at Essex Junction High School. Used with permission.

Global Perspectives

Global interdependence is the theme that binds cultural studies. Diane Ravitch (1991) asserts that the purpose of public schools should be to instill in children our shared, not our separate culture, particularly because American culture is an amalgamation of all the cultures that have contributed to its emergence. In part, the movement toward global education extends "citizenship" education to encompass the whole human community, including the cultural, economic, linguistic, racial, social, and technological systems that bind us as one people (Peters, 1986).

Teachers of global perspectives emphasize that our future depends on the resolution of issues that are global in scope rather than regional (Randall, 1990). In 1984, a survey of members of the National Association of Secondary School Principals and other groups elicited responses and profiles of international education programs in rural, suburban, and urban areas in 49 of 50 states (Dembo, Feigenbaum, & Morehouse, 1984). Program profiles reveal a wide interest in global connections and a growing awareness of global interdependence.

FIGURE 3.8   PROJECT 3: Using Math to Travel—Fusing Spanish, English, Social Studies, and Science

ESSENTIAL QUESTION: Is it necessary to learn how to measure?

You are about to take an exciting trip from your house in Seville in the seventeenth Century. The skills and materials you will need to embark on this journey will be provided in your classes. You must complete one level before you can on to another. Keep all your work together in your log book.

FOUNDATION LEVEL: Preparation

1. Choose one of the following locations and figure out from the coordinates where you are going. Once you have chosen your destination, you must stay with it for the rest of the project but you can do all three levels with this destination. The points are based on the math processes needed.

   A. 45W25S or 75WW 35N or 10W 10N

   You will need to know how to measure and use the appropriate tools (rulers, etc.). You will need to tell how far away from Seville this place is, using measurement and scale. The skills you will use are basic math: how to draw to scale, figure area and perimeter, transpose figures from one system to another, and find square roots.

   B. 73E 20N or 115E 33S

   For each one you must make a pit stop at 20E 34S. The math skills will include those from part A plus some geometry and basic algebra. (10 points)

   C. 123E 31N

   For this one you will need two pit stops: the same as above 20E 34S plus 106E 10S. The math skills will include all in parts A and B above, plus a comprehension of geometry and algebra. (15 points)

   In parts B and C, you will need to be figuring out your distances using coordinate geometry.

2. All students will have to figure out how long it will take them to get to their destinations by figuring out the theoretical hull speed. You will also have to change the distances to nautical miles and your speed to knots. (You will get this information in class.)

3. You have $300.00 for the trip. Create a budget that includes materials for the boat building, food, tools, and salaries for the crew. You will receive a list of goods and prices.

4. Include a scale model drawing of your boat. (10 points)

5. Explain why you are leaving and who is going with you.

6. Keep a daily log of your experiences. You will need five entries and each must be one page and include:
   • weather, climate, wind, etc.
   • health/nutrition
   • social interaction
   • course you travel, spottings at sea, events of the day
   • record of what you learned this day

INTERMEDIATE LEVEL: At Sea

1. Describe what stars you can see on your journey and what season of the year it is.

2. Give a brief summary of the history of clocks. Tell why you could or could not use a pendulum clock on your boat.

3. Write a letter to one of the fictional nautical characters about whom you have read.

4. Write five more log entries
   • Groups A and C need to write two of the entries in Spanish
   • Groups B and D need to write one of the entries in Spanish.

(Continued)

FIGURE 3.8 *(Continued)*

ADVANCED LEVEL: Landing

1. If you have landed in the 'A' destinations, plan a house that is appropriate to climate and location. You will use local materials so you need to state what these are. Draw a floor model to scale that shows area and perimeter. Include a list of tools and materials necessary. Include a sketch of how the dwelling should look.

or

   If you have landed in the 'B' or 'C' destinations, make a list of ten questions you will need to know in order to set up a life there or trade. Be sure this list is checked. Then answer these questions by going to the library and writing a report for your superior or sponsor about your findings.

2. Write five more log entries.
   - Groups A and C need to write two of the entries in Spanish
   - Groups B and D need to write one of the entries in Spanish.

ASSESSMENT:

Have a conference with one of your teachers to discuss the essential question. Then talk about what you did, what you learned, and how you fulfilled the outcomes. Both you and the teacher should take notes. Use this discussion and the notes to write an assessment of your project. This could help you prepare for our June Round Tables.

Assignment from Paul Allison, University Heights High School, Bronx, NY. Used with permission.

One reliable way to emphasize global interdependence is to focus on regions of the world and their connection to each other. Guides for regional studies have become commonplace, with notable development occurring for Canada (Joyce, 1985; Freeman, 1981), Latin America (Sable, 1983), China (Parisi, 1982; McBride, 1984; Gross & Wang, 1991), and Africa (Asante, 1991). Because the span of global perspectives is so great, many teachers have used one discipline as a primary lens for regional studies and regional comparisons, including art as a basis for cultural comparison, philosophy as a basis for a "great ideas" curriculum, or anthropology as a basis for analysis of cultural artifacts. At Drake High School in Larkspur, California, the Communications Academy uses the genre of the novel to help students view human experience from a global perspective (see Figure 3.9). Students work in groups to study a country, read a novel, and present the perspective they have gained to the class.

More important to some high school teachers, global studies allow some disciplines, such as language and ethnic studies, to find a place in an integrated curriculum when they might otherwise remain isolated. In a global context, language study gains a clear purpose. At St. Charles High School in St. Charles, Illinois, focusing on the cultures of Mexico allows Debbie Kling and Gretchen Hargis to teach Spanish in a living context. These teachers use visual and dramatic art as a platform for the development of a second spoken language. As Figures 3.10 and 3.11 show, their students create their own expressive works of art, compare Mexican artists, and recreate celebrations and rituals from Mexican culture. The objects they create or observe can be labeled with Spanish vocabulary. Dramatizing Mexican customs lets them practice Spanish syntax. By integrating Spanish with art and anthropology relating to Mexican culture, they avoid the deadening memorization that can make language learning such a dreary activity for high school students. Because a global curriculum can expand indefinitely, problems result when courses lose focus and resort to "cov-

FIGURE 3.9   World Literature Presentation

Project

Present a five to ten minute scene that captures some important quality of your novel and makes it come to life for us on the stage. You might center on theme, character development, setting, or even style. You may use dialogue and description directly from the novel, but this is not a requirement. Before you begin your scene, introduce the audience to the novel by giving the title, author, setting (both time and place), and a brief statement of what your scene is about.

   Please hand the teacher a copy of the script of your scene before your presentation begins. Head the paper with the names of the group members.

The Novel

Nigeria: *Things Fall Apart,* Chinua Achebe
India: *Nectar in a Sieve,* Kamala Markandaya
Mexico: *Chronicle of a Death Foretold,* Gabriel Garcia Marquez
South Africa: *Cry the Beloved Country,* Alan Paton
China: *Joy Luck Club,* Amy Tan
Russia: *One Day in the Life of Ivan Denisovitch,* Alexander Solzhenitsyn
Japan: *The Sound of Waves,* Yukio Mishima
France: *Harvest,* Jean Giono
Brazil: *The Violent Land,* Jorge Amado

From the Communications Academy, Larkspur, CA. Used with permission of Sheila Girton and Theron Cosgrove, Sir Francis Drake High School, San Anselmo, CA.

ering" a certain number of regions in the same way a conventional history curriculum might try to cover dates, kings, and wars. Clear focusing questions can reduce the tendency to allow breadth to overwhelm depth in the study of cultures.

A wide-ranging "perspectives course" can develop cohesion simply by asking students to search for patterns in the relations between religion, economy, philosophy, art, and history in areas that share some similarities (Ozturk, 1991). Martha Ozturk at Champlain Valley High School in Hinesburg, Vermont, asks her ninth grade students to focus on aboriginal peoples who developed a coherent culture before the arrival of outsiders: "What can we learn about being human by looking at different people who shaped their culture to the world they saw in their own region?" Her students work in small groups to find similarities among indigenous people from Africa, Southeast Asia, Australia, and the Americas, seeking patterns and connections that may reveal the essential nature of humanity. All groups focus on similar questions:

- How did these people communicate? (Languages)
- How did rituals serve the people? (Religion/Culture)
- How did they make a living? (Economics)
- What was their worldview? (Philosophy/Art)
- How did they organize themselves? (Sociology)
- How did they respond to change? (Adaptation/Survival)

As Figure 3.12 shows, her students create bark paintings, devise ceremonial masks, enact rituals, and write the stories or myths that contain the wisdom of the human tribe. If a group studies the Grass People of India, the whole class boils grass to eat. What happens to a class of people who disposed of excrement when toilets arrive in the village? Student projects and presentations cover the walls, express-

FIGURE 3.10   Integration Worksheet for a Two-hour Spanish I and Beginning Art Class

Unit concepts: Systems, diversity, structure/function, change, balance sustainability interdependence and valuing.

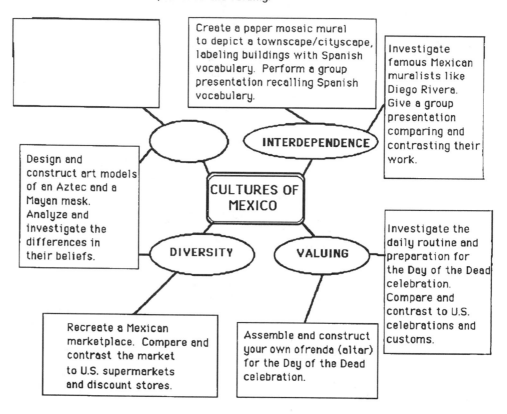

Outcomes

Students will:
Access and use information
Think critically
Communicate effectively in Spanish

Exhibit creativity, global responsibility, interpersonal skills and ethics

From cultures of Mexico class, "La Frontera." Used with permission of Debbie Kling and Gretchen Sue Hargis, St. Charles High School, St. Charles, IL Excerpt as permitted under the United States Copyright Act of 1976, no part of this publication may be reproduced or distributed in any form or by any means, or stored in a database or retrieval system without the prior written consent of the St. Charles Community Unit School District #303.

ing the joy of individual discovery and communicating answers that groups have discovered—"Does our society use masks to protect or to express individual identity? What does your mask look like? How does it serve you?"

American Studies: Civilization AND Culture

American history has long been a requirement in the high school curriculum. As the United States has grown more diverse, however, a uniform focus on history has given

FIGURE 3.11   Fusing Spanish I with Art and Design

DEAR

¡FELICIDADES! (CONGRATULATIONS!)
You have been selected to "make history" at St. Charles High School! You will have the opportunity to participate in a newly developed class called "La Frontera" (the border) that combines your Design Drawing and Spanish I classes.

During our time together you will find yourself surrounded by a new way of learning which includes creative group work, individualized attention and new relationships. Does this sound like fun? YES!!

WE ARE IN THIS TOGETHER! This class will become an unforgettable part of your freshman year and you will be responsible for making this happen! WOW!!

As your teachers, we are really excited about this new opportunity that we can bring to you and we look forward to meeting you at our special class picnic on Thurs. Aug. 26th from 6:30 - 8:00 p.m. at Pottowatomie Park Pavillion. We will send you a postcard in August with all the details about what to bring!

¡NOS VEMOS PRONTO! (We'll see each soon!)

Gretchen Hargis   *Debbie Kling*
Gretchen Hargis, Spanish   Debbie Kling, Art

FIGURE 3.12   A Student Paper for a Perspectives Course

"Harmony"

Susan Parsons
11·4·93

The people in my tribe - the Arapaho tribe - have ancestors who were the first people living on this land; the very land on which my teepee sits. I have talked to the old and wise one, the one we call Sacred Moon. I asked him what he thought would become of our land many years from now. He said to me, "Sweetgrass, I fear the future of our land lies in the hands of foreigners from far away places. Many tribes as our own will be forced to live in smaller lands than the open space we have now. If only the future were avoidable, my child."

I thought to myself; we are such a unique nation! We have our own land, we have our own language, our own culture. Doesn't that make us our own people, equal to any foreigners? I couldn't help but wonder, "Sacred man, if what ya say is true, then what will become of our people?"

"Not only will they move to smaller areas of land, some of us will also have to live in crowded places. They will have to work in white man factories. While some of them will still live on our sacred land, they will be threatened by white man construction and productions."

Used with permission.

way to a focus on many different histories of the many different people who have come to live here. Focusing on the people of the United States, in turn, tends to shift attention away from the chain of events toward the people themselves and the cultures they represent. In many integrated curricula, American multiculturalism has infused the curriculum with energy: "Is the United States a melting pot, blending all ingredients into one thick stew? is it a Salad Bowl, tossing different ingredients into a colorful but unblended heap?" The question is by no means simple. Each region and period yields a different answer.

American Civilization

American civilization courses trace the path of development from precolonial times to the present. History provides the skeleton for such courses, but art, philosophy, literature, economics, and sociology provide the muscle. What beliefs hold a culture together? Architecture can provide clues as can newspapers and museum collections. "How did we come to be as a nation? What problems did we face? Which ones did we overcome? What problems remain today?" Questions like these lead students toward the present, helping them use research to find answers that may make a difference in how they choose to live. Literature provides a close companion to history in American civilization, focusing students on the experience of a historical period beyond the events themselves. Historical novels personalize history (Gallo & Barksdale, 1983), but any good literature can provide insight into how people respond to the age in which they live (Hellenbrand, 1988). American drama reflects the growth of ideas and gives students a chance to role-play characters who reflect aspects of the past.

American civilization as a course leads students away from textbooks as a source of information toward primary materials. Looking at Civil War letters lets students understand the confusion and personal agony behind the generals and their campaigns (Olcott & Lear, 1981). In women's studies and ethnic studies, oral histories, street interviews, and student-designed surveys helps students see effects in the present that they can tie to the past (Moses, 1981; Women's Support Network, 1983). Family history is a good starting point for studies of immigration or ethnicity, particularly in a diverse classroom. Studies of music and the media initiate inquiry with familiar and evocative evidence of a living history (Levine, 1981; Cooper, 1981). Rather than relying on "cooked down" text materials, the most effective teaching units on American culture and civilization assign students to collect and examine primary materials from which they draw their own conclusions.

Using primary materials collected by students frees the teacher to focus on questions and connections among the materials gathered. The individual project sends students out to find information, then brings them back again to present what they have found, conducts a discussion, and makes connections to the projects that other students have completed.

American Cultures

Teaming literature and social studies teachers usually creates a beginning for studies of American culture, though art, music, philosophy, and cultural anthropology may easily find a place. American culture courses emphasize immigration and the contribution of ethnic groups to American culture, including African Americans, Hispanic Americans, Asian Americans and Native Americans (Rosenfelt, 1982; Fine, 1991) as well as most of the European immigration eras (Social Studies Development Center, 1983). A heritage curriculum provides a different kind of structure from an American studies curriculum. Heritage studies use artifacts from existing ethnic groups to study the interaction of world cultures.

In New Brunswick, New Jersey, teachers developed an American studies course that uses three basic themes to fuse social studies, English, math, and science—identity, freedom, and change. The course asks students to predict what it will mean to be an American in the twenty-first century (Spicer, 1986). A focus on culture also allows language studies to contribute to an integrated curriculum (Hoffman & Young, 1985). Multicultural education, aiming to reduce ethnocentrism and racial conflict, can direct the curriculum to the support of broader school and community goals (Webb, 1990).

In developing a multicultural focus, perhaps the easiest region in which to begin is one's own school. Eliot Wigginton's *Foxfire* has long made the study of one's own culture the beginning point for extended inquiry (Wigginton, 1991). Working in multicultural Los Angeles, Marie Collins and her team have organized a course around three simple questions:

- *Who am I?* (Personal ethnicity)
- *Who are you?* (Differences and similarities)
- *Who are we?* (American culture)

While the first question encourages personal research and reflection, the second and third questions bring a wide variety of sources to bear: literature, art, philosophy, and language. The sequence of questions also allows the team to emphasize basic writing and reading skills. In a sense, student writing becomes the subject of the curriculum, making the process of "inhabiting other lives" the focus of study (Goswami, 1993).

Studying one area encourages comparison with other areas. The "New York and the World" humanities program in Brooklyn, New York, uses the multiethnic population of the city as a microcosm of the world (Fuentes & Weinberg, 1993). Each student in the school thus provides access to the cultures of the world. Students can meet and interview Japanese Americans, but they can also examine Japanese art at the Metropolitan Museum to discover the origins of Japanese ideas. In one assignment, Fuentes and Weinberg (1993, p. 16) ask their students to adopt the perspective of a Japanese visitor and write a letter back home:

> Imagine that you are either Hatsue or Shinji from *The Sound of Waves*. . . . Write a letter to your friend back in your village. Compare the Japanese and American art that you saw in the museum. Which American works did you like? Why? Which Japanese works did you like? Why? How did the American students respond to the Japanese art? . . .

Comparing Japanese art to American art lets them recognize realistic as opposed to symbolic motives. In adopting the perspective of a Japanese visitor, they may critically assess both Japanese culture and their own.

A focus on American culture encourages active learning, particularly through field research and artistic expression. Using ethnographic observation and interviews, high school students can study their own culture, as well as the culture of other students. Including popular music in studies of American culture allows students to look objectively at expressions of youth culture from a critical or aesthetic perspective (Cooper, 1981). Helping students make observations and draw inferences about their experiences can help students objectify the forces that might otherwise control them (May, 1986). At Newcomer High School in San Francisco, Gilberto Sanchez and his students created and produced a play called This Hard Rock as part of a drama-based program introducing folklore, ethnic studies, literature, and writing (Sanchez, 1993).

The purpose of Las Vegas, New Mexico's Currents Team is to "teach New Mexico," not as a geographical area as much as a point of intersection between the old world and the new—a European tradition and a Native American tradition—and between *written* text and the *living* text of a energetic modern culture. In four high schools in the state, teachers and administrators have developed four variants of an interdisciplinary humanities curriculum that uses local culture as a lens toward world culture and world issues. At Taos High School, an initial study of modern culture— "Who am I?"—becomes an examination of global issues, meshing with the International Studies Program (Taos in the World: 1492–1992—Columbus, Kokapelli, Coronado, and Carson) (Melendez, Love, & Gonzales, 1993).

Robertson High School in las Vegas, New Mexico, experimented for several years with a cultures curriculum, then fused their departments into five "Interdisciplinary Learning Groups" of faculty that could further fuse curriculum in their related subjects (see Figure 3.13). Teams of eight to twelve faculty in any of the five areas have the flexibility to schedule classes, plan special activities, and design multidisciplinary learning projects that connect Las Vegas to its origins and to the rest of the country.

FIGURE 3.13   Interdisciplinary Learning Groups at Robertson High School

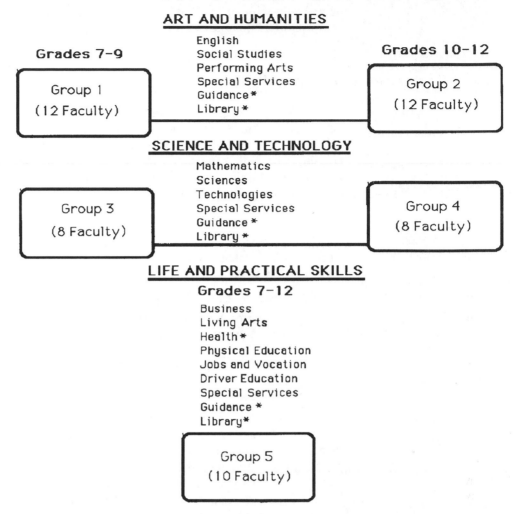

ART AND HUMANITIES

Grades 7-9

English
Social Studies
Performing Arts
Special Services
Guidance*
Library*

Grades 10-12

Group 1
(12 Faculty)

Group 2
(12 Faculty)

SCIENCE AND TECHNOLOGY

Mathematics
Sciences
Technologies
Special Services
Guidance *
Library *

Group 3
(8 Faculty)

Group 4
(8 Faculty)

LIFE AND PRACTICAL SKILLS

Grades 7-12

Business
Living Arts
Health*
Physical Education
Jobs and Vocation
Driver Education
Special Services
Guidance *
Library*

Group 5
(10 Faculty)

*Individuals representing these services will rotate among the groups to meet curriculum needs. Health teacher may need to provide advice to all groups as needed.

From James Gonzales and the Robertson High School Currents Team, Las Vegas, NM. Used with permission.

The historical research class (English/history, communications), led by James Gonzales, has produced materials for the school and for the community at large:

> In 1992, the class wrote *El Ferrocarril La Cultura De Las Vegas History of Las Vegas from 1821 to 1900,* a fifty-page history book consisting of text, art, puzzles, and activities for use in the school and community;
>
> In 1993, the class developed an *Historic Las Vegas Calendar,* noting the important dates in Las Vegas history, with old maps, drawings and illustrations of the areas main features;
>
> In 1994, the class developed a second calendar, including old photos and historic buildings as well as a coloring book for elementary school children that features familiar places and events;

In 1994, the historical research course focused on the advent and the influence of the railroad between 1880 and 1930. The high school team is planning to develop print and video documents for use in the school and the community at large. Students in the course present much of the information through their projects, skits, interviews, and visual productions. In the historical research course, students begin with an examination of their questions and learn to pursue their own answers (see Figure 3.14).

Moving from Group to Individual Projects

To accomplish something as large as a history book for one's community or a Civil War Museum, students need to take active roles in developing and communicating what they have learned. In a fusion curriculum, individual student projects have increasingly become the medium for both learning and teaching. As students take on more responsibility for communicating information, the teacher becomes a manager, organizer, and guide, supporting projects and organizing the sequence of presentations. Preparing to teach one's friends or community adds motivational force to student work that no teacher or grade book can provide.

To become active communicators, students need a clear framework in which to work. At the Communications Academy in San Francisco, teachers have dedicated each semester to the examination of two themes in American life:

Fall Semester: Diversity in America

First Quarter: Immigration and migration
Second Quarter: Civil rights

Spring Semester: Beliefs and Values

First Quarter: At home in America
Second Quarter: America looks abroad

Literature is the focus for cross-cultural studies at the Communications Academy, with history and the arts providing additional lenses (see Figure 3.15). Within these themes, each student follows an Individual Education Plan that includes two major projects, two media projects, and a special project, each with research and support from the teaching crew. Each student follows a plan that fits her or his preferences but also fulfills the requirements of the curriculum. As students complete their plans and qualify for a grade, they are also performing for others in a full range of media. The process of managing information, rather than the information itself, has moved to the center of the learning enterprise.

The Challenge of Cultural Change: ATLAS in Arkansas

Developing a fused curriculum can move a school toward more general reform, and also raise problems that do not come up until a school begins to change the culture of schooling. In Perryville, Arkansas, teachers and school administrators have been developing a fused approach to teaching global studies, English, art, life skills, and communication since 1987, supported by the International Center at the University of Arkansas. Evelyn Harless and Karen Derrick-Coleman worked as a teaching team for the core subjects, supported by Barbara Glover in Art and Patsy Smith in Life Skills. With experience in interdisciplinary teaching, the faculty discovered further changes that would make learning accessible and meaningful for all the students involved:

- *A Focusing Question:* "What is culture?" used to introduce a full year of study and to mark progress in the final exam;
- *Block Scheduling:* 2.5 credits for two hours of blocked class time;

FIGURE 3.14   Nuestras Culturas—A Course Designed for Robertson High School Students

Our Questions

- What happened in Las Vegas (and San Miguel County) from the railroad through boom times to its evolution into a small town?
- What didn't happen? What could have happened?
- What do we want to happen?
- Who were the people of Las Vegas—their names, occupations, origins, stories?
- Who made up the various communities and why the divisions exist?
- Who are we, the members of the class—our backgrounds, our current lives?

Our Stories

Genealogy/Census: Students develop their own family trees; map regional origins; share their own stories with each other and with their teachers; begin developing autobiographies and family stories; create personal coat-of-arms; investigate changing role of the census; visit archives for primary documents

Other Activities: Students learn about inhabitants of Las Vegas during the period in question; assume roles of fictitious inhabitants for the semester (preparation for writing a play to be presented at the end of the semester)

Our Past

Reading/Research (literature and historical sources): Students read Gateway to Glorieta (Las Vegas history); read and discuss Bless Me Ultima (literary source for cultural studies)

Other Activities: Students read primary and secondary historical sources pursuing interests related to overall theme, using books, newspapers, legal documents, local records, etc. as sources of information

Students learn techniques of oral interviewing, develop formats for interviews, seek out human resources, and organize ways to use knowledge (writing letter to editor)

Our Community

On Site Research: Students visit cemeteries and historical buildings; in-town tours and trail hikes

Other Activities: Students map and catalogue cemeteries; sketch, research, and map buildings; conduct interviews and assemble material on school and local "history in the making" for publication in newsletters; create models of buildings studied; make "what if" maps showing potential development of Las Vegas from 1882 map

Culminating Activity: Preparation and presentation of play, "Nuestro Pueblo: A Story of Old Las Vegas; design and painting of mural, "Nuestras Culturas," on wall in school building.

Methods of Assessment

Weekly log summary (filled in daily); research paper; projects and activity reports; tests and quizzes; quarterly self-evaluations, class evaluations

Course design by James Gonzales. Used with permission.

FIGURE 3.15 **Communications Academy Literature Study**

Diversity in America—First Quarter Theme: Immigration and Migration *Key Questions: Who are we? What is an American? How did we get here?*		
History	I N T R O D U C T I O N	Immigration, Migration, Westward Expansion, Urbanization: causes, dreams vs. reality, results. Native Americans, African Americans, Puritans, Latinos, Go-Getters, Oakies. Reactions to Diversity: intolerance, xenophobia, acculteration, acceptance
English		*Grapes of Wrath* (novel/play/film) *The Crucible* *Tom Paine* *Are You Now or Have You Ever Been?* *Young Goodman Brown* + other short works
Arts		Theatre: Production on Immigration (written by guest artist) Video: Oral History Interview Projects Multimedia: Family Tree Projects Audio: Special Projects—TBA
Misc.		Begin ComAcad jobs
	(2 wks.)	(9 wks.)

Used with permission from Sir Francis Drake High School, San Anselmo, CA.

- *Team Learning:* Cooperative groups conducting research related to the focusing question and reporting back to a panel of teachers;
- *Student Exhibitions:* Units of six weeks or so aimed at helping student groups prepare a final performance for the rest of the class;
- *Socratic Seminars:* Class meetings dedicated to critical examination of deeper questions in each unit—student led, student focused, and student directed;
- *Heterogeneous Grouping:* Cooperative groups of mixed ability worked on a six-week unit, changing so that each student cooperatively worked with every other student during the course of a year;
- *Unit Portfolios:* Collections of students work from a unit from which students selected one or two "best pieces" for final drafts;
- *Student Evaluation:* Portfolio components evaluated first through student reflection and then through application of grading criteria.

Blocked schedules and team teaching increased the team planning time available to core and satellite teachers. By planning together, teachers and students gained understanding, not only of their differing expectations, but of each other and the succession of problems they had to solve together. They could also plan to include student ideas and preferences in the units they were developing. The process of fusing curriculum has triggered vigorous challenges from the community and from non-participating teachers that eventually made the education of the whole school community a necessary extension of the fusion initiative.

The West Africa unit from the Arkansas ATLAS project is a good example of a history-based fused curriculum in which regional units let students examine both culture and the process of change (Arkansas International Center, 1992). History provides an organizing thread for student inquiry. Nevertheless, as the exhibition guide in Figure 3.16 shows, "What is culture?" remains the focusing question for this unit, tying it to others in the curriculum. Student projects, group inquiry, guest speak-

FIGURE 3.16 Exhibitions for West Africa Unit

Answer the Question "What is culture?"

Suggested Ways to Present

1. *Perform a Play:* If you and your group are only going to do a play, then it must meet certain requirements:

   a. It must give information about ethnic groups and segments of their culture—weddings, dances, superstitions, religion, ceremonies, etc.

   b. In the actual presentation, the "actors" must not read directly from note cards; they should only be referred to if memorized lines are forgotten.

2. *Focus on Ethnic Relations:* A presentation on a country of Africa and how ethnic groups of that country relate to each other is another possibility. Give incidents of specific encounters. These may be found in the books the groups are reading. (A compilation of the information from the books that the members of the base group have read would be a possibility here.) The method used to present this information would vary according to the abilities of the participants. (This may be taped and edited.)

3. *Predict the Future from the Past:* A presentation on where Africa is today in terms of culture and economy and where it is going, as well as what has happened in the past. How have we been affected by Africa in the past? What effect has that had on our culture? What effect has America had on African culture in the past? What is the impact on the two cultures presently? How will we be affected by Africa in the future?

4. *Focus on One Country:* Take a country from Africa. Dissect this country in terms of ethnic groups, government, education, religion, or any other topic that relates to the country. How do these topics mold together to form the country? What is the country's relation to others in Africa?

Note: You should not have to do a lot of research in the library except on the third option; however, you may do as much as you feel is necessary. Use what you and other members of the group know from reading the books and other information that you have obtained through study of the unit.

Time limit: 30 minutes

Used with permission from Evelyn Harlers and Karen Derrick-Coleman, Perryville High School, Perryville, AK.

ers, and extensive writing assignments add depth and a skills dimension to the unit. Students use their classroom study as a basis for individual exhibitions that are the primary means of assessment and of student-to-student teaching. Students use a set of common criteria to judge their own exhibitions and those of others in the class.

Seminars on the "deeper questions" require that students take a stand on the issues that arise in the study of any culture—race relations, civil rights, and world poverty, for example. To prepare for a seminar, students develop a perspective on a focusing question and gather information from group and individual work to support their opinions. During a seminar, a group of students poses a question and leads discussion of a difficult question. All students are expected to participate; following a seminar, they all evaluate their own contribution:

> I think the topic was a good one. Would you turn yourself black? This was the first question asked and a good one. Most people said no, but if anyone was willing it would be an adventure. You would see life differently. It was exciting and I couldn't wait to tell the next class what I thought.

> I think that I played a mediocre part in the seminar. I didn't talk as much as Travis, but I talked quite a bit. One way I encouraged discussion was everything I said Travis would correct. I like to do seminars. It is a fun alternative to doing tests.

> I brought out points that others argued against and posed questions at others' opinions. I would give myself 100 percent. I think everyone should be given 100 percent for expressing their opinions and participating.

I believe I did an excellent job of giving new points of view on each subject. I contributed a lot of input by expressing my thoughts on each subject. I also listened to each person and tried to keep order in the room.

Seminars give students a chance to synthesize information, weight points of view, and practice managing a large group discussion.

Despite university support and faculty commitment within the interdisciplinary teams, change did not flow smoothly as Perryville developed its integrated curriculum. Groups of parents and teachers opposed changes early and increased their resistance as the program took hold; they felt that aspects of the new curriculum were too "humanistic":

1. Replacing global history texts with controversial books, such as *The Underdogs* and *One Day in the Life of Ivan Denisovitch,* persuaded some parents that the school had adopted an excessively liberal, "New Age," philosophy;
2. Moving from tracked to heterogeneous grouping seemed to threaten standards of performance and behavior some parents had set for their children;
3. Moving from grammar-based English to writing-based interdisciplinary learning was seen as an assault on the basics;
4. Cooperative learning and student-to-student teaching suggested to some parents a threat to individual student responsibility (and the onset of an age in which teachers were no longer asked to "teach";
5. Conversely, some students did not initially regard group projects, seminars, and presentations as "work" appropriate to school (until they had gained some experience with self-evaluation);
6. Portfolio-based evaluation with student involvement in assessment seemed to threaten the drive toward college of students with college-educated parents.

Parents also complained that the kids were working too hard in the new curriculum.

After parent discussion groups sprung up around the community, teachers and parents began to meet to discuss these issues over lunch or at evening meetings with outside speakers. Increased interaction between teachers and parents increased parent understanding of the curriculum and also resulted in regular meetings between parents and a planning committee. Presentations by college professors, state Department of Education officials, program teachers, and school administrators, who had collected favorable statistics, helped alleviate the strain. A volunteer program brought nonsupporting community members into the school to work with the kids while the teachers and students planned new units. This also raised the level of community awareness. In short, changing the school curriculum required an intentional effort to involve and educate the whole community.

Nonparticipating teachers in the school also resisted the changes brought about by the ATLAS project. Some complaints resulted from disruption of business as usual—increased noise in classrooms introducing the idea of student-as-worker; invasions of space previously reserved for certain faculty members; and erosion of faculty prerogatives in text selection, discipline, and grading. Although several personnel changes occurred during the controversy, the restructuring program may simply have outlived the problems it faced early in the change process. As the program grew from a new program to a "regular" program, the number of "big" discipline problems in the school began to drop. School attendance began to rise, followed by improved test scores and more positive student attitudes. As students took more responsibility for their learning, their ability to communicate with teachers also improved. As they became sophisticated seekers of information, their research skills improved too. Students began to demand courses that stressed higher-level thinking skills and student-based inquiry began to infuse new energy into conventional courses in the school. ATLAS had initiated a process of schoolwide adaptation and then it had to struggle to survive resulting tumult in the change process.

FUSION SHOWCASE

Humanitas Program: Richard Rorty and Postmodernism

Nina Gifford, Ray Linn, Neil Anstead, and Chris Biron
Grover Cleveland Humanities Magnet High School,
Los Angeles Unified School District, Los Angeles, CA

The Cleveland Humanities Magnet High School in Los Angeles started in September 1981. Along with other magnet schools in the Los Angeles Unified School District, it was a result of the desire of the Board of Education to take meaningful steps to fully educate all students. The Magnet was established with two primary aims: (1) to provide high-quality instruction in the humanities, and (2) to promote the integration of students from varied ethnic and racial groups and of different socioeconomic backgrounds. As the Magnet Program developed, each primary aim was further articulated into more specific objectives. Working with all kinds of students from all over the city, we are still trying to accomplish both of these goals.

Program Organization

The Cleveland Humanities Magnet High School provides an interdisciplinary program with courses in literature, aesthetics, history, and philosophy each year in grades nine through twelve. Students have two humanities periods each day. During the ninth-grade year, while students make the transition to high school, three teachers provide all core instruction. In grades ten through twelve there are four teachers per grade level, each with expertise in a particular field of the humanities. Within a chronological framework, instruction is based on thematic units designed to ensure that students recognize the interrelationships between all four fields of study.

Every week, the three or four teachers in each grade level meet to evaluate units in progress, coordinate instruction, discuss research and curriculum materials, and share observations regarding the progress of individual students. There are also periodic meetings of the entire magnet faculty to coordinate overall instruction, evaluate progress, keep faculty members informed, and, most of all, sustain a "community of inquiry." It is vital to the Program that each faculty member remain dedicated to personal intellectual growth; it is equally vital to prevent the professional isolation so common to high school teachers.

Figure 3.17 illustrates the way the instructional program is organized in grades nine through twelve. While Group 1 receives instruction in history and philosophy, Group 2 studies literature and aesthetics. After five weeks, Groups 1 and 2 switch teachers so that both groups explore all four core disciplines in each ten-week unit.

All major examinations are in essay form. The mid-term and final exams require that students integrate concepts from all core disciplines in discussing the assigned topic. Teaching teams devote considerable thought and discussion to the preparation of good essay questions, including writing, exchanging, and critiquing their own responses in order to better understand the effectiveness of the questions. Since grades on report cards are determined by all grade-level teachers acting as a group, success in the program requires that a student demonstrate competency in each field.

Showcase text and figures used with permission.

FIGURE 3.17   General Schedule for Thematic Units

	Five weeks	Five weeks		Five weeks	Five weeks	
History (1st hour)	Group 1	Group 2	*Mid-term* *Essay*	Group 1	Group 2	*Final*
Philosophy (2nd hour) *Essay*	Group 1	Group 2		Group 1	Group	
Exams *Aesthetics* (1st hour)	Group 2	Group 1	*Exams*	Group 2	Group 1	
Literature (2nd hour)	Group 2	Group 1		Group 2	Group 1	

An Introduction to Richard Rorty and Postmodernism

This year at Cleveland Humanities High School the twelfth grade teachers decided to develop a unit on Richard Rorty and Postmodernism. The curriculum focuses on the history of modern western thought, beginning with the rise of capitalism at the end of the Middle Ages, the discovery of perspective in art, the Scientific Revolution, *Hamlet,* and the philosophy of Descartes; we end with the present-day world. Our approach to this history is thematic, focusing on specific themes we think are important, not only to the time periods being studied, but to us today. It is an interdisciplinary approach, studying these themes from the standpoints of history, literature, art, and philosophy. At the end of the year we try to present radical alternatives to the mainstream western tradition. In the past the alternatives have included Buddhism, Taoism, Ayn Rand's Objectivism, and A. A. Neill's radical approach to childrearing and education, but this year we decided to present Richard Rorty and Postmodernism as our "radical alternative." (See Figure 3.18.)

One reason we got interested in teaching a unit on postmodernism is that it is obviously a major cultural development that is reflected throughout the contemporary world (e.g., in architecture, literature, art, philosophy, city planning). It is also a cultural development that can—and we think should—be presented at the high school level. We are especially impressed with Richard Rorty's version of postmodern thought, and thus he has structured our approach more than any other postmodern thinker. Incidentally, *postmodernism* has also been defined as a "condition" and as "a structure of feeling," but we think it makes more sense to think of it as a "new cultural development"—a new way of thinking about the world and what we should do in it. As a cultural development, it is full of diversity, but it is especially marked off by its treatment of several interrelated themes, especially themes such as reason, science, truth, self, the relation of language to the world, the relation of language to thought, and creativity and the aesthetic. As we see it, a postmodern way of thinking about these themes begins with Nietzsche toward the end of the nineteenth century, but postmodernism as a major cultural development didn't get underway until the 1960s. From then until today it has increasingly influenced how people think about the world and what we should do in it.

It should be emphasized that our approach to postmodernism has been greatly influenced by Richard Rorty. Rorty has written several books which take a postmodern view of Western philosophy, and our unit is centered on readings from his

FIGURE 3.18 Humanities Magnet Theme Unit (Grade 12)

Team Members:

Philosophy—Teacher #1   History—Teacher #3
Literature—Teacher #2   Aesthetics—Teacher #4

Part I—Themes/Outcomes   Unit Theme: Postmodernism

Rationale:

Postmodernism is a major contemporary intellectual development that has influenced the study of history, art, literature, and philosophy. In that it is a move away from Marxism, it is also important in political science.

Outcomes for Students (cognitive, and may include affective):

- Students will learn the critical difference between modernist (Enlightenment) thought and postmodernist thought
- Students will learn the great importance of language in shaping human lives
- Students will learn to value imagination and fiction as well as reason and science
- Students will become more open-minded and flexible about what is possible

Part II—Curricula

Teacher:	#1
Subject:	Philosophy
Materials/ Activities:	• Chapters from *Consequences of Pragmatism,* Rorty • Chapters from *Contingency, Irony, and Solidarity,* Rorty • Excerpts from *Twilight of the Idols,* Nietzsche • Excerpts from *Beyond Good and Evil,* Nietzsche • Excerpts from *Philosophic Investigations,* Wittgenstein
Teaching Strategies:	• Socratic dialogue • Handouts from books listed • Oral reading of some parts of handouts • Essay exams
Teacher Subject:	#2 English/Literature
Materials/ Activities:	• *The Unbearable Lightness of Being,* Kundera • *Breakfast of Champions,* Vonnegut • *The Trial,* Kafka • *Victims of Duty,* Ionesco • Poems of Wallace Stevens

These possible choices of literary works are postmodern in the sense that they question whether language can accurately represent nature or express the self.

Teaching Strategies:	• Analysis of literary works—question and answer • Occasional group work • Oral reading • Essay writing
Teacher: Subject:	#3 Aesthetics/Art History
Materials/ Activities:	• Chapters from *Postmodernism and the Cultural Logic of Late Capitalism,* Jameson—deal with Frank Gehry's house in Santa Monica, California, and John Portman and Associates' Bonaventure Hotel in Los Angeles • Slides—to study pop art (Warhol: "Art doesn't have meaning") and appropriation art (art is a picture of a picture)
Teaching Strategies:	• Handouts of chapters listed • Slide presentations with study questions • Studio project on postmodern architecture • Field trip to postmodern architectural sites in Los Angeles • Essay exam

(Continued)

FIGURE 3.18   *(Continued)*

Teacher	#4
Subject:	History/Social Studies
Materials/ Activities:	• Chapters from *Postmodernism and the Cultural Logic of Late Capitalism,* Jameson—discuss the historical developments that made postmodernism possible • Essays by Baudrillard on postmodern society and the media • Essays by Foucault on power
Teaching Strategies:	• Discussion of main ideas presented in readings • Handouts of readings listed • Oral reading of some parts of handouts • Essay exams

Part III—Essay Question

Where would a postmodernist differ from a modernist in discussing the following topics: truth, reason, and science; language; multiculturalism; aesthetics and art; hope? What social and economic developments help to explain the emergence of postmodernism? Should we adopt this way of thinking about our situation in the world?

modern view of Western philosophy, and our unit is centered on readings from his *Consequences of Pragmatism* and *Contingency, Irony, and Solidarity.* Many other postmoderns disagree with Rorty's pragmatism, but in our opinion it is precisely Rorty's pragmatism—the pragmatic slant of his discussion of the major postmodern themes of reason, truth, science, language, self, the other, and creativity—that makes him more important than other postmodern writers, including Lyotard, Jameson, Foucault, and Baudrillard. By connecting postmodernism with American pragmatism, and by insisting that democratic institutions are the great part of our Enlightenment heritage, and by writing in an exceptionally clear, democratic style, Rorty has rescued postmodernism from the absurdity, nihilism, and obscurity found in so much postmodern writing, and he has given us a version that is particularly useful in the high school classroom. After the unit on pragmatism, Richard Rorty visited our high school and talked to students in the library. He gave a half-hour talk to 150 seniors and then engaged in a twenty-minute dialogue, an excerpt from which is shown in Figure 3.19.

So what is the moral of this story about postmodernism—the moral for high school high school teachers? To begin with, we should not throw philosophy and reasoning out of the classroom just because they cannot deliver on truth; the distinction between good and bad reasoning continues to be important because it often fosters successful action in the world. If we follow Rorty, we will certainly emphasize the limits of good reasoning, but we will not try to get rid of it! Nor will we throw out empirical science because it cannot discover the truth about nature, for it too obviously leads to successful action in the world.

On the other hand, we should discourage the modernist tendency to idealize science as the solution to all of our problems, social and moral as well as material. Instead of idealizing, we should present science as just another language game that human beings have created, a game that is useful for some purposes such as reducing tooth decay, but not useful for other purposes such as improving moral behavior. We should also discourage the modernist tendency in education to think that the creative artist is less substantial than the scientist because he is soft on truth. Rather, we will make the creative artist our major cultural hero—not because she gives us truth, but because her creative use of old words in new ways is essential to the solution of problems and to the creation of a better life with greater solidarity and less cruelty.

FIGURE 3.19   From a Dialogue with Richard Rorty

Image the following: One-hundred-fifty twelfth-grade students gathered in the Cleveland HIgh School library in Reseda, California, waiting to talk about pragmatism with Dr. Richard Rorty, one of the most respected philosophers in the Western world. Once Professor Rorty finished his introductory remarks, the questions began.

STUDENT: You say that human beings don't have a nature to be true to, that there is no intrinsic truth. Do you think there are any intrinsic values at all?

RORTY: I don't think there is anything intrinsic. Roughly, anything can be made to look good or bad, true or false, by putting it in a different context. What we humans are good at is inventing new contexts. There is no limit to what recontextualizing can do.

STUDENT: You encourage feminists and other oppressed groups to redescribe themselves and suggest that doing so might strike a chord in the minds of the oppressors. What is that "chord"? Is it some unifyinghuman center?

RORTY: No. The explanation has to be in much more concrete terms. Consider the civil rights movement of the 1950s. The whites in the South listened to the same passages form the New Testament as the blacks listened to in their churches. When Martin Luther King began reciting relevant passages and when white seminarians from the North went to the South and talked with black and white seminarians, there were common references to Christian doctrine to go on, and that helped a lot. There isn't a human nature or something deep within us to appeal to, but there are lots of cultural references that make up the common hords, and the oppressed can use them, and sometimes success fully.

STUDENT: When you talk about liberal utopia, you say solidarity should be based on "similarities with respect to pain"; but you also concede that pain is a linguistic phenomenon. If that is so, on what should be base solidarity?

We should also point out that our imaginative, poetic nature is even essential for scientific revolutions, as Newton proved when he first used *Gravitas* as a metaphor.

With regard to Homo sapiens in general: if we follow Rorty, we will try to destroy two key modernist ideas: first, that we are born with an essential nature or self that gives determinant shape to our thoughts, feelings, and lives. Instead we will describe ourselves as "centerless webs" of beliefs and desires that are shaped by our community's language. Second, we will destroy the modernist idea that we are a truth-finding species, and we will replace it with the idea that we are the imaginative species that creates and recreates worlds through language and redescriptions. Finally, we should tell students that we are the only animals who live in a symbolic world which we have made, a world that can be improved because, as Rorty says, "Anything can be made to look good or bad, important or unimportant, useful or useless, through being redescribed."

As students studied postmodernism, we also asked them to extend the implications of the philosophy into related realms, using pictorial rather than written forms. Their assignment was to create, from a page of examples of modern and classical architectural motifs (see Figure 3.20), a pastiche which retained qualities of both forms without letting one form dominate. In other words, they were pushed to recognize that there is no single solution to a given problem. The resulting projects show postmodern fragmentation as against rational unity, and—as our students found—there is great pleasure in shattering modernist unity. In our program, the main tool of evaluation is the student essay exam, and at the end of the unit on postmodernism, we gave a two-hour essay exam that was written in class without notes.

FIGURE 3.20   Postmodern Architecture Assignment: Four Student Connections

Results in Student Learning

In 1991, Pamela Ansbacher and Joan Herman from the center for the Study of Evaluation (CSE) at UCLA completed a study of the Los Angeles Unified School District Humanitas Program. The Program creates a community within a school with opportunities to develop critical thinking, writing, and discussion skills, and it offers teachers a chance to collaborate on a thematic, interdisciplinary curriculum. Cleveland Humanities High School was the model for this successful Program.

The effects of the Program on students—specifically, evidence of high student motivation and enhanced individual and group work—was an important focus of the final CSE report. Humanities students were found to write essays with better overall quality, more conceptual understanding, and a greater ability to see interrelationships between different disciplines than students in comparison groups. Further, traditionally low-achieving students made gains in essay writing quality equivalent to those of higher-achieving students. Absenteeism was lower among humanities students than in the comparison group, and the dropout rate among traditionally low-achieving students was lower for humanities classes (1%) than for comparison classes (7%).

Students who were questioned about the Program said that humanities teachers had higher expectations for their work, that their humanities classes required more reading than other classes, and that the work was harder but more interesting. They reported that the Program strikingly influenced their writing skills, their understanding of history, and their ability to synthesize ideas. Furthermore, they enjoyed their humanities classes more than other classes and felt more willing to work hard in them. Teachers and school administrators shared this view of the Program.

CHAPTER 4

Teaching Themes

Organizing Learning Around Ideas

In 1993, Ernest Boyer, President of the Carnegie Center for the Study of Teaching, joined others in calling for the elimination of the Carnegie Unit, an august institution that once brought uniformity and perhaps higher standards to high school learning. The academic division of content areas, coupled with Carnegie units required for high school graduation, has frozen into place a conception of learning that emphasized the separateness of knowledge and the divisibility of knowing. Boyer (1993) says,

> It's enormously revealing that very young children keep on asking "why?"—they're searching for connections—but as students climb the academic ladder, they stop asking "why?" and start to ask, "Will we have this on the test?

When they cannot see connections and meanings in their classes, passive students may choose to comply but active students often choose to rebel.

Teachers typically spend the majority of the time used in thematic unit design on the development of activities. This is understandable, because we want the experiences to be engaging for our students. However, presentation of cleverly conceived activities does not necessarily result in a powerful learning experience. Pointing out the need for thoughtful, explicit instruction, Lipson et al. (1994, p. 261) state:

> Frequent and thoughtful explicit instruction may be required in order for students to develop the higher-order thinking abilities essential for applying knowledge acquired from the theme to authentic situations. Clearly, *students can and do learn from experience as well as direct instruction* [emphasis added]. Instructional activities should be well selected and employed so that students and teachers are spending their time wisely.

Our message here is that the activities need to be well thought out, but we should give attention to somewhat more fundamental questions. Before "going public" with a thematic unit, consider addressing the questions listed in Figure 4.1.

Setting Clear Purpose

A thematic unit can provide a broad framework for linking content and process from a variety of disciplines. If well chosen and well developed, it capitalizes on students' natural interests and involves them directly in activities. In this respect, research conducted by one of our colleagues has found that a recurrent problem in the development of thematic units was the tendency to equate themes with activities. They caution that activities frequently are creative and interesting; *however,* units built on activities rather than themes often lack substance and come untangled when the mechanics overwhelm collective purpose. Certainly, our goal in thematic unit construction should be to find activities that are interesting to students, to present the

FIGURE 4.1 **Thematic Unit Checklist**

1. Does the theme selected provide *coherence,* that is, does it give a *focus* to the activities that accompany the unit?
2. Does the theme help students see *meaningful connections* across disciplines or skill areas?
3. Has the theme been selected to accommodate both *breadth* and *depth* in the unit, that is, does it permit study of the "big picture" as well as closer scrutiny of particular aspects of the theme?
4. Do the planned activities make effective use of instructional *time*?
5. Can the *learning outcomes* be identified and are strategies in place to *demonstrate attainment in contexts that are realistic (authentic)*?
6. Do the activities of the thematic unit provide for students with *varying learning styles*?
7. Will the theme convey a *clear, compelling purpose* to students, teachers, and parents, linking ideas to actions and learning to life.

world as it really is, to honor various learning styles, *and* to foster the development of important concepts and skills. As Lipson (1994) and her colleagues point out: "Unless there is a strong relationship between the activities and some clearly visible student goals or outcomes, we cannot be sure that the theme will be worthwhile."

Developing an educational purpose for thematic units is the necessary first step. To focus on the mechanics of change without having a purpose compelling enough to provoke effort over the long term is to invite failure at the outset. Figure 4.2 and Figure 4.3 represent two schoolwide thematic units developed in Vermont during the last few years. One flew (4.2) and one nearly crashed (4.3). The Wellness Unit had the purpose of gathering a whole school community around investigation of health and lifestyle issues at a time when the community was experiencing considerable strain. "How can we sustain ourselves while experiencing stressful schoolwide change?" was the question that held the unit together over a full schoolyear, involving parents, teachers, local citizens, and every student in a variety of health activities.

The second example, "Winter in Vermont" (Figure 4.3) began without a clear educational purpose and perhaps caused more strain than it cured. Rather than pursuing a clear educational purpose, "Winter in Vermont" aimed to give students and teachers a change of pace just prior to mid-term. The elaborate mechanics required to set up a schoolwide thematic unit, even in a short, relatively simple four-day format, quickly developed into a nightmare vortex of quirky schedules, unattended events, unstaffed classes, and undirected activity among students. Even so, the enormous detail of such endeavors can prove as alluring to committed teachers, who may exhaust themselves in troubleshooting, as it proves discouraging to the halfhearted. Schoolwide-integrated teaching is simply too difficult to attempt without a theme to focus on that inspires everyone to think. We include "Winter in Vermont" here to show how the risk of planning a schoolwide thematic unit when the theme is not sufficiently compelling to gather a whole community around learning.

There are numerous stories that might be told about thematic teaching ventures. Some had difficult beginnings and happy endings, while others started with great excitement yet never attained a satisfactory conclusion. As Deal (1994) points out: "The worst flameouts make the best stories." There is something to be learned from each story. Listening to teachers tell their stories gives us insights on how difficult it is, in most schools, to set aside the planning time necessary to put curriculum dreams into practice. In fact, the romance of thematic teaching is far more alluring than the reality when it comes to how many themes can be developed by a teacher or teachers during a schoolyear. Most secondary school teachers try one or two such thematic

FIGURE 4.2   Rationale for a Year-Long, Schoolwide Thematic Unit in Cabot

Why the Theme of Wellness?

A SUMMARY OF REASONS FROM AN EARLY JUNE TORRENT

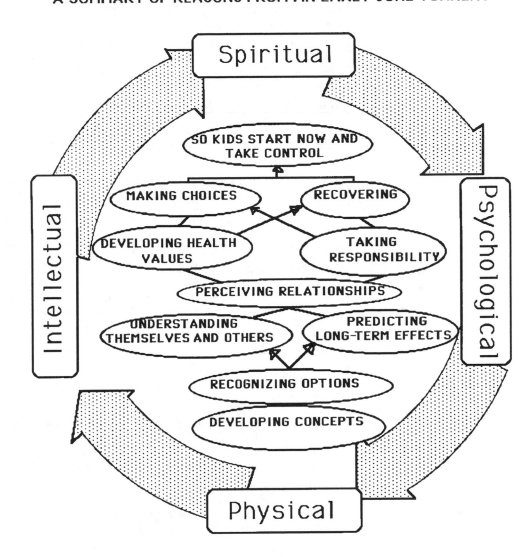

units annually, while maintaining a home base or comfort zone in the ongoing curriculum of their department. Increasingly, they find that such approaches improve the school, and they seek ways to garner the resources to more aggressively continue that work.

The short descriptions of teaching projects that follow represent the wide range of successful thematic teaching units that are going on in high schools across the country. Each story has a purpose that makes it different from others, as well a structure that reflects local conditions.

Vignette 1: Motivating High-Risk Students

Unmotivated high school students often find it easier to recognize the importance of learning when it is organized around a theme. Burlington High School, as urban a

FIGURE 4.3   Winter in Vermont: A Schoolwide Thematic Project

December 10: Physical Education teacher manages to get Jay Peak to offer very reduced rates to 290 of our 287 students over a period of four days this winter. The teacher proposed that we incorporate the skiing with our schoolwide project and study the topic "Winter in Vermont." The proposed project was presented to the faculty and accepted, though not enthusiastically.

December 17, 1991: Before classes began this morning, we were informed of the dates Jay Peak had set aside for us and that there are only three days instead of four. They are sooner than we had planned and closer together than we would have liked them.

December 18, 1991: The afternoon discussions were to be spent brainstorming ideas for activities to be offered within the context of Winter in Vermont. We had to change that this morning because the band instructor let us know that today was the worst possible day because of the dress rehearsal scheduled for the Christmas Concert tonight.

January 5, 1992: Over the Christmas vacation we went over the lists of activities generated in the brainstorming sessions, then categorized the activities into five major categories: indoor, outdoor, in/outdoor, weather, area economics. We then listed the activities appropriate to each category beneath them.

January 30, 1992: After students selected two major categories and prioritized them.

Observation: Given a free range of brainstorming and choosing possible activities, the students, 287 of them, generated about 100 activities. Another bomb hits. We found that there are only going to be two days of skiing and the mountain informed us that snowboarding would cost $15 per student, when we thought it would be $5. The list of snow machiners was posted today and started with 40 students and quickly reduced down to 16; but, it is expected to finalize at 20 or 25 students.

February 2, 1992: Snowmachining: We are still waiting to see if they are all licensed, registered, and have the means to transport their snow machines to and from school.

Swimming: We have to check with the school nurse and now the health department about the dangers of the meningitis epidemic in Quebec since the Stanstead pool is just north of the border.

Carnifest: This is now a mixture of in/outdoor, indoor, outdoor and named after student-generated categories of Winter Carnival, Winter Olympics

February 4, 1992: All lists are finalized. Right now there is an air of excitement. As a result of our blending different activity choices, Hunting/Fishing/Trapping includes winter survival, how fish live under ice, seasonal affective disorder—the title has frightened a few.

February 13, 1992: Teachers express a need to meet with their students in their activity for last-minute details. We will end period seven on Monday, the seventh, at 2:45 p.m. and meet for ten to fifteen minutes and then again on Wednesday on a six-day schedule. Maps of the outdoor Carnifest activities layout are needed. A list of indoor Carnifest activities and room numbers needs to be given out and all lists and maps need to be posted. We are working on collecting permission slips and checking those that have been returned and those that have not.

Those students crossing the border must be reminded to have some identification with them. We need to check with the kitchen and janitor to see that lunch, snacks, and barbecue necessities are all in order. The Hunting/Fishing/Trapping group still has not given us their agenda.

There is a new student; guidance tells her to do what she wants for the project. We remind two swimming groups to take their students for a snack since they will be coming back for lunch late. We need to tell the lunch ladies how many hambugers, hot dogs, and checken need to be kept warm for these two groups—one day after we get the information together.

We walked the fields and will draw up a map locating the various Carnifest activities. We will enlarge the map and hang one up by the assistant principal's

(Continued)

FIGURE 4.3 *(Continued)*

office and a second copy by the nearest outside door. We need to arrange for a bucket loader to mound up the snow for making igloos and snow sculptures. When will we send the money to the Standstead pool? They want Canadian money, so we must go to the back to convert U.S. dollars into Canadian dollars and then take a ride to the pool in Standstead. What will the weather be like? Outdoor Carnifest will be quite a challenge without snow, or with mud. Rain is predicted.

Project Day 1, February 20, 1992: The outdoors is dangerously icy. One never knows when their feet will step on snow only to pass into rain water underneath. On the early morning snow machine ride to blaze the trails for the snowmachining students to trace, we realize the original map must be changed to avoid the lake that has developed over night and is situated on part of the trail. The assistant principal is not coming in to school today due to a family emergency. Carnifest students had to be coerced to set up the various activities such as the golf course, obstacle course, and others. The outdoor students kept disappearing into the school and wandering about looking for friends or joining in the indoor activities. Guests came and went, buses came and went with students out and about in the community.

   All were photographically recorded and mounted for the rest of the school to share. Only by tracking problems can we understand what has to be done and sharpen our problem-solving strategies.

Excerpts from the journals of Felicia Woolsey and Gerry Ballinger. Used with permission.

high school as one can find in northern Vermont, developed Project Aspire to serve fifteen first-year, at-risk (homogeneously grouped) high school students. A social studies, English, and science teacher volunteered for the assignment, assisted by a special services coordinator. Block scheduling was established during periods 2, 3, and 4 each day, with period 5 used as a common teacher-planning period. During the remainder of each day, students attended regular, non-Aspire classes for mathematics, physical education, and electives.

   Because of limited funding, the program began without extensive planning before the students arrived for the start of school in the fall. Planning during the school day involved finding ways to weave the three disciplines (social studies, English, and science) together. The Aspire teachers developed several thematic units during their first year. Topics included Africa, *The Odyssey,* and photography. Perhaps the most notable thematic unit focused on Ethan Allen Homestead—the farm of the American Revolutionary hero. The unit culminated in a field trip to the site where Allen once lived. Students toured the old farmhouse and nearby museum; ate a colonial meal of greens collected along the Winooski River; saw one of their teaching team, in costume, dramatize "the women of Ethan Allen's time"; played colonial games; and did some writing.

   The teachers typically did not work in the classroom together, but tried to teach separately with an interdisciplinary flavor. Clearly, the emphasis of this program for "basic skills" students was on providing a setting where they could succeed. In fact, a hope of the program was that students would remain in school and be able to move up an ability level in classes in the tenth grade, ASPIRE continues to attract students who do not thrive in a content-based curriculum.

Vignette 2: Fusing Ideas and Applications

Carol Paskiewicz and Susan Fennelly, a mathematics and a physics teacher from Wethersfield High School in Connecticut, worked together to develop a thematic unit entitled, "Graphical Analysis of Body Physics." Designed to illuminate the theme of "motion," it encouraged the collection of data through the performance of physical activities such as a long jump, high jump, walking, and running. It also helped students organize the data, construct appropriate graphs, and analyze the results. The unit was put together in such a way that a math and science teachers could work cooperatively in its teaching, or it could be used by an individual math or science teacher working independently. Fennelly and Paskiewicz (1993) characterize their work as cooperative:

> The data collected in the science class could be taken to the math class where the data could be expressed graphically. The graphs could then be taken back to the science class where analysis is done and conclusions are formed. This type of cooperative, interdisciplinary approach can vitalize both a math and science lesson and can make work done by the student in both disciplines more meaningful in a real way.

While the disciplines remained largely separate, the theme gave students a chance to put abstractions into action.

Vignette 3: Linking Learning to Life

Patricia Millette and Kathryn Woodsum, ninth grade science and mathematics teachers at Mt. Blue High School in Farmington, Maine, found math and earth science frequently meaningless and irrelevant to high school students because they often see no relationship between those subject areas and life outside the classroom. The teachers realized the critical connection between life inside and outside the classroom and attempted to increase student motivation by interrelating the two areas within the context of their individual classes. One unit they developed to do this involved the use of algebraic formulas to teach specific concepts in surface and groundwater hydrology. With the help of a state geologist, the teachers created a number of groundwater problems actually found in their area of Maine. Buoyed by the success with this single unit, they decided to expand their efforts in an attempt to encompass the entire ninth grade curriculum (Millette & Woodsum, 1993). Using water as an organizing theme brought relevance to both subject areas.

These three stories are representative of the types of approaches teachers have taken in working toward thematic teaching. Reasons for their development vary, and some are clearly more ambitious than others. The teachers who developed the thematic units described in the vignettes found connections between subjects and consciously exploited them. Sometimes two subjects, sometimes more. They tended to remain grounded in their traditional subjects but were willing to "break away" to focus on a common idea and make learning meaningful. However, they also felt that they were still honoring the integrity of their academic specialty. None of these stories were as radical as would have been the case if integration of the curriculum took place. Thematic teaching, as described here, offered them a way to probe the edges of integrated curriculum. Short thematic units give teachers a chance to try sharing instructional responsibility with one or more colleagues, to reflect seriously about the philosophical issue of "what knowledge is of most worth," and to search for ways to better serve students.

Today, many school administrators, informed by contemporary best practice, actively encourage teachers to initiate interdisciplinary teaching. Because thematic teaching may require adjustments in the way the school day works, thematic teaching thrives when administrators and teachers work *together* to take advantage of the learning opportunities inherent in interdisciplinary teaching. Experimenting with thematic and interdisciplinary teaching may ultimately change many dimensions of a high school: (1) philosophy; (2) scheduling; (3) student grouping practice (tracking); (4) certification/licensure and inservice training requirements; (5) assessment of student work; (6) allocation of money for instructional resources such as media, field trips, and speakers.

Most thematic teaching reported in the literature results from the effort of two or more teachers to make schoolwork meaningful for themselves and their students. Susan Drake traced the evolution of one such planning effort by a six-person team in an Ontario (Canada) school district. They represented English, history, geography, science, graphic arts, special education, physical and health education, and environmental studies. Not unexpectedly, she found that when teachers arrived at a place in the planning process where they couldn't find personal meaning, they reverted back to what they knew best.

The challenge of the curriculum development process became one of "dissolving the boundaries" that existed because of the ways in which each teama member had been taught to view the world. A breakthrough took place when teachers acknowledged that certain facts did not need to be taught in certain grades. By working together, more and more natural connections across the curriculum were identified. As Drake (1991) put it: "Eventually, we may become 'connection experts' rather than subject experts." Indeed, letting go of curriculum that is familiar can be a painful process. Fortunately, a special virtue of thematic teaching is that the sacrifice of closely held content and instructional time can be modest. Many excellent thematic units can be completed in a week or less.

Schoolwide thematic units promise to bring an entire community of students and teachers into meaningful contact. Brief, schoolwide thematic units may be strategically placed during the schoolyear, sometimes during a week of community celebration, or perhaps before a vacation period. Although this strategy is not a universal recommendation, it can be a valuable experiment to determine who might assume leadership in future efforts, and to identify trouble spots that will need to be accommodated. If conducted whimsically, and the results turn out badly, that poor outcome can set back future interdisciplinary efforts.

Choosing Themes for Development

The development of themes is not novel to high school teachers. In his lexicon of interdisciplinary curriculum terminology, Gordon F. Vars (1993) regards theme as, "a generic term for any title, topic, concept, issue, or problem that is used as a unifying focus in curriculum designs." In fact, any discipline can be represented in terms of the core ideas that bring purpose to information. For example, Figure 4.4 represents the themes that teachers at the School without Walls in Rochester, New York, found in the discipline of history. On close inspection, one sees the promise of these themes transcending history with attention to anthropology, law, the arts, politics, geography, and the environment. When ideas such as these force us to cross disciplinary lines for information, the whole school curriculum may become thematic. Of course, breaking away from one's own discipline and finding connections with other teachers is much more challenging than teaching themes in a single classroom.

Some commonly taught high school subjects, such as history, have an expansive focus and loose boundaries that make it easy to find connections with other content realms and academic specialties. Fortunately, some national curriculum groups—the National Council for the Teaching of Mathematics, The National Science Teachers Association, as well as the National Council for the Social Studies—have recognized the need to help students find connections with the real world, and have developed guidelines that support thematic teaching. These national initiatives buttress the plans of teachers and schools who have chosen to move toward interdisciplinary teaching.

Ernest Boyer (1983) recommends eight themes to tie the subject areas into meaningful bundles based on "human commonalties" that cross all age and cultural lines.

FIGURE 4.4   Themes that Emerge from a Curriculum in U.S. History

> The themes identified below are central to all eras and represent the most signif-
> icant movements and ideas from our past. These themes enable students to
> evaluate what ideas, what documents, what leaders, and what events played
> significant roles in our nation's history.
>
> **Society:** The gathering and interaction of the nation's people and culture—the
> understanding that all groups have played a vital role in our history.
>
> **Politics:** The evolution of American Democracy, its ideas, institutions, practices,
> and controversies. The role of the Constitution in U.S. history.
>
> **Economics/Technology:** Economics and technological changes and their
> relation to society, government, ideas, the geographic setting, and environment.
>
> **Artistic Expression:** The way in which citizens have artistically expressed
> themselves. The relationship between art and society. The change and continuity
> in artistic styles. The development of a U.S. style.
>
> **International Relations:** The changing roles and interactions of the United
> States in the world.
>
> **Local History:** The changing roles and interactions of federal and local govern-
> ment. The relationship between local events and national history. The growth and
> development of the Rochester area.

These themes are heavily based on the findings of the National History Project, July, 1993, administered by
the National Center for History in the Schools.

Used with permission of Andrew Nagel, School Without Walls, Rochester, NY.

From his perspective, themes can help teachers focus directly on what it means to be
an educated person.

1. *The Life Cycle:* Reflection on birth, growth, and death, emphasizing responsibility for
   one's own body functions;
2. *Language:* Symbols and communication across the subject areas;
3. *The Arts:* The universal language of self-expression;
4. *Time and Space:* Western civilization to understand the past and non-Western civilization
   to understand the future;
5. *Groups and Institutions:* The social web that shapes our lives;
6. *Work:* The simple economics of producing and consuming;
7. *The Natural World:* Our connections that govern survival on this planet;
8. *Search for Meaning:* How we fashion commitment to ourselves and each other.

This construction of themes, and many others, subordinate facts to questions and
help students construct a personal view of what things mean and how things work.
Boyer's themes give teachers a chance to redirect their planning toward integration,
first by linking and fusing subject areas (as described in the previous chapter) and
then potentially by reorganizing curriculum around the themes themselves.

At York High School in Newport News, Virginia, four ninth-grade teachers, representing English, science, mathematics, and social studies, formed an instructional
team and agreed to work cooperatively with a block-scheduled cohort of 100 heterogeneous ability students. As they began, some instructional time was used traditionally, although teachers actively looked for *connections* between their disciplines.
Additionally, the teachers agreed to employ the theme, "Human Connections," to
more consciously bypass the disciplines and present students with what Ernest Boyer
had identified as attributes of an educated person. Thus, seven sub-themes were studied over the course of the year: (1) the life cycle, (2) language, (3) aesthetics, (4) time
and space, (5) groups and institutions, (6) producing and consuming, and (7) ecology.

The teachers combined their classes from time to time to draw attention to the "Human Connection" theme, which counted as 10 percent of a student's grade in English, social studies, science, and math. The teachers felt empowered by the flexibility they were given by school administration to put this program together. The team tried to provide real-world experiences, producing instructional products and services that reflect what students will do as adults. As Charles Gilliam (1994), a member of the team commented: "We see 'Human Connections' as a *work in progress,* something that will continue to change as we go along."

The National Center for Improving Science Education (1989) offers a set of conceptual themes for looking at change in science and related disciplines:

Cause and Effect	Change and Conservation
Diversity and Variation	Energy and Matter
Evolution and Equilibrium	Models and Theories
Probability and Prediction	Structure and Function
Systems and Interaction	Time and Scale

It is not difficult to find similar or supporting themes in most disciplines.

Large themes may also lead teachers toward a global perspective for their classes. Trade, food, environment, war, technology, and human rights are all thematic issues that cross borders and defy purely local treatment. In an interdependent world, local events have global effects. David Shiman's (1993) teaching guides help students develop an understanding of human rights that they can use to examine specific events in any region, including their own classrooms (see Figure 4.5). How can we protect human rights? The question can be applied to a classroom, a government, or a world body. Human rights issues in South America become migration issues in North America, with economic, cultural, and social consequences. Issues that once were local and isolated have now become global and pervasive in the experience of being human.

The Themes of Motion and Visibility in New York

Some high schools are using a few themes to organize a distinctive and comprehensive curriculum for their schools. In New York City, International High School serves a student body composed entirely of immigrant students. In a curriculum organized around two themes each year, "Motion" and "Visibility/Invisibility," students practice language skills as they make connections among four subject areas. The Visibility/Invisibility and Motion programs bring physics, mathematics, English, and physical education into one curriculum structure. Focusing on a few large themes helps the faculty organize language development around ideas that are recognizable in the lives of their students. Final portfolio entries ask students to use information from the four central disciplines to solve a problem related to the organizing theme.

The International High School faculty worked collaboratively with LaGuardia Community College over several years to develop their schoolwide thematic design, increasing the level of integration at each iteration and gradually produced a thematic curriculum called *The Motion Program* (Hirschy, Lopez, Rugger, & Krull, 1991). Initially a way to integrate mathematics and science for inner-city students, the program now incorporates English and physical education as well. The course activities guide for the Motion Program is now nearly 330 pages long, and growing. The physics component of the program includes physical laws and experiments related to motion from the experiential to the molecular level, all of which students experience directly and measure using mathematical techniques. Literature that describes the experience of motion, as well as language studies related to action, connects math and physics to human experience (see Figure 4.6). In a Project Adventure compo-

FIGURE 4.5   **Framework for the Initial Examination of a Human Rights Theme**

Human Rights Squares				
A human right	Country where human rights are violated	Document that proclaims human rights	Group that was persecuted in the past	Group in your country that wants to deny rights to others
Country where people are denied rights because of their skin color	Country where groups make conflicting rights claims	Organization that fights for human rights	Film that is about rights	Country where people are tortured
Singer who sings about rights	Right your parents have that you do not	Country where human rights situation has improved recently	Type of human rights violation that most disturbs you	Country where there is not freedom of speech
Right denied to you in school	Books about rights	Person who is a fighter for human rights	Rights sometimes denied to women	Right all children should have
Country where people are denied rights because of their religion	Human rights not yet achieved by everyone in your country	People denied right to establish their own nation or homeland	Human rights being achieved around the world	Right of yours that is respected

From Shiman, David A. (1993). *Teaching human rights.* © Center for Teaching International Relations, University of Denver, Denver, CO. Used with permission.

nent, students work through physical tasks that test their strength, decision-making ability, knowledge of physical movement, and cooperation. The math and physics are offered in a block of back-to-back class periods, while the English and Project Adventure components can take place at various times in the daily schedule.

Expanding the program to include literature and Project Adventure was a key element in the development of The Motion Program. Linking the entire program and creating a small learning community serve to integrate not just the math and science learning but students' whole school experience. This community creates a natural support group for each student academically, socially, and emotionally. Planning for the course leads teachers to plan collaboratively for instruction based on student needs and interests. These factors, taken together, lead toward student success. As students experience success, they are more likely to view themselves as able to enter careers based on science or math. Further, students who are weak in math have an alternate, experientially based road to develop these math skills (Hirschy et al., 1991, p. 1).

Having succeeded with the theme of motion, teachers at the International High School took on an even more promising challenge, a curriculum that would link the visible world of the senses with the invisible world of the mind's constructions. Converting information from the senses into ideas to think about is surely the work of the English language, but it is also an enterprise common to all work in the disciplines. The materials for the Visibility/Invisibility program were first developed and piloted by three physics/math teachers, two literature teachers, and a Project Adventure teacher,

FIGURE 4.6   A Measurement and Motion Exercise

The Theme of Motion

The word that sums up the theme of your four classes is **Motion**. Before we start the literature part of the class, we are going to look at a variety of words which relate to the word **Motion**. The job of the people at the table is to look at the words below and divide the list so everyone has an almost equal number of words. Then, assign each person to write down the meaning of his or her word and draw a picture using stick figures to show its meaning. Decide on a way to present your group's work to the class.

> MOTION
> EMOTION
> MOVEMENT
> MOBILE
> MOTIVE
> MOTIVATE
> MOTIVATION

Group Task

When you finish, answer the following questions together and be prepared to hand in and present your answers.

- What happened in the group that caused the work to get done? For example, how did the group decide who would do each words, or who would speak, or whose answers to questions would be handed in? Be specific and use names of people in the group.
- What problems did the group have and how did you solve them? If you didn't solve them, what ideas do you have on how they could have been solved?
- When you work as a group again, what would you like to do differently to make the group work at its best?
- Which words on the list could be used to describe what happened in the group? Use them in sentences to describe what happened.
- What questions do you have about the theme of motion in literature?

From *The Motion Program*, The International High School/Middle College, New York, NY, 1991. Used with permission of Philip David Hirschy.

working with an instructional development person (Hirschy et al., 1993). The program uses extensive group work to build both trust and language proficiency and introduces the library for information, but its core remains experimentation with connections between the world of objects and the world of ideas (Hirschy et al., 1993, p. ii):

> Students use the writing process to produce academic and creative writing connected to the theme. This class supports the development of communication skills which enable students to share their feelings, emotions and individual lives. The class emphasizes generalization, creative thinking, and the ability to move from the literal, concrete world into the figurative, symbolic and abstract one.

The theme of Visibility/Invisibility merges three distant worlds: physics and math, were scientists scrutinize physical phenomena hoping for a glimpse of invisible laws and forces; literature, in which readers scrutinize fictitious characters for a glimpse into the human heart; and Project Adventure, where our dreams help us carry out physical tasks that first seem impossible. Many Visibility/Invisibility exercises ask the student to examine the interaction of the physical world and the world we construct in our minds.

In a typical classroom at International High School, groups of four or five students work simultaneously on different projects or exercises located at several stations around the room. As they cycle from station to station, they develop an increasing sophistication about the central themes, as well as language skills, that let them express relationships between different events and ideas. As they complete their work at any given station, they "debrief" continuously—with other students, with the faculty, then perhaps with the whole class. As Assistant Principal Sue Ellen Weiner explains the process, students use their high school experience to construct content knowledge as well as a language system in English that stresses the meaning and connection in experience. Facility in English results from the whole thematic experience, rather than from an isolated class aimed at English fluency.

To connect the wide variety of learning activities to the theme of motion, the faculty developed a portfolio system that lets them hold the theme central, but vary the requirements to meet individual needs and abilities. Their cumulative portfolio for each student includes feedback from themselves, from their peers, and from their teachers. The summative portfolio assignment in Figure 4.7a asks students to compare their achievement to their original goals and then make connections between the experiments they have conducted, the measurements they have taken, the literature they have read, and the group challenges they have faced and mastered. Student portfolios are judged by teachers, peers, and the students themselves, using criteria students helped develop.

FIGURE 4.7a   Motion Program Portfolio Assignment

Personal Evaluation:

Please write about your progress. Your portfolio will have both a personal statement and a part that demonstrates your mastery of the ideas in The Motion Program.

Personal Statement:

- What personal goals have I achieved?
- What are my goals now?
- What am I especially proud of?
- What have I learned about working with others?

Mastery Statement:

How are the four classes of motion connected? How are they different?

In "To Build a Fire," Autobiography," "Southbound on the Freeway," "Being Moved," "The Paw," and "Graphing Lives," you saw the concept of motion used in a variety of ways. Select two of these activities and describe in detail how a person or character can be in motion in ways that are physical and not physical.

When an object falls, describe its motion as carefully as you can: What happens to it? Why does it behave as it does? You may wish to use charts, graphs, and formulas to explain the distance, velocity, and acceleration.

When we do experiments, we usually take measurements. What is a measurement? What are units? Explain how measurements have errors. When we make a graph of measurements, sometimes the curve doesn't go through all the points. Explain. What does the curve represent?

A scientist who studies fish goes to a small lake with a net. Describe a good procedure she might use to learn about the fish in the lake.

In Project Adventure, we are working to develop:

- self-expression/sharing,
- being comfortable with others/self-confidence, and
- respect/trust

Describe an activity which we have done to develop each area. Explain how each activity helped develop the skill.

How does the class contract support these goals?

How do these skills help you in your work in the other classes?

Use as many pages as you wish to answer these questions.

Please insert your personal statement, your mastery statement, and all activities listed on your cover sheet.

FIGURE 4.7b   Motion Program Student Evaluation Form

Evaluation Guidelines

Reader's Name: _____

The following categories and descriptions were generated by the Motion class to be used in self, peer, and instructors' evaluations. For a person to deserve an A in classwork or portfolio, they should get an A in most of the categories, not necessarily every one. For a person to deserve a B, they should get a B in most of the categories. They may be an A in some and C in some.

Classwork:

Attendance, lateness

    A   None except for emergencies
    B   2 3
    C   4–6
    D   7–8
    N.C. 9 or more

Mark _____

Working with others

    Leader, supports others, helps others
    A   almost all the time
    B   most of the time
    C   sometimes yes, sometimes no
    D   rarely, needs improvement
    N.C. not acceptable

Mark _____

The amount of work completed

    Has completed _____ activities
    A   14–15 activities
    B   12–13 activities
    C   10–11 activities
    D   8–9 activities
    N.C. not acceptable

Mark _____

Concentration

    Works on activities, does not fool around
    A   almost all the time
    B   most of the time
    C   sometimes yes, sometimes no
    D   rarely, needs improvement
    N.C. not acceptable

Mark _____

Understanding of classwork

    Can explain almost all the work to others
    A   almost all the time
    B   most of the time
    C   sometimes yes, sometimes no
    D   rarely, needs improvement
    N.C. not acceptable

Mark _____

Communication growth

    Progress in the ability to write, speak, and understand English, or consistent mastery
    A   excellent
    B   good
    C   fair
    D   poor
    N.C. not acceptable

Mark _____

Classwork Mark: _____

Figures 4.7a and 4.7b are from *The Motion Program*, The International High School/Middle College, New York, NY, 1991. Used with permission of Philip David Hirschy.

Cautions and Caveats

In their zeal to move toward interdisciplinary teaching, schools risk moving forward too aggressively. This hop-on-board-a-moving-train tendency, often experienced in curriculum and instruction, can result in learning outcomes that are unclear or ill-defined. According to Moore (1988), because the development and use of thematic units is relatively easy to do, it *can* be accompanied by a litany of bad practices:

- Teaching with no direction (every direction is no direction)
- Too many tangents
- Failure to establish clear goals and objectives

- Unmotivated students become discouraged
- Lack of attention to basic skills
- Superficial teaching
- Conceptual confusion

The pressure to ensure state- and district-mandated learning outcomes *can* serve as countervailing force against the wide use of thematic teaching. However, we continue to be impressed with how effectively teachers find ways to make interdisciplinary efforts conform to standards. In fact, many teachers and administrators today are trying to change these standards to what they believe will more appropriately characterize learning in the future. That work, necessarily, is political.

These potential problems not withstanding, thematic teaching can be a first step for working through the many challenges presented by a comprehensive interdisciplinary or integrated approach to secondary schooling. Lest we go too far, we are reminded that, ". . . we must examine under what circumstances activities, subjects, and/or content areas might need to be taught independently, that is, out of the integrated framework" (Vermont Institute for Science, Mathematics and Technology [VISMT], 1994). Finally, when we ask teachers to collaborate in producing interdisciplinary units, it would be well to remember Jacobs' (1991) advice: "Good teams, like good marriages, are voluntary."

Teachers who have developed interdisciplinary units can offer us important *process* suggestions as we begin to attempt similar work. Judy Moore, a language (Spanish) teacher who has considerable experience in thematic and team teaching, shared the tips in Figure 4.8 with her colleagues at Hartford High School in Vermont. This list can serve as useful suggestions for possible approaches in any school.

Why Not Total Integration?

Today, the integrated teaching movement in the United States, as exemplified by the work of Susan Kovalik (1994) and her "Integrated Thematic Instruction" (ITI) approach, takes schools well beyond the thematic teaching described in this chapter. Her adherents in numerous ITI-sanctioned schools, throughout the United States and internationally, will be satisfied with nothing less than a radical transformation of K through 12 education. A thematic unit here and there is seen as the cliché, an insignificant "drop in a bucket," and doesn't come close to achieving the substantive change needed in high schools. Kovalik has, for example, urged the elimination of the seven-period day and all textbooks, promoted year-round schooling with significant teacher planning/inservice time, and advocated for the use of a single, year-long theme for students.

In Kovalik's view, interdisciplinary teaching simply selects from traditional disciplines—that is, it still gives inappropriate attention to the traditional categories or disciplines of learning that have dominated U.S. schools (Kovalik, 1994). The integrated curriculum school would be "real-world" based, and not attempt to rationalize adherence to traditional academic structures. As James Beane (1994) points out, the integrated curriculum movement seeks nothing less than a radical transformation of schooling. School systems must acknowledge that the traditional curriculum preserves the elite, dominant (largely white male), official knowledge of Western culture. That curriculum will not serve the schools of today with their diverse student population. Beane, then, views the full extension of integrated curriculum representing a "paradigm war" being waged in schools between its advocates and those finding meaning in traditional disciplines as defined in the high school curriculum.

We believe in the notion of "successive approximation"; for example, we often settle for less than we desire in our personal and professional lives, hoping to move

FIGURE 4.8   Considerations in Getting Underway with Thematic Teaching

1. Be aware of subject matter being covered in other disciplines so you can refer to it when it applies to your own teaching. Students understand issues better when they are tied to previously learned material.
2. Develop an interdisciplinary unit or quarter with another teacher whose class meets at the same time as yours. The unit will need to meet the objectives of both classes and can be taught to the two classes jointly or separately by each of you.
3. Offer USEFUL faculty inservice on interdisciplinary teaching.
4. Carefully establish your goals and objectives and make sure that a strong discipline base is either taught in your class, or already exists.
5. Consider teaching a certain unit or thematic approaches across the curriculum (in applicable courses): environment, nuclear war/peace, the enlightenment, great works, great men and women, good and evil, love and hate. Or, a different cross-curricular subject could be taught each year in four-year cycles.
6. Cluster the registration of students in courses with parallel concept development so that similar skills can be taught in several disciplines at the same time. For example, students in a writing course should take other courses that require writing so they can apply knowledge from the writing course to what they are learning and doing elsewhere.
7. Concentrate on teaching your present classes with emphasis on integrative teaching styles; have the cognitive development of your students as your goal; encourage problem solving, abstract thinking, etc.; design a stimulating environment.
8. Consider offering a course during "off" science lab days to combine the discipline of that science with another discipline: design and development/ science and society.
9. Offer a two-week, schoolwide mid-year study of a certain theme, unit, question or issue: drug abuse and health, nuclear/peace, etc. Try to involve all departments.
10. Establish ways that skills will not simply be repeated in class after class, but that the learning will actually spiral . . . grow from one subject to another and from year to year.
11. Discuss what you are doing in your classes with fellow teachers on an ongoing basis—share ideas and excitement.
12. Be aware of curriculum in feeder schools and colleges when establishing a need for interdisciplinary versus disciplinary courses.
13. Establish ways mathematical concepts can be applied to other classes.

By Judy Moore, Hartford High School, Hartford, VT. Used with permission.

from one small success to a larger one. In the context of curriculum, this means that all teachers may not be part of the reconstituting of schools as the curricuolum integrationists have urged. The purpose of this chapter has been to clearly illustrate how teachers, working individually or with one or more colleagues, have broken away from traditional, discipline-bound teaching through the use of *thematic units*. Sometimes the development and teaching of these thematic units *is* motivated by a desire to transform the school along the lines advocated by Kovalik and Beane. However, at other times, teachers have not moved into such a socio-political context. They may simply believe that students can be better served and that a new approach is warranted in their teaching. Teachers do not initially need tight, ideological positions to improve the educational experience of the students they serve. In short, we do not devalue what some advocates of integrated curriculum might characterize as the "modest" curriculum efforts described in this chapter.

Beginning Thematic Design

For a teacher or school convinced that breaking disciplinary boundaries is worth considering, thematic teaching provides a reliable way to begin. While such efforts work most effectively when teachers collaborate, individual teachers can be successful in this instructional approach. Such teaching usually begins by selecting the content that will be packaged into an appropriate framework. There are numerous "planning frameworks" being advocated by workers in the field. Heidi Hayes Jacobs has developed one such comprehensive guide to unit development (Jacobs, 1989). Jacobs (1991, p. 27) suggests designing thematic units such as these within a larger planning framework that will help the school and community adapt while the curriculum changes:

> 1) *Action research:* looking inside and outside the existing curriculum for models that have worked; 2) *proposal:* creating a proposal for the board, administration and faculty explaining the purpose and long-term prospects for the innovation; 3) *running a pilot* to see what works and what doesn't; 4) *adopting a revised program:* passing the changed curriculum through the formal channels of the school.

There are numerous commercially produced interdisciplinary curriculum available, many of them excellent. Also, educational literature, the Educational Resources Information Center (ERIC), and professional conferences provide countless examples. The work of building interdisciplinary units "from scratch," while perhaps inefficient, is a highly effective way to build confidence in the kind of teaching that supports integrated learning.

Thematic design requires a commitment of school resources to the enterprise. The joy and anguish (angst) of first-hand experience should help a teacher argue persuasively for the *resources* that will be required to tackle interdisciplinary teaching in a more substantial way later. By resources we mean things such as time for planning, library media, access to (computer) technology, community people and locations, and money for instructional supplies and equipment.

THEMATIC TEACHING SHOWCASE

Team Zenith: Integrating Teams, Themes, and Projects

Tom McGuire
Thayer Junior/Senior High School,
Winchester, New Hampshire

Discrimination: A Theme

Winchester is an economically deprived town in southwestern New Hampshire. The town takes pride in Thayer Junior/Senior High School, and truly tries to fund the school to the best of its abilities. In spite of this, there is very little money to lavish on extras. Thayer High School has received national attention as a result of its gifted and charismatic principal, Dr. Dennis Littky. Dr. Littky has not only drawn the attention of educators for his innovative methods but also because of a legal battle surrounding his unlawful firing by the school board several years ago. The story has been recounted in a book and later a television movie entitled *Doc* and "A Town Torn Apart," respectively. Because of Dr. Littky's successful grant writing efforts, Thayer has access to a moderate degree of technology in the form of an in-house computer network consisting of about 50 computers to serve 340 students. To some degree this helps mitigate shortages in other resource areas.

Thayer is a student-centered school. One is unlikely to see students in rows receiving information from the teacher. Student-as-worker and teacher-as-coach is not just a buzz phrase at Thayer. We live it everyday and endeavor to "coach" students deeper and deeper into what it is they are working on. Courses of study are hung on the foundation of Thayer's nineteen skill areas. These skills have been defined by the staff over the last several years. When a project is designed, often with student input, a great deal of effort goes into ascertaining how the project will enable the students to become more proficient in these skills. The completed project is then reviewed in relation to these skills and put into the student's skill portfolio. Cross-reference sheets are used to illustrate which other skills have been met by this process as the work is placed in only one of the nineteen folders. Students are regularly encouraged to update their portfolios as work is handed back to them. Each year only their best work follows them to the next grade.

Welcome to Team Zenith

Zenith is the name of the eleventh grade class at Thayer, consisting of English, economics, and history. The Team Zenith is comprised of Mike Brown, Jean Kennedy, and myself, Tom McGuire. Early on in our time together we knew that the personalities were right to really push and develop what we wanted the class to look and feel like. We knew that if we carried out the total integration theme well enough these courses' labels would become obsolete, and indeed they have. Zenith is much more than just about integrated projects; it is about creating an atmosphere of open communication, student inclusion into decision making, extension of trust, and uniform expectation of respect.

Zenith is really rather simple in its goals. We are trying to create an educational experience that is infused with some real-life elements. Our students learn that they

Team Zenith Project used with permission.

do have a voice and that their voice can and does matter. They learn where to look for information and how to apply this information in areas of their lives where it matters. By allowing the students a voice in the decision-making process, it becomes an authentic exercise. This authenticity takes knowledge out of the vacuum of the classroom and into the minds of students. During a bright May day last year, a Zenian came up to me and said, "If we had a history teacher, would it be you?" This was the indication I was looking for—integration was complete.

A key element of the program is our daily class meeting where a typed agenda is presented (see Figure 4.9). This agenda may range from a simple review of what the next few deadlines are to a challenging discussion of any one of a myriad of human relationship issues. Students also are required to write a piece for this agenda each day so that it does not solely reflect the Elders' point of view. We refer to our selves as the "Elders" and the students are referred to as "Zenians." As a way of including

FIGURE 4.9   Daily Agendas Built to Fit the Need

One Day

8:56–9:05—Perhaps it is because it is pre-vacation week or perhaps it is because a few of you suffer from a moderately bad case of rudeness, but the conversations which take place during the introduction of material during ZENITH time are disconcerting and time consuming. You all demand to be heard yet you cancel out this right for others! Think.

9:05–9:20—Journal redo—others may begin work on parallel projects.

9:20–10:10—Type up project forecasts.

10:10–10:20—BREAK

10:20–11:25—Go over term paper stuff.

11:25–11:32—Attendance period. Be here please so we don't have to send out posses.

No, I wasn't crabby when I wrote this Kristy! In fact I'm sitting here with my lovely headband feeling light as air!

Another Day

8:56–9:10—Announcements

9:10–9:30—Short Story Assessment—two groups will meet in each of the three rooms and will explore the status of the very important short story project from the English seminars. Each group will have about six students.

9:30–10:00—Short Story writing sessions with group

10:00–10:10—BREAK

10:10–11:02—Continue work on Quarterly projects. If your part is complete or you are waiting for paint to dry or an inspiration from the heaven, then you should be working on the new project or your short story. There is no long downtime built into this schedule.

Today's Guest Writer is Paul Fournier—be here by 2:25 please.

A Third Day

8:45–9:05—Announcements and other pertinent stuff

9:05–10:20—Last seminar of Session I

10:30–11:30—Meet with exhibition groups to plan exact course and to develop materials list and work assignments. *HOW* you work is a graded component just as the final product is. Our goal is excellence and not just a monument to mediocrity!!!

students in the daily agenda, we require all of them to write an item each day that becomes part of the record and part of the discussion. Here are two examples:

> Dear Zenith:
>
> I am an LD student in your class and I would like to tell you I feel now that I am in the eleventh grade. I feel more comfortable because I feel closer to each and every one of you. I know it was hard for me to get used to being in mainstream classes, but you all have made me feel welcome and I thank you all very much for that
>
> This year started out easy compared to last year. The projects and group activities help make the time go by faster. Zenith has good ideas and I think the structure of the team allows everyone to work things out.

The student writings have run the gamut from a basketball player recalling of the last game's highlights to a student sharing how adversely her family has been hit by her father losing his job and the health insurance that went along with it. Most important, perhaps, it just gives a chance to inventory where we all stand as a group and to clear the air of issues that are too emotionally charged before they have a chance to amass. The daily meeting also helps us gather coherence around the central theme we are using to organize individual and group work.

Focusing on Themes: The Discrimination Project

An example, which may give a good insight into Team Zenith, is the Discrimination Project. This project was an offshoot of a first-quarter theme which was dominated by a reflective look into the social fiber of the United States. We kicked off the Discrimination unit with a series of one-week seminar classes. Every student had to take each seminar but was free to choose in which order they were done. The English seminar was based on readings of poetry and short stories that are illustrative of the different faces of discrimination in our nation. The Economics seminar was centered around the theme of what role economics plays in creating and perpetuating discriminatory practices. The History seminar was a multimedia primer of the major periods of discrimination since the Civil War (see Figure 4.10). The seminars were intense and demanding. It was understood by all that these classes were setting the foundation for the next project.

Theme: "The Road Less Traveled, Voices of the Oppressed"

> Hello ZENIANS!
>
> We are all about to enter some uncharted waters, to go where no team has gone before, so to speak. You all will be asked to see the human experience from vantage points which differ significantly from the one you currently possess. This growing process will encompass us all and there are no guarantees as to what conclusions you'll draw from all of it. One thing is quite clear, you will probably not see things quite the same as you always have if you immerse yourself in this exploration process.
>
> For this second quarter, there will be a change in your schedule. We will begin a series of one-week seminars within the confines of our ZENITH schedule. Each person must take each of the three seminars. When all is said and done, however, in which order you sign up for them is up to you. Mrs. Kennedy, Mr. Brown, and Mr. McGuire have been designated as the instructors for these seminars, but as usual, they will be a team collaboration. Each seminar will run about one hour a day for the week, to be followed by team time and an interdisciplinary project tying it all up. Exact course offerings will be distributed on or before 11/26/94. As of today, the courses look like this:
>
> *English:* Literature Survey of Discrimination Theme
> *Economics:* Economic Discrimination Issues Research
> *History:* Civil War through Civil Rights: The Black Experience

We have three periods a day together, from 8:52 to 11:24 A.M. A typical day would see our class meeting last for fifteen minutes, then we often break into our

FIGURE 4.10   Focusing History on a Theme—Subtitled: Where Is It Written That Its a White Man's World?

HISTORY SEMINAR I
Must Something Be Destroyed
in Order to Save It?

11/30

Welcome to this sample of America's struggle with civil rights. As you are bound to see, it is an ongoing affair. It is one that you are part of now and into the future.

Outline

A. Introduction, laying the foundation: understanding the basics

B. Discussion and group "fact finding" session

C. Read Abraham Lincoln's First Inaugural Address and begin assignment due tomorrow at the start of seminar. Assignment is:

  1. Read piece

  2. Answer the following questions:
      a) What is Lincoln's stated position concerning slavery in the Southern states?
      b) What issue is of much more concern to Lincoln than that of slavery?
      c) Does the Constitution, according to Lincoln, flatly state whether slavery is allowed or not? Find a quote, and write it down, that sufficiently answers this concern
      d) According to Lincoln, whose hands was the Civil War in?
      e) Specifically, what advice does Lincoln give to the dissatisfied Southerners?
      f) What is the only substantial dispute between the Northern states and Southern states, again according to Lincoln?

Assignment

For a 3- to 5-page paper, start thinking of topics for further review. You may choose concepts, personalities, battles, court decisions, speeches, etc., to research. As the week unfolds, be prepared to discuss this. Due 12/11.

---

three rooms to write in journals for ten minutes. Topics may be selected by the Elders and by Zenians, or the Zenians may free write if they wish. The journals are collected regularly, but not always, and we respond to student writings as appropriate. After this time, students will then settle into the rooms to continue work on their current project or projects. If students need to use the library for research, they are asked to sign out on the board.

Each student was given a project packet and asked to declare a theme for further study. This initial packet included "Essential Questions," project requirements, due dates, and final exhibition expectations (see example in Figure 4.11). Because students were told throughout the seminar week that they would be asked to declare their topic for further study, most were indeed ready to write their abstract for our approval. Student projects have been permanently mounted in a public display area here at Thayer High. One young woman wanted to create a directory of the most influential woman in America's history. Her project turned out so beautifully that she had an offer to publish it. Her "book" has become part of the permanent collection at several area libraries.

On occasion, students travel the twelve miles to Keene, New Hampshire, to do research at Keene State College's library as well as at the Keene Public Library. Our extension of trust to these students has been rewarded by many comments from librarians and staff who couldn't believe that unaccompanied adolescents could be so focused and serious in their research efforts. Students revere this trust and freedom so much that they are by and large in charge of policing it themselves. They have let us know if someone has been abusing the privilege to the point where it might ruin it for everyone.

Time spent together in class has the purpose of providing background knowledge for student projects. At Thayer, however, both Elders and Zeniens have the responsibility of gathering and explaining information to the rest of the group. Elder-made assignments can follow conventional-looking questions:

1. Why was Kansas bloody?
2. What did Lincoln and Douglas debate?
3. Why did the South secede from the United States?
4. What did the Civil War cost the United States?
5. Was "Abe" really honest?
6. Why did the North win the war?
7. Who killed Lincoln?
8. What was reconstruction and how did it affect the South?
9. Who were the carpetbaggers?

With this background, students pursue their individual and group projects, based on their interests and bring back to the whole group the flavor of their individual discoveries. To center the school on learning, students become their own teachers and teachers for the rest of us. Part of the assignment of each theme is a set of lessons, with tests and guides, designed by students for us and the rest of the group (see Figure 4.12).

A group of students wanted to find an inner city school to begin a real dialogue in an attempt to break down to some the degree the barrage of misinformation they obtain through the media. A teacher in our school, Elliot Washor, knew of an all-

FIGURE 4.11   Essential Questions for a Biography Project

From a List of 200 Civil Rights Leaders

Some of the ESSENTIAL QUESTIONS your projects will focus on are:

1. How would the world be different if this person never lived? We will assume for this exercise that what they did would not have been done by someone else.
2. How are their life and contributions viewed by the world today?
3. How were they reacted to by their contemporaries? Were they considered to be successful or unsuccessful by the world they lived in?
4. How would they react to today's world?
5. Why did they make the top 200 list?

Zenith can help with some of the projects in the form of materials. You must let Tony know early on what you need so he can plan our finances.

By Wednesday we need to know your person and which grade you plan on trying for. You may always change the grade plateau as time unfolds. As we did last quarter, these projects will wind up with a parent night performance!

FIGURE 4.12   Student-Designed Lesson and Test

A) *Write a lesson plan for one week* and a follow-up test designed to assess level of knowledge attained. This lesson will include:

1. Content
2. Activities
3. Goals
4. Materials needed
5. Assessment

Included in the assessment will be:

1. 10 paragraph questions or
2. 25 fill-in questions AND 25 multiple choice questions

For both a and b you must include the answers.

B) *Individual Oral Defense:* Design an Essential Question with the ELDERS that must be defended orally to a panel of ELDERS.

C) *Debate:* Any topic on this quarter's theme may be debated with another student or teacher advocate as required by topics and pairing of debater. Exact requirements for preparation will be distributed to interested parties as the need arises. Successful entries will receive a speech credit.

D) *Write a Paper:* Write a 4- to 6-page paper. It must be prepared on a typewriter or computer to be acceptable. Because so many groups have selected the Civil War as an area of study, the topics have been selected from this era. Using three references, research and respond to one of the questions.

black school in the South Bronx that was trying some innovative educational methods. After a series of letters and phone calls, a visit was arranged for all fifteen students who wanted to attend. Another Thayer teacher, Karon Marsh, and myself, along with our students stayed in a youth hostel in Manhattan; culturally, we might as well have been ten thousand miles from home. The meeting was emotionally charged and explosive until our new friends began to see that the students had many of the same fears, aspirations, and drives as they did. On the second day a meaningful dialogue took place and our trip "wore a smile." To this day these fifteen students view this as the most intense learning experience of their lives. I agree.

The Elders then have the task of "coaching" each student to ensure that the student is centered in the project and is attempting to reach deeply into the subject matter at hand (see Figure 4.13). To be done effectively, this coaching process has to have a few key components in place. It is crucial that a rapport be established between the student and the coach and that the coach become intimately aware of the student's learning needs and style. Far from the scatter shot of a lecture, a deep personal commitment must be present. Sometimes this can be a grueling process if a given student is not apt toward trust. The Elders must also trust that the other thirty-five students are where they say they were going to be, doing what they said they were going to be doing. With a very few exceptions, our trust has been warranted.

The Elders

The Elders meet daily to clarify purpose and the theme, share ideas, and set agendas for the flexible schedule. When our coaching is at the level of excellence that it should be, the Team Zenith structure represents a rigorous and demanding challenge for students. A fatal flaw in creating a system such as Zenith would be if a teacher/coach made the mistake of assuming because a student looks engaged that she or he is working at a level of rigor and depth that is sufficient to bring about a rewarding

FIGURE 4.13   ELDERS and ZENIANS Go on Up to the Big City

By now many of you already know what the ELDERS decided to do about the Bronx Project. Everyone who turned in an essay is able to go on the trip! There is a TREMENDOUS amount of work to be done in a short span of time. This is the one and only time we are going to say this; if you think the Bronx exchange is an essay project, don't do it! There are no second chances. If you are seen to be riding on the efforts of others, you will be removed from the group and will fail your exhibition! You are all representing our school and ZENITH. We have to be as blunt and straightforward as possible concerning this issue.

Things we need done IMMEDIATELY:

1. Contact Bronx Regional and decide on a date. See Mr. Washer for people and numbers to contact. He will be a very important person in helping to pull this together. We are grateful that some of you will get to know Mr. Washer better during this project! *Dr. Littky needs a date ASAP so he can advise the School Board.*

2. We need to arrange for host families from Bronx Regional students. Tentatively our trip will be for two days and one night. Please be aware that not all Bronx Regional students live in the Bronx and that we will probably not all be together as a group at night. If this is a problem for you, we need to know that. You must also help to arrange housing for interested Bronx students.

3. There must be a follow-up project to include your observations and insights. This is an EXTREMELY challenging project! It also could very well be one of the most rewarding things you do in your time here at Thayer!

Areas for Further Study:

a) Write a brief, one to two page history of New York City's five boroughs.

b) Describe the major periods of immigration into New York's Ellis Island. Outline the different groups, when they entered, and in what numbers. How many stayed in New York and how many left for other parts of the United States?

c) Outline major civil rights disturbances in New York City during the last 30 years and give a brief description as to their cause.

d) How did blacks and Hispanics come to largely inhabit the five boroughs of New York City and many other northern cities? Describe their journey?

e) Research at least three myths about blacks that are known not to be true by scientific means (i.e., blacks are inferior to whites intellectually). This myth is still widely held to be true by some people. Science has long ago disproved this as racist propaganda. Find and research three more of your own.

learning experience. The fine art of coaching has become so in tune with the students' endeavors as to know when to push them deeper and when to pull back and support, using positive praise and encouragement as the tool of choice.

The ELDERS have on many occasions this year told you all about their efforts to define and refine ZENITH goals and the methods used to fine tune these goals. The effort is an ongoing affair and will never reach a conclusion as long as there is room for improvement. The quest is enduring:

What is EXCELLENCE? What is MEDIOCRITY? Which feels better? No matter how much progress we/ve all made as group there is ALWAYS room for improvement.

As a major side issue to the above is our constant effort to go deeper with the subject matter in an effort to ascertain exactly what students have gotten out of a particular project or quarterly theme.

The development of these habits of mind has been the one side of Team Zenith that has allowed us the extraordinary freedom to totally integrate the curriculum. It has made many students partners in our efforts. Each project begins with a discussion of what we all want to see as our end product and then we "backward" plan from there. Along with these backward planning sessions is the formulation of how the students are going to exhibit (see Figure 4.14) the skills they have attained and how to demonstrate what else they have learned during their journey.

Our common planning period is not enough time to iron out projects in these initial formative stages. At this stage we may have to go on for a while after school, during lunch, and on the phone at night. However, without this common planning period during the day, it would be nearly impossible to plan and implement a multi-faceted project of the depth we desire—one that includes the essential elements of English, economics and history.

An enterprising student stayed late one day and became an "ear witness" to a somewhat typical Elder meeting. The meetings often become animated and decibels elevate, but we never treat each other with disrespect. All of the team feels passion-ately about creating a special atmosphere of learning and respect for Team Zenith. We all have different viewpoints on how to achieve these ends. This is the beauty of the Elders; we all care for each other deeply and try to translate this mutual regard into an environment that fosters exploration and positive socialization. So, if you see us (or hear us) having an exchange of philosophy, please see this as an extension of a desire to make pure the process!

A Zenian who had been in a traditional school before coming to us had a very difficult time making the transition into our way of doing things. This young man is very, very bright and had always done well on the "stuff" and "test" method of teach-

FIGURE 4.14 Quarterly Exhibitions

> The following projects will utilize the skills you will have obtained during the seminars along with a good deal of individual and group research effort.
>
> It is not essential that the people you choose to work with are from the seminar groups you have selected. There will be ample time during designated work periods to accomplish the interfacing required. These projects will culminate with a *Parent Night performance and presentation.* There is an overt expectation that these exhibitions will encompass research, planning, editing, negotiating, writing, deducation, logic, art and performance skills, among a host of others. We will all have to begin to live and breathe these projects as the quarter unfolds. ZENITH's search for excellence is reaching for new heights!
>
> 10:30–11:32—Begin work on assignments from seminar classes and or start formulating plan for Exhibitions.
>
> *Project/Exhibition Choices:*
>
> 1. *Debate:* A cogent, well researched debate of an issue centered around in-equality or discrimination including the role of the government.
> 2. *Play:* Produce a prepared or student-authored play based on an event or issue. Must be based on historical, social, emotional, and economic FACTS.
> 3. *Speech Recitation and Biography* of a person who represents a minority voice of note.
> 4. *Map, Pictorial Display and Timeline:* Charting of Civil War battles and civil rights demonstrations on an accurate and final product.
> 5. *Bronx Regional Exchange:* LIMIT 5 students—plan and implement student exchange program

ing. He later told me, when finally exasperated by the expectation that he take an active role in his educational experience, that he was angry at our insistence that he actually put effort into his education. "Why the hell don't you just tell me what you want me to know and give me a test?" This statement finally broke the ice between us; because he is so bright, he immediately recognized that his time to be a bystander in his learning had come to an end if he wanted to graduate from Thayer High. Later that quarter the same young man turned in a brilliant research paper on the early years of Adolph Hitler and how his family structure may have influenced who and what he became. Figure 4.15 shows how one student summed up the Team Zenith experience.

FIGURE 4.15   Who Says Things Can't Change?

```
Keep Your Eyes on the Prize: Words to Live By
              From Cris Newell

   I have been on the Zenith Team all year long and have
griped and complained about the way the Elders do things
and about the assignments we've been given. But now that
they've told us we might be together next year I see that
life isn't so bad under the Elders.
   During the first part of the year, I hated the work
and I didn't like project after project after project
after . . . . . But somewhere along the line I've changed. I
have no idea where, but I can see it now. I've finished
all my work and handed it in ahead of time. Now that, for
me, is strange. I not only finished the projects, but the
teachers were surprised by the quality of it [we were not
surprised, we KNEW you could do it blindfolded: ed.]. I
am known as being lazy. If I came around this much in
this one area, I wonder what kind of change will come
about, in time, in the other area. I need to work on: my
negativity.
   I just thought I'd share with all of you how I've come
full circle. If you don't care, fine. I don't either!
```
Thanks Cris: You have so much to feel proud of. We ALL support you in your continuing efforts to make personal change. Everyone should have your courage!

Used with permission of the student.

PART II

Focusing on Process

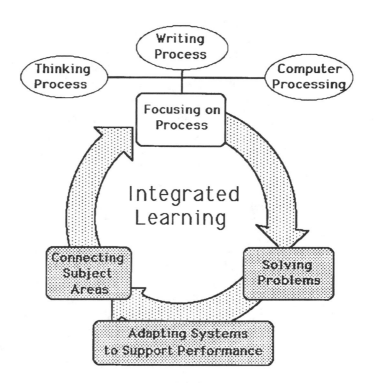

Integrated teaching in Part I relied largely on making connections among discrete subject areas, resulting in a shift of focus away from subjects toward the process of learning. Integration in Part II focuses more directly on learning processes, including computer-based processes that extend human ability. By focusing on the process of learning as a discipline or subject area, teachers are finding ways to increase student awareness of the work their minds can do. Engaging students in different kinds of processes, and helping students recognize the different effects that are possible, supports the development of transferable cognitive skills—ways of knowing that students will continue to develop for a lifetime. As information continues to explode in all subject areas, focusing on learning process may result in increased adaptive skill to manage information.

Chapter 5, The Thinking Process: Multimodal Intelligence—The idea of "distributed intelligence" has begun to revolutionize the teaching of thinking. If intelligence is not a set of innate abilities locked up in our boney skulls, but is instead a flexible capability that finds its form by interacting with the environment, we can shape growing intelligence by shaping the kind of interactions students have with their surroundings. When Howard Gardner (1985) described seven kinds of intelligence that take form as the mind interacts with its surroundings, teachers began designing activities that deliberately activated one or more of these intelligences and helped students understand a new way of "knowing" about something. Others began to experiment with the shape of knowledge itself—the graphic organizers that represent different intellectual processes. By activating many forms of intelligence rather than one or two, teachers aim to improve the quality of learning and open many points of access to learning.

Thinking Process Showcase: Teaching Conceptually with 4MAT*
  Steve Boyle, Brian Nelligan, Kevin Martell, and Brian Walsh, Essex Junction High School, Essex Junction, VT

Chapter 6, The Writing Process: Writing to Learn—Writing is surely one of the oldest techniques teachers use to help students represent the way their minds work. While our minds jump around and leave no footsteps, the written word sits on the page for all to see, exhibiting simultaneously the shape, the process, and the content of knowing. Teachers can use the stabilizing feature of writing for two purposes: (1) in writing to learn, students write to represent to themselves the way they are thinking about a subject so they can further adapt both the process and the content; (2) in writing for a specific audience that is not necessarily the teacher, they shape what they know to fit a purpose they have imagined beforehand. Writing shows writers how knowledge is constructed. It also represents the act of knowing as a personal enterprise, measurable not against absolute standards of truth, but against internal standards of consistency, power and quality.

Writing Process Showcase: Writing to Understand Local History and Culture
  Mary Elyn Carroll, York High School, York, SC

Chapter 7, Computer Processing: Using Electronic Information—The idea of distributed intelligence has been electrified. In computer-based simulations, data management software, and communications technology, students can interact with a startling array of different "ways of knowing." The communications revolution has given students a medium for learning that is both flexible and personal. Students can use computers, modems, and interactive software to gather information from a variety of sources. They can reconstruct and present what they learn in a wide variety of formats. While the ability to benefit from the content of this chapter requires resources, it represents the future and reality *today.* This chapter shows how technology has brought all knowledge within reach of everyone, radically changing conventional roles in teaching and learning.

Computer Processing Showcase: Learning about Technology by Using Technology
  Priscilla Norton, University of New Mexico, Albuquerque, NM

*© Excel, Inc.

CHAPTER 5

The Thinking Process

Multimodal Intelligence

The Work of the Mind

When Project Zero began at Harvard University in 1967, it took a name worthy of its meager origins. At that time, not much was known about how the mind works, particularly how it manages to create unique objects and performances in the arts (Project Zero, 1993). Until recently, research and teaching focused on our ability to replicate and control aspects of the environment. Researchers studied memory more than other faculties the mind develops. In their turn, teachers taught in ways that help students recall, comprehend, and apply well-established facts and principles. Guided by behaviorism, the dominant educational paradigm of the sixties and seventies, the mind was just a black box—a seat of mysteries beyond our ken. With the mind viewed more as a replication system than a construction process, teachers and researchers aimed to manage "inputs" and learning conditions in a way that would let them predict and control the "outputs" of learning. What mattered was what the mind reproduced in measurable form on standardized tests or analytic essays.

At the same time, human intelligence was conceived to be a unitary entity related to one's ability to reproduce inputs as outputs with high reliability. On standardized tests, some of us were found to have lots of intelligence, while others had little (Gould, 1981). That measures of unitary intelligence seemed to reflect directly inequities in surrounding social conditions—with respect to race, gender, ethnicity, and socioeconomic class—coexisted quite comfortably with the belief that schools exist to certify for the larger social system the assumed preexistence of "intelligence" among individuals rather than to create it among students of all backgrounds. It also reinforced the conception of a classroom as rows of desks at which all students receive the same information and then reproduce it in a distribution pattern that also fits the "normal curve" for unitary intelligence. Students found it easy enough to convert classroom performance into a label for themselves: C+, honors, or dummy (Rosenholtz & Simpson, 1984).

The conception of intelligence being planted in the "black box" of the human mind as a preordained and immutable capacity could not last forever in the face of evidence from many quarters. Initially, the unitary concept of intelligence was founded on the weak relationship between measures of student intelligence and measures of later adult performance. When Guilford's theory of intelligence came forth with 120 separate components, the ability to process information became as important as the ability to remember it (Guilford & Hoepfner, 1971). In addition, teachers and researchers began to notice that intelligence was not a static quality but an ability that can either grow or decline through schooling. Intelligence also seems to change its character in relation to different kinds of challenges. As the idea of intelligence changed to become not one thing but many, teachers and researchers began to shift their attention toward techniques that increase the ability of different young people to use different aspects of their intellectual ability to achieve different purposes (Bloom, 1981).

Current theories of intelligence stress the flexibility of the human mind to connect to its context and to create novel responses to the challenges it perceives. By encouraging students to use multiple sources to achieve a unique product that fits a distinct purpose, teachers are relying on a conception of the mind as a flexible system capable of analyzing and then recreating the larger context of which it is a part.

Mind as Model-Maker

In a constructivist view, students use their classroom experience—all of their experience—to construct a model of the world that lets them understand and manage their own lives (Sigel, 1984; Clarke & Biddle, 1993, Ch. 3). Early models are simple, giving names and actions to faces and things in the vicinity of crib, playroom, and neighborhood. Adult models grow to become highly complex, using abstractions and causal rules to predict the future, plan strategies and imagine new solutions to the complex and often unpredictable problems that occur. The process of elaboration that creates highly complex and individualistic models of the universe is visible in students conceptions of their own minds from early grades in school to high school (Clarke, 1994). Because all new learning depends on prior learning (Ausubel, 1968), teachers need to be able to show students how to adapt their existing models of how things work and to create elaborate models that are more powerful in analysis and more productive in creativity and problem solving. Teaching students to develop elaborate models of the world—what things mean and how things work—throws the focus of classroom teaching toward thinking itself.

Shifting the focus of instruction toward thinking does not mean that we can dispose of content knowledge. In fact, content knowledge—organized information gathered through reliable processes of inquiry—creates the basic playing field in all the thinking processes (Perkins & Salomon, 1989). In teaching thinking, however, knowledge from many sources becomes a means to an end rather than the end in itself. When teachers teach thinking, students have to locate relevant information, organize it so it has meaning, envision new ways to use established facts and ideas, and plan out a sequence of steps that makes knowledge work in a real situation. Focusing on thinking through real questions or problems forces students to search through information more than they would if knowledge alone were the aim of education. In a "thinking classroom," students cross the boundaries of disciplines to find what they need. In a thinking classroom, the teacher become less a purveyor of information and more a planner, coach, team consultant, resource manager, and evaluator.

Lauren Resnick (1987) derives her view of thinking as the aim of education as much from the demands of adult living as from research on cognitive process (see list at the end of this paragraph). The adult world calls for careful analysis of unfamiliar situations. It requires us to entertain alternative points of view. It confronts us with situations in which imagination and forethought have as much value as knowledge. It poses problems that do not yield to routine answers, but demand the deliberate planning of a strategy and recycling back through the steps to troubleshoot and design new techniques.

Thinking as the Aim of Education

- Is nonalgorithmic—the path of action is not fully specified in advance
- Is complex—the total path is not mentally "visible" from any single vantage point
- Often yields multiple solutions, each with costs and benefits rather than unique solutions

- Involves nuanced judgment and interpretation
- Involves uncertainty—not everything bearing in the task is known
- Involves the application of multiple, sometimes conflicting criteria
- Involves self-regulation of the thinking process, not regulation by others
- Involves imposing meaning and finding structure in apparent disorder
- Is effortful

Teaching students to think in ways that prove essential in adult life has become an organizing framework for integrated teaching. Although a multitude of techniques exist for teaching students to think (Nickerson et al., 1985; Costa, 1992), two phases appear essential: (1) proposing challenges that require students to use multiple sources of knowledge and multiple processes for acquiring and expressing what they have learned; and (2) guiding reflection on thinking so students learn to recognize and manage the many capabilities they are developing.

In this chapter, we emphasize the vast number of teaching strategies that help students develop multiple intelligences and the graphic organizers that help them recognize and control the processes of their own minds. The showcase for this chapter is based on 4MAT, an integrating technique in which teachers can emphasize different thinking modalities while showing students how to process information (McCarthy, 1990).

Thinking as Quality of Mind

Teaching thinking as a way to integrate secondary school learning shifts our attention from indicators of quantity known (test scores, percentiles, and norms) to the quality of a product and the process that created it. The question becomes now "How much do they know?" but "How well can they use what they have learned?" The kind of thinking that is the aim of integrated teaching is most visible in the student productions that teachers like to brag about. It is unique to students' concept of relationships and is built to fit their conception of the world around them. The defining characteristic of thoughtful learning must be measured in terms of quality rather than quantity. Defining *quality* in learning is a new enterprise for teachers.

Focusing on thinking as the aim of education forces us to define quality more closely than we have in the past. In the Rutland Northeast Supervisory District, 230 teachers gathered from across the school district to define quality in student work. Rather than to define quality from some abstract perspective, however, they wanted to derive a definition of quality from the kind of work they most prized among their students. To focus the one day of inservice, with the aim of defining quality as the goal, each brought one example of student work representing what they most desired and encouraged among their students. "Bring something that represents quality in student learning," we asked. Films, geographic maps and tabulations, models, books, computer programs, essays, scientific studies, songs, and games appeared that day. The variety was astounding.

Working in cross-grade groups, we asked each teacher to describe the student work she or he had brought. Each teacher demonstrated the student work and explained its virtues. We then asked the small groups to work together to assemble a definition of quality in learning that would serve as a goal for the whole school system. Figure 5.1 is the collective list of four of the quality indicators developed by the district teachers that day, organized into five general categories:

Uniqueness: The work is infused with individual spirit.

Communication: The work has an impact on others.

FIGURE 5.1   What Are the Characteristics of Quality Student Work?

Results of Districtwide Analysis of Quality Products

Uniqueness: Infused with personal motivation, enthusiasm, initiative, conviction, and pride

- reflects elements of risk and joy
- thought provoking, insightful, and inspiring
- goes beyond the expected
- reflects personal experience, individuality, originality, personal investment, and personal responsibility
- reflects and inspires curiosity
- demonstrates creativity, reflection, and self-assessment
- reflects student as well as teacher direction

Communication: Reflecting a clear sense of audience

- the product communicates/shares information clearly, in a way that demonstrates its value to others—so it is neat, accurate, coherent, carefully prepared with age-appropriate attention to grammar, usage, and mechanics; as written work, it is a finished, polished product that is organized coherently to fit a clear purpose and goal
- reflects planning

Integration/Connectedness: Reflecting the students' use of multimodal, cross-disciplinary resources to collect and convey information

- use of human, print, and technological resources to collect and convey information
- process requires the ability to listen and observe
- process and product connect current learning to prior learning
- reflects the application of learned skills, strategies, and concepts to new and unfamiliar situations
- process and product reflect a connectedness to real-life skills and abilities

Challenge: Reflecting an element of risk through which the achievement of success leads to increased self-esteem

- reflects perseverance and self-discipline
- reflects the ability to solve problems
- reflects the application of higher-order thinking skills
- reflects the ability to make decisions and choices

Integration/Connectedness: The work employs multiple sources and multiple media.

Challenge: The work results from invention with some risk.

Growth: The work reflects a process by which the student has changed.

In this collective definition, quality has little to do with test scores against a norm or any of the conventional measures we use to assess learning. Instead, it has the look of life itself—in the workplace, in the home, and in the community (Clarke & Cornell, 1994). The definition also has the look of intelligence. Quality work is a product of student thinking.

As the Brandon teachers assembled a definition of quality student work, they were also creating benchmarks for the qualities of thinking they hoped to teach. Quality serves a purpose. Quality finds an audience. Quality brings parts together to make a new whole. Quality expresses an individual perspective, changing the creator and the community of viewers at once. In short, quality in student work is no different from quality in any work, except, perhaps, that it reflects the educational purpose of teachers within a school district. Quality results from an elaborate, self-directed thinking process. If the aim is quality, teachers must teach the kind of thinking that produces quality. To aim for quality, we need to conceive of the mind as an entity that extends into the environment, appropriating and reconstructing parts of its surroundings to better fit purposes it devises for itself. The kind of thinking that produces work of high quality results from complex processes in the human mind.

Distributed Intelligence: Mind as Work, Medium, and Product

Some current views of intelligence include the mind's work as extensions of the mind's intelligence. No longer do psychologists see thinking as a fixed entity, capped and sealed within the boney fortress of the skull, contained, predetermined in structure and measurable in its potential. Intelligence—all the intelligences—reach out through the spinal column through all the lesser channels of the nervous system to each of the senses and into the world, where the tools of the mind's work become extensions of mind itself. If the chimp, the stick and the bunch of bananas were once seen as separable and distinct entities, now all become aspects of intelligence as soon as the chimp reaches for the bananas with the stick and peels one back for lunch. Distributed intelligence is a concept that explains how the things we make increase the power of our minds. The mind finds its way free of flesh and blood and, to become real, joins the surroundings, changes them and then refits itself to better control the work it has accomplished.

In interaction with our environment, we have grown much larger than ourselves. As David Perkins (1992, Ch. 6) points out, distributed intelligence includes the things we use (needle, thread, or computers), the people we interact with (friends, teachers, and cooperative group members), and the symbols we manipulate to represent ourselves in the environment (words, pictures, computer programs, or concept maps). Throughout this book we represent thinking as a cycle, a convenient metaphor that allows division in an infinite number of ways. Through the metaphor of the wheel, we can see that half of the mind's power results from its ability to model the universe in which it finds itself (conceptually and procedurally); the other half results from interaction with its setting, where the mind tries to make things work (creatively, experimentally, and practically).

Clearly, the internal models of how things work direct the way we use our hands, feet, and bodies to reshape the universe around us. Success in managing the affairs in the world then reshapes our model of how things work. Success begets success. The wheel turns. Elaborate and accurate models of how things happen allow greater control and creativity in the world of work than do simpler models. They also increase our ability to "remodel" conceptions—or "learn" from experimentation with objects, people, and symbols (see Figure 5.2). If we are successful in finding and cleaning sludge from a filter in the carburetor of a car, we are suddenly empowered to drive. We are also empowered by a new conception of carburetors (that now includes filters) to repair some of the dead engines that fill a lifetime of experience with cars. Some of us develop such elaborate models of cars and carburetors in our heads that we can actually "hear" the site and cause of most malfunctions. The quality of our mental models (in any form of representation) plays out directly in our ability to control the setting in which we live.

None of us attempt to model all aspects of the universe in which we are living. Attempting verisimilitude would simply overwhelm our processing ability. Our minds are built to reduce impressions from the senses to abstractions—handy chunks of concept, vision, or procedure—that we can manipulate internally with great speed,

FIGURE 5.2   A Conception of Distributed Intelligence: (Re)Modeling and (Re)Making the Universe

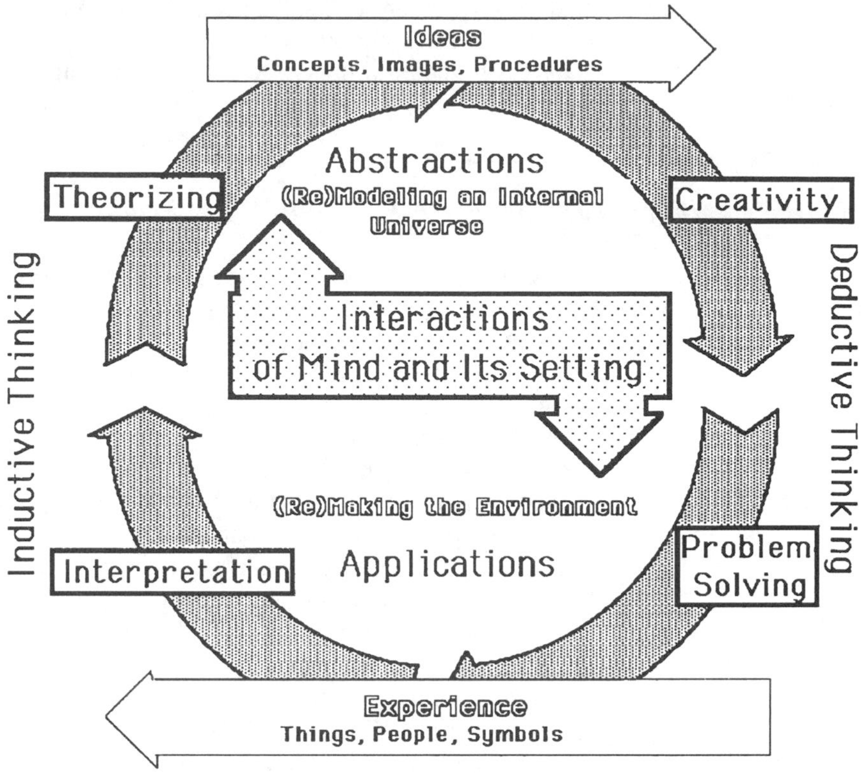

testing the models of what we know against the reality of what we experience. If our abstract models are sufficient to the tasks we face, we succeed in those tasks. If they are not sufficiently elaborate or accurate, we can achieve success only by chance, imagination, or experimentation. Having succeeded by experimentation, we adapt mental models to explain our success. In short, we learn.

In view of a distributed conception of intelligence, it becomes easy to see how some students, born into chaotic settings where there is little help in modeling a manageable universe, experience failure in school. As Bloom (1981) points out, success and failure in school soon achieve their own momentum. Kids who fail in second grade become likely to fail or drop out of ninth grade. "All new learning depends upon prior learning," David Ausubel (1968) insists, a proposition that clearly favors knowing a great deal and foreshadows great frustration for those who do not go to school already knowing much.

What is most liberating about the distributed conception of intelligence and the circular model for learning is the number of points of access it opens for teachers. If "works" are extensions of mind, why not make student work the point of classroom activity, shaping the classroom activities and assignments so as to guide the growth of intelligence? If the mind is a natural model maker, why not directly assist students in developing more accurate and elaborate mental models of how things happen and what things mean? Much of the experimentation with multiple intelligences aims to increase the variety of experiences students have in school, increasing their access to materials they can use in modeling themselves in their environment (Gardner, 1993). Much work with graphic organizers aims to help students construct visual representations of complex relationships in their experience (Clarke, 1990; Perkins, 1987, 1988; McTighe & Lyman, 1988; McTighe, 1992; Hyerle, 1992). Helping students activate their intelligences and represent the processes of thinking aim to extend the awareness and control students exert over the work of their minds.

Teaching Dimensions of Learning

A focus on learning and thinking becomes most explicit in the Association for Supervision and Curriculum Development's (ASCD) general framework, *Dimensions of Learning*. Robert Marzano and his colleagues (1993) developed a framework for learning-based instruction that can be adapted to any discipline or interdisciplinary subject. The dimensions begin with positive and aggressive attitudes toward learning, and then include four groups of strategies (Marzano, 1992) that extend learning from the classroom to the world where thinking makes a difference:

Thinking involved in acquiring and integrating knowledge;
Thinking involved in extending and refining knowledge;
Thinking involved in using knowledge meaningfully;
Productive habits of mind.

Each dimension of thinking can be used in conventional classroom teaching. The Marzano model also integrates nicely with an adaptive, learning-styles approach, such as 4MAT (McCarthy, 1990), and with techniques that rely on graphic organizers to show students the processes of their own thought (Clarke, 1990). *Dimensions of Learning* is designed to help students learn meaningfully, but it also recognizes the strategies they can use to make learning work (see Showcase in this chapter).

To help students recognize the thinking strategies they employ, and to help teachers assess student progress on the various dimensions, Marzano, Pickering, and McTighe (1994) have collected examples of learning tasks that engage the thinking process, with rubrics teachers and students can use to assess performance and set new directions. Because ASCD's *Dimensions* emphasizes transferable metacognitive control rather than simple cognitive skills, the assessment strategies give students and teachers a chance to look again at how students have thought their way through a situation so they can replicate and refine the process. The Marzano et al. ASCD book contains rubrics teachers can use as is or convert to fit related purposes. *Dimensions of Thinking* expands the conception of cognition to include a full range of tasks for which the minds must prepare.

Integrating Intelligences

Focusing secondary teaching on thinking should engage not one kind of intelligence, but many. Howard Gardner (1993, p. 15) argues that "an intelligence is the ability to solve problems or fashion products that are of consequence in a particular culture or community." Gardner proposes seven kinds of intelligence that we can hope to engage in secondary teaching, including conventional linguistic and logico-mathematical abilities, along with spacial, kinesthetic, musical, intrapersonal, and extrapersonal (Gardner, 1985). Gardner's research on brain-damaged individuals points to the independence of these intelligences in brain function. What is clear to teachers who design authentic learning activities, however, is that a complex challenge elicits multiple forms of intelligence in a group or an individual. The more complex the challenge, the greater the number of intelligences that can be brought to bear in useful ways. Authentic learning tasks give students more opportunity to use different parts of their intelligence in patterns they devise for themselves.

As James Moffett (1992) points out, people who work in schools have been the least receptive to the idea that important kinds of thinking involve much more than symbol manipulation in mathematics and English—a proposition that seems obvious to the rest of the population. "But no one needs research to tell them that some other kinds of intelligence are operating when they compose music and choreography, paint and sculpt, act, sail a boat or grow corn" (p. 42). As members of the information age by birthright, high school students also recognize the excitement of learning or expressing learning through dance, dialogue, music, or design. Most high school students are naturally reflective about themselves and naturally curious about others.

Teaching to multiple intelligences involves teaching students to access different kinds of information for presentation through different kinds of media. To integrate different aspects of the mind's power, teachers invent assignments that call on movement, color, group interaction, music, and personal insight as forms of expression for thinking (Gardner, 1985). Bruce Campbell, Linda Campbell, and Lee Dickenson (1992) describe alternative modes for the seven intelligences in detail in their book.

Activating each intelligence makes students look at what they are learning from another perspective and personalize what they know. As the following examples illustrate, creating a unique expression involves accessing and analyzing available information, as well as creatively designing a response that fits. In each example, high school students are using some intelligence beyond verbal language and mathematical symbols to represent their understanding of the relationships they are studying. For each of the examples, the teachers have created feedback sheets that students use to guide the development of a unique performance and to assess what others in their class have done.

Alternative Perspectives in Song

Before printed script made literacy commonplace, music was the vehicle for knowing. Wandering bards, singers, and players brought stories to the people that connected those people to the general culture. Song once gave voice to the wisdom of the tribe. The Singer of Tales was, in part, a holy person, partly entertainer and partly priest. When Marilee Taft and Steve Dowd of Essex Junction, Vermont, make assignments for their fused American studies course for sophomores, they include assignments that evoke different kinds of intelligence. Songs, skits, dialogues, and dances are then enacted before the merged class, enriching the content and helping students reframe what they have learned into a special kind of intelligence. Rebecca Reilly wrote the ballad in Figure 5.3 to help herself imagine how a slave ship must have appeared to a young white person who was personally implicated in slave trafficking. Her song is based on knowledge, but it is also infused with qualities that define thinking. Figures 5.4a and 5.4b show two other students' conceptions of slave trade.

Great Ideas: Putting Color to Concepts

Mike Hornus teaches a social studies class at Essex Junction High School on the "great ideas" that lend purpose to life on this planet. The purpose of the course is to let students "see" their experience and the course of human events through lenses provided by thinkers in different cultures. The reading list for "Great Ideas" course includes:

FIGURE 5.3   A Student Ballad

Truth Revealed (A Song About Middle Passage)

A young man, a captain's son, writes of a journey with his father:

So bonny were the rolling seas
and so lovely was the mist,
as with a voyage to the Ivory Coast
my father I did assist.

I had asked of him when we struck land
might I go ashore?
Alas, no more, I feared could I withstand
the ship's stench I did abhor.

As he allowed and bade me go
I left the ship that day.
Took I a walk along the coast
though scorching was the way.

Longed I for home when first the sight
arrested fast my soul.
Ne'r before in the darkest night
had I seen a sight so cold.

My countenance, I'm sure, quite fell
As natives were before me marched.
Men blacker than mine eyes beheld
while the sun all throats did parch.

Led were they by a well dressed few
as black as were they.
By thieves or tradesmen, a motley crew,
they were roughly dragged away.

Kidnapped and sold by kings. I found,
All chained from feet to neck,
Traveling where no love abounds
they sadly came on deck.

The voyage was a more gruesome tale
than ever I did read.
Every person, whether female or male,
was in some way made to bleed.

Each day for purpose of merriment
the men set the slaves to dance
Death, if a slave did anger vent,
Would rarely get a second chance.

If one of two men by chance, did die,
both to the sea were tossed
Though the dead was chained to the one alive,
If one was dead, the pair was lost.

The women were bid to wander above
Only men were chained below
Greatly they missed the land they loved
When the sailors their cruelty did show.

I was never allowed to go below
But heard it was quite a place
The abundant fumes, waste and moans
put fear and illness in each face.

The picture of the children, it's sure,
Is with me, never lost.
Ill bodies and souls that had no cure
sold for high price, but at higher cost.

Reached we at our destination
With so fewer than the departure.
Fevers, flus, sad souls, starvation
Took heavy tolls from Africa's shore.

"Was it worth it?" I asked of the man
"To make a profit from another,
To take a people from its land,
To take a child from its mother?"

If there's ever a time to sit and think,
Remember Africa's Ivory Coast,
Humanity's pushing itself to the brink
And falling into innocence lost.

By Rebecca Reilly, Sophomore, Essex Junction Educational Center. Used with permission.

Heaven and Earth
  (A Computer Game)
Heraclitus
I Ching
Lao Tsu
Plato's Cave
The Tao of Pooh

Tao Te Ching
Turtle Quarterly (A Native American
  periodical
The Way of the Peaceful Warrior:
  Dan Millman
Zen for Beginners

His students read about ideas that have guided human history but they also enact them in the classroom. Within a semester, his students may represent a new perspective through role-playing, paper construction, graphic organizers, rap songs, dance, poetry, song, or martial arts. Hornus's students also portray themselves and their growth in drawing and mask ceremonies. Over the schoolyear, students work with all their "intelligences" and come to recognize their contribution to knowing and thinking.

FIGURE 5.4   Two More Student Conceptions of the Slave Trade

Top drawing was done by Destiny Saxon; the bottom one is the work of Brian Smith. From Marilee Taft's tenth grade class, Essex Junction High School. Used with permission.

In the Great Ideas course, dominated by abstractions and anchored to many different forms of expression, synthesis is a challenge. How can students in a course emphasizing multiple sources of information and multiple forms of expression put what they learn into a form that has meaning, for themselves and others? Where would it all fit? Students were able to find the answer to this question on the rear wall of their classroom—a naked expanse of cinder block painted in numbingly familiar institutional green. The class produced a painting to represent the connections among all that they had read and discussed as a final project. "It might just fit on that wall," a student offered. And so it began. The Great Ideas class worked cooperatively, as they had all year, to design and paint a mural expressing relationships among all the ideas they had confronted during the year.

To compensate for the absence of photographs here, we will describe the essential features of "The Wall":

> Whirling into being out of chaos, a fetus hangs suspended between a harsh sun and the fathomless ocean depths, where sea creatures circle in the dark. The embryo is encased in a mandala of swirling colors, a womb of life and thought. To her right, a deep forest grows, surrounding a plush garden where figures wait and watch. Far up the Wall, a river tumbles from the mountains, a prophet speaks and others listen. To her right stretches the desert and pasture land, overseen by a Sphinx. Countless figures populate the scene, some human and recognizable from literature or modern culture, others more mythical and imposing. The Wall includes creatures of the earth and creatures of the imagination. The whirling fetus is being born in a maelstrom of undifferentiated color—reds, pinks, purples, blues, yellows, and greens. The colors all find recognizable form in the particular scenes that make up the mural.

The wall exists, now, but what does it mean? Clearly, the wall had to have some organizing meaning for the class that designed it. The wall will mean different things to the students who come into that classroom in the years that follow. What is most important about the wall, perhaps, is the meaning that each of the Great Ideas students ascribes to the work as a whole, and their own contribution. Mike Hornus asked each student to explain what the wall means as part of their final project. Figure 5.5 contains a sample of some of their reflections, with reference to parts of the course that inspired parts of the mural. As his students reflected on the wall, they made reference to each of Gardner's (1985) intelligences, emphasizing the intrapersonal and extrapersonal abilities they developed in the process of painting.

African Dance: Moving Toward Meaning

Kevin Martell and Carol Willey teach an integrated English/social studies class called "World Perspectives for Ninth Grade Students" at the Essex Junctional Educational Center in Vermont. While more conventional world civilizations courses cover the entire span of human history, their purpose is to show students how to view history and culture from different perspectives. Working in cooperative groups, their class of forty-five students reads selections from texts, but spends more time conducting library research and working through problems in study guides such as those included in the curriculum showcase of this chapter (Clarke, Martell, & Willey, 1994).

For each section of the course, the final days are dedicated to a "production" in which students give personal expression to what they have learned in front of the whole class. To complete their Africa unit, the World Perspectives class studied photographs of ceremonial masks, then prepared ceremonies in which they would celebrate for the whole class some aspect of African culture in relation to their own individual spirits (see Figure 5.6). In preparation, they constructed masks for themselves from wood, cardboard, clay, feathers, paint, and household paraphernalia. In class they were assigned at random to a cooperative group to create one ceremony expressing the relationship among all the masks. Martell and Willey provided feed-

FIGURE 5.5   What Does the Wall Mean?

Twelfth Grade Students in Essex Junction, Vermont, Describe Their Art

The wall means unity to me. It combines the thoughts of different people in different ways. The class "Great Ideas" is generally an eye-opener, allowing each individual to challenge her/his mind to her/his own extent. I personally have learned to think more freely and I have also learned about myself.

N. Audette

To Me, the painting represents a positive development and collaboration of the class, illustrated by each person's individual character. . . . Faced with paint and brushes, a kind of equality settled over the group. We saw new aspects in peers that had never been exposed before. Glimpses of our personal lives are included with the ideas from class. Yet, just as with people, the exterior is just a cover for more complex and amazing content.

R. Rowley

To stay in line with all we have discussed this year, such as Taoism, we tried to balance the picture. Since everything in the universe can be broken down into mandalas, we decided to put a mandala right in the center. The fetus in the center represents the beginning. On the top and bottom are night and day, the sun and moon, the Yin and Yang. They are there to balance the picture.

A. Donehower

The general overall meaning is life. It gives life to me. It has many meanings. I look at this painting and it is filled with energy. The energy is soaked up by my body when I look at it. It is divided up into parts of nature, with each part having its own symbols and meanings. The parts of nature are desert, sea, outer space, forest and mountains. In the middle is a mandala. The colors of the mandala represent the different complexities of life. In the middle is a fetus.

C. Bordeau

Even though some people were not gifted with an ability to draw, they all helped out in some way that furthered the production of the wall. In our group, I would say there are a wide variety of "cliques." So, in a way, the wall has made friends for people. The wall basically brings nothing negative with it. I was proud to be a part of it.

Mike L.

This wall was created for the purpose of demonstrating virtually all that we learned this year. We met and agreed on how to present our ideas. For example, on a desert island there is a shaman to show our interaction with Native American culture. In the night sky with the moon is a Yin and Yang planet to represent time spent on Eastern philosophies. Pooh Bear shows our alternative approach to Taoism. On the edge of the forest where the wild things play sit two main characters from our discussion, Dan Millman and Socrates. They were our teachers on The Way of the Peaceful Warrior. Also, you will see various creatures of fantasy all throughout the painting to represent the joy and humor of life.

R. Grannis

Students' class work used with permission of Mike Hornus.

back sheets to each student for such occasions so they could tie what the cooperative groups expressed to other ideas from the unit being completed.

Real-Life Theater: Acting It Out

Peter Ryersbach teaches a class in social problems to high school students at Middlebury Union High School in Vermont. The purpose of Real-Life Theater is for students to investigate topics of importance to them and their school, and to express what they have learned to the whole school community. Each unit occurs in two parts—a research section in which they use the library, popular media, and literature to understand a modern social problem and a second part in which they reshape what they have learned into a theatrical performance. Whether they are preparing a "Guerrilla Theater" for a short run in the cafeteria or hallways, a public service announcement video for the local community, or a stage production for presentation in the auditorium, students work up their script from classroom improvisations in which

FIGURE 5.6   A World Perspectives Ceremony—Learning Through Dance

---

African Culture: Creating a Ritual

Two days before Spring break, the freshman inter-disciplinary class had finished most of their work on African cultures. They had studied the history of Africa from prehistory to the precolonial civilizations. They had compared Bantu civilization with that of the northern cities. They had traced trade routes down rivers and across the plains In all of this, they had focused on cultural adaptations that followed trade and the role of religion in holding a people together. As a final exercise, each student was assigned to create a mark, based on historical African masks, relating their own spirit to larger forces at work in the environment. Then, working in groups of four, they would develop a ceremony for the whole class to watch, linking all four masks into one central theme.

"As you present your ceremony," Kevin Martell instructed, "we should be able to identify your individual spirit, as well as the spirit that holds all of you together—the spirit of your affiliation. Give shape to what you have learned. Surround it with some form." The students spent half of their double period devising a ceremony and half presenting a ceremony to the rest of the class. In the hallway and in separate corners of the room, small groups worked intensely to develop and refine a ceremony that their classmates could understand, bringing individual masks into larger relationship.

I have followed a Sun mask, a Night Moon mask and two Human masks, divided dark and light, into the hallway. What could they celebrate as one people? The Sun mask and one face mask were radiant. The Moon mask and the other Human mask were contemplative. As they examined the masks they had made, the brooding Human mask noticed a similarity. All of the masks were somehow split, dark from light, joy from sorrow. Sometimes lightness prevailed; sometimes sadness. This dividedness was one theme, but it led them quickly to a second. "I meant to show how quickly I turn from one mood to another, from person to another," one girl explained. Another agreed. "Changes" was the theme. They wanted to recognize in a dance how one thing becomes its opposite, from light to dark, from dark to light, from sun to moon, from shade to heat. They choose to dance to the changes that mark our moods, our days and our lives.

Quickly, the four fashioned a dance in which one member rose to dance while the others sank back into themselves. Then, they danced in a line. Then, two moved forward and the others fell back. Then, they split out into separate dances. Then all whirled in a circle. "How did you figure out your dance?" I asked. "It was easy," one replied. "We just figured it out from our masks. How we felt. The dance came to us from that." Other dances followed: "Birth of the New Gods," "The Surprise of Spring," "War, Death and Rebirth." "It was easy. We just figured it out from our masks."

From Kevin Martell's ninth grade class at Essex Junction High School. Used with permission.

they develop an understanding of different perspectives on a problem. They are ready to perform in public when any student can play any role in a performance.

Developing scripts from improvisations takes practice in listening. At the beginning of the course, they practice with short extemporaneous scenes. "We sit in a circle and one person says one word. The person next to him or her says a second word, trying to link up to the first word, until they are making coherent sentences with a brief story line." Scenes with two characters follow, each with a different perspective:

- A recently unemployed woman with her six-year-old in the toy aisle of the local supermarket
- A pacifist missionary visiting the jail cell of a man who has just murdered his wife
- A social activist trying to recruit participants from the high school cafeteria for a memorial march on Martin Luther King Day

The actors begin with one role, listen to the comments of their classmates, then take the other role. When Peter Ryersback calls "freeze," characters hold their positions while he and the rest of the class examine the perspective of the speaker and make connections to the ideas they have studied in the library.

After initial exercises, Real-Life Theater students begin their public service announcements. From library research, they write a storyboard. They then shoot 30 to 60 minutes of videotape and spend several days editing. Their final product must not exceed 60 seconds of airtime. Recent productions have focused on AIDS, drug abuse, teen pregnancy, racial strife, street violence, world hunger, and a teen suicide prevention tape for a local counseling service. The tapes include reenacted scenes from the newspaper, music, computerized graphics, art, and photographs. For an effective 60-second public service announcement, students quick-cut their shots, emphasize juxtapositions of color and action and focus everything on one message.

The final production of the year is a play in which students develop a focus on one problem, develop a script, create and refine characters to represent different perspectives, and perform for a live audience of high school students and teachers. In 1993 Real-Life Theater presented "The Man, The Act, The Revenge" in which a lone male chauvinist restricts the choices of several female characters and is then condemned to adopt the perspective of a female as punishment for his transgressions. The actors put on the play in half a period, and then answered questions from the audience. Asked to assess the effect of Real-Life Theater on their thinking, the students uniformly agreed that the most important part of the course involved taking the perspective of another person and working through that perspective until motivation, action, and values achieved a coherence of their own.

For a final exam, students write a complete five-minute monologue, using the same criteria for evaluation as they used during earlier parts of the course. The evaluation is conducted by the whole class, stressing the concepts of thesis, multiple perspectives, coherence, planning, and design that form the organizing framework for the whole course. As one student said, "In Real-Life Theater, you get pleasure from the product when you finally get it done right."

Engaging Intelligence

Engaging multiple intelligences has proven a fertile strategy for integrating learning and for involving students with different kinds of ability in classroom learning. Emphasizing different ways of knowing and many different modes of expression clearly makes student learning the center of classroom activity. Harvey Cohen at Colchester High School in Vermont has begun to catalogue the kinds of activities that fit the high school classroom, based on the ideas of Howard Gardner (1985) and models provided by Project Zero (1993) (see Figure 5.7). Focusing on different kinds of learning processes brings high excitement to conventional subjects. However, making student thinking the center of classroom activity requires a degree of disorder not tolerated in every high school and creates management problems that require skilled teaching. Also, time devoted to a proliferation of student "expressions" in the classroom reduces time available for "covering" a specified amount of content. Finally, the effect of multiple intelligence instruction on standardized tests, which rely on simpler conceptions of thinking, has not been determined. Still, if involvement is the key to learning, multimodal teaching creates a depth of learning not possible through conventional teaching.

Graphic Organizers: Displayed Metacognition

Focusing on thinking entails creating problems or situations for which students have to work out their own solutions using as many forms of intelligence as possible. Mak-

FIGURE 5.7   Engaging Multiple Intelligences with Conventional Content

Intelligence	Traits	Sample Projects/Ideas
Verbal Linguistic	Language production. Including: storytelling, humor, poetry, reading and writing, abstract reasoning	Write a dirty poem. Write a science fiction story based on scientific fact.
Logical Mathematical	Scientific thinking/inductive reasoning. Including" recognize patterns, work with abstract symbols (numbers and geometric shapes), discern relationships and/or see connections between distinct pieces of information	Make your own weather map Graph the relationship between kinetic and potential energy of a rock falling off a cliff.
Visual Spatial	Visual arts, navigation, map making, and architecture and games such as chess. Includes the ability to form mental images and pictures in the mind. The key sensory base is the sense of sight.	Write a children's science book. Make a flip book illustrating a scientific process. Video creations. Computer graphic interactions such as Linkways/Hypercard
Body Kinesthetic	The ability to use the body to express emotion (dance/body language), play a game (sports), create new products. Learning by doing.	Build a Rube Goldberg machine that illustrates the simple machines or energy transformation. Create a dance/play that illustrates a scientific process (The life of a rock).
Musical Rhythmic	Rhythmic and tonal patterns, sensitivity to sounds in the environment.	Write a rap song that illustrates a scientific process and perform it. Interpret a musical piece (Grand Canyon Suite). Listen to an environmental music piece; list how it reminds you of a particular process.
Interpersonal	Ability to work cooperatively with others, as well as the ability to communicate both verbally and non-verbally with other people.	Any group project/performance. Combine this with the five intelligences listed above.
Intrapersonal	Knowledge of the internal aspects of the self, such as feelings, range of emotional response, thinking process, self-reflection.	Any ideas on this one?????

An adaptation of the multiple-intelligences projects/ideas for earth science teaching used by Harvey Cohen, Colchester High School, Colchester, VT.

ing growth in thinking ability durable in the human mind requires a second step, making students aware of the strategies they have developed so they recognize the processes they have used and can adapt them to novel challenges. *Metacognitive awareness* and *control,* as psychologists have named the mind's ability to direct its own work, develop as students practice new strategies and then recognize how those strategies can be modified to gain different effects. Helping students recognize invisible strategies of thought is a special challenge for integrated teaching, especially when the social and intellectual excitement in an integrated classroom—projects, ceremonies, vivid walls—can overwhelm less visible parts of the thinking process. Productions, exhibitions, and other displays give purpose and structure to integrated learning, but students need to recognize the processes they have used in these productions in order to gain control over the work of their minds.

Gardner sees three phases in the development of any of the intelligences: (1) *raw patterning,* in which we make basic distinctions in the tumult of sensory experience and recognize organizing elements; (2) developing a *notation system,* in which we create a language for representing the relationships we see; and (3) a *vocational pursuit,* in which we put what we know to useful work, solving problems, and creating new things (1993, p. 28). The development of a notational system for the work of the mind, caught between the excitement of seeing (patterning) and the excitement of doing (vocational pursuit), requires a special kind of teaching effort. To succeed in teaching thinking, we need to help students represent the process they develop to solve problems in some form.

Each of the intelligences Gardner (1985) describes, as well as each of the disciplines taught conventionally in high schools, has developed its own notation system or language. *Body language,* for example, may be seen as an intrapersonal notation system. Choreography is one of many kinesthetic languages. The color wheel and perspective give structure to a language for spatial learning. Among the disciplines, mathematics has developed its own special notation system to describe relations. Computer science has adapted the language of logic to fit its programming needs. Chemistry has adapted algebra to describe chemical transformations. In school subjects, learning most often depends on being able to manipulate one or more of these language systems to understand a situation or solve a problem. Unfortunately, the formal language systems supporting expression in the disciplines do not reflect the processes of thought that produce learning as well.

Graphic organizers are being used as an informal language or notation system that lets students recognize the processes of thought they are using as they approach a learning situation (see Figure 5.8). Art Costa (1992) calls graphic organizers *displayed metacognition*—visual representations of different thinking strategies. Graphic organizers give shape to the invisible patterns of thought, helping students separate as well as integrate analytic and creative patterns that help them carry out different purposes. As McTighe and Lyman (1988) point out, they "cue" students as to strategies that can be used to work through tasks with different intellectual purposes.

The Wisconsin Department of Public Instruction (1989) has also developed a general framework for teaching patterns of thinking in which focusing questions guide student planning, monitoring progress and reflection. Differences between the focusing questions lead teachers to design different teaching strategies and introduce study-skills tactics that fit student questions. In the Wisconsin conception, study skills that were once taught in isolation become part of an organic system motivated by questions. Clarke (1990, 1992, 1994) describes graphic organizers that support different aspects of the thinking cycle that also organize the chapters of this book. Research suggests that graphic organizers have proven useful in giving students a sense of purpose, as well as a path to learning (Mayer, 1989). They may support higher achievement among low-achieving students, but not among successful students who have already developed a reliable set of organizers for learning (McKeachie, 1984). As the ninth grade graphic (Figure 5.9) from Brian Walsh's Global Perspectives class shows, students can learn to develop graphic representations that convey a personal sense of knowing something. When they present their graphics to the class, other students find the substance familiar but see the form as unusual and provocative.

Hyerle's "Thinking Maps"

How can teachers show students how they can think about a question or a topic? David Hyerle and his associates in Cary, North Carolina, have developed a set of Thinking Maps* for the basic thinking strategies (Hyerle & Lipton, 1993; Hyerle,

Note: "Thinking Maps" is a trademark of the Innovative Learning Group in Cary, NC.

FIGURE 5.8 **Graphic Organizers for Thinking**

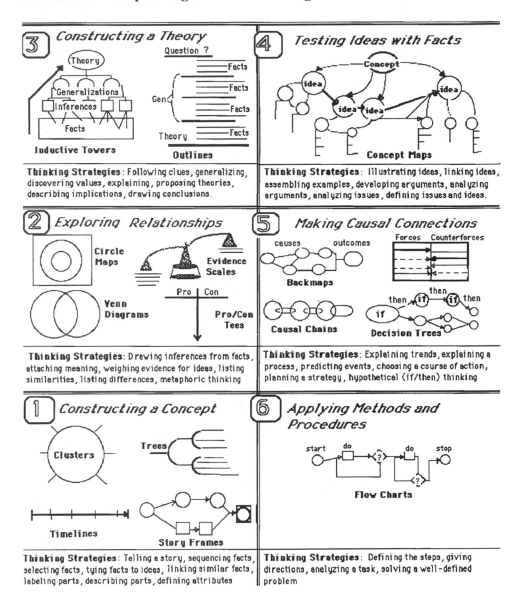

1990, 1994). Hyerle introduces the eight basic Thinking Maps™ directly to students as a notational system for thinking—for answering different questions. Each map represents a basic thinking process and a set of questions that can be answered through use of such a map. Thinking Maps™ constitute a graphic language that is both consistent and flexible. Each map carries its own message. The maps are tools that guide students through analyses of concept (establishing a frame of reference, a definition, or classifying parts to whole relationships), as well as analyses of sequence (operations, sequencing, or cause and effect). Hyerle (1990, 1994) uses graphic organizers to focus both curriculum design and classroom teaching on the kinds of thinking required for academic success.

Hyerle (1991) developed the sample thematic guide on "Scarcity, Conflict and Choice" in Figure 5.10 to help teachers "map" the thinking tasks making up the North Carolina standard course of study. The guide integrates content from five areas (com-

FIGURE 5.9　Global Perspectives Class Graphic

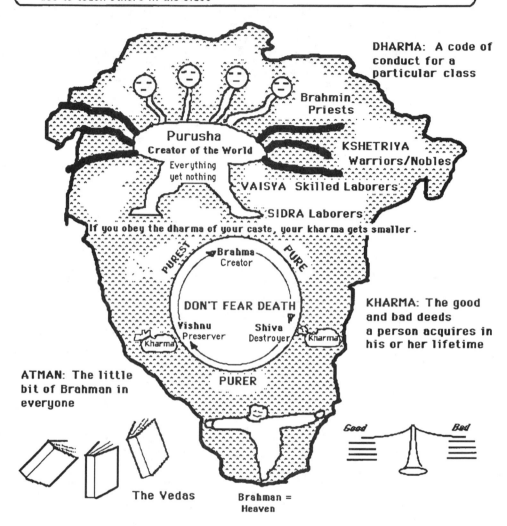

By tenth graders Laura Daigle, Selden Houghton, and Janessa Reinblatt for Brian Walsh's Global History class at Essex Junction High School. Used with permission.

munication, social studies, mathematics, science, and health) using existing texts and curriculum goals. In addition, the North Carolina guide describes the thinking processes teachers can emphasize, given the theme and the content focus in each of the ninth grade subject areas. By representing the embedded thinking process with the content focus of the curriculum, teachers can understand and teach the *what* of the subject areas in connection with the *how* of thinking about them (Hyerle, 1992). Within this thematic framework, teachers can develop graphic organizers that help students link parts of the content they are studying. As they struggle with facts, principles, and theories related to conflict and scarcity, they use the Thinking Maps to explore basic relationships and generate useful questions. Figure 5.11 describes Thinking Maps that help students organize answers for different questions teachers ask.

FIGURE 5.10   Thinking Maps™ for Helping Students Think about Questions

Thinking Map™	Mapping Metacognitive Questions
Circle Map	**Center Circle:** How am I naming this thing? How is this affecting the definition I am giving to it? **Outside Circle:** What is the context information that supports the definition for this thing? **Frame:** What is my frame of reference? What is influencing my point of view on this subject?
Bubble Map	**Center Circle:** How am I naming this thing? **Outside Bubbles:** What *adjectives* am I using to describe this thing? Are the adjectives more factual (sensory), or based on an opinion guided by reasoning (logical), or based on personal judgment (emotional/aesthetic)?
Double Bubble Map	**Two Center Circles:** How am I naming the two things that I am comparing? **Middle Bubbles:** What are the most important common qualities of these things? Why? **Outside Bubbles:** What are the most important unique qualities for each of these things? Why?
Tree Map	**Top Line:** How did I identify this main idea or general category name? How is this influencing my ideas? **Middle and Lower Lines:** Where did I get these supporting ideas and details?
Brace Map	**Far Left Line:** Is this the only name for this *physical* object? Is this part of another, larger object? **Middle Lines and Far Right Lines:** How did I decide which were the major and minor parts?
Flow Map	**Large Boxes:** How did I decide what were the major stages of this story or event? **Small Boxes:** Could any of these substages of each major stage be understood as a major stage?
Multi-Flow Map	**Center Box:** What do I think was *the* most significant event in this story or sequence of events? **Far Left Boxes:** What were the immediate and distant, historical causes of this major event? **Far Right Boxes:** What were the short and long term effects and my predictions about the future?
Bridge Map	**Bridge ("as"):** What is the common relationship between the related pairs of things on the left side and the right side of the bridge?

The interdisciplinary matrix shown here is based on the 1991–92 North Carolina Standard Course of Study; there have been revisions to it since then. Used with permission of David Hyerle, Director of Curriculum and Staff Development, Innovative Learning Group, A Division of Innovative Sciences, Inc., P.O. Box 5509, Cary, NC 27511.

To practice using maps to represent different kinds of thinking, the ninth grade English teachers of Winston-Salem, North Carolina, focused on "The Interlopers" by Saki (see Figures 5.12a–5.12d). The first Thinking Map (5.12a) is a circle diagram that helped students understand the feud between the two main characters in its human context and also as a reflection of natural forces. The "double bubble" or comparison map (5.12b) let them identify similarities and differences in the main characters. The flow map in Figure 5.12c helped them trace the course of action through five

FIGURE 5.11   Thinking Maps™ Developed by Ninth Grade English Teachers to Support the 1991–1992 North Carolina Course of Study

GRADE **9**

Theme: **Scarcity, Conflict, Choice**   *using thinking maps for connecting content, concepts, skills, and thinking processes*

	COMMUNICATION SKILLS	SOCIAL STUDIES	MATHEMATICS	SCIENCE	HEALTH EDUCATION	CONNECTIONS
CONTENT FOCUS	world literature (p.278)	economics (p.329)	consumer math. (p.237)	biology (p.278)	drug abuse (p.183)	**Concepts:** resources, scarcity, choices, conflict, interdependence
CONTENT CONCEPTS AND SKILLS	read types of world literature	economic choices–groups and individuals; scarcity	credit; availability of money	behavior and survival	nondrug alternatives to meeting human needs	
COMMON THINKING PROCESSES	representation, frame of reference, metaphor	frame of reference cause-effect	cause-effect systems dynamic	frame of reference cause-effect	frame of reference cause-effect	**Processes:** frame of reference, cause-effect, systems

THINKING MAPS:

ORGANIZING CONTENT

SYNTHESIZING CONCEPTS

TRANSFERING THINKING

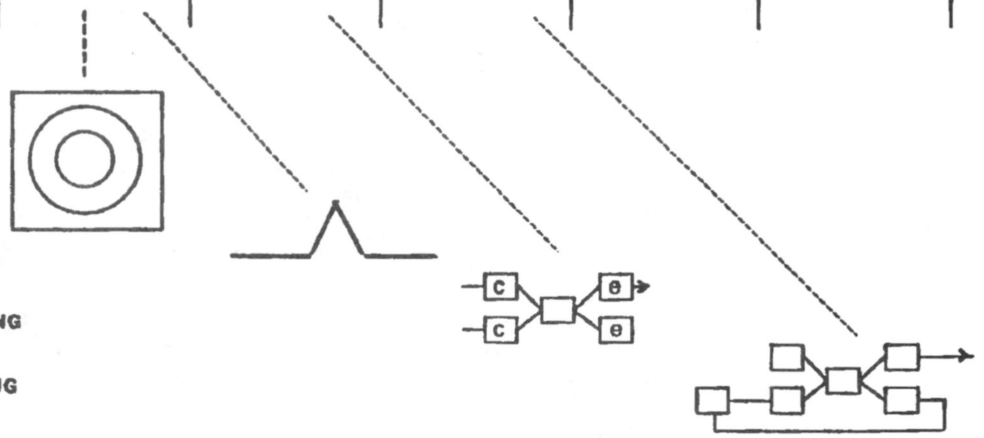

Used with permission of David Hyerle, Innovative Learning Group, Cary, NC.

parts of the short story structure. Finally, the inductive tower in Figure 5.12d helped students select specific parts of what they had read, connect them in thematic groups, draw inferences, and propose a theme for the story: "Hatred causes destruction" (Clarke, Gilbert & Raths, 1990). The graphics did not teach them to think in an unaccustomed way. They simply created a playing field for thinking purposefully as a group. By sequencing the graphics from simple to complex forms, Hyerle (1992) helped the teachers achieve a sophisticated level of analysis in which all were equal contributors.

Teacher as Designer, Guide, and Coach for Thinking

When thinking becomes the focus of classroom teaching, teachers reduce their reliance on "teaching as telling" and increase their effort in planning the management of learning projects. Designing different kinds of tasks engages different aspects of stu-

FIGURE 5.12a Circle Map to Help Students Understand the Context of Saki's "Interlopers"

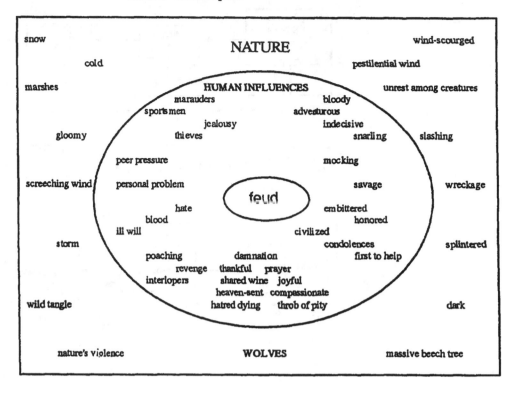

FIGURE 5.12b Double-Bubble Map for Analyzing Character Conflict

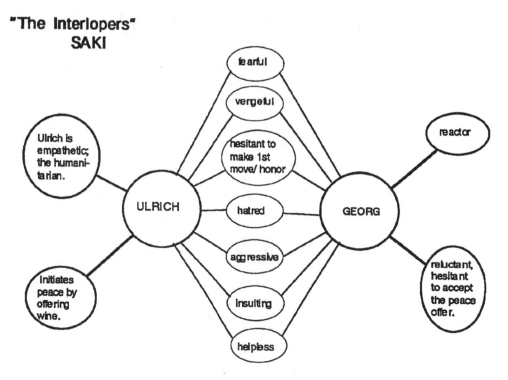

Used with permission of David Hyerle, Innovative Learning Group, Cary, NC.

FIGURE 5.12c   Flow Map for Analyzing Plot for Cause and Effect

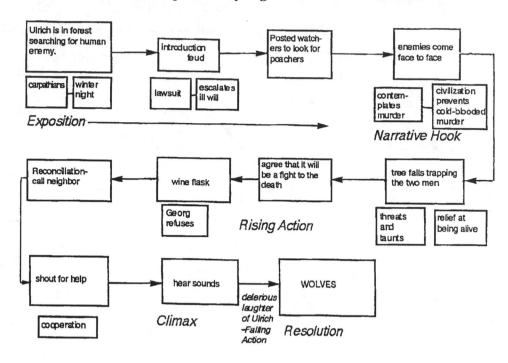

FIGURE 5.12d   Inductive Tower for Analyzing Connections Among Details in the Saki Story

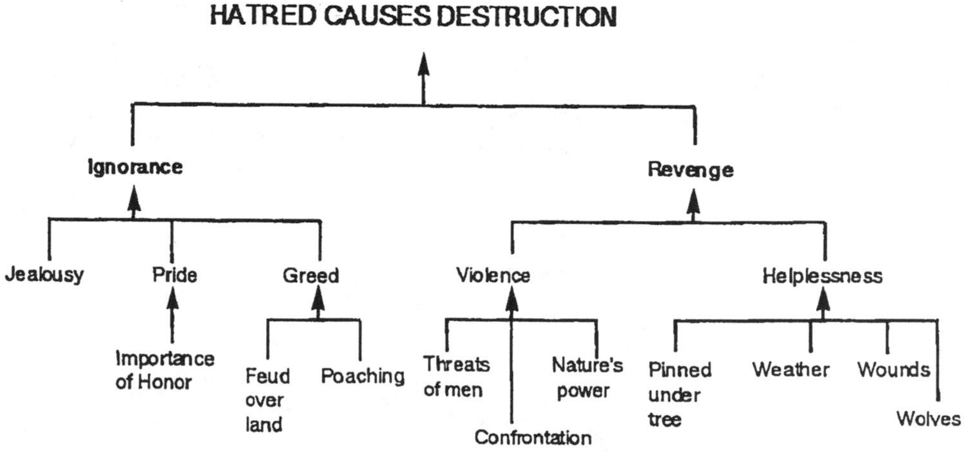

HATRED CAUSES DESTRUCTION

Ignorance

Revenge

Jealousy   Pride   Greed

Violence

Helplessness

Importance of Honor

Feud over land   Poaching

Threats of men   Nature's power

Pinned under tree   Weather   Wounds

Confrontation

Wolves

Used with permission of David Hyerle, Innovative Learning Group, Cary, NC.

dent intelligence and provides routes of access to students with different preferences or styles. Clearly, a great deal of effort goes into designing "work" for students to do, aiming for products or performances that will expand their estimation of their own "intelligence." Because different students build different models of their setting using different kinds of materials, opening access to resources become essential.

Creating graphics and guides that let students "see" a representation of their mental work increases the control they can exert over those processes. In the classroom, the teacher tries to keep the purpose in view, help students define a set of steps and a sense of their outcome, maintain learning teams or groups, set standards for success, and help students assess their own work in light of standards and criteria. When thinking is the focus, the excitement of individual initiative is the payoff; a more reliable system of management is the price.

In the Showcase that follows, Bernice McCarthy's 4MAT system has become the organizing pattern for teaching that includes all seven intelligences and graphic organizers for many different thinking patterns. The unit on nationalism was developed by the social studies department at Essex Junction High School and a team of interns from the University of Vermont who were working together to create a professional development school at Essex. Today, student work lines the hallways in the English/ social studies corridors at the Essex Junction Educational Center. In the classrooms, students are engaged in bringing new life to their learning and expressing their own developing intelligence.

THINKING PROCESS SHOWCASE

Teaching Conceptually with 4MAT:
A Case Study on Nationalism

Stephen M. Boyle, Teaching Intern; Brian Walsh, Lead Teacher;
and Students Katie Ross, Shawn Machia, and Jennifer Myers;
Brian Nelligan, Chair, Social Studies; Kevin Martell, Global Studies Team
Essex Junction High School, Essex Junction, VT

As educators have struggled to develop goals and objectives for content-driven curriculum, the process of learning has been largely ignored. Curriculum design is greatly enhanced when the "what" of teaching is combined with the "how" of learning. Since learning involves both content and process, a narrow focus on content may no longer be enough, particularly when a school aims to involve all students in developing thinking and learning strategies. The students who fill the rows in high school classrooms bring vastly different repertoires of background knowledge, skill, and approach to learning. To teach all these students requires a framework that addresses different learning styles, and learning styles are at the heart of Bernice McCarthy's (1990) 4MAT system.

Within 4MAT, students are taught to approach a subject using each of four major learning styles, emphasizing: (1) concrete experience, (2) reflective observation, (3) abstract conceptualization, and (4) active experimentation. In addition, each of the four styles may be approached from one of two models—a "left brain" mode that employs reasoned or deliberative tactics and a "right brain" mode that relies on an intuitive sense of texture, context, and relational perceptions. By designing units in an eight-step sequence, teachers can ensure that students begin their study by reviewing their established knowledge, activating different facets of their intelligence as they work with the content and complete the unit with a personal expression of their own understanding. Figure 5.13 shows McCarthy's 4MAT system as eight steps in a learning cycle that balances a focus on content with a focus on learning.

While each student may favor one style over others, engaging all four styles ensures that each student has a chance to approach the content from a preferred style and also works in styles less often employed in learning. Because students share their understanding at each phase, they benefit from seeing how others have chosen to represent facts and ideas from the subject under study. In Quadrant 1, sharing an experience related to the subject allows students to activate prior knowledge, reflect as a group, and realize the source of different perspectives on the same event. In Quadrant 2, they integrate personal experience with new information, expanding what they know to include facts and concepts from lectures, texts, films, and library sources. In Quadrant 3, students practice using the new concepts and facts to make meaningful connections and to propose possible relationships. In Quadrant 4, students analyze all they have done in earlier quadrants and synthesize ideas in a project of their own device—and make them their own. What emerges from the cycle is a product,

Note: Essex Junction and the University of Vermont have created a Professional Development School, where high school teachers, UVM teaching interns, UVM professors, and Essex Junction students collaborate to develop new approaches to teaching and learning. Showcase materials used with permission of teachers and students.

FIGURE 5.13   The 4MAT System

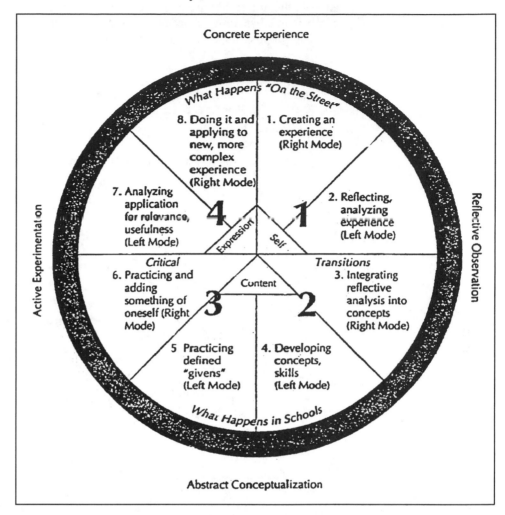

From *The 4MAT System: Teaching to Learning Styles with Right/Left Mode Techniques* by Bernice McCarthy. © 1980, 1987 by Excel, Inc. Used by special permission. Not to be further reproduced without the express written permission of Excel, Inc. Those desiring a copy of the complete work for further reading may acquire it from the publisher, Excel, Inc., 200 West Station Street, Barrington, IL 60010, (708) 382-7272.

designed by teacher and student, that adapts prior knowledge of each student to new information and expresses it in a unique formulation. Using 4MAT as a framework, students demonstrate not only what they learn, but also how they learn in a variety of measurable ways.

Nationalism in Four Phases

This chapter describes a unit on nationalism, team-taught by six social studies teachers at Essex Junction High School—three teachers and three student interns—who use 4MAT collaboratively to design units and to teach them to students of different abilities. By addressing the four major learning styles, the unit balances thinking strategies and content acquisition, using different assessment tactics in each quadrant to obtain multiple views of student learning. Developed for heterogeneous classes at the sophomore level, the unit engaged approximately sixty Global History students in examining the origins and nature of nationalism. Teachers working in the team also adapted the unit to fit their own conventional classes. Figure 5.14 represents the goal of the nationalism unit, carried out in eight phases, based on McCarthy's 4MAT system.

The purpose for each quadrant may be expressed separately:

Quadrant 1: Defining nationalism from a common experience—flags, myths, creeds, anthems, and an airplane race

Quadrant 2: Political, religious, and economic facets of nation-building—1066–1715 (England, France, and Germany)

Quadrant 3: Nationalism in three contemporary conflicts (Quebec, Palestine, and Northern Ireland)

Quadrant 4: Exploring nationalism in a student's country-of-choice

FIGURE 5.14   The Goal of Nationalism Based on McCarthy's 4MAT™ System

Title: Nationalism
Grade level: Sophomore   Duration: 3-5 weeks
Subject: Nationalism
Author(s): Stephen M. Boyle
Concept: Loyalty, leadership, power, values, social control, nationalism.

— Overview —

Objective: Students will evaluate the relationship between the individual and the State, and come to conclude that the meaning of nationalism changes over time.

Required Resources: Filmstrip of nationalism

Course materials prepared using *The 4MAT System* by Bernice McCarthy. Used with permission.

After students formed nations that helped them define nationalism (Quadrant 1), they were reassembled in their respective classrooms for a series of lectures on the religious, economic, and political aspects of nationalism (Quadrant 2). Students were then asked to convene as nations to put nationalism into historical perspective (Quadrant 3). Through timelines, students place bits of information into the framework of history. Finally each student in each "Nation" presented their own ideas of contemporary nationalism (Quadrant 4).

Quadrant 1: Creating a Nation and Reflecting on Nationalism

How was the unit implemented? What actually happened? The unit began with a random assignment of students into various groups or "nations." Grouped randomly by the months of their birth, each student was asked to contribute to the "creation" of their country. Shy or disinterested students invariably held back, at least initially. However, by having a specific duty within a cooperative "nation," each student eventually contributed to giving their nation a name, motto, pledge, and anthem. For much of the rest of the unit each student became an independent citizen within one of those nations.

By the end of the exercise, each nation put forth a unified front when it came time to present to the class. One pledge read:

> We, the great people of Tirrices, pledge our loyalty to our most awesome land. We will give all we can to help it grow and become the most powerful nation to ever exist. In return, we expect and know we will receive equality, peace and all the power in the land.

Even without an obvious reason for unification, such as external threat or intern turmoil, the student–citizens of Tirrices had come together to form the basis of a unified nation.

The approaches students took to nationalism varied. Some student–citizens seemed eager to demonstrate national unity while others did not. As they worked through the unit, student–citizens were confronted with some of the problems inherent in nationalism: coping with zealous fellow student–citizens, rallying citizens unwilling to participate, and negotiating conflicts between the national interests of other nations. At the risk of occasional classroom chaos, educators and students developed an experience showing how nationalism unites and troubles the human experience.

As one of the first, and most important steps toward nationalism, student nations created a national mythology. One nation, Aquaria, took an almost biblical approach to the creation of their country:

> Once, a very long time ago, the water Goddess Aqualina made the tiny island of Aquaria. At that time, the world was a very desolate place. The Goddess was saddened by this barren wasteland, and she decided to make a place that would have all manner of plants and creatures. So she made this small land, and she saw that the animals needed someone to watch over and protect them. So she then made many men and many women to populate this land, and to protect the creatures.

Once Aquaria had established its own creation myth, a strong sense of national unity could not be far behind. The appearance of a unified front during these presentations may have actually helped bring students together.

In another class, however, students were anxious to express their individuality. On the verge of anarchy, while professing peaceful coexistence, the "Independent Nation of Individuality," or INI, sought unification through laisse-faire individualism.

After creating the basis of a nation out of randomly selected citizens, students prepared paper airplanes for homework. Complete with each nation's logo, airplanes were flown for prizes in the gymnasium. Winners were crowned in three categories: longest individual toss, greatest national average, and single most colorful airplane. Victorious nations were positively reinforced with candy bars. The activity resulted in great fun for citizens cheering on fellow citizens, even those ill-fated sorties that landed *behind* the take-off line. Back in the classroom, as numbers were being tallied for the official results, students discussed the activity. Who did they think won? Why? Who cheated? Is a strong air force important in defining your nation? What is more important? Why? It was determined that the winning team, Sagio, cheated to gain victory. Rivalries developed between nations as it became apparent that Sagio was disdainfully proud of its tainted victory. Confronted with justifying themselves, losers accused the winner of cheating. Immediately a classroom "balance-of-power" struggle ensued as other nations joined in to accuse Sagio of aerodynamic deception.

Student–citizens rallied around the need to justify their behavior in the airplane race. Teachers asked each student to write to the folks back home explaining their results. Some blamed erratic gymnasium wind currents for their poor performance. Other nations downplayed their lack of productivity by limiting the importance they placed on an air force. Still others placed the burden squarely on Sagio, while Team Sagio gloated over its own aeronautical effort. Quadrant 1 ended with student–citizens finding their own paths to national unification. Emotions that led students down the road to nationalism could include the following: having to explain themselves and their actions to other citizens, accusations or threats from other nations—or perhaps it was as simple as needing to belong. In a sense, many of the same emotions that unify countries in the real world existed to unify these makeshift countries. Almost without knowing, student–citizens fed the fires of patriotism.

Quadrant 2: Gathering Information—Politics, Economics, and Religion

To seek historical analogs, Quadrant 2 sent each class back into their original classrooms for a short filmstrip on nationalism and a series lectures on the rise of nationalism. One teacher and one student intern joined forces to present two weeks of lectures on either the political, economic, or religious aspects of nation-building. For example, one teacher and one intern were designated religious experts. Their job was to present a lecture on religion to each of the three classes. Likewise, one teacher and one intern teamed up to present lectures on the impact of politics and economics on the creation of the nation-state. Three or four days were allotted for each lecture, and then the teams rotated to give the same lecture to a new class. The religious aspects of nationalism covered the Crusades, the Inquisition, and the Reformation. Politics dealt mostly with England and France from William the Conqueror's invasion at Hastings in 1066 to the end of Louis XIV's reign in 1715. Although each lecture took on its own flavor, students were provided with the same general framework of knowledge in each of the three categories.

To engage the intuitive component of learning about historical instances of nationalism, the teaching teams asked students to develop a project that expressed a central idea from the lectures and readings. To express the economic origin or nationalism, one student turned to poetry and another to the visual arts to represent economic growth in the age of nationalism (see Figure 5.15a). Here, in a nutshell, is the economic origin of nationalism. Increased food production, the growth of trade, and the power of a new, urban middle class, all provided for a stronger economy. Also apparent are the seeds of capitalism and political power based on wealth, not wealth of land.

In the visual approach to many of the notions, the student captured the growing economy just as powerfully. All students accompanied their artistic work with a written explanation (see Figure 5.15b) of their purpose. Note the kneeling King at the center of Figure 5.15a, representing decreased monarchical power. The King bows toward a peasant thinking of agricultural improvements. These improvements helped spur a food production surplus that would lead to increased trade. The broken sword represents the dead feudal notion that power lay only in military might. A rising middle class, whose wealth was based on money, seems to be saying "the coin is mightier than the sword."

FIGURE 5.15a   Student Poster Showing Nationalism Replacing Feudal Order

FIGURE 5.15b   Shawn Machia's Description of a Nationalism Poster

The late Middle-Ages

My drawing represents the biggest changes that took place in the late Middle ages.

The kneeling King in the center of the page shows that the power of lords and kings was greatly decreased. They no longer owned people.

The figure of the man thinking symbolizes the public in general. People were thinking more. There were new advances in agriculture, and that led to businesses which led to trade.

The broken sword on the bottom shows how strength didn't necessarily proclaim the ruler anymore. The people had more of a say in what went on. This power came from money. With businesses and trade, the new middle class gained power. Some made almost as much money as the King, and many partnerships made as much. The money, and the figures coming out of it represents how businesses and money gave the citizens more power.

Drawing by Shawn Machia. Used with permission

Quadrant 3: Extending and Personalizing Knowledge of Early Nationalism
To begin Quadrant 3, we chose to assign a Timeline of Nationalism: "On as long a piece of butcher block paper as you need, write down the names, dates, and events that marked the emergence of nationalism from the end of the Roman Empire to 1715. Different student groups worked on different sections of the timeline. The wealth of information obtained in Quadrant 2 was thus transferred into a visual for students to use in making some chronological sense of the ideas presented. Most student timelines were 6 to 10 feet long, with important clusters of events and people noted in different colors, creating a final display from which they could explain how nation-making over a millennium had contributed to the rise of nationalism.

After students completed their section of the timeline, they were asked to help write the history of their fictitious "nation," including a sufficient number of "great moments" to justify national pride. As they wrote their history, students could be as creative with the concept as their imaginations allowed. Fabricating a timeline gave students the opportunity to visualize the history of nationalism, as well as practice working with the concept of causation.

We completed Quadrant 3 with a role-play involving all six teachers. In pairs, teachers and student-teachers played out three contemporary conflicts concerning nationalism. One pair provided the background for Northern Ireland's religious-based nationalism while another pair acted out the cultural nationalism of the French versus the English in Quebec. The last pair of teachers played out the tortured Middle East's Arab–Israeli split. Each teacher argued from a nationalist perspective—one as a belligerent Palestinian and another as a militant Israeli. Wearing the Intifada–Palestinian head-dress and carrying stones, one teacher argued for Palestinian autonomy while another teacher argued for Israeli control.

Students could now appreciate the painful choices involved in nationalism. Religious, economic, and political aspects of nationalism merge to become one, and it is no longer possible to separate one aspect of nationalism from another. The role-play took the spirit of nationalism into the twentieth century, setting the stage for 4MAT's fourth quadrant.

Quadrant 4: Viewing their World through a New Lens—Nationalism
In Quadrant 4, the burden for learning was placed almost entirely on the student. At this point, students had become quite familiar with the concept, and they were ready to synthesize the idea into their own network of knowledge. The activity we chose involved group research and presentations. In choosing their final project, students randomly shouted out countries whose nationalism they might be interested in studying: Bosnia, England, Vietnam, and Israel were just a few. As countries were listed on the board, students signed up. Every student, as one might guess, opted to study with their original classmates—their "nation." More important than who students chose to work with was whether students understood what was expected of them.

Quadrant 4 allows each student to evaluate his or her own learning while interpreting the concept in their own way. Of the final two weeks of the unit, we devoted one week to research and the last week to presentations. Consequently, more than at any other time in the unit, teachers acted as facilitators in Quadrant 4. In a chaotic scramble for information, we spent one week with sixty students in the library. Students researched the economic, political, and religious facets of their chosen nations, and tried to make sense of the model of nationalism that they had developed throughout the unit. In every group, the nature of nationalism appeared to change, forcing students to update and revise the model they had just learned.

Oral presentations were graded by students and teachers on a rubric. Based on quality of research, content knowledge, presentation, and effort, the rubric consisted of a scale from one of four, with four representing exceptional work. Predicting the future is a large part of all Quadrant 4 activities, and the rubric of assessment needs to reflect this. Questioned by teachers and students, those presenting had to explain just how nationalism changed over time. Was economic nationalism leading Vietnam to open her doors to trade? How was Northern Ireland to get beyond religious wounds that simply will not heal? Would ardent nationalism allow peace to flourish in the Middle East? The purpose of the nationalism unit was to help students see how nationalism, emerging gradually over 100 years, might direct the future course of history—the section of history yet to be written by these students.

Aftermath

Was it a success? Which aspects need to be improved for the future? In employing the team approach to 4MAT and the nationalism unit, the social studies department was setting a schoolwide precedent. Without any set time to organize and plan, one can imagine the coordinating problems that might arise. As the unit began, most of the problems centered around student involvement. Students appeared tentative at first, and Quadrant 1 began slowly. However, with an eager department chairman at the helm, the plan went forth without any noticeable disasters. Certainly one of the greatest challenges involved nervous student interns, green with inexperience, plodding through lectures as cooperating teachers patiently filled in the historical gaps.

As they experimented with cooperative learning in their team-taught class, teachers were confronted with the prospect of presenting similar material to their own individual classes. Each teacher had at least one other global history course in which to present a nationalism unit. As the teachers soon found out, activities that worked well in a team-taught class of sixty students did not necessarily translate to a class with one teacher and twenty-five students. And yet, teachers somehow tailored each assignment to fit the needs of their conventional classrooms. Thus, the unit was not only an experiment in cooperative teaching, it was a lesson in creative teaching as well.

CHAPTER 6

The Writing Process

Writing to Learn

Why Write?

During this decade, writing has reasserted itself as a medium for learning as well as a medium for communication. Teachers have turned to writing with increased interest not simply because writing has become more important as a skill for jobs and personal advancement, which it has, but because the process of writing gives teachers and students a powerful vehicle for integrating learning and thinking. Writing to learn, as opposed to writing to communicate or express feeling, has become a basic tool in interdisciplinary teaching because writers may cross many boundaries, from math to science to English, pursuing answers to the questions they ask of themselves. Writing to learn is reflective writing. This chapter describes two kinds of writing-to-learn activities—journals that help students process new information, and writing projects that help them synthesize and present information from a wide variety of different perspectives. Writing to understand one's own thinking and writing to have an impact on one's surroundings both give the writer a physical medium for exploring the power of the mind in understanding or managing a complex world.

Writing is by far the simplest way to begin crossing boundaries in a quest for understanding. In interdisciplinary classrooms, writing lets students focus on big questions, then search as widely as they are able to find answers. Answers may come from any source—personal experience, contact with others, or facts and concepts from subject areas. Writing to learn usually starts with what students already know from personal experience. It can then reach out to incorporate ideas from other students, as well as facts and concepts from text, observations, and reflections on class discussions. Words on a page reflect what students know and how they have come to know it. A writing journal, or thinking log, helps students and teachers keep track of what they find out about a subject, make connections to what they know already, and push on toward further questions and problems.

Unit-length student projects or short writing-to-learn exercises both have advantages for classroom teachers:

Empowering Every Student: Writing is a personal enterprise. It forces every student to become active in learning, whether they are working alone on some part of an investigation or sitting together in a class-sized group.

Creating Common Focus: Written projects on a common theme and short written exercises during class both bring focus to the idiosyncratic process of individual learning.

Forcing Commitment: Informal writing makes students take a stand on what they know, reducing the extent to which they remain passive while the class goes on around them.

Activating Learning: Whenever a student is writing, the center of classroom work becomes the individual mind, trying to raise questions, gather facts, or propose new ideas.

Making Connections in Content: Written language creates connections between facts and ideas, through the magic of syntax. On a written page, learning becomes more than a collection of isolated facts; it becomes a process of making meaning.

Mirroring the Work of the Mind: Writing allows students to practice an enormous number of intellectual strategies, including data gathering, categorizing, logical inference, theorizing, creating, predicting, planning, and problem solving.

Teachers who use writing in the classroom can create assignments that shape the processes students use to think.

In their writing, students construct a mental model of what they already know in addition to information they are learning that is visible to themselves and to others. In their physical form on paper, thoughts can be revised and reconstructed toward greater accuracy, detail, and meaning. Without a stabilizing medium, thought is fleeting. It comes and goes. Without form, thought is shallow, only bright flashes on oily water. Thoughts half hatched become full on paper, raising questions for further pursuit. Questions betray convictions and lead to new perspectives. In turn, new ideas take on physical form, attaining a temporary stability while new questions arise. Teachers can use writing to help students explore their world and their own minds, fashioning for themselves a comprehensible and even more manageable universe.

Informal Writing: Writing to Clarify Knowledge

Toby Fulwiler (1987b), among others, has proposed two roles for informal or expressive writing. One role occurs in the composing or draft stage of formal writing, where ideas and relationships come into focus and find their shape before students turn to a final draft. The other is in *writing to learn*—writing with the singular purpose of focusing the mind—during which students explore what they know and clarify questions about what they do not know yet. A well-kept journal comprises a record of what a student was thinking as the process of learning unfolded. Writing to learn usually does not end in a "publishable" piece; its purpose is only to push students into the unknown. When students learn to share their exploratory writing with others, they become their own teachers. The validity of their opinions, the connection of facts to ideas, the logic that brings meaning to facts, and the questions that open the door to new learning become objects of study on the written page. Writing gives teachers a simple mechanism for creating a community of learners in a high school classroom.

Figure 6.1 shows how teachers can use expressive writing to move students toward formal prose, or toward learning and thinking across disciplines. That expressive or informal writing can support idea formulation, decision making, problem solving, self-discovery, understanding, retention, and inference is often visible in formal student writing. Writing to learn captures and exploits the curious, unresolved quality in most student writing. Interdisciplinary teachers can use informal writing at any moment in a conventional classroom, stopping the action momentarily to force independent thought. They can use a two-minute journal to begin a class: "In your reading last night, Huck Finn and Jim were floating down the Mississippi on a raft. Open your journals and write for two minutes about a time in your life when you had to spend time alone with someone you didn't know." Writers explore and consolidate their perspective.

Once discussion has grown warm or a debate has begun, teachers can use short writing exercises to bring everybody in: "This is a tough question. Let's take a minute to write out what we think. Has Tom become the slavemaster on the raft?" When the

FIGURE 6.1   Two Roles for Expressive Writing

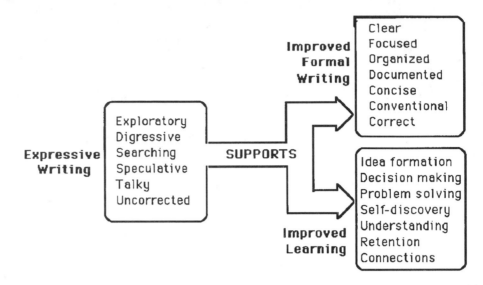

Adapted from Toby Fulwiler (1987), *Teaching with writing,* p. 13. Montclair, NJ: Boynton/Cook. Used with permission from author.

debate resumes, all students will have developed a point of view. Teachers also use writing to summarize a class and lead toward the future: "In these last minutes before the bell, try to predict what will happen between Jim and Huck as they travel down the river." Prediction writing gives students a clear purpose as they continue their reading.

Focused writing can be used as homework, creating a launching pad for the next class, but it has a more immediate effect in short two- or three-minute breaks within the class period. If a class period is lagging and student eyes have begun to droop, a short writing-to-learn assignment brings energy back to the topic. If a class has become fractious with dispute and individuals have stopped listening to each other, writing can focus energy on personal clarification, setting the stage for more organized inquiry. Writing turns eyes inward, where the search for connections and cohesion is an individual enterprise. If students collect their journal entries with other class notes, the journals constitute a record of the individual's attempt to make sense of the subject matter (Fogarty, 1991).

As John Bean points out, effective writing-based teaching depends largely on the assignments a teacher creates to help students probe facts and ideas from the disciplines (see Figure 6.2). A sequence of coherent and purposeful assignment questions can help students explore connections between complex ideas. In the name of cohesion, writing to learn often requires a learning journal—an ongoing record of ruminations and insights that drive individuals deeper into the meaning of subject area knowledge.

Informal Writing in the Classroom

Figure 6.3 represents four ways short writing assignments can support classroom teaching and learning (Biddle & Clarke, 1990). In this four-step cycle, writing is simple a mirror to thinking:

FIGURE 6.2   Eight Ideas for Designing Writing-to-Learn Tasks

1. Create tasks that link concepts in your course to personal experience.
   Example from mathematics: Write a short essay on the topic "My Mathematical Autobiography." Include anything you consider significant about your past or present associations with mathematics.

2. Create a list of controversial theses in your discipline.
   Example from history: Caesar was (or was not) an ambitious demagogue. (Refer to primary sources.)

3. Create assignments that pose an interesting question or problem, perhaps posing the question from an audience other than the teacher.
   Example from physics: A sand glass is being weighed on a sensitive balance, first when sand is dropping steadily from the upper to lower part and then again when the upper part is empty. Are the two weights the same or not?

4. Create paragraph-length "frame assignments," providing a topic sentence that students then illustrate with examples or explanations.
   Example from philosophy: Socrates and the Sophists differed in their beliefs about truth. Socrates argued that . . . On the other hand, the Sophists argued that . . .

5. Create assignments in which you present students with data that they must convert into a short essay or argument.
   Example from current affairs: Basing your argument on the attached statistical table, support or deny the assertion that "Women (blacks) have made significant progress toward job security since 1972."

6. Create assignments that require students to role-play an unfamiliar point of view.
   Example from fine arts: Look at any of the cave paintings (on board). Imagine you are the ice-age artist who created the painting. What motivates you to paint this figure?

7. Have students write summaries of your lecture, of articles, films or arguments related to the content.
   Example from biology: Write a one-page summary of the argument (C. S. Lewis) that the earth itself deserves to be categorized as a living organism.

8. Have students write dialogues or miniplays in which characters take various positions on an issue.
   Example from political science: Write a dialogue between Socrates and Robert Oppenheimer at the Los Alamos compound during the development of the A-Bomb.

Written by John C. Bean, Director of Writing, Seattle University, Seattle, Washington (February 1988). Used with permission.

1. *Clarifying Prior Knowledge:* Teachers can create short writing-to-learn assignments at the beginning of a class to find out what students already know—and how they have come to know it—creating a launching pad for further learning.

2. *Setting Purpose:* As a class progresses, they can ask students to generate questions about the lecture, film, experiment, or discussion that is the topic of the class.

3. *Supporting Analysis of Facts:* To gain depth in a discussion or to force connections between an assortment of facts, teachers can ask students to write descriptively about details and their relationships, driving further analysis and further questioning.

4. *Clarifying a New Perspective:* At the end of a class period, a teacher can assign a short journal exercise, asking students to take a stand on what they have learned, perhaps from a new perspective that balances competing ideas.

Short writing-to-learn assignments scattered throughout a class period underscore the main purpose of a class and encourage independent thought (Olsen, 1991). They

FIGURE 6.3   Writing to Learn: A Cycle of Activities that Support Integrated Learning

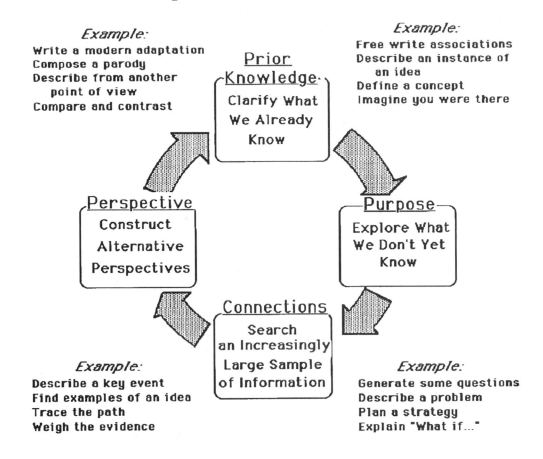

Example:
Write a modern adaptation
Compose a parody
Describe from another
    point of view
Compare and contrast

Example:
Free write associations
Describe an instance of
    an idea
Define a concept
Imagine you were there

Prior Knowledge
Clarify What We Already Know

Perspective
Construct Alternative Perspectives

Purpose
Explore What We Don't Yet Know

Connections
Search an Increasingly Large Sample of Information

Example:
Describe a key event
Find examples of an idea
Trace the path
Weigh the evidence

Example:
Generate some questions
Describe a problem
Plan a strategy
Explain "What if..."

also direct individual energy toward learning and give the teacher a chance to look at the situation and make new plans.

Writing to Clarify Prior Knowledge

"All new learning depends upon prior learning," the psychologist David Ausubel wrote in 1968. "Ascertain what students already know, and teach accordingly." The advice seems simple enough, until one realizes how few means exist for finding out quickly what students already know. Short writing assignments or journal entries at the beginning of a class period are easy ways to focus class attention on a specific focusing question.

> When was the last time you had to make a moral decision? (Such a question might lead into a discussion of *Of Mice and Men*.)
>
> What does it take to solve a real problem? (Such a question might introduce word problems in algebra.)
>
> What do you think a chemical bond looks like up close? (Such a question might prepare students to think about ionic and covalent bonding.)

When students have expressed some part of what they know quickly, they have also prepared themselves to learn more. Writing to assemble prior knowledge lets students start on their strongest footing and share what they know with others. From that point, they can move with confidence on to what they do not know as well.

To begin a unit on reading and study skills, we asked a class of high school students, grades 10 to 12, to reflect on their own expertise. "Write for three minutes about something you do very well," we asked. We wanted the students to develop new reading skills, but we also wanted to start them off on their best footing. None of them were counted among the school's successful students. To become more successful, they would have to look at skills they had already developed to a high degree. Their responses reflected the astounding diversity of any high school class.

> In high school, I am really good in mathematics. Yes, it is my subject. I have gotten all A's since I came here . . .

> I am an expert in playing cards and making money on the weekends. I enjoy the competition and the happiness that it brings out . . .

> Well, there are many things I am good at. One is shooting. I shoot quite often when I get the chance. The other is hunting. I have two deer to my name. I also love to draw.

> Something that I am really good at is hockey. It is all that I think about and do. I have spent many hours working on the sport.

> I am really good at listening to people, helping people. I know what to do if they are in a certain situation. I help them find help.

> I seem to have the touch when it comes to little kids. When I was in 6th through 8th grade, I used to come in to help the teacher with gym class.

> I am really good at reading. I can read very fast and I understand what I read . . .

What does it take to get really good at math, cards, hunting, hockey, reading, or helping others? For different areas of expertise, the class developed a common list of necessary ingredients. Practice, dedication, love, imagination, persistence, strategy, and focused effort. The list of factors they have developed gave us and them a sense of things they needed to apply to their high school classes. What students already knew suddenly became a bridge to what they did not know as well—"the skills of English," "my biology class," "my grades in dental technology," or, as a basketball expert said, "Life science is a big problem" What would it take to help kids transfer skills from their area of expertise to an area of frustration? The next writing assignment asked them to transfer their established knowledge to an academic class where they were not succeeding.

Writing to Raise Questions and Set Purpose

As most writers recognize, the act of writing often produces as many questions as firm conclusions. As words lie on the page, they may provoke as much discomfort as satisfaction: "Is this really true? How does this happen. Can I find any evidence that I am on the right track? How many ways are there to look at this phenomenon?" Writing pushes us forward, to explore, to connect ideas, and to raise further questions. Individual students in any classroom raise different issues and concerns around the same topic, creating tension that teachers can use to move discussion or debate. This "pushing forward" opens the door for further inquiry in the classroom.

At the School Without Walls in Rochester, New York, Andy Nagel makes all his students keep a record of their thoughts and observations in science. Students' journals, maintained over a full year, help them find connections between the experiments, readings, films, and discussions that take place. Over time, the journal becomes a record of learning in science and a source of information for a whole class. Individual students ask individual questions, like these from Tangy Hall's 1994 notebook, and find the answers that make sense for them:

> I never knew that they could put the genes of a mouse into an elephant or a sheep in a human, or vice versa, without the offspring coming out with some appearance or characteristics of the animal. But I found out the answer (I think). To make it short and quick,

they replace a certain gene with another gene in the host; for example, a protein gene, instead of replacing the gene in the egg with appearances.

But also another thing that crosses my mind is "What animals should or shouldn't be used for human research?"

Questions beget answers that then beget more questions. In a well-guided journal, the process of asking and answering can probe ever deeper into the meaning of the subject.

Writing to Search a Sample of Information

Do facts ever really "speak for themselves?" More often than not, each of us sees the same facts from a slightly different perspective. Looking at a wide array of facts, each of us may choose a different sample to use in making inferences or drawing conclusions. In higher-level learning, it is often the connections between facts, rather than the facts themselves, that leads us toward understanding. When we think students are being lazy about reading a chapter or listening to a lecture, they may simply lack a reason to look closely at the facts. A three-minute focused journal exercise puts a whole class to work on making connections.

Focusing Questions

- After seeing this film, describe three incidents that represent the origins of prejudice.
- In chapter 6, find three characteristics that Roman tyrants had in common.
- Looking at the results of your experiment, locate any events that might make you suspicious of your own conclusions.
- Write about three words in this poem that you think carry the main message.

Focusing students on the details helps students find the whole idea in an assemblage of pieces.

At the School Without Walls, Andy Nagel's student journals include a vast number of observations, linked to the questions an individual has asked in previous assignments:

Today, myself and a partner dissected a grasshopper. I really shouldn't say dissect because we never found any of its internal parts, but we did cut it up pretty good. When first looking at the grasshopper, I noticed it was a female. Its body cavity was very flexy, meaning when I pushed it in and out it seemed like an accordion instrument. Its back, last two legs have little spiky looking sticks on them. I think they are probably for jumping and sticking on certain objects like leaves and stems. When looking at our grasshopper under a scientific microscope, I could see little hair follicles. The wings both inner and outer look like leaves, but the outer ones were darker than the inner ones. I think that if I had a more willing partner, I could have observed some internal things such as the heart and stomach. Maybe if we had bigger specimens like RATS, the internal parts would have been easier to recognize.

Tangy Hall's Notebook

For this student, making sense of the details of grasshopper anatomy could not take place early in the observation. The journal builds its own momentum, working through early problems and details to more intricate problems.

Writing to Develop Alternative Perspectives

Teachers can use writing to help students adopt a new point of view on a topic or question.

How would it feel to arrive in Canterbury with Chaucer's pilgrims? Write a brief description of your arrival from the perspective of any one of the travelers.

> The golden spike has just been driven into the last tie on the railroad linking the East and West coasts of the United States. You are there. Describe the event from one of the following viewpoints: the President of the United States; a Chinese laborer, Sitting Bull, Andrew Carnegie, Belle Starr.

> It is 1957. Russia has just announced that Sputnik has been launched into space. Describe this event from a political, social, economic, educational, or scientific perspective.

Writing from a new perspective forces students to look freshly at events. They must select details to describe what have importance to a particular viewer. They must also use the lens of a different value system from their own. "What is important?" The question suddenly has as many answers as there are viewpoints.

In time, a notebook becomes much more than a record of facts. It becomes a cycle of questions, large and small, that push the student forward. At the end of Tangy Hall's notebook, questions, assertions, factual observations, and interpretive statements have found a synergistic relationship. In a journal entry from a simple reading assignment, ideas, questions, facts, and interpretations flow easily from one to the next, driven forward by the desire to make some connections in biology:

> ### Chapter 6: Insects
>
> *Idea:* I have doubts about the statement "People seem to adopt a negative attitude toward small size, even in people." My impression of this human society is that the majority strive to be small.
>
> *Question:* How can a biologist actually perform surgery on a fly without causing, one: death and two: a loss of blood?
>
> *Facts:* A hungry fly has less sugar in his blood than a fed fly.
>
> *Interpretations:* It is not possible to feed a fly with a stomach tube, also to administer an enema. Another way to test whether or not a portion of the body is engaged in some activity is to interrupt the nervous communication with the brain.

Of course, this line of inquiry generates new questions:

> I wonder did this fly eventually blow up? Can their skin—whatever it is—expand? Is there a certain average size, weight, etc. for flies? . . . Excessive surface area usually means excessive water evaporation and heat loss.
>
> *Tangy Hall's Notebook*

Once students have learned to recognize the importance of their journal in their personal quest for meaningful information, they begin to value the opportunity to write as they learn.

Some students easily recognize the power of writing as a tool in learning and begin to use it widely in their academic classes. Others resist the labor of writing or the personal risk of putting their thoughts on a page. Asked to explain her success in high school in a short journal assignment, one college sophomore wrote about writing as the main vehicle for learning throughout her high school experience.

> More than anything, I used my writing to steer me through my high school years. At age thirteen, I began to write poetry, observational essays and what I called "free-writes." This helped me digest the world around me and made me interested in any classes that required writing. In this way I was generally interested in many of my classes, especially English.
>
> *Student Journal*

Some students seize on writing as a learning strategy. Others fear the exposure writing brings to them and need to separate it from formal writing before they can use it to learn freely and effectively.

Communication Strategy: Writing to Make a Difference

Converting informal writing to formal prose triggers a second group of thinking skills related to the idea of strategy: "How can I say what I mean in a way that will affect people who clearly think differently than I do?" The concept of "audience" beyond the classroom has an organizing effect on expressive writing. By changing the nature of the audience, a teacher can redirect student learning toward different kinds of purpose. Aiming writing toward a larger audience also brings new energy to the process. When the teacher is the only audience for student writing, motivation flags. What purpose is there in writing to someone who already knows the right answers? On the other hand, when students have to consider a larger audience for their writing, they are forced to consider strategy as well. A strategy has a clear purpose, based on both the subject itself and on sensitivity to how others may perceive the subject. It organizes thought to achieve its purpose; and, it tries to remove any barriers in itself that would reduce the chances of failure on behalf of its purpose. Writing to learn becomes "formal" when students have enough confidence in what they have learned to turn their attention from the issue itself to the challenge of persuasion: "How can I show others the meaning of what I have learned in a way that will change someone's point of view? In formal writing-to-learn exercises, students have to work creatively with the basics of effective writing: thesis, rhetorical structure, and grammar.

A compelling audience for student writing exists right in the classroom. Once they have recognized the disparity of opinion in their class, students can aim their writing toward teaching their friends. In teaching problem solving in mathematics, writing is being used extensively to help students look carefully at a problem situation before they begin plugging in numbers and to communicate with each other about strategies that work (Wajngurt, 1993). G. Horgan at Otter Valley Union High School in Brandon, Vermont, asked her first-year algebra class to guess the number of Ping-Pong balls that would fit in their classroom. Their first estimates, done without calculation, showed an enormous range of possible answers. Then, she asked each student to develop a method for finding out a good answer and to write out the process so others could check for reliability (see Figure 6.4).

In a class of twenty-five students, there were twenty-five different algebraic equations expressing useful processes for figuring how many Ping-Pong balls would fit into a large uneven space. Some students crammed some into a shoe box to estimate the volume consumed by spheres in rectangular space, then divided the shoe box volume into the volume of the room and multiplied by the number of balls. Others, like the student did in Figure 6.4, concentrated on obtaining a good estimate of the volume of the room, then simply divided by the volume of one ball. One question generated many answers, and many ways to "model" a real-life problem using algebra. Students could share their writing and gain respect for ambiguity in problem solving. The quality of any answer depended on the quality of the algebraic models students used to get answers. "Which answer is best?" There is no best answer to the Ping-Pong ball question. The question of accuracy depends on the question of audience and purpose: "How much accuracy do we need to build into our algebraic model?"

Jim Burke, who teaches tenth grade English at Burlingame High School in San Francisco, has developed a social issues class in which students carefully research an issue of importance to themselves and then try to persuade a public official to adopt their view. The student who wrote a letter to Governor Pete Wilson (see Figure 6.5) was struck with the disparity between unmarried teen-fathers, who "sleep peacefully" and go about their business, and teen-mothers, who are up all night taking care of the baby, supported by the state. Kyle Woolf used his personal experience first as a source of inspiration, and then as a basis for persuasive writing.

To prove convincing to Governor Wilson, Kyle would have to observe the conventions of letter writing, validate his point of view with clear examples, and struc-

FIGURE 6.4 **Writing to Develop Problem-Solving Strategies**

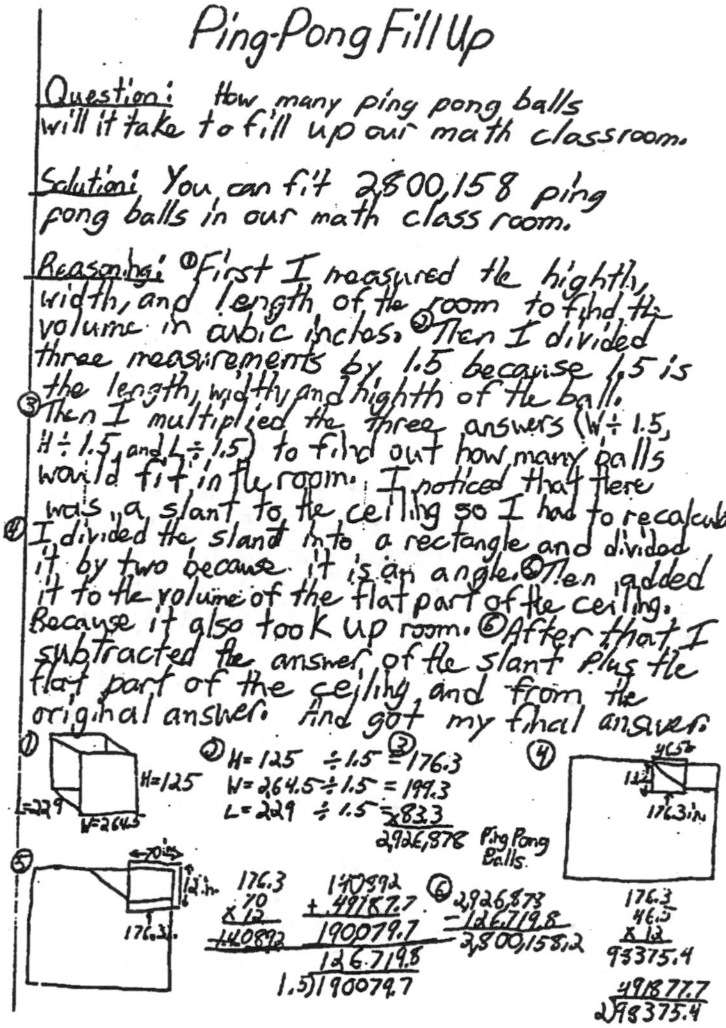

Ping-Pong Fill Up

Question: How many ping pong balls will it take to fill up our math classroom.

Solution: You can fit 2,800,158 ping pong balls in our math class room.

Reasoning: ① First I measured the highth, width, and length of the room to find the volume in cubic inches. ② Then I divided three measurements by 1.5 because 1.5 is the length, width, and highth of the ball. ③ Then I multiplied the three answers (W ÷ 1.5, H ÷ 1.5, and L ÷ 1.5) to find out how many balls would fit in the room. I noticed that there was a slant to the ceiling so I had to recalculate. ④ I divided the slant into a rectangle and divided it by two because it is an angle. ⑤ Then added it to the volume of the flat part of the ceiling. Because it also took up room. ⑥ After that I subtracted the answer of the slant plus the flat part of the ceiling and from the original answer. And got my final answer.

Work of G. Horgan, Otter Valley High School, Brandon, VT. Used with permission.

ture an argument that would lead the Governor toward a recommended "solution." The existence of a powerful "audience" outside the classroom empowered the writer as well, and it forced him to consider his writing style carefully. As his teacher, Jim Burke, commented,

> Kyle's letter combined the virtues of personal writing with the conventions of public writing. It seemed to me to be the perfect combination of personal and official; it is all the more appropriate since Kyle is one of those students who defined himself by his hate of writing throughout much of the year, all the while growing until now, at year's end, he has matured into a very fluent writer—when he has something to write about that concerns him

Martha Ozturk at Champlain Valley Union High School in Hinesburg, Vermont, asks her ninth grade students to write stories for children in local elementary schools. As her class finishes a unit, they create stories that will represent what they have learned to younger people. The collection of pages in Figure 6.6 are from different student books resulting from her unit on "Myths." On a designated day, Martha's

FIGURE 6.5   A Student's Letter to Governor Wilson

May 25, 1993

Governor Pete Wilson
Office of the Governor
State Capitol
Sacramento, CA 95814

Dear Governor Wilson:

Since I am doing a project for my tenth grade
English class on a significant social problem, I am
writing to you regarding an aspect of teen pregnancy
that deeply troubles me. This is a subject very close
to me since my 17-year-old cousin (who is more like my
sister) just had a baby. I am concerned not only for my
cousin and her baby, but for our state and its taxpayers too.

One of the things that disturbs me the most is the
total lack of interest and support by the father. While
my cousin has left school to stay home and care for
their child, the father is enjoying his senior year and
all the activities that go with it. While my cousin is
up hours every night and stuck in her house all day,
the father of the child is sleeping peacefully and able
to come and go as he pleases. While my parents and
neighbors (as taxpayers) are paying for the upkeep of
his child, the father is free to take his wages from a
part-time job to spend as he wishes.

This whole situation makes me angry and frustrates
me. Can the state really afford to be supporting all
these teen mothers and their babies? Since we keep
hearing that the state is in deep financial trouble,
why aren't programs being developed to address this
problem and others like it???? Instead of constantly
cutting back on the things we really need, such as
education and caring for our elderly and disabled,
etc., let's hold people responsible for their actions!

I am not just writing to complain. I am suggesting
one solution: in order to ease the burden on the state
and taxpayers, a program should be developed where a
teen father who is not going to contribute to the support of his child is responsible for a set number of
community service hours per week until he is able to
accept responsibility and the taxpayers don't have to
do it for him anymore. We can put him to work in our
day-care facilities, United Way or Red Cross. I am sure
with all your consultants, you can come up with even
better ways to employ these fathers. Also, this might
keep them busy and out of trouble.

Thank you for taking the time to read this. I hope
that the state will look into this issue.

Sincerely yours,

From English class work done by Kyle Woolf at Burlingame High School, San Francisco. Used with
permission.

FIGURE 6.6   High School Students' Myths Written for Grade School Readers

Horses became a part of the people and their families. They were given names by the name-giver of the people. The warriors and older people all had special horses. They even had herds of their own. When a brave would ask a father for his daughter, they often used precious horses for trade as well as traditional gifts.

The water was the only thing in the beginning. Water circled the earth, never ending, never breaking. Endless. This was the dawn of time, the time when Warramurrungundji, Mother of the Earth, came to be. She appeared out of the water, and with her came the first sun rise, and where she stepped there was land. Soft, smooth sands, whispering grasses, sharp, rough stones, and brown earth grew beneath the touch of her feet. When her heels pressed down into the softer land, they created depressions that filled with clear, fresh water. Her toes traced winding rivers into the landscape.

Drawings done by Sera Harford and Kate Fink. Used with permission.

students travel to local schools and read their stories to the children. It is a practice that breeds respect for writing among older and younger students.

Although proposing a particular audience can sharpen students' attention to the finer points of writing, proposing a general audience of peers and adults in the community can have a similar effect. At Soquel High School in California, David Casterson, Charlene McKowen, and Tim Willis (an English/social studies/biology team) use student writing projects as a student performance that organizes the investigation of critical issues. The writing assignments all follow an "I-Search" format, as opposed to "Re-search" (see Figure 6.7). Whether working alone or in cooperative groups, students use a similar reporting format for all their public writing: (1) cover/title page; (2) table of contents; (3) why I chose this topic; (4) what I already know about this topic; (5) searching: How I went about finding my information; (6) new information; (7) creative page; (8) interview; and (9) bibliography. The format ensures that students observe the conventions of writing (title = focus; contents = outline; "why?" = thesis) and also helps them personalize their writing in the name of power and creativity. Stories about places and people in the community have a wide readership.

Learning by aiming toward written productions that are published for the whole community produces lively writing that has value to others. Still, the value to learning extends beyond the project itself. As the teachers (Casterson, McKowen, & Willis, 1993 Letter) explain it:

> Why do we do this? 1) It gives three teachers who love their jobs a chance to work together, creating cross-curricular relevance and peer support for each other. 2) It gives the students the opportunity to link course content and to learn "globally." 3) It gives students and teachers the chance for flexible scheduling according to the needs of the lessons, within the three hours (scheduled). 4) It gives students the benefits of teacher coordination of field trips, homework, evaluation, guest speakers, films, class projects, and countless other activities where authentic learning is stressed. 5) It gives parents easy access to an innovative program (There has been phenomenal parent participation!). 6) It gives teachers the opportunity to see fewer students per day. . . . Most important to us is the fact that our students are LEARNING, PERFORMING, and PRODUCING just as we had envisioned.

The Soquel High School Team hands out the grading criteria at the beginning of each project. The grading criteria are specifications of elements of success in each outline area:

- Flow, sequence, organization
- Overall creativity
- Inclusion of all elements
- Thoroughness of each element (depth)
- Bibliography

When projects are being conducted by cooperative groups, the team uses a peer evaluation form to assess the contribution of individual students (see Figure 6.8). Writing about a subject helps students find meaning; assessing writing helps them understand their own learning processes.

Making the News

The newspaper provides a convenient format for collecting student writing aimed at an audience. Because newspaper writers have to assume relative ignorance among their readers, they have to describe "who, when what, where, why, and how" in sufficient detail to drive home a clear point. When Steve Dowd and Marilee Taft completed their American Studies unit on the prerevolutionary period, they began looking

FIGURE 6.7   Front and Research Pages of a Soquel "I-Search"

The Present and Long Ago of the Daubenbiss House

III.   The Search

I began my search on Tuesday, November 17, 1992. During fourth period, Mr. Willis graciously let me and Holli Smiley, to make sure I looked before crossing the street, go to the Daubenbiss house. The purpose of our trip was to take pictures of and admirer the house. When we saw the majestic, grandeur house, we knew we had to get a closer look. Taking pictures, every step of the way, we approached the porch with caution. After noticing the oval blue historical plaque lying on the floor of the porch, I wrote down the information. Holli offered to take a picture of me on the porch, in front of the door, with the plaque. Before she did, I picked it up and held it in front of me. I realized it signified a historical accomplishment.

After wiping my tears away, I decided to knock on the door. A rather young lady answered and said, "Hello." I told her I was a student form Soquel High and was assigned to pick a local historical place and do a report on it. "After passing by your house several times a day, I want to find out more information about it", I said. I went on to say that I was wondering if I could interview her? She then said that she really didn't know very much history of the house, but that she would be more than happy for me to interview her. I asked her how about if I came back at about four thirty. She said, "ok, I'll see you at four thirty." Holli and I walked back up "the trail" and responsibly went back to class.

Before my appointment at the Daubenbiss house, my mom took me by the Porter Memorial Library. There, I found two

Project done by Charlene McKowen and Tim Willis at Soquel High School, Soquel, CA. Used with permission.

FIGURE 6.8   Peer Evaluation Component of Student-Made Books

Yosemite Book Individual Grade Tally Sheet: In all honesty, circle the appropriate number for the effort shown by each member of your group. Do yourself first. Do your own thinking; pay no attention to what others in your group think.

Your name: _____   Person being evaluated _____

1	2	3	4	5
Did basically nothing	Did very little a minimum	Did average work	Gave a decent good effort	Outstanding responsibility

Your name: _____   Person being evaluated _____

1	2	3	4	5
Did basically nothing	Did very little a minimum	Did average work	Gave a decent good effort	Outstanding responsibility

From David Casterson's class project at Soquel High School, Soquel, CA. Used with permission.

for ways to make students search for connections between all the events and names they had studied. "How can we help students understand the reasons for the rebellion without memorizing a list of causes?" they asked. Writing a colonial newspaper for one of the years between 1760 and 1770 might force students to assume the perspective of a colonist. Figure 6.9 shows a sample of headlines from several colonial newspapers for those years. When the separate newspapers were lined up chronologically, the class of forty-five students could "read" the accumulating record of royal transgression from beginning to end, as they themselves had written it. From that point on, reading Tom Paine or the Declaration of Independence simply clarified what they already knew.

Science is an area in which students may soon tire of the facts and the terms used to organize those facts. Biology, for example, can easily degenerate into rote memorization of classifications and the components of life systems. After Nancy Smith finished the "Fungus" unit at the Essex Junction Educational Center, she felt strongly that her students needed a chance to work through the taxonomy again, looking for connections among the varieties of fungi and locating specific species that offer some value to humanity. "Why not get the students to write a newspaper for the Fungus Community?" she thought. "They could exchange their newspapers with other classes and use the results for review."

Nancy organized her students into four editorial teams and set them to work. Her criteria were twofold: (1) the newspapers had to convey specific information about fungi, and (2) the newspapers had to have conventional newspaper sections—front-page news, editorials and features, advice, entertainment, book reviews, horoscopes, sports, Letters to the Editor, personals, comics, puzzles, and classifieds. To write features, reports, or even cartoons, her students poured through their text looking for reportable quicks in the fungus family. The front page of *The Fungal Gazette* (see Figure 6.10) reflects the sum of the ingenuity her students brought to their work. More minute connections are visible throughout the papers published after four days of research.

"New Parcivota Film Ignites Controversy" a headline blared beneath the banner of *The Morning Mold.* Secondary news reports included "Sporothrix Arrested" and "New Ascospore Born to Marasmius." Individually, students wrote quick articles that connected small bits of what they had learned about fungi. Collectively, small groups assembled that knowledge into newspaper form, a humorous overview of the topic. Each group edited its copy to ensure factual accuracy. As a class, Nancy Smith's

FIGURE 6.9   **Headlines from Ninth Grade Colonial Newspapers**

Colonial Free Press

Nov. 3 1764

SUGAR ACT TOO SOUR FOR COLONISTS

"The price of sugar was already high, but how can I afford it now with this added tax?"

Boston Baker

Boston Times

March 6, 1770

MASSACRE!

Firing started when Crispus Attucks threw down a British soldier...

The Intolerable Times

BRITISH PASS UNFAIR "COERCIVE ACTS"

Yesterday, the British parliament passed the "Coercice" or Intolerable Acts, including the Boston Port Bill. Any loading or unloading of ships in any Boston port will be prohibited.

I WANT YOU

FOR THE COLONIAL MILITIA

Slave Auction

Three ships expected

Town Wharf

Tuesday, Oct 20 1763

Colonial Enquirer

STAMP ACT TO PAY FOR ELVIS' SURGERY!!

Money from the Stamp Act was supposed to be used to support troops occupying the American Colonies. Reliable sources, however, have told the Enquirer that the majority of the funds will be saved for eventual liposuction...

Class project done by Merilee Taft and Steve Dowd for American Studies, Essex Junction High School, Essex Junction, VT. Used with permission.

FIGURE 6.10   Student Newspaper for a Sophomore Biology Unit

The Fungal Gazette

Tuesday, March 24, 1992 — Matt Clark

Campaign '92: The Good, the Bad, and the Winner

Washington— President Marasmius was elected to a second term in office yesterday with a landslide victory over democrat Pleurotus Ostreatus.

Marasmius's victory was somewhat in doubt after his alleged affair with Nancy Smut in February. He almost had to drop out of the race earlier this month when it was discovered he suffered from stem canker.

After his operation President Marasmius's popularity increased. He won 87% of the vote.

President Marasmius shown here after delivering a speech to the public outside the Whitehouse, yesterday.

President Marasmius was a big favorite of the Basidiomycota and Ascomycota. He split with the Deuteromycota and was a slight loser with the minority Zygomycota. ~A.R

CLASSIFIED 'SS

REAL ESTATE

MOLD MANOR
For Sale: Bread stored in plastic bags. Fairly moist in dark area. Call days only (we work in the dark of the night)

ASCOMYCOTA REALITY
For Sale: Aquatic property in tropical climate. Great for budding fungi. Yeasts, molds, mildews, and morels welcome.

EMPLOYMENT

Needed: Seeking members of the Phylum Oomycota to start a potato famine in the U.S. Good hours. No experience needed.

We are in desperate need of a Basidiomycota. Training is available if necessary. Must be able to attack cereal crops (wheat & oats) within a week. We have already started to infect wheat. Must be a rust!?

PERSONALS

SWM (single white mushroom) looking for love or conjugation. No need for both. Meiosis resulting in a zygote would be an added bonus.

Fungus in need of mate. Starting to form fruiting bodies (first time). Needs mycelium to share the joy.

Lichen in need of a mutualistic partnership. If you help me I'll help you. Call 555-MOLD.

Fun guy looking for a fun gal. Please, no saprophytes. Either uni- or multicellular. Call 55-FUNGI after 5:00.

HELP ME FIND MY MEANS OF SEXUAL REPRODUCTION!!!!
I'm confused and scientists haven't been able to help. I am Deuteromycota. I have about 10,000 species which need help also. I live in a terrestrial habitat. Stop by any time.

LINDSEY PALASCIANO

Class work done by students at Essex Junction High School, Essex Junction, VT. Used with permission.

biology unit published three newspapers, each with a different slant on the fungus world, each with its own specific information. Read as a whole, the three class newspapers constituted a fairly comprehensive review of the whole fungus unit.

Teachers at the Cabot School in Cabot, Vermont, sent out "time travelers" to explore different decades in the twentieth century. "the greatest journey ever taken by man." Four students on ten teams set out from the school in a miraculous time machine developed for them by Professor E. Ray Loomis (see Figure 6.11). Each team had to select a particular decade, design an itinerary of their two-week exploration, collect artifacts, and bring everything back to the classroom for exhibition. When all the journeys had been completed, the class could begin writing articles for the *20th Century Times*—features, news stories, interviews, and analyses. "What were the pivotal moments in the twentieth century?"; each team had a different answer. As the decades were lined up in order, distinctive trends became evident—science, global politics, and the arts. The class had constructed a record of the major influences driving change in our time.

Making Writing Central

At the School Without Walls in Rochester, New York, over several years, Charles Benoit discovered that he could teach the entire sequence of U.S. history by making news writers out of his students. For each ten-week quarter, each student becomes a writer specializing in one year of history. A whole class would thus "cover" a whole era—1812 to 1860, for example. On a daily basis, his students plumb the library, CD-ROM disks and assorted primary sources for "stories" to write up. Old woodcuts, lithographs, daquerotypes, and student art illustrate the pages of their work. At the end of the quarter, students lay out one full issue of their newspaper and publish it for the rest of the class. Arranged in sequence again, student newspapers can become the subject of large questions—"How did resistance to slavery begin?" "What stopped Native Americans from setting up their confederation?" Students can trace a specific issue over an extended period of time, counting on each other to provide specific information about a specific time.

To force some class cohesion, Benoit asks his students to focus on themes that span the eras of U.S. history and to search for stories related to those themes. "I believe that it is more important to understand the major themes prevalent in U.S. history than to recall data," he wrote. "Therefore, I chose six themes to concentrate on: society, politics, economics, artistic expression, international relations, and local history." Student newspapers must contain articles that reflect these themes, and contain the following sections:

Main story: The most important event of the year you selected

Society: A story about the ignored "average person" of your era

Artistic expression: An article about a specific work of art at the Memorial Art Gallery (in Rochester)

Editorial: Based on a crucial issue of the year

Everyday object: A story about everyday life and what it tells us about people

These section heads also push students toward depth as opposed to breadth in their coverage. The class uses simple design software to lay out and print reproducible copy.

As they publish each issue, students also create a matrix that connects their "Contents" to the six themes. A quick review of some headlines suggests the depth to which individuals dig in their search for good stories:

FIGURE 6.11 Cabot Calls for Time Travelers to Research the Twentieth Century

20th CENTURY TIMES

Cabot, Vermont

"All the news that was fit to print."

March 19, 1993

TIME MACHINE WORKS!!

Startling news has just arrived from Central Vermont where inventor E. Ray Loomis has unveiled what he claims is the worlds first time machine. Loomis claims that the machine, which looks very similar to a 1963 Peugeot sedan, can transport its occupants to any destination in time. "A few bugs will have to be worked out of it," says Loomis. "At this point I'm pretty certain it can handle going back and forth to the year 1900, but beyond that, well, I can't guarantee a successful return. I sent my dog back to the years 1949, 1913, and 1893. He was fine on the first two trips, but on the last one he got lost on re-entry. Last time I saw him he was chasing Ty Cobb around a locker room."

When asked how he built the machine, Loomis was a bit hesitant about revealing many details. "Let's just say that I did start with a thirty-year old Peugeot. It certainly doesn't look like much, but I'd rather not draw much attention. Can you imagine showing up at one of FDR's fireside chats in a DeLorean? I converted it using parts from a Frigidaire, a Victrola, a discarded PowerBook disc drive, and a sunken sub. I won't say how I put them together."

Loomis has not yet tested the machine on himself. He's hoping that he can convince a few people to try it out with him. Skeptics believe otherwise. "Can you imagine sending back a team of guinea pigs". Loomis believes otherwise. "Can you imagine sending back a team of people to witness events of the last ninety-three years? Why, we'd be able to answer so many questions that continue to bug us. We'd find out why Neal Armstrong almost didn't make it to the moon, what may have happened if the Navy had known about the attack on Pearl Harbor ahead of time, and why the Red Sox traded a kid named Babe Ruth for twenty bucks and a bag of broken bats. We could rewrite history!"

It's believed that Loomis will be putting out a call for "time travelers" in the next few days. We'll certainly be following this story very closely.

Professor Loomis' Time Machine

Trivia Quiz

In which decade was this photograph taken?

20th CENTURY TIMES

Cabot, Vermont

"All the news that was fit to print."

March 22, 1993

TIME-TRAVELERS NEEDED

Professor E. Ray Loomis, inventor of the world's first successful time machine, has unveiled his plans to send teams of explorers into the past. At a news conference outside the barn that houses his machine, Professor Loomis stated that he is seeking volunteers willing to travel back through the last ninety-three years.

"I'm hoping to put ten teams of either three or four explorers together for this project. I've chosen ten teams since that's the number of decades there are in this century. I refuse to send anyone back before the year 1900 because of the problems I've had getting the time machine back from the nineteenth century.

"Each team will spend about two weeks exploring the decade they've been sent to. It promises to be the greatest journey ever taken by man. Can you imagine being able to witness the events that made these times what they were? Being able to listen to Louis Armstrong play his trumpet, or watch Lindbergh depart for Paris; I truly envy these explorers for what they're about to do."

When asked why he wasn't going to travel with any of the teams, Professor Loomis explained that his job is to see that the travelers safely return.

"I have a second time machine that I've nearly completed that will be used in the event of an emergency. I built it using the body of an ambulance."

It's expected that the teams of explorers will be announced very soon. Already, Loomis has had hundreds of inquiries from would be time-travelers.

WELCOME-BACK CELEBRATION BEING PLANNED

Plans are underway for welcoming the time travelers back from their journey. It is expected that the teams will be returning with information, artifacts, and exciting tales to tell about their two weeks in one of the decades of the twentieth century. An entire afternoon, and possibly an evening, will be scheduled for mid-April at which time the travelers will be feted at Professor Loomis' research facility.

"I will expect the travelers to return with written accounts of their experiences, photographs, documented interviews with individuals, and even a few artifacts," Professor Loomis recently stated.

"It is also my hope that this team will be able to discover some of the reasons why people are the way they are today. For example, why are there hardly any houses built with front porches anymore? And are people better off now that most everyone has an automobile?

"The celebration will have the appearance of a museum exhibition. It will be the event of a lifetime that I'm sure no person will want to miss."

Tickets for the event will be available soon.

- Tecumseh: An Interview with One of the Greatest Shawnee Chiefs Yet
- Old Ironsides Does It Again
- Book Review on *Pride and Prejudice* (and a little about the author)
- Kitchen Corner with the Kitchen Queen (Rotary Roaster, 1790)
- West's Secrets Unveiled, St. Louis, 1804
- Update: Mission Systems Being Built in California

A home medicine column, "The Doctor's In" (see Figure 6.12), combines questionable 1815 advice with a review of equally suspect surgical and physical techniques for the novice. Selecting the information to be presented and also writing opinion pieces forces students to adopt multiple perspectives on the year being studied. The Editorial sections of one newspaper contained a polemic against slavery, some disputes on "right sizing" the U.S. Navy of 1804, some gossip on White House affairs, and a clip from Sheridan's play, *School for Scandal*.

In effect Charles Benoit found ways to use writing to replace most of the activities that make up high school teaching.

> Do they miss key events in U.S. history by concentrating on one year for ten weeks? Undoubtedly, but they miss just as much when they are in a class that tries to cover a hundred years in ten weeks. With this course, they were able to research a year well enough to create hypotheses, draw inferences, reach conclusions, and report their findings clearly. And isn't that what "doing history" is all about?
>
> *Charles Benoit's April 26 Letter*

At this point, Benoit has given up virtually all of his class time to student research, writing, and publication. Competition between students to present improved forms and more interesting substance continues to force quality upward within the whole class.

Still, simply reporting about the year is not sufficient if the goal is improved learning. At the end of each quarter, Benoit assigns his students the task of assessing "What I learned about U.S. History by Studying this Year." Using the four reflective questions shown in Figure 6.13, he asks students to take a broader view of events, tying them to modern times and focusing on change. Following the publication of the newspapers, he makes out his own evaluation, using a computer-based form that the School Without Walls has developed to capture and assess student learning in the school. How can we assess the changing teacher role in a writing-based classroom? "For me, the hardest part was learning to stay out of their way," Benoit writes. "Most students worked exceptionally well independently and enjoyed the chance to research what they felt was important rather than what someone else told them was important."

Writing in a Community of Learners

Writing to learn gives teachers a bridge across subject areas, and a connection between groups and individuals in any classroom. At first, informal writing serves to clarify the thoughts of individuals. Because each student thinks differently about a topic, a collection of student writing raises questions for a whole class to consider. What are the big issues? What do we need to know? How many ways can we approach the questions? Working alone or in cooperative groups, students can then use writing to collect the information they need. Different students in different groups collect different kinds of information. To make sense of it all, they have to share what they have written and reconcile the differences if they can. With writing as a medium for learning, reflection, questioning, searching for facts, and adopting new perspectives become community norms. By confronting differences in perspective, students can learn to tolerate ambiguity and to respect the viewpoints of others.

FIGURE 6.12 Student Newspaper Column for a U.S. History Class

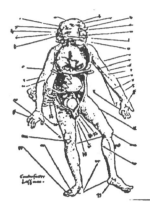

The Doctor's In

Dear Dr. Schengal,

I am a practicing nurse in small town in, Indiana Territory. I just happen to be the only nurse/doctor in a three-hundred mile radius. I have recently been bombarded with an outrageous number of gunshot victims. I am writing to you, asking can you provide me with any information for this dreadful things.

Ms. Scotts
Indiana Territory

Dear Ms. Scotts,

It is indeed a dreadful thing, with all these recent gunshot victims. In fact most of them die within months if not properly treated, and rechecked.

Because clothing and splinters are carried into the wound with the ball, tissue fibers and vessels are destroyed. Inflammation, possibly turning to gangrene, may make amputation necessary. First, search for the ball with a probe, finger or forceps as little as possible, for it will increase the pain and inflammation. It is best not to go after anything beyond the reach of the finger. Then dilate the opening made by the ball to free matter from within. If the ball goes straight through, widen both wounds, do not remove any balls if seen late. Wait until the inflammation is over and good digestion appears. Dress with lint dipped in oil to allow fluids to escape more easily, with the second dressing, use a mild digestive-and where the wound is large, a bread and milk poultice.

Dr. Schengal Ph.D.

Dear Dr. Schengal,

Two months ago my husband was involved in a horse accident. At the time we were only aware that his injuries were to his head. Recently he has just started to complain of pains and aches to his left knee, and left forearm, possibly fractures. If these ills my husband is suffering from are in fact fractures or not, what is still the best procedure to use, to ensure a quick and healthy recovery?

Mrs. Jabsten
Virginia

Dear Mrs. Jabsten,

If indeed the accident your husband was involved in, was that of a hard fall to the ground, it is quite possible that his pains are fractured bones.

As with all fractures you must at first relax the muscles. Make sure the fractured area can be seen and felt, then the bandage should lie smooth and even, and give as much tightness when wrapping it as possible. For a fracture to

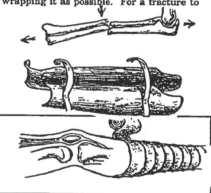

the forearm, the inner splint is longer to hold the palm, a sling supports the arm. For the knee cap,, the wrappings must be extended by wrapping with compress and bandage.

Dr. Schengal Ph.D.

Dear Dr. Schengal,

I own a small farm in Tennessee, and at the present time, my wife and myself can not find the common means to afford any unnecessary bills. This is why I am writing to you for desperate help. My son was wounded badly by a raccoon, a few weeks ago. His wounds consist of punctures to the back, arm and leg areas, all showing the bone, they have still not changed to heal. My wife is currently changing the wounds twice daily, with cotton wrappings and water. She is now worried about the chance of him getting a fever. Can you please help us?

Mr. Olson
Tennessee

Dear Mr. Olson,

The best advice I would give to anyone in your situation, is to go and get immediate help from a local doctor, but because you can not do that, I will try to provide you with as much information as I can, so your son can start on a speedy recovery.

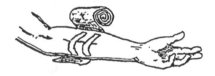

As for the fever, Antipyretics or Febrifuges are used to prevent or reduce its effects. Emetics are also used to check a fever in its early stages, before bed confinement. Because with all deep wounds and punctures, there is a great loss of skin and tissue, the first best thing is to always defend them from the air, with dry soft lint. A soft mild ointment may be used to arm a pledget of tow to cover the wounds. If a laceration heels with unequal lips, it may be later excised with a scalpel, or kitchen knife.

Dr. Schengal Ph.D.

Used with permission.

FIGURE 6.13   **How to Write Up "What I Learned about U.S. History by Studying . . . "**

THE ASSIGNMENT

1. *Read over all your new stories.* Are there *any recurring themes?* slavery, war, constitutional issues, treatment of Native Americans)? What do the attitudes and actions of the time tell you about society?

2. *Are there any stories that stand out* because they are so unusual? When something is newsworthy because it is rare, that too says something about a society.

3. *How is the era you are studying similar to our era?* In what ways is it remarkably different? Remember, history is changing over time. What changes have occurred since your year and what do they tell you about U.S. history? There are many types of changes: technological, religious, societal, governmental . . . The longer you think, the more you will spot.

4. *How do I write it?* You might want to start by citing the BIG changes you noticed—or the BIG similarities. You can also go through each story and write about how it reflects that society. You can make it personal, "Why I wouldn't want to live then . . ." There are many ways to approach this, but the important thing is that you have already done the research. Reread your stories. The answer lies there. This essay should be at least 500 words long.

Charles Benoit

A RESPONSE

```
"What I Learned about U.S. History
     by Studying the Year 1804"
```

While writing this paper, I learned many things. I learned that many things in history are forgotten as time goes by. My Science and Technology article illustrates this. What was important a hundred years ago, we laugh at now. For example the trundle bed. To the people in the year 1804, this type of bed was important for conserving space. Now, although we still have them, they're more for convenience than for importance.

The lifestyles are nothing like ours are today. Things have also changed in the way we look at women. A women's role has changed a lot. In the early 1800s, women did not go to work. They stayed home and took care of the children, or if you were rich, you had tea with your friends. The job for a women then was being a teacher or taking care of the home.

Our government has also changed a lot. Now, there are more secrets and more things that the government keeps from the people. In the editorial, I talk about the injustices to the Indians. Not many people know how we treated the first people to live here. They think we just came over and it was like, yeah, you can use our land. That's not how it was at all. We just came and forced them out of our way because we wanted to have the control and the power of a new land.

I will not like to live in this time period. I guess in some ways, it's better than time periods before it but they still had a lot of ideas and traditions that I disagree with. Their technology was far behind ours. I me, if you gave them a television or a compact disk player, they probably wouldn't know what to do with it. I also don't like the way their women were treated. Personally, I wouldn't want to stay home and watch the children all day, or cook and clean to my husband's approval.

(Continued)

FIGURE 6.13 *(Continued)*

I also learned not to look at things in the past and laugh.
Just because something may seem funny or stupid to us, doesn't
mean it's not important. Looking at my interview with Alexander
Hamilton's widow, I think it's stupid to die in a dual. I know
it's got something to do with ego and dignity, but why take the
chance of dying just because you disagree with someone.

This era is similar to ours, because we still are always looking for ways to get ahead. Conquer a new idea, be the best in
what we're pursuing. We can't settle for second best. In 1804, it
was the search for land, who had the most and got the most money.
Now it's the search for answers. We've already conquered all the
land, so we try to make the most money, win the most awards,
anything. It's part of the human race. We will always be looking
for something better. Our sights are always set on the future.
That's just the way life is. And if you don't go with the flow,
you're left behind.

From Charles Benoit's U.S. history class at the School Without Walls, Rochester, NY. Used with permission.

In such a formulation of classroom teaching, the teacher becomes an editor: mentor, guide, evaluator, and coach. If the audience is clearly drawn, students begin to see that their conception of audience makes the difference in the way they choose to write. If the audience is themselves, their writing can be exploratory, infused with assertions, questions, and the energy of not yet knowing. If their audience is other than themselves, they must consider persuasion as an art form. Pictures? Photos? Direct quotations? Fiction? Poetry? What will it take to change another person's point of view? Writing, as informal exploration or formal persuasion, can activate the whole mind and make students aware of how they are thinking.

WRITING PROCESS SHOWCASE

Writing to Understand Local History and Culture

Mary Elyn W. Carroll
York High School, York, SC

Dear John Clarke,

I cannot pinpoint *exactly* the time when I began using writing as a way of learning or a way of thinking. Most certainly, it has always been so. By its very own nature, writing achieves this purpose and requires thought processes. In my class students examine the writing of others, ponder, speak, compose, examine, discuss, converse, think, write, critique, revisit, rewrite, and learn. Although literature can successfully and easily be taught and studied by genre and/or structural and rhetorical devices, I find thematic units, concept development, analysis, shared inquiry, exploration, and discovery more useful for my purpose—reaching the language arts objectives and goals set for my students—having them receive and produce language so that it has meaning for them and for others. My classroom has become a WRITING PLACE.

One does not have to be a good writer to teach good writing or to allow students the privilege of using writing to learn or to afford them the opportunity to read. A student of mine said to me recently, "It's not knowing all the rules, but knowing how to break them and get away with it that makes a good writer." Who knows? Certainly, it's more than that, and the conventions of our language, rules of punctuation, etc., are necessary signals to aid in understanding meaning. I ditched parsing, diagramming, labeling, and the naming of parts, and buried them—except for those students who were truly fascinated with grammar, usually girls, sometimes a boy or two [Several of my young colleagues don't know what parsing is.]

I wasn't too long in the classroom when I realized that—as fascinated as I was and am with the grammar of our language—the study of usage and vocabulary were the important tools for manipulating language to best serve whatever purpose or assignment or goal I had for my students or my students had for themselves. I reasoned that if the knowledge and analysis of grammar, mechanics, and usage were the keys to good writing, then all English teachers should be good writers and maybe even published writers and could open any door in the world of the printed word. But they are not! Nor do I believe they could be . . . the art is sometimes missing in the soul and grit of a person.

Writing as Learning

The two driving forces of my classroom are effective, efficient language production and language reception. Using that as the premise, I began analyzing my objectives for students and quickly eliminated anything that did not lend itself to those ends. This became an ongoing thing, and my course of study is revisited and revised each year. The units of study that I have developed as a consequence of my analysis are total language arts packages which embrace the skills of speaking and writing, read-

Showcase materials from a letter, a unit plan, and student histories written by Mary Elyn W. Carroll. Used with permission.

ing, and listening. Among the themes and concepts are units on The Faces of Friendship, Growing Up in the South, Growing Pains, Parents Are People Too, The Me Nobody Knows, Pariahs, Fatal Flaws, War, The Evil Men Do, Odyssey, A Touch of Greatness, Prejudice (see Figure 6.14).

The initial unit each year is a self-exploratory unit I call "The Me Nobody Knows," a title stolen from the Broadway play and book. I find that students enjoy and are surprised by an exploration of self. They think about many things they have never thought about before as they engage in self-examination, comparison, and contrast with both real and fictional people, and write. Through this unit, I get to know my students and they get to know themselves—their strengths and weaknesses, their yearning, their interests, their memories, their yesterdays and tomorrows. For the first time, they are exposed to conferencing with a teacher about the things they write, about their ideas. Each student's ideas are important; each student's ideas are worthy. Each activity or assignment requires each student to think, to explore, to deliberate, to decide, to compose, to list, to web, or to network. At the end, each student is prepared for a different kind of "Odyssey" through the units that follow, but each is equipped with a tool called "the pen" and a computer called "the human mind."

Fortunately, several years ago, the Rockefeller Foundation made grants available to rural school districts (Rural Education Alliance for Collaborative Humanities [REACH] Grants) for the purpose of increasing reading and writing skills through an exploration of nearby history, heritage, and culture. Three other teachers and I applied—two English teachers, one French teacher, and one art/humanities teacher. As a frame for our grant, we chose York and the 1940s, specifically World War II events and the fact that the Wallace Brothers' Circus headquartered in York for the winter. As the only native of the town on our REACH team, I was able to make contacts with other natives and residents to aid in our research. In addition, we chose Fumel, France, as a sister city because it is basically the same size as York, South Carolina.

Through CUFAN, a computer network at Clemson University, students were able to engage in a correspondence with students at a high school in Fumel. They shared what they learned about the WAR II. They compared and contrasted the war as felt by the French who lived it and the Americans who learned about it through newsreels, letters home, newspapers, radio, etc. What an enlightening experience for my students to explore something they had only read about in a book and to learn from children of families in a place occupied by the enemy during the WAR. Bomb damage is still visible in Fumel.

I became the initial resource for students during the first year of REACH. I was born in 1940 and have memories of the late World War II years, the soldiers who bivouacked outside our small town or stayed with families in town as they awaited transfer overseas or to some other station or practiced at being soldiers. I also remember vividly the wonderful circus people and animals. In fact, I rode an elephant in the circus parade on several occasions even though members of my family were not circus people. Many things that I think I remember are things that have been told to me so often in family reminiscences that I can't separate what I remember from what I don't.

In any event, to engage my students in participating actively in the REACH project, I energetically told many stories about growing up in the forties—stories of the elephant named Alice that Santa rode in our local Christmas parade, stories of the blackouts and how frightened I was that Hitler would see the fire on the end of my father's cigarette and would bomb our home as we rocked in a hallway, stories of my mother jumping on a firetruck to practice first-aid maneuvers, stories of the fear I had of the Little People from the circus who ate regularly at my grandfather's Greek restaurant and how I would press myself against the glass at the end of the candy counter and peep around to find myself face to face with a Little Person, the story of speaking to President Truman on the telephone on Christmas Day 1948 . . . anything that would

FIGURE 6.14 Writing as a Vehicle for Critical Thinking Objectives

Purpose: To promote compositional proficiency; to develop competent, versatile writers; to develop the basic principles of effective, efficient writing; to embrace and utilize writing as a way of thinking and learning; to find the stimulus that will awaken interest and generate the necessary energy to communicate in the written word.

Exposition

The student will communicate a logical explanation.

1. use factual information
2. write a topic sentence
3. write supporting details
4. research information and gather relevant details
5. write coherently—sequentially and logically
6. use ideas, opinions
7. analyze a topic
8. write a thesis statement
9. write supporting information
10. write evidence
11. write clear, complete, coherent explanations
12. generate broad statements incorporating a group of specific details
13. judge relevancy of details to a statement
14. isolate each step needed to write clear, complete, directions
15. write step-by-step instructions

Description

The student will communicate a meaningful representation of something experienced

1. use sensory details to describe an experience
2. select specific, vivid, varied details to communicate a complete and precise sense of what is being described
3. express feeling about a subject
4. use the five senses to gather data (observational acumen)
5. utilize the most effective, descriptive language
6. select varied, specific, concrete language
7. discriminate between words with the same denotation but different connotation

Critical Thinking

1. process information
2. set goals
3. achieve goals
4. attain concepts
5. develop concepts
6. synthesize
8. reason analytically
9. evaluate evidence
10. examine values
11. make decisions
12. elaborate
13. solve problems
14. create and invent
15. power-think
16. infer
17. determine cause and consequence
18. critique and analyze
19. categorize

Narration

The student will communicate a clear sequence of events:

1. determine the purpose of the piece of writing
2. use the most effective language to establish voice
3. analyze the audience for whom she or he is writing
4. determine events to be included and arrange these events in clear order
5. elaborate by using details
6. establish the most effective order of presentation
7. use sequential indicators and transitional devices
8. understand clearly the place of any one event in the context of an entire sequence of events and present it appropriately and effectively

Persuasion

The student will communicate major contentions and supporting reasons for the purpose of influencing a particular audience to take a desired course of action or support the ideas presented:

1. communicate a convincing argument with evidence
2. state a contention (point of view)
3. state support: reasons, factual evidence, opinion, psychological appeal
4. determine audience in order to choose effective, appealing argument

163

generate questions, curiosity, and excitement about the decade . . . stories of the German prisoners of war who were incarcerated at a prison whose location later became that of a high school and then an elementary school that most of my high school students attended as third through sixth graders . . . stories of the oldest buildings and homes and the eccentric and wonderful people who lived there and live there now or worked there or work there now, and the story of famous Jefferson Davis "who slept here." We looked at my baby book and students speculated about why my first word was "soldier." I shared my memories, and we wrote about them as we engaged in shared inquiry.

These stories became the meat for memory writing. My stories sparked the memories of my students and they began asking their own family and friends about the forties and later years. Students were looking at their own baby books and asking questions. Suddenly and surprisingly they became energetic about "that old subject called English" because they didn't recognize it anymore. We had so much reminiscing going on! And it was beautiful. Students have no trouble with oral language, like Southerners who have no trouble with the oral tradition. We talked, we shared, we wrote, and we learned.

In 1990, I developed "Growing Up in the South" as a unit and have used it with basic, general, and college preparatory students (see Figure 6.15). I feel that it is extremely important for young people to have a sense of place; to be aware of their roots, culture, heritage; and to be aware of the commonalities they have with each other even though their families are unique and their fellow Americans far away. Although the activities were developed specifically for Southern teenagers, each can be modified for use in any section of the country—village to national region—by the choices of literature and a simple semantic change in directions. For example, the bulletin board theme for the unit is "Southern Ain't a Synonym for Stupid."

FIGURE 6.15   Growing Up in the South: A Humanities Unit for Grades 7 to 12

Sustained silent writing accompanies most activities (SSW—writing as a way of thinking and learning) by reacting, responding, interpreting, inferencing, surmising, concluding about the concept of *Things that Are Southern.* The order in which unit activities are presented will depend on the choice of activities and the timespan.

Activity One: Concept Development—Brainstorming and Discussion

Students list either individually or orally as a whole class "things that are Southern"—similar to word association. When you think the word "South" or "Southerner," what comes to mind? After the list is compiled on the board, the class discusses the items to determine validity. Items which are determined to be regional are retained. Students read "Saying Grace" by Jennifer Greer from *Southern Living's* "Southern Journals: Moments in Time." We talk about the tradition of always saying grace before we eat and share other similar family traditions. After the discussion, students engage in sustained silent writing. Reading *To Kill A Mockingbird* by Harper Lee, students are given themes, customs, ideas, concepts to look for as they read. Each student is given a different aspect of the novel—the role of the father, prejudice, superstition, the role of women, etc. Students keep a double-entry journal during their reading.

Activity Two: Concept Development—Bulletin Board

The bulletin board theme is "Southern Ain't a Synonym for Stupid." Students bring articles from newspapers and periodicals and any other source (calendars, etc.) that feature Southerners of achievement. The people or groups of people featured do not have to be well known or public figures such as the President and Vice President, both Southerners. Students may bring articles about students in their own school. The only criteria for inclusion is achievement and being Southern. Each student is required to submit a minimum of five articles for the bulletin

(Continued)

FIGURE 6.15   *(Continued)*

board. The subject of the article must be achievement—social, economic, educational, political, athletic, academic, etc. Students read and share their bulletin board items. During SSW, students in the class make notes of their classmates' articles by writing a very brief summary or reaction.

Activity Three: Concept Exploration—"The more things change, the more they stay the same."

Students with a partner peruse yearbooks of an assigned decade dating from 1935 to the present to glean information for a "Then and Now Chart," noting how what they have discovered supports the concept—the constants, the cycles, the new, the old, the same, the different. Each set of partners is assigned a particular decade: the thirties, the forties, the fifties, the sixties, the seventies, the eighties. Students look for data in the yearbooks in the areas of academic curriculum; vocational/business curriculum; extracurricular: sports, clubs, student government, superlatives, publications, hairstyles; clothing styles; faculty; administration; class size; school size; etc. Using newsprint, each set of partners lists and makes notes on what they find. This information is shared with the class. A king-size chart is created in chronological order—each set of partners contributing to the chart as they share with the class what they have gleaned. Individual students engage in SSW.

Activity Four: Concept Development—Nearby History

Each student identifies in a yearbook from the thirties, forties, or fifties a citizen who lives in our school district. Students make appointments to interview these people. Some of the interviews are videotaped, some are tape recorded, some handwritten—all are transcribed. Students develop their own interview questions. Students use as a resource the book *Nearby History.* From interviews with these people, some of the students write articles and compile a book of nearby history; others, using dummy sheets, paste up a newspaper. Some students do a slide-tape show of the historic district and use interviews with people who live in the homes now or work or own the buildings to create a program with a sense of history felt by present occupants. Students also visit the courthouse and research the deed books for additional history on the homes and buildings included in their work. One student went on to stage a "This Is Your Life" for a grandparent, contacting people from the yearbook who were contemporaries, using tape recordings, letters, notes.

Activity Five: Dialects/Lifestyles/Names of Places

Dialects: Students choose states outside the South to obtain information for their dialect comparisons.

Letter Writing: The first letter is to the Department of Education in each capitol city to obtain the name and address of a high school in the state with the same or close to the same demographics as ours. The next letter is to the principal of a high school requesting cooperation by a teacher. The teacher is asked to have a student(s) respond to the survey which is enclosed with the letter explaining the project. The teacher in the other school chooses a volunteer who establishes a penpalship with a student working on the unit so that lifestyles, etc., can be noted. Students in my class keep a log of information gained from the pen pal. From these logs, discussions are held (fishbowl style) and conclusions are drawn about things that are uniquely Southern and things that are universal.

A compilation of all dialect survey responses is made and shared with the cooperating teacher from the other state. A Southern dialect section is included, compiled from students' responses to their survey. Students discuss the concept of transplants to the South and dual allegiance. SSW: students summarize what they have learned from this activity in relationship to Southerners and people from other sections of the country.

Names of Places: Students read the article from *Southern Living,* "It's All in the Name" by Steve Bender, featured in the section Southern Journal. The article lists towns, villages, and cities with strange or unusual names. Students use an atlas to locate the quaint names of towns, villages, cities in each of the Southern states and write to city government officials or Chambers of Commerce in those

(Continued)

FIGURE 6.15   *(Continued)*

towns to find out how the place got its name. For example, South Carolina has a Fair Play; North Carolina has a Kill Devil Hills; Virginia, a temperanceville; Arkansas, an Evening Shade; Mississippi, an Alligator; Kentucky, a Flippin; Louisiana, a Lucky; Florida, a Frostproof; Georgia, a Need More; Tennessee, a Difficult; Alabama, an Equality; Texas, a Goodnight. Usually the responses to the students' letters of inquiry include brochures and other information we use in the display.

Activity Six: Following Directions—Southern Recipes

Students, parents, and teachers choose an evening for a covered dish supper. Students peruse recipe boks like *The Flavor of the South* and *Southern Memories* and others to choose a recipe to prepare. Students who want to share a family recipe bring a copy of the recipe to school; however, another student prepares it. Students, with parental permission, bring utensils and ingredients for the recipe chosen. Using the school kitchen, the recipes are prepared by individual students. The students have a "Southern Night Out" for supper. After the meal, students watch a video with a Southern setting, such as *Driving Miss Daisy* or *Twain and Me.*

Activity Seven: Southern Places, Southern Families, Southern Communities, Southern Stereotypes

Students have an extensive list of novels, short stories, short essays, excerpts from books, and the book *Growing Up in the South,* which includes stories with various themes such as loss of innocence, sexual awakening, family relationships, social adjustment, schools and teachers, religion, values, initiation, emotional development, growing responsibility, love of storytelling, preoccupation with family, support of close-knit community, suffocation of close-knit community, race relations, gender roles, social classes, passion for place, code of honor. The student reads the selection and (1) writes a double-entry journal, (2) writes a response to "How is the theme developed?" (3) makes notes of dialect oddities (special to the South) such as "ain't studying you"—chile—playing the book, (4) writes a critical analysis.

Activity Eight: Field Trip to Cemeteries

Supplied with newsprint and crayon, students visit a local cemetery and do rubbings of the gravestones. Many of the gravesites date back to the 1700s. Interesting epitaphs are shared. For example, "Killed by the Sioux at Wounded Knee—He was a soldier, and a good'un." Rubbings are displayed, discussed. Students make a list of things they would like said about them if they were to move away to another place to live.

Activity Nine: Creating Poetry

Using Nikki Giovanni's poem "Knoxville, Tennessee" as a model, students compose their own personal poem about the season and place they like best. Students draw from their own experiences during some special season of the year.

Activity Ten: Memory Writing

The teacher shares a memory with the class, an anecdote from his or her past. The students recall the significant events and the order in which they occurred. The class discusses the story and the idea that time changes our perception of things; that often we draw conclusions incorrectly because we weren't old enough to know the truth or others thought we were aware of things that we weren't; that sometimes because we come to an event with a different frame of reference, we draw a different conclusion or picture of what we experience and remember; that we hurt unneedfully because we don't ask, we live with our myths and misconceptions, and any other concept that arises. Students share their memories with a small group. They discuss the memory, question, recall. Each student writes her or his own memory as an anecdote, or one student may write another's memory.

(Continued)

FIGURE 6.15 *(Continued)*

Activity Eleven: The Family Calendar—Engaging Others

Students, using their own format, create a family calendar, exclusively for their family. The calendar includes family members' birthdays, anniversaries, memorabilia, recipes, anecdotes, family firsts—first words, first steps, first dates, proposals, "baby book stuff," family pictures. The calendar is made as a gift. The objective is to get students to listen to others, to get away from the audio-visual world of TV and video games, sound systems, etc. . . . to recapture the rich oral tradition and make a concrete record of it. The calendar is supposed to be a surprise for the family—a gift. The calendar must be original, no computer-made calendars—a process and a project!

Activities for Use with the Book To Kill a Mockingbird

The major activities to complete with Harper Lee's book include:

1. comparing Maycomb, Alabama, of the thirties with York, South Carolina, of today (Similarities are remarkable)
2. engaging in the activities in Perfection Form's Masterprose unit on Lee's book
3. comparing Boo Radley with the tree in Shel Silverstein's *The Giving Tree*
4. writing about the various themes
5. analyzing a transume of Scout
6. group talks
7. double-entry journals
8. comparing the film and the book
9. comparing Atticus with the father in Dorie Sander's book *Clover*
10. writing Harper Lee a letter (Key West, Florida)
11. making a list of the superstitions
12. discussing and writing about the heinous KKK
13. analyzing why Atticus Finch was a man ahead of his time
14. analyzing why Atticus missed the boat about the KKK

Closure for the unit includes an original essay by each student who chooses her or his own topic about the South—being a Southerner, etc. Our own Moments in Time Journal is compiled from these essays. Students are required to free write an answer to the question "What have I learned?" before writing the essay.

Different regions have stereotypical descriptions held by those living outside the region; depending on that stereotype, a bulletin board phrase can be chosen and the items used on the board presented and posted to refute the stereotype. The unit engages students in language production and reception, with a strong emphasis on composing and reading. Listening and speaking activities are inherent in the assignments; the assignments are the science of the unit. The teacher adds the art. Closure for the unit includes an original essay (see sample in Figure 6.16) by each student who chooses a topic about the South—being a southerner, etc. We publish the *Moments in Time Journal,* a compilation of these essays. Students are required to free write an answer to the question, "What Have I Learned?" before writing the essay.

Teaching as Constant Revision

I find that conferencing with young writers is the most effective way to teach sentence skills, unity, support, and coherence without interfering with the art of writing. During a writing conference, it is important that a teacher does not become a collaborator unless collaboration is an objective. Through the use of journals and sustained

FIGURE 6.16   A Final Student Essay for a Unit on the South

PAULINE FLOYD

The person that I interviewed is Pauline Floyd Gill. She was born on July 26th, 1929. Her mother gave birth to her in a house in the country. Pauline Gill has one brother and five sisters, two of whom are deceased. The schools that she attended were Jefferson Elementary and then City Grove Elementary for the fifth grade. She had to quit school at an early age in order to keep her family well. She was the oldest child and took care of her brothers and sisters. Back then, life was tough; she had to chop wood, work on a farm for 75 cents a day, and wash dishes.

She took an old dishpan down a big hill in order to get water from a spring to wash with.

She has attended Fishing Creek Baptist Church since she was only 12 years old. On a mission trip she and her sister won a wheelchair award. Fannie Ann, her sister, won the "1981 Wheelchair Award" in which they represented South Carolina in Columbus, Ohio. She rode elevators and escalators, went window shopping, and the people were especially friendly.

On that trip she was dreaming about going back to school and getting an education. In 1974, she started night school and finished with a GED in 1976. She was proud of what she had accomplished and savored every minute of it. She treated herself to a trip to Harrisburg, Penn. She saw beautiful gardens and big markets of fruit stands, clothing stores, window stores and the people were friendly.

I asked what kind of entertainment she enjoys. Pauline says, "Just good clean fun, gospel music and being with the family." Her hobbies are cooking recipes and visiting the handicapped. I asked, "When will you retire?" and she said, "When I get 62 and on my own."

"Times really have changed since I was a teenager back then," she said. Pauline went to church and was allowed to go to the movies once a month. She had to be home before the sun set, which was very early.

The last question I asked her was if she could change any situation that exists presently that wasn't present when she was growing up, what would it be and why? "Children on drugs and the young men and women to respect for one another and change the attitudes of some young folks," she said to me.

Sean Collins

Used with permission.

silent writing, students find ammunition for their pieces, answers to their questions, concepts and ideas, solutions to their problems and the problems of others, and a forum to pose questions for exploration and ideas for discovery. At the conference, which is handled in pretty much the same way as the old country doctor whose patients sign in and are called in on the first-come-first-served basis, the student and I discuss his piece—we disagree, agree, I suggest, he accepts, he rejects, I succumb, he relents, and so it goes.

Teaching is also, or at least should be, an evolutionary process. Evolution in the classroom occurs simultaneously with evolution in society; thus assignments and activities, the purposes-goals-objectives, the processes—techniques and methods, learning and teaching styles, and evaluation procedures evolve. Adaptation! Lessons evolve with the times, with the challenges, and with new faces entering the classroom each year. The constant is the teacher's art. The evolution is the teacher's science. The teacher is the fine tuner, the honer, the creator; students are the energizers and the lumps of clay. Although one may like to think that students are students, when I compare the access to any and everything that students have today with the access my students did not have years ago, it is astounding. And that makes all the difference!

I am retiring this year after thirty-three years in the classroom. How I will miss it—I already miss students not born yet whom I will never know, whose energy I won't be a part of. The thing I will miss most is watching as students learn through writing, share through writing, and engage in giving permanence to their thoughts through the written word. I will miss chuckling or crying or laughing or seething over and about what students have to say. Oh, how I will miss it!

CHAPTER 7

Computer Processing

Managing Electronic Information

A high school sophomore whom we know quite well, like other sophomores we also know, enjoys talking with her friends. At fifteen she sees conversation as a favorite thing to do. On a weekend, she can meet a friend down at the town pizza shop and they talk. Most days, however, she resorts to the phone. When we got a modem for the phone line and computer, she found a whole new population of other fifteen-year-olds to talk to on a countrywide computer bulletin board based in one of the local high schools. They adopted network names to accentuate their separate network identities. Our fifteen-year-old became the wire-based "Goddess of Wisdom." Soon, her friends had established a number of topically focused bulletin boards—about friends, music, and ideas—and she found her way to them. Over the modem, she and her new friends devised a whole new class of gossip since they had never met, that treated parents, school, and friendship on a more abstract level, a more interesting level than they could achieve at the pizza shop.

Over a vacation, she discovered that she could get on the EDNET from her house too, where a few cybernetic corners had been set aside for high school students looking for quality gossip with a philosophical bent. Or musical preferences. Or old records to sell. Or old cars to fix. She joined right in. The Library of Congress, six publications, the AP Wire Service, the stock exchanges, and some fairly bizarre "personal" sections opened to her touch. Around the dinner table, we raised big metaphysical questions about just how large the human mind might be—attached by wire to human events and human minds distributed in a huge web around the world.

The same wire that brought information to the house could send it out as well. She and one of her friends started a "zine," a kind of computer-made magazine, written by one or two high school students and consisting entirely of what they happen to believe at the moment. Access to her "zine" is currently restricted to fifteen-year-olds. When we told her that there was the Internet waiting for her through the EDNET, she knew immediately that she could find precisely the kind of talk—and the kind of audience—she wanted right there. And so it is, this fifteen-year-old mind may converse with any kind of mind she wants to contact, in this country or even in others, whenever she wants to do so. (We offered her unlimited cash backing if she could find out what's actually on the Internet and tell us in a language we can understand.) And what lies past the Internet? The Cosmonet, perhaps, in which we all converse with each other at once, sharing in distant events from our homes, while knowledge flows back and forth across the world like a wind?

The information highway stretches out ahead, limitless and unmanageable in any conventional sense. What this fifteen-year-old has already learned has yet to be felt fully by us or by her teachers: She can share her thoughts any time with all kinds of people and in sharing thoughts with people who have related ideas, she will grow. Not only will she learn, she will enjoy learning. The interaction is joyful to her. Controlling the flow of her learning reinforces her sense of control. She aims her days toward the evening when time on the computer will let her communicate with her friends. Before she has learned to drive a car, she knows that the larger highway is coming into view and she is on the road toward it. She knows that command of this highway does not depend on what you know but whether you can find what you need. The answer to knowing content lies in the process of finding and reconstructing it electronically. On the information highway, content is unlimited in quantity. Can you recognize a need and find information that meets that need? That's the question. Control over circumstance lies in control of process: making connections, managing thought, and solving problems.

In this chapter, we show how teachers have taken advantage of the technology that has brought knowledge within reach of everyone. The emergence of this flexible and personal medium for learning has been characterized as the "information superhighway." Students can use computers, modems, and interactive software to gather information from a variety of sources. They can reconstruct and present what they have learned in a variety of formats. Resisting the temptation to be encyclopedic in coverage, our purpose is to show how technology has been employed in *giving students control over information*—what they choose to learn and how they choose to represent what they have gathered—to an audience that may be scattered widely across the globe.

Getting Started from Where You Are

The awkward process by which computers entered the schools created two classes of teachers—those who felt relatively comfortable with the computer and those who did not. When micro-computers became available for school use in the mid-1970s, pioneering teachers blazed the trail, constructing a washboard road marked with such names as VIC-20, Commodore 64, and TRS-80™ (Tandy Corp.), introducing a technolanguage that thoroughly frightened or alienated great numbers of teachers. Anyone interested in technological history can view the chronology of computer development at The Computer Museum in Boston, which houses the modern equivalent of the Edison Museum's Victrola collection.

Early users have slowly drawn others into using technology, now enhanced by Apple Powerbooks™ (Apple Computer Corporation), CD-ROMs, modems, file servers, and satellite dishes. Of course, new instructional and administrative roles have been created for technology coordinators in school districts, causing further division within the faculty. "User friendly" interface programs, such as Windows™ (Microsoft Corporation) and Apple's homey icons, give the computer a human look and make computers accessible to everyone. Clearly, young people raised on Nintendo have been quicker to make their way toward the information highway than have older people—such as teachers. To exploit the educational potential of computers, teachers have to make up the distance between their familiarity with computers and that of their students. Further, the principle of equity that guides high school teaching requires equal access to information for all students.

Because computers and electronic communication will play such an important role in the future, high school teachers need to become involved, starting where they happen to be right now. Today's problems with the new technology fall into several categories:

1. Technophobia
2. Memory of early computer programs/technology that were not very good
3. Teacher training efforts that have been piecemeal and not optimal in meeting desired goals for the technology
4. Frequent changes in the technology, accompanied by inherent obsolescent and the need for ever-increased capital expenditures (fiber optics)
5. Inequity in access, with schools in poorer communities often excluded, yet again, from the resources to provide best-practice schooling
6. Lack of clear purposes for why the technology should be used—just "having" the capability for inter-school or district posturing
7. The cost of equipment and supplies to conduct education with the technology, particularly involving breakout to individual classrooms once the external signal enters the building

For these reasons, well-intended educators and taxpayers may be reluctant to get behind "computers in the schools" to the extent that technology-buffs might wish.

We acknowledge these challenges but are unable to imagine learning in the twenty-first century that does not place technology in a prominent position. Whether current students pursue careers in the insurance agency, the car shop, the fast-food chain, or the multinational corporation, the rewards will go to those who recognize the place of computers in modern life and know how to access electronic information. Our task as educators is to take the best of what is available today, use it critically, and become involved in designing the network of roads in the future. This chapter presents illustrations of teachers who have taken exploratory trips on the information superhighway and, to continue to push the metaphor here, have not become lost. Instead, they have altered their teaching to accommodate computers and the highly individualized learning that computers bring to the classroom.

Fundamental Skills for Highway Travel

Computers, software, and the electronic network simply extended existing human capabilities—an electronic version of the "distributed intelligence" described in Chapter 5. Word processors extend our ability to edit and amend what we know. Spreadsheets help us represent and manage connections among numerical values. The modem extends our personal capabilities to others who might be interested and gives us access to their ideas. Computer software is built to help us do something with our minds that we do anyway, but to do it more quickly—and perhaps more effectively. To show how computers support human thinking processes, we have fit various computer applications to the "thinking wheel" that organizes this part of the book (see Figure 7.1). In using a particular software package, we are amplifying one or two aspects of intelligence that already exist in the human mind.

Adapting Chip Bloom's taxonomy of technological skills to the model of learning we used earlier, we imagine a technological highway that is circular in form (Bloom, 1992; Clarke & Biddle, 1993). As Figure 7.1 suggests, the skills students develop in one part of the cycle soon become applicable in other areas. Students who first develop skills using data-gathering software, such as spreadsheets and interactive library catalogs, may find it easier to adapt to simulations and mathematical modeling programs such as STELLA® (High Performance Systems, Inc.) and LOGO® (Terrapin, Inc.). Students who design their own instructional programs through HyperCard™ (Apple Computer, Inc.) or Linkways may soon want to communicate those ideas through an interactive bulletin board or electronic mail (e-mail). Being able to psych out a software package usually follows a need for the application represented by that software. Comfort with one medium leads toward the exploration of

FIGURE 7.1   Computer Technologies in the Learning Process

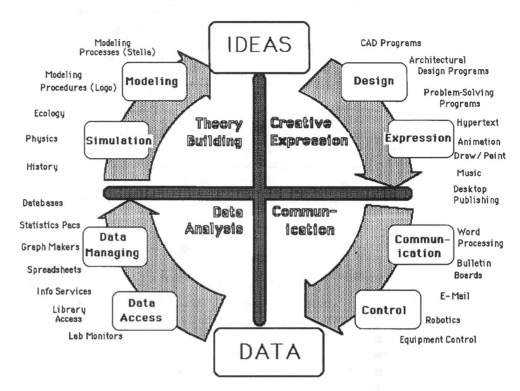

Adapted from work done by Chip Bruce (College of Education, University of Illinois, Champaign, IL) and Clarke and Biddle (1993). Used with permission.

others. The computer is simply a vehicle for "distributing intelligence" beyond the human cranium into the human community.

Despite the fact that most high school computer use is now confined to programming or work within subject areas, a number of states have identified what is called a common core of knowledge that all students must have before graduating from high school, including a separate category for technology. Usually derived from an extensive process of public participation, these goal statements are intended to chart the direction for schooling in the future. In Vermont, an organization of those interested and knowledgeable in technology has identified skills all students should have in information technology. We see the competency list in Figure 7.2 being achieved in interdisciplinary study far more simply than they might be achieved separately or in single disciplines. Computers pay no attention to the artificial lines that divide high school subject areas. Students learn computer skills more readily when they develop those skills as a part of a larger effort to find something out or make something known.

To make effective use of the technology available today, many teachers may need to add to their repertoire of skills. "Foundational skills" for competencies and experiences in information technology have been identified by the International Society for Technology in Education (ISTE), a professional and advocacy group in the field. The ISTE competencies represent what experts in the instructional technology field think all teachers need in order to be competitive in their teaching. Their listing was intended to "empower students by providing teachers with the power of knowledge about those technology tools that are so rapidly changing our world." Like other

FIGURE 7.2   Vermont's Essential Skills in Information Technology

---

Word Processing—Students will be able to use a word processor to:
1. Communicate ideas.
2. Create, modify, and output documents.

Databases—Students will be able to use an electronic database to:
1. Access useful information.
2. Create, maintain, and use a collection of information.

Spreadsheets—Students will be able to use an electronic spreadsheet to:
1. Manipulate alphanumeric and numeric data.
2. Create, modify, and output documents.
3. Organize, analyze, interpret, and test ideas.

Telecommunications—All students will be able to use telecommunications to:
1. Access distant resources.
2. Exchange information.

Visual-Audio Output—Students will be able to:
1. Create, express, and interpret ideas in the arts.
2. Communicate ideas using computerized multimedia.

Simulations—All students will be able to use computer simulations to:
1. Develop modeling tools to explore situations in controlled environments.

Desktop Publishing—Students will be able to use publishing software to:
1. Create and present a document combining text and graphics to communicate ideas.

Input Devices—Students will be able to use appropriate input devices to:
1. Accomplish a task or solve a problem.
2. Collect data.
3. Understand the use of alternative or specialized input devices.

Programming—Students will:
1. Understand that a program is a sequence of instructions to accomplish a task.

Compiled from information distributed by the Vermont State Technology Council.

taxonomies, its bulk alone may inspire more timidity than conviction. None of us should set out to master all of it; instead, we should seek access through any aspect of the list of teaching skills that supports our own teaching goals.

What Teachers Should Be Able to Do*

1. Demonstrate ability to operate a computer system in order to successfully utilize software.
2. Evaluate and use computers and related technologies to support the instructional process.
3. Apply current instructional principles, research, and appropriate assessment practices to the use of computers and related technologies.
4. Explore, evaluate, and use computer/technology-based materials, including applications, educational software, and associated documentation.
5. Demonstrate knowledge of uses of computers for problem solving, data collection, information management, communications, presentations, and decision making.
6. Design and develop student learning activities that integrate computing and technology for a variety of student grouping strategies and for diverse student populations.

*These ISTEs recommendations for initial teaching certification or endorsements are from Abramson, G. (1993). Used with permission.

7. Evaluate, select, and integrate computer/technology-based instruction in the curriculum of one's subject area(s) and/or grade levels.
8. Demonstrate knowledge of uses of multimedia, hypermedia, and telecommunications to support instruction.
9. Demonstrate skill in using productivity tools for professional and personal use, including word processing, database, spreadsheet, and print/graphics utilities.
10. Demonstrate knowledge of equity, ethical, legal, and human issues of computing and technology use as they relate to society and model appropriate behaviors.
11. Identify resources for staying current in applications of computing and related technologies in education.
12. Use computer-based technologies to access information to enhance personal and professional productivity.
13. Apply computer and related technologies to facilitate emerging roles of the learner and the educator.

In many instances, teachers using technology have been "self-taught," picking up ideas and options from colleagues, conferences or journals, or perhaps even from a book such as this. Many teachers adopted the computer for personal use long before they began looking for classroom applications. Across the teaching profession, the process of adoption has been largely random, but the results have already enhanced the effectiveness of instruction at the schools involved. None of us "measure up" perfectly on this extensive list of competencies. Our experience has been, however, that we pick up things we need to know as we go along a personally selected route. The trick is getting started. The examples that make up the bulk of this chapter represent access points for teachers who want to do a better job than they are doing now with some aspect of information management in the classroom. The path toward the information highway also leads toward the integration of high school subjects, creating further momentum toward integrated teaching.

Technological Support for Integrated Teaching

In the last decade, computers have changed from instruments that needed to be programmed to information processing systems that need to be used. After a few years of COBOL and BASIC, the medium quickly became the message. Software packages, designed for a myriad of reasons, now shape the way we learn and leave what we learn largely up to the individual learner.

Chapter 5 shows how the idea of intelligence has expanded to include the things we do and create. Extended electronically, intelligence can stretch to fit highly complex intellectual processes organized into software programs. Over a modem and on the electronic network, we may share our intelligence around the world. The examples that follow are organized to show how the computer can augment the four basic intellectual processes—data analysis, theory building, creative expression, and communication and problem solving—represented elsewhere in this book. Because the computer and the network link these functions, we see the electronic highway as a perfect place for young people to develop and extend their intelligence.

Supporting Data Analysis

Labs, Databases, and Spreadsheets

The computer is a far more powerful machine for gathering and sorting information than is the human mind. A computer data bank can store huge quantities of information—the U.S. census for 1990; the works of Shakespeare; or the catalogue of paintings in the national museum, indexed by artist, date, and subject. With a modem and searching software, any high school student can collect any amount of this information and bring it back to a personal disk or hard drive. From there, a number of statistical packages are available that help students analyze numbers and an equal number of data management programs help them make meaningful connections between separate pieces of information, stored as text, pictures, or numbers. Database programs are available to help students sort what they find into useful categories and connect those categories to a larger purpose or question.

Spreadsheets and Statistical Packages

Computers can gather information with infinite patience. Joyce Marris, one of our colleagues, was a secondary school science teacher for many years in the Bronx, New York. She often moved beyond pure "science" to help her ninth grade students see the application of science instrumentation and technology to people. One technology she employed was the "microcomputer-based laboratory." In this *add-on-kit,* wires (probes) are attached to an existing computer to permit the collection of data, over a desired time interval, on temperature, sound, and light intensity or heart-rate. These data can be plotted on a computer screen, or printer, using an axis system selected by the student. Once the information is in the memory, students can group and analyze it in ways they find meaningful. The flexibility of this system allows students to test different hypotheses within a very short period of time.

Using data from their own experiments or from other studies, high school students can ask and answer questions that would prove impossible without a computer. In Figure 7.3, Joyce Morris presents the results of her student's investigation of the question, "Which pair of gloves gives us the best protection against the cold?" This activity models the research conducted by consumer welfare organizations as Consumer's Union in their product testing for *Consumer Reports.* It represents the efforts of a teacher to use available technology to help connect students with real-world situations.

The amount of information available to students is astounding. The topic of earthquakes usually attracts student attention, especially when they make the TV news or papers. Tom Vaughn, a high school teacher in Billerica, Massachusetts, used earthquake epicenter data obtained from the U.S. Geologic Survey 800 number to get his students in on the action of locating tremors. Gerald Larson, one of Vaughn's associates at a high school in Wisconsin, in a NSF-supported project to encourage use of such data, developed and used a "Where Was that Earthquake" activity. The data arrived at the high school over a computer/modem connection.

Once teachers become aware of how real-time and archival data can be accessed, they find the network connection an invaluable resource to advance learning. Word gets out, perhaps on electronic bulletin boards, of how to access the sources of such information. Dictionaries, encyclopedias, many periodicals such as *Omni* and *Discover,* raw reports from the wire services, stock market quotations, special interest centers—many of them are public domain, are available for just a toll charge, or better yet, through a 1-800 number without cost. Others, like The Source, Delphi, Prodigy, and America Online, entail monthly and line charges. One such for-a-fee information source, CompuServe, posted actual satellite-relayed data to track the progress of sailboats circling the globe during the Whitbred Race in 1992. Teachers and their students who used this service received latitude, longitude, distance made good, weather, and current information as the race went on. Over the modem, they had access to better information, and less salt in the eyes, than the sailors who won the race.

Databases

After word processing, one of the first uses of a computer that teachers employ is often databases. Data organizing software, such as Microsoft Works, ClarisWorks™,

FIGURE 7.3   Scientific Method Used to Choose the Best Gloves

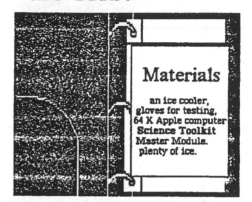

Which pair of gloves gives us the best protection against the cold?

Materials

an ice cooler,
gloves for testing,
64 K Apple computer
Science Toolkit
Master Module,
plenty of ice.

Questions to Answer

Can you help me discover which pair of gloves I should buy for the winter?

How could you design an experiment to *verify* your *prediction?*

Why is it important to begin all the gloves at the same temperature?

How can you *generate* a temperature of 82 degrees?

Why is it important to measure the time?

How does the direction of the line change as the thermistor cools?

What does the angle of the line mean?

Why does the temperature in the glove decrease?

Followup Activities: Test & compare other insulated items such as mittens, hats, socks or different body coverings such as wool, hair, fur, feathers and hide.

PROCEDURE

Select **TOOLS** from the **Science Toolkit** menu.

Select the **strip chart** tool to work with.

The scale we will use is the (°F) one and the speed of the experiment should be set for " 1 " hour.

Make sure that the thermistor is plugged into socket "C" of the interface box.

Place the thermistor all the way into the middle finger of the glove. Place it well under the ice.

Start the experiment by pressing the space bar. Take temperature reading of the glove for 2 minutes and 40 seconds. Push the space bar to stop the experiment.

Push *esc* three times, until you are at the screen with the **DISK** option to save your results. Use your name followed by *.gv*

From a project done for Joyce Morris's class at JHS 143, Bronx, New York. Used with permission.

PFS-File, and Lotus, includes programs that let students file information, add new records, and remove ones no longer needed. From a data file, the program can find and organize the information students need to answer any question, letting them generate numerous reports from one set of information. While databases can be preexisting, perhaps located in a library or resource center, increasingly teachers are helping students create their own files of information for use in research reports and in computer-based exhibitions. What is especially useful about databases is that different students can contribute to a class-owned database, greatly expanding the base of information that will be analyzed by other individuals.

Databases can support the inquiry process. As Hancock (1993) points out, a database can quickly sort data in specified ways to assist perusal; it can present information in lists and graphically, thus allowing for quick scanning; reorganizes information for particular purposes; it carries out searches rapidly and accurately; it can present findings in numeric and graphic forms; and can be readily updated so that information is current. To make any of this happen, a student must be able to define a search in precise terms.

CD-ROM

CD-ROM disks contain archival information assembled to fit one idea or event. Compact disks (CD-ROMs) have the ability to store tremendous amounts of data—nearly 650 megabytes of information—the equivalent of about 270,000 pages of text. They are read by a drive that is either built into the computer or available as an external unit. Using patented processes, such as *QuickTime,* students can playback video and animation, creating meaningful connections within the information.

Teachers have an ever-expanding source of material from which to choose on CD-ROM. Apple Corporation's CD-ROM brochure suggests the range of possibilities for school use:

The View from Earth [Time, Warner Interactive Group]

Classical CD Companion Music Series [from Voyager]

Audubon Discs [from Creative MultiMedia Corporation]

Shakespeare [from Creative MultiMedia Corporation]

Biology of Life [from MDI]

Great Literature [from Bureau of Electronic Publishing]

U.S. History on CD-ROM [from Bureau of Electronic Publishing]

U.S. Wars [from Quanta]

As the amount of information stored on CD-ROM disks increases, the ability of students to seek out information with a clear purpose in view also increases.

Supporting Theory Development

Simulations and Model Makers

Just as the computer can store vast quantities of information, it can also represent ideas and the connections between ideas and events so as to "model" some part of the human condition. With so much factual information available, students need to develop theories or "models" that let them organize related facts and ideas. Software packages such as STELLA allow students to develop abstract models that mimic complex systems—food chains, economic systems, or the weather, for example— letting them create simple systems that become increasingly complex as they add in new factors. STELLA helps students create their own simulated systems.

Predesigned simulations are also widely available, giving students a chance to experiment with different models of human experience. Computer-based simulations are prebuilt to reflect forces, trends, and general laws at work in our experience: salt marsh ecology, Wall Street, or an ant colony, for example. Software has been designed to make the models appear real: the air war over the Pacific in 1943, the battle of Gettysburg, or population ecology in a small pond.

At Essex Junction Educational Center in Vermont, Mike Hornus has the students in his World Perspectives course play the simulation "Civilization" as they study the entire record of human experience. To reach the modern era, his students have to invent stone implements, create an alphabet, and form unifying governments. They cannot become rich traveling along the Mediterranean trade routes until they have mastered navigation. Navigation requires geometry. Geometry requires basic tools and language. As students labor to create their own civilizations, they gain increasing insight into the names and events that mark the many histories of civilization in their texts. They also see the modern world as a direct extension of the ancient world. Building civilization one block at a time, students gain respect for those who lay the basis for modern culture.

Stephen Martin's students at Vergennes Union High School accompanied their study of Western civilization with simulation of a modern city called "Sim City™" (Maxis). To become the mayor of a flourishing urban environment, his students had to plan out the industrial sections that will support the city, the residential sections that will house the citizens and the latticework of services that will maintain health and order. If they raise taxes too high, the citizens may cause mayhem in the streets. If traffic gets tied up in the residential sections, their "approval rating" may go down. Both building and destroying what has been built entail "costs" to the city. The simulation includes a number of disasters that may surprise the most farsighted mayor and cause social or economic collapse (see Figure 7.4). Students may create their own city from scratch or work from an established structure based on Tokyo or New York. To help students make connections between the simulation and their own world, Martin developed a set of reflective journal guides that focus on the major issues in urbanization.

Like Steve Martin, Mike Hornus's purpose goes beyond the game called Sim City. He wants his students to recognize and respect the innumerable forces at play in the development of any civilization. In their debriefings, the students discuss the implications of their decisions: What is the best tax policy? What role does religion play? How much money should you put into "infrastructure?" How much into recreation? As a final project, each student designs an ideal city on large newsprint based on what they have learned. As the map of Long Eyeland in Figure 7.5 suggests, their creations attain a high level of complexity. As Mike's students describe the virtues of their city to the rest of the class, they face a wily and astute audience—other students who have struggled with the design implications of economics, public opinion, and import/export ratios. Even the most dazzling design does not escape careful scrutiny.

Fish Banks* is another microcomputer-based simulation designed to improve academic achievement and increase communication skills while teaching the principles behind management of renewable environmental resources. During the simulation, students form teams that represent competing ocean fishing companies. Each team has to make decisions about increasing the size of their ship fleet and allocating their ships among offshore and near-shore fishing areas. Each "company" of students records its actions on a decision sheet, and the teacher enters the information into the computer program that accompanies the simulation. Fish Banks provides detailed accounting of financial transactions and computes the interactions of fish catch, births, and deaths to account for changes in the fish population (see Figure 7.6). The time required to complete the simulation, including the critical *debriefing,* is three hours.

Willette Harbor, a science teacher at Northern High School in Baltimore, Maryland, used the "Fish Banks" simulation to help his students envision the complexities of any economic activity. The issues students typically confront range from concepts of fisheries, biotic potential, carrying capacity, limiting factors (science), to social and economic policy, communication and group skills (social studies), ethical behavior, mathematical operations and graphing (mathematics). As students compete in the real-life drama on the fish banks, they also begin to recognize the economic, political, social, and technical forces that dictate survival. Although students become

*© Dennis L. Meadows.

FIGURE 7.4   Student Reflection on What It Takes to Create a City

SimCity
In-class discussion and analysis

List at least 5 things that a successful city must have.

1) Enough funds to support the people in your town such as police, fire department, and transportation. 2) A power plant of some sort, prefferably a coal one because they don't cause as many problems. 3) You also need to have enough industrial zones and commercial zones. Everybody needs to work and no one wants to go many, many miles for groceries if they can help it. 4) Everyone needs to be hooked up to electricity. 5) Make the area pleasing to the eye (playground, parks, water)

Choose any two items from your list above and think about how they relate or effect each other. Now write a brief paragraph (3-5 sentences) that explains this connection.

Commercial and industrial zones relate to a pleasing city. I know that I and many other people would want to live in a town, city etc. that was both pleasing to the eye (parks) and go to work nearby. Many people today in the real world complain that they have to go to far to shop or work and want to move to a place that's nearer.

Based on your experiences as a city planner and leader how would you try to solve the following problems while still trying to keep a high approval rating:

Your Simcitizens are repeatedly and loudly complaining about traffic congestion. *Make more optional roads. That way if one way is crowded then they could take another one. You could also put in a railroad as an optional form of transportation.*

Industrial and automotive pollution has resulted in a dull haze of smog over your once clean and prosperous city. (If you choose to bulldoze industrial zones how will you replace the jobs and tax income they provide?) *If you bulldoze them then you can put a controled amount back in further away from the town or city and put in more houses a ways away too. The industrial zones can go where no one's living and that way it won't bother them.*

Do you think you better understand how real cities like Vergennes operate after working with SimCity? Briefly explain *Yes, I think so because now I understand how important it is to balance your funds and provide enough houses and roads. I also know how often things need to be fixed and enough industrial zones provided.*

From a project done by Stephen Martin, Intern, Vergennes Union High School, Vergennes, VT. Used with permission.

heavily invested in the competitive mode of the simulation, the teacher must derive meanings from what transpired through careful processing or debriefing of the students after the rounds of fishing are completed. Fish Banks, Ltd., has identified the stages of this debriefing that can be appropriate for any simulation that attempts to capture a portion of real life for analysis. It is critical in using the many simulation programs on the market to acknowledge that they do not teach themselves; to help students find the meanings that are latent in any computerized activity, the teacher must be at his or her best.

FIGURE 7.5   Student Project Based on Computer Simulation

City Plan For Long Eyeland

Final project after working with Sim City, an interactive simulation
of factors affecting urban design and development.

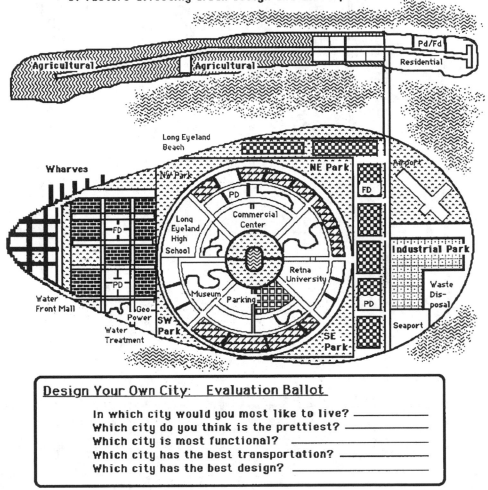

Adapted by John Clarke from original produced by Jothan Cashero, Essex Junction High School, Essex Junction, VT. Used with permission.

Stages of Debriefing Process in a Simulation

Connections

1. Identify problems and events that occurred in the game
2. Connect analogous events in the real system
3. Identify factors responsible for what happened in the game
4. Identify factors that also determine the real system

Reflections

5. Which changes in the game could solve the problem?
6. Which changes in the real system could solve the problem?
7. Gain commitment from players to seek solutions for the problems in the real system.*

*From materials produced by Karen Burnett-Kurie. Used with permission.

FIGURE 7.6 Fish Banks Opening Scenario and Role Description

FISH BANKS, LTD.
ROLE DESCRIPTION
AND OPENING SCENARIO

Congratulations! You have just been hired to manage one of the principal fishing companies in your country. Together with the others in your company - captain and crew members - you will operate your fishing fleet each year according to policies you design to maximize your assets. The rules and information required for your success are provided below.

CRITERION OF SUCCESS

Your team's goal is to achieve the greatest possible assets by the end of the game. Your assets equal the sum of your accumulated bank balance plus the salvage value of your ships at the end of the final year in the game.

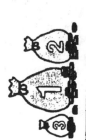

RESOURCES

You begin the game with a fleet of ships, a bank account of ($200) x (number of ships), and access to two offshore fishing areas.

DECISIONS

Each round you must determine your fleet size by deciding whether to bid for ships at auction, make ship trades with other teams, order new ships to be constructed by the shipyard, or maintain your fleet at its current size. Then you must decide how to divide your ships among the Coastal and Deep Sea fishing areas and the Harbor. You will be most successful if your decisions are based on a long-term strategy for fleet size and allocation. You must also take into account the actions of the other teams and modify your strategy accordingly.

Fish Banks, Ltd. © 1991 Dennis L. Meadows

SHIPS

You may change the size of your fleet by buying ships at auction, negotiating to buy or sell ships from another company, and ordering new ships from the shipyard.

Ships cannot be lost or damaged, and used ships purchased in an auction or trade are as good as new ships ordered from the factory.

AUCTIONS:

From time to time a fishing company in a neighboring country will go bankrupt. Its ships are then sold in one lot to the highest bidder, and they may be used immediately.

Only one company can win the ships, but two or more teams can agree ahead of time to divide the ships later (during the trading session) at a negotiated price.

TRADES:

During the trading session all companies are free to negotiate the purchase or sale of ships. Ships that are traded are available to the purchaser for fishing immediately.

Rentals can be arranged by a prior agreement to buy ships and sell them back for a lower price in a later year.

CONSTRUCTION:

Every year the shipyard accepts orders for new ships. These are available at a fixed price of $300 per ship. The ships are picked up and paid for at the end of the year, so there is effectively a one-year construction delay before the ships may be used.

SALVAGE:

At the end of the game your ships will be scrapped. Their salvage value, $250 per ship, is included in your total assets. You may not scrap ships before the end of the game.

R-1

From materials produced by Dennis L. Meadows, Institute for Policy and Social Science Research, University of New Hampshire, Durham, NH. Copyright © 1991, Fish Banks, Ltd. Used with permission.

Supporting Creative Expression

CAD and Hypermedia

Perhaps the greatest promise in computer-based teaching and learning resides in the design software that students can use to express their learning or create new ideas. Computer-aided design (CAD) revolutionized the machine-tool industry before it invaded the high school classroom. Computer-aided design software lets students create drawings of objects that exist now, or that could exist in the future. Instructional programs for CAD lead students from simple drawings to complex figures with multiple parts. Teachers are using CAD software to help students design or invent their own ideas.

The mechanical drawing classroom of fifteen years ago—featuring 4H pencils, sloping tables, Dietzgen instruments, gum erasers, and T-squares—has subsequently disappeared, replaced by the use of CAD drafting labs. Frank Saccente, a teacher at Roselle Park High School in New Jersey, has described how technical drawing at his school not only uses that new equipment, but has moved out of the school to provide dramatic field experiences. After using CAD to create aeronautical models, his students had a chance to study real-world application of the principles and concepts covered in class by seeing a three-hour demonstration—featuring a U.S. Coast Guard helicopter that landed on the school's athletic field. At another time, following their use of AutoCAD to draw cam patterns for automobiles, his students toured a local facility that designs, fabricates, and assembles race cars for a national racing circuit.

Saccente also has students in a technical writing course use desktop publishing—Adobe Systems' PageMaker™ DPT software—to produce a document which, combining text and drawings, describes the operation of a machine or mechanism. This traditional vocational subject has, thus, meaningfully used technology to help students develop a basic understanding of concepts and skills in mathematics, science, library research, information retrieval, writing, and drawing. Design software exists for a number of specific applications such as designing a house, arranging a landscape, or creating patterns for clothing.

Design software for multimedia presentations, such as HyperCard and Linkways, lets students gather, organize and present information they find or create in any digitized medium. Using a simple system of connection-making buttons and icons to tie one idea or picture to another, they can assemble cartoons, slide shows, movies, photos, and text into unique expressions of their own understanding. What doctoral students used to accomplish using 3 × 5 cards and a shoe box, high school students can now accomplish with less effort, using visual, musical, and spoken forms as well as written script. Using a linking software, such as HyperCard for Apple or Linkways for IBM, students can stitch together a multimedia presentation using any source, connected in any pattern they want to create. Fred Myers, who teaches at Mt. Abraham Union High School in Bristol, Vermont, assigns students the task of creating multimedia presentations using Linkways on most of the regions they study in the ninth grade social studies curriculum. Linkways presentations include elements of formal essays, maps, movies, cartoons, and music. As Figure 7.7 shows, Fred Myers's assignments help students expand their content knowledge while they develop new ways to work with multimedia.

In earlier times, design and invention required either vast amounts of money or a set of preliminary skills that had to be developed over a long period of time. Computers make designing new ideas and producing novel expressions of thought a relatively painless endeavor. Supported by new kinds of hardware, such as digitizing scanners, video cameras, and various audio systems, students can assemble creations of their own that include music, photography, video clips, and drawings as well as written text. Because a computer disk condenses large quantities of information into

FIGURE 7.7   Social Studies Projects that Use Linkways to Integrate Media

Africa

First Page
Draw small-scale map of Your country on the outline map of Africa. Label your country. Put a Link button over your country's name that links to the second page.

Second Page
Draw a large-scale map of your country or region. Include rivers, lakes, mountains, climate divisions. You will notice that there is a menu bar at the top of the page with the words culture, art, history, and current issues. You will place a link button on the word culture that links that word to page three. You will also place a link button on the word art that links that word to page four. You will then create a document button for the word history which links that word to a document that you have typed in Word Perfect. This document gives a brief summary of the history of your country or region. For the words current issues you will create a text pop-up that explains some of the current issues of your country or region.

Page Three
On this page you will put a picture that you have Zap-shot using the electronic camera. You will expain how this picture represents some aspect of your country's culture using a text pop-up button.

Page Four
On this page you will put a picture that you have Zap-shot of an example of the art of your country. You will then use a text pop-Up button to explain the cultural importance of the object.

From a project done by Fred Myers, Mt. Abraham Union High School, Bristol, VT. Used with permission.

manageable sizes, the computer helps teachers and students overcome the logistical problems that would make working live or on paper an impossibility.

Software supporting expression makes the idea of a student portfolio a practical possibility. Harry Chaucer at The Gailer School in Middlebury, Vermont—a private school member of the Coalition for Essential Schools—has designed a HyperCard framework that will allow students to create and maintain a complete file of their own work, linked together to represent connections they have found in their learning. The electronic portfolio has clear advantages over its physical counterpart: (1) an electronic portfolio lets students trace their development along different paths, using one body of illustrative work; (2) an electronic portfolio allows easy editing so students can add or link new productions as they complete them; and (3) an electronic portfolio promotes browsing by reducing bulk. The Gailer School asks students to determine what is most important to know. As Chaucer says, "The information highway is meaningless without students who have become motivated to search for ideas and information upon which their minds can work."

Using information technology does not eliminate the need for great teaching, but it does change the character of teaching and learning. As Harry Chaucer explains it:

> At the Gailer School in Middlebury, we view teachers as travel agents preparing students for their journey on both the high-tech information highway of the near future and in their conventional explorations in the world of libraries, museums, laboratories and studios. Like any good travel agent, we ask questions. We ask students about their destination while providing them with a chart showing them the paths that humanity has traveled over its millions of years of evolution and cultural development. We ask how they most enjoy traveling. We ask students to determine for themselves what is important to know.

A sample "card" from the Gailer School's DaVinci curriculum is shown in Figure 7.8.

Supporting Communication and Problem Solving

Networks and E-Mail

As the vignette at the beginning of this chapter showed, computers let students hold a conversation with others without fear of interruption. Any high school student—or any adult—can create a bulletin board on a computer network that will make others aware of an interest and invite them to join in on a conversation. They may ask questions, answer them or rave on about their own ideas. Using an online service, students can send e-mail to each other and receive a prompt reply. Left to their own devices, conversants on an electronic bulletin board tend to wander a bit and develop an argot for their electronic community, closing off access to newcomers who may have no idea how a conversation started. The ability of the computer to identify an area of common interest and open access to all who want to participate has obvious applications in education.

At South Burlington High School in Vermont, an interdisciplinary team of French, social studies and English teachers created units on various social issues such as AIDS. To obtain an international perspective on the problem, and to practice the use of French, they made contact with a similar group of students at the Lycee de Loure Gatel in France. Using the telecommunications system, the students in both countries began a dialogue on AIDS, aiming to develop full reports they could share through a modem and over the network. Writing in two languages, they could exchange information; chit-chat; ask questions and answer them; and practice writing, language, and social science skills simultaneously. A printout of their dialogue for January 30, 1992, contained a multitude of facts gleaned by students through research in both countries, recommendations for a film on AIDS, and a wide variety of questions beamed out across the ocean. The students wrote questions and answers in both languages, often jockeying to receive a reply in the other person's language.

As Ann Sorrell's students communicated with their French counterparts (see Figure 7.9), informal dialogue evolved toward more formal inquiries:

- Do you know how AIDS is contracted?
  I think so: 11 students; Not sure: 0 students; Don't know: 0 students
- Are you concerned about AIDS?
  Very much: 8 students; A little: 3 students; Not concerned: 0 students

Between students of different cultures, or between students in a single classroom, writing questions is a simple icebreaker. Because questions lead naturally to answers,

FIGURE 7.8   Sample from the HyperCard Portfolio

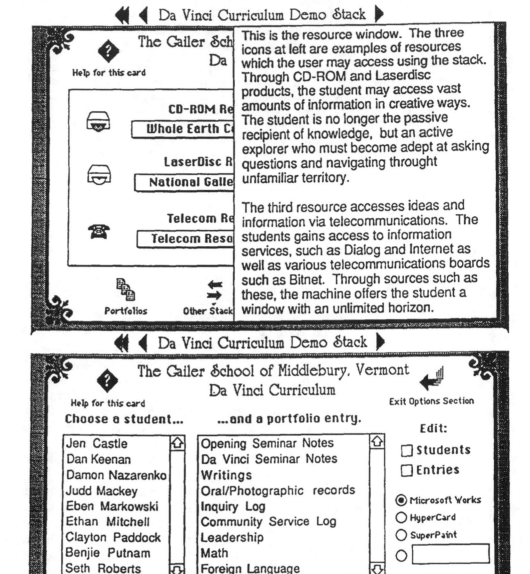

Used with permission from Harry Chaucer.

and further questions, conducting an inquiry on the electronic network can do a great deal for integrated teaching.

Joyce Morris, mentioned earlier for her work with a microcomputer-based laboratory, has also used telecommunications between her school in the Bronx, New York, and a school in Great Britain. Between the two countries, she found substantial student interest in acid precipitation, a topic in which interdisciplinary connections are

FIGURE 7.9   Conducting an Interview via Computer Across the Atlantic

Student Questions from the United States:

Do you have a class like ours?

What kind of research are the French undertaking currently? Do you hear about AIDS in the media every day the way we do?

Est-ce que vous pensez que la même chose doit se passer en France?

Est-ce qu'il y a beaucoup d'élèves qui les utilisent?

Est-que cette épidémie a changé votre mode de vie?

Comment est-ce que le virus de cida a commencé, est venu en France?

Are people with AIDS discriminated against in France?

Are men who sleep around considered macho and women considered sluts (who do the same thing?)

Are men who contract AIDS considered differently from women who contract AIDS?

Student Questions from France:

Can you ask a question and we'll answer directly?

The Secretary for Women's Rights would like condoms to be sold in high schools for twenty cents. Does this exist in the USA? Where can they be bought in the USA?

Ça pourrait aider à les utiliser. Sont-elles remboursées?

From class work done for Ann Sorrell in the French Department at South Burlington High School, South Burlington, VT. Used with permission.

readily visible and in which comparative study is useful. Eventually, student work on acid precipitation in the Bronx was compared with the same experience at a school in Exeter, England. Working cooperatively, British and U.S. students designed science experiments that both could carry out in their separate environments: devising acid rain collection containers, studying the effects of acidity on living and nonliving matter, and determining and validating the pH of common liquids.

Students analyzed and interpreted articles and confronted different perspectives on this controversial issue. As Figures 7.10a and 7.10b show, both acid precipitation and the telecommunications connection were equally important parts of the student experience of this curriculum. Using the modem to communicate findings they had derived from the scientific method increased the impact of Joyce Morris's acid rain unit and changed the nature of her relationship with her students. In association with students in Great Britain, her students gained an understanding of the global implications of their study and of their own connections to world events.

> Being exposed to another culture in such a personal and expedient way, students were able to compare and contrast a number of social behaviors and values and reflect a little more on their own. Some of the students have exchanged "Snail Mail" addresses (i.e., stamp and envelope) so they can continue their correspondence when school is out. . . . Being a teacher of science and computer, the opportunity for my students to express themselves usually extends to explaining scientific phenomena. Having students write about themselves and their class, and reading the correspondence to other students, gave me an additional perspective and a better understanding of the students I work with.

Perhaps because they provide a protective, mediated layer in one-to-one communications, computers sometimes seem to accentuate the personal aspect of learning.

FIGURE 7.10a   Assignment Sheet for Acid Rain Research: Bronx, New York, and Exeter, Great Britain

---

ACID RAIN INFORMATION SHEET

You must RESEARCH the answers to the following questions. Include any other relevant information about the Acid Rain problem that you come across. You will need at least two pages (handwritten) of information. You will be using this information in computer class to write your own newspaper using Appleworks and then PUBLISH-IT!

1. What causes it? Be specific. Tell about the natural and man-made sources of acid pollution. What chemicals are involved and how are these produced?
2. Where it is a problem? What areas of the world are most affected? Where is the problem the worst? Why are these areas most affected?
3. Why is it a problem? How does acid rain affect the environment? How does it interfere with the food cycle? How has it affected the forests in the Northeast United States? How does acid rain affect fish?
4. What is the normal pH of rainwater? What is the pH of acid rain?
5. What is being done about it? What can be done about it? Who in the United States is responsible for monitoring and studying the problem?

KEEP A RECORD OF ALL of your sources of information. You must document all your facts.

FIGURE 7.10b   Framework for a Study of Radish Growth in New York and London

---

```
                        TIMETABLE

BY: Joyce Morris
FOR: Telecommunications Project
PROJECT: A Comparison of Radish Growth in New York City and London

Week:
1.   Introduce the class to the concept of telecommunications and
     the project. Introduction of Appleworks word processing pro-
     gram. Refamiliarize myself with the workings of the modem
     and telecommunications equipment. Review the concept of a
     controlled science experiment and scientific method.
2.   Teach the class Appleworks word processing; saving to disk
     (normal and ASCII) and printing hard copy. I will get on-line
     with the teacher(s) from London.
3.   Introduction to the use of Appleworks database. Set up class
     database and discuss methods of exporting this information.
     Continue correspondence with London teacher.
4.   Practice in utilizing database information. Send off packet
     of pictures and personal notes to class in London. (Perhaps
     include a sample of New York soil for analysis and a few
     sample science tests).
5.   Discuss possible projects with class. Introduce the use of
     the spreadsheet function of Appleworks. Introduce procedure
     for use of modem and telecommunications software. Have five
     students a day save on disk and correspond with London
     students.
6.   Introduce use of Visualizer to graph spreadsheet information.
     Have five students a day save on disk and correspond with
     London students.
7 &  Students research information necessary for conducting the
8.   science project. Two students a day will compile research
     and relay it to London.
9,   Begin science experiment. Two students will compile individ-
10,  ual results each day and send them off to London. (Radishes
& 11. take only three weeks from planting to maturity.)
12.  Analyze and compare results and evaluate.
```

From a project done for Joyce Morris's class at JHS 143, Bronx, New York. Used with permission.

Sources of Skepticism

Those of us who work in secondary schools and look to the information highway will encounter many tricky turns, detours, and just plain "road closed" signs along the way. At the outset, a generation of young people raised on Game Boy, Sega Genesis, and Dungeons and Dragons has clear advantages over its elders in basic familiarity with the computer medium. Without extensive exposure to electronic media, teachers have a hard time telling the difference between an educational experience and a mindless diversion. More immediately, when students are working individually or in pairs at a computer screen, teachers have little access to the interaction—Are the students on track? Is the interaction valuable? Is the content "suitable?" Will they arrive at a destination on time? Computer-based education fundamentally changes the nature of learning and teaching, shifting responsibility to the students and rendering obsolete most of the conventions of control that bring order to conventional classrooms. The same medium that frees students to pursue their own learning seems to render teachers powerless. How can teachers take responsibility for student learning if the students are wandering around the superhighway all by themselves?

In addition, teachers who are wedded to a conception of learning based on face-to-face human interaction question the validity of mediated interaction. Many Americans have discovered the capacities of communication over networks, subscribing to such services as America Online, Delphi, or Prodigy. A March 7, 1994, *Boston Globe* editorial sends a cautionary note to those who embrace such technology, warning that the superhighways may simply add one more layer of protection against authentic interaction between us and our surroundings:

> Our automobiles provide us with a protective, anonymous shield from human contact on the road, encouraging all manner of antisocial behavior. Now the information superhighway threatens to do the same. Logging on to the Internet has given us a safe, therapeutic forum that is being celebrated as the new electronic hearth. There are computer bulletin boards for people suffering with cancer, for closeted gays, overeaters, feminists, fundamentalists, music fans, birdwatchers, lonelyhearts. More than eleven million Americans are using them. The call and response from a wired-in audience gives the illusion of intimacy, but the contact is as glancing and insubstantial as a rainbow. Rather than forging honest bonds of care and compassion, the technology gives us one more way to disconnect. . . .
>
> Now we chatter anonymous and alone in a darkened room, behind a scrim of cursors and bytes, watching the electronic fire burn. We inhabit a place with 500 channels and nobody home. It hardly seems like progress.

Teachers have reason to be skeptical of the promise technology offers to transform schools when technology has also contributed to increased isolation of individuals from their culture.

Preparing to Drive the Information Highway

No one we know is adequately prepared to use the technology currently available to enhance student learning in all the ways that are possible. Facing different groups of people, we all start at different places. English teachers may begin using simple word processing software and end up helping student publish their own newspapers and brochures using page layout software. Mathematics teachers may begin with spreadsheets, adopt visual geometry, move to statistical packages, and end with elaborate "modeling" software such as STELLA. Science teachers may begin with an ecological simulation and work toward a CD-ROM disk containing "wave theory" in physics and engineering. Even if we ourselves feel woefully unprepared to drive the information highway, our students, who can sample all of these applications during a high school career, will be better prepared. In traveling with them, we may gain more skill and speed than we ever imagined we would have.

What high school students can do on a computer is impressive. From our perspective, what high school teachers do to get ready is even more impressive because change has moved into the schools so rapidly. The Curriculum Showcase in this chapter chronicles Priscilla Norton's work over a ten-year period, as she and colleagues in New Mexico gradually introduce computer technology to their classrooms. Norton began working with simulations without a computer. Now, experience has led her toward a fully integrated curriculum in which the computer serves almost all the functions outlined in this chapter. Her story shows how we pick up the necessary skills to utilize the information highway as we go along, provided that the necessary support systems are there—mentors, sympathetic administration, and the financial resources needed to take the ride. Norton's showcase illustrates how ongoing experimentation with technology brings increasing benefits and also inspires the quest for more powerful ways to enhance student learning. All anyone needs to do is to get started.

COMPUTER PROCESSING SHOWCASE

Using Technology to Learn about Technology

Priscilla Norton
*University of New Mexico, Innovative Programs
in Education, Albuquerque, NM*

When I was a social studies teacher, schools closed their doors against the information world—no television, no radio, no telephone—of students. Today, with limited computer access, schools often do not open this world to students; instead, they close out the students' world. My frustrations led me to seek a doctoral program in curriculum and instruction. While studying, I explored technology.

For the last ten or so years, I have been working on making technology a medium for a powerful high school curriculum: (1) *developing problem-centered learning* related to technological development (1984); (2) *integrating technology* with the study of technological development (1988); and (3) *integrating problem-centered, technology-based learning with high school restructuring* in a five-course school-within-a-school for sophomores (1992). The following story describes my collaborations over those ten years with six secondary teachers who were willing to wrestle with the roles of technology in the learning process and to design learning experiences that ask high school students to use technology to solve problems in the world they will manage.

1984—Problem-Centered Simulation for Learning about Technology

One afternoon in the middle of August, Denny had just completed a Summer Institute on Technology in the Social Studies Curriculum. Denny knew he was a successful teacher as measured by conventional standards. His students did well. He was an influential model; many students had returned to share their victories with him. Yet, he also knew he was a fairly traditional teacher. His classes were planned around the progression of ideas inherent in the organization of his students' text with an emphasis on lecture, discussion, homework assignments, and traditional end-of-chapter tests. Denny wasn't satisfied. His students left each year informed but not invigorated. One night as he and his wife watched the national news, he had what he describes as a "defining insight."

On that particular night, each major news item had presented a dilemma reflecting the disparity between scientific and technological advances and the society's ability to cope with those advances. The first news item had concerned a small infant girl named Baby Fae who had just received a baboon heart. The second news item spoke of the arrest of an alleged spy accused of selling high-technology secrets to the Soviet Union. The third news item reported the condition of a man who had received the first artificial heart while the fourth item told of four California teenagers who had been arrested for a series of "prank" computer break-ins. Denny asked himself that night and we continue to ask ourselves, "How does a society respond to the social impacts of a rapidly changing, high-technology culture?" Is it possible to bring these debates into classrooms—not just on a current events day—but as an integral part of the ongoing process?

Denny called me early one August morning. In an excited voice, he stated that he was interested in using my problem-centered model for curriculum design and the notion of mushroom management.* Denny had heard a presentation in which I had outlined the model shown in Figure 7.11. He asked if I would be willing to work with him in planning a problem-centered unit on ethical issues related to high technology.

FIGURE 7.11   A Problem-Centered Curriculum

A problem-centered curriculum is one that is built around the solution to a real-world problem of interest. Educators select appropriate problems, problems that are contemporary, nontrivial, and real—complex enough to engage students and amenable to concrete solutions. The students' abilities to solve the problem, to present their solution, and to revise their solutions in light of additional information become the goals. Placing the problem at the center emphasizes students doing rather than mastering discrete bits of information. [See the next chapter in this book for an explanation.]

Mushroom Management: A Problem-Solving Strategy

When educators choose to create a problem-centered curriculum, they must structure educational environments consistent with problem solving, adapting classroom and curriculum organization to be flexible, innovative, and collaborative.

How do educators create such environments? In his book, *The Soul of a New Machine,* Kidder traces the development of a new computer, following the people and ideas involved in its creation. The frame for the management of this project is what Kidder describes as mushroom management. In the search for an overall strategy, Kidder's description of "Mushroom Management" presents itself as a viable framework for creating educational environments that support a problem-centered curriculum. For Kidder, mushroom management is summed up in four phrases: put 'em in the dark, feed 'em manure, stand back and watch 'em grow, and chop off their heads and ship 'em. To implement a problem-centered curriculum using mushroom management as a planning strategy:

Put 'em in the Dark

Plan to put 'em in the dark by identifying a viable problem around which to organize instruction and determine activities that engage students with the problem.

Feed 'em Manure

Plan to feed 'em manure by asking what it is that might help students solve the problem. What content knowledge do students need? Draw on any and all relevant disciplinary concepts. What skills and processes do students need to be able to do? Include mathematics, reading, writing, drawing, locating, and organizing information and the like.

Stand Back and Watch 'em Grow

Plan to stand back and watch 'em grow by asking what projects, presentations, and activities students can do that bring together what they have learned. Support students' use of their knowledge and skills to solve the problem. Encourage a range of solutions. Focus on students supporting their solutions rather than students finding the "right" solution.

Plan to Ship 'em

Plan to ship 'em by identifying culminating activities that engage students in bringing the pieces together, sharing results, and obtaining feedback by which to judge the results of their efforts.

---

*Although these ideas were still in the development phase when I first began collaborating with Denny, I have since written a three-part article that builds the rationale for and provides examples of several problem-centered units organized using mushroom management as an organizational framework. The reader is referred to Norton, 1992a, 1992b, 1992c.

Denny arrived at my office armed with his government textbook and an animating idea. We talked for several hours, drew webs on my office board, plotted, and, finally, agreed to collaborate on the design of a simulation. Our simulation would meet three specific goals: (1) teach students about the U.S. government and the process by which legislation is devised and then becomes law, (2) develop problem-solving strategies relevant to making ethical judgments, and (3) engage students in consideration and discussion of contemporary issues related to emerging developments in science and technology.

Denny read and I reread Tracy Kidder's (1981) book, *The Soul of a New Machine.* This book presented a real-world example of a problem-centered approach to resolving a dilemma—the invention and development of a new computer. In Kidder's context, a research and development lab, the learner is guided through four stages analogous to raising mushrooms. That is, they are put in the dark, fed manure, left alone to grow, and, finally, their heads are chopped off and they're shipped." A rather strange notion of teaching, Denny thought, until he saw it modeled. Armed with a new understanding of simulations, the development of moral reasoning, and the design of a problem-centered curriculum, Denny and I began the creation of what culminated in "The First Intergalactic Congress" simulation (Norton, 1986). Built around mushroom management, the simulation asked students to organize themselves to solve the kinds of problems we face in an information age.

Put Them in the Dark: Posing Dilemmas
To engage students with the ethical dilemmas confronting society today, we chose Ray Bradbury's (1980) short story, "There Will Come Soft Rains." The story describes the automated running and final failure of an electronic house. The story ends with the ultimate collapse of not only human life but human artifacts as well. In the early years of the simulation, students almost unanimously believed the disaster to be the result of a nuclear war. More recently, nuclear attack is only one of their possible explanations with environmental disasters of one sort or another high on the list. In all ten years, a student has always recommended legislation as a regulatory solution. And that gives us the opening to ask, "How do we, as a society, formulate and enact laws protecting human interests?" One year, Denny overheard a parting conversation between two students: "Why haven't adults taken care of this already?" asked one student. "Probably 'cause they don't have time," remarked his friend.

Feed Them Manure: Information
When we first designed this simulation, we planned three weeks for feeding them manure. Prior to beginning the simulation, we spent a great deal of time deciding on "the manure" students would need to begin wrestling with these difficult dilemmas. First, students would need to learn how to discuss issues without "right" answers. So, we wrote ten short dilemma stories using the framework and procedure outlined by Galbraith and Jones (1976) (see Figure 7.12). Second, students would need to learn about the structure of the federal government, about the roles and responsibilities of those charged with legislative duties, and about the process by which possible legislation becomes law. So we wrote the tales of Estabol in journal form.

The journal describes a world in which five planets have been colonized—each with a different perspective on the role of individual rights, punishment, and the place of technology in human life. The journal ends with the election of Estabol as the first president of the Intergalactic Union, and details about the speech he plans to deliver as the First Intergalactic Congress convenes. In this speech, Estabol will ask the newly elected senators and representatives to prepare "Bills of Technology" to establish laws to govern the use of technology in the new Union (Figure 7.13).

Following the discussion of each day's dilemma, students read selected excerpts from Estabol's journal. Because one set of strategies students will need throughout

FIGURE 7.12   Sample Dilemma Stories

Computerizing Man's Best Friend

Johnny was a very lonely boy. He found it hard to make friends and often spent a great deal of time by himself. To occupy the hours that he spent alone, Johnny had become quite an expert designing and building computers. Late one night, he had an idea that would solve his dilemma. The next morning he got up early and began to design a computerized companion. Several months later, Johnny had created a look-a-like for man's best friend, a computerized dog. This dog became Johnny's constant companion and made it possible for him to be very happy without ever socializing or interacting with another human. Soon Johnny was making lots of computerized dogs and selling them in the stores. Parents who bought these computerized dogs discovered that their children were very happy with their new friend. However, the children quit talking to other children and to their parents. Should Johnny be allowed to continue building these computerized dogs?

Animal Donations: A Small Parts Factory

The United States Medical Association has proposed the creation of a special factory designed to provide animal organs for people who need them. In this factory, live animals will be raised so that doctors can take their hearts, kidneys, livers, and brains and transplant them into humans. The Society for Cruelty to Animals has objected to such an organ bank stating that this organ factory poses cruel and unjust treatment of animals. The United States Medical Association has replied that the animal organs are vital to preserve and extend human life and that there is nothing wrong with using animal organs in humans. Should the United States Medical Association be stopped from developing the organ factory?

Robots Do It Better

Dan Smith has just been informed that new robots are about to be installed at the factory where he works. He has learned that once the robots are in operation, he will be laid off, since the robots will be able to do the same job he does. When Dan went to complain to his boss, the boss said that he was sorry but there would soon be no work for Dan. The company was sure that production costs would be less using robots, and that it was essential for the company to make as much as possible. Later that night, Dan met with his fellow workers. Most of the workers agreed that they should sabotage the robots every chance they get in order to preserve their jobs. Should Dan help?

The School's Best Athlete

David was a member on his high school's wrestling and weight lifting team. He was a good athlete, but he wasn't the best. David wanted a college athletic scholarship, but he knew he would have to be number 1 on the team. David had read in the newspaper about a new artificial device that could be used to strengthen the arms and legs of people who were paralyzed. David thought he could use this artificial device to win athletic competitions and get that scholarship. So, he went to see the doctor working with the devices. He explained that he was not weak or paralyzed, but that he wanted to secretly use these new artificial devices to become the school's best athlete. He offered the doctor a great deal of money to go along with his plan. Should the doctor agree with David's plan?

FIGURE 7.13   A Sample Entry from Estabol's Journal

At last! I have decided to call a special session of the Intergalactic Congress. I will address a joint session in four days and propose a new set of laws. These laws will be the first ones added to the new constitution. I think I will suggest that they collectively be called "The Bill of Technology Rights." I plan to suggest that these laws be appended to the constitution in order to guarantee the citizens of this union their basic freedoms. It is time that the constitution be expanded so that the issues of technology which confront us can finally be settled. In my speech, I will propose that congress ensure the passage of at least five bills:

The First Bill of Technology (Privacy): This bill must be written to deal with the issue of our citizens' privacy. It is time we decided once and for all what information should be private; who can have access to what information; how we should protect information from those who should not have it; and how we will punish those who break this law.

The Second Bill of Technology (Piracy): I will ask congress to pass legislation that determines guidelines for deciding what information, books, television programs, movies, holograms, and music can be copied or used by someone besides the author. We must know as a Union what belongs to whom and who and how information is to be made accessible. This legislation must outline under what circumstances these things can be copied, under what circumstances these things can be sold, under what circumstances the author(s) has exclusive rights, and how offenders will be punished.

The Third Bill of Technology (Nuclear Energy): The third law I will ask congress to pass centers on the nuclear question, both for military use and for domestic use. Congress must help us determine what weapons can be used; whether nuclear weapons can be used; whether weapons can be put in space; whether the planets can spy on each other; and what weapons can be used against the enemies of the Union. In addition, are we going to sanction nuclear power plants; how are we going to deal with nuclear disasters; how are we going to deal with nuclear waste? How will offenders be punished? Who will oversee compliance?

The Fourth Bill of Technology (Robots): I intend to propose to congress that there be two laws dealing with the role of robots in our society.

> **Part One**—This bill must decide who can produce robots, what limits must be placed on their production and their design, what jobs robots can perform, and what jobs must be protected. Can robots be used for such occupations as parenting, teaching, doctoring, and nursing?

> **Part Two**—This bill must decide how to protect people from robots. Specifically, it must determine whether computers and robots can be allowed to make decisions and to think, whether a robot that looks like people must be labeled as robot, and whether a robot's identity may be kept secret.

The Fifth Bill of Technology (Biomedical Ethics): I intend to propose to congress that there be two laws dealing with the role of robots in our society.

> **Part One**—Laws must be made to deal with organ transplants. This law must also provide guidelines in the same areas related to artificial organs, such as implanting computer devices to make people stronger or smarter.

> **Part Two**—This legislation must make laws governing how humans can be created. It must make laws that decide about the acceptability of growing babies in test tubes, about what rights and responsibilities biological parents have, and whether scientists can change genes to create altered plants, animals, and humans.

Well, tomorrow is the big day—my speech. I wonder what will happen!

their lives as they wrestle with technology is the ability to collect, organize, and use information, we designed three small group activities to help students understand the information in the journal more clearly. These activities model three different ways to organize information. (1) To understand the worldviews of each of the five planets as metaphor for attitudes and beliefs that influence our discussions about technology, students construct *outlines*. (2) To help students understand how the new government is organized, students create *mind maps*—visual representations of the elements of government (see Figure 7.14). (3) To help students understand the process established for writing and passing legislation, they construct a flowchart. Flowcharting is presented using a chapter from Robert Bly's (1983) book, *Ronald's Dumb Computer.*

The last entry in Estabol's journal identifies five technology issues. Once we are clear that students have a preliminary sense of the challenges confronting them, students are asked to write down which bill they would like to help write, listing their most interesting choice first. The class is divided into six political action committees

FIGURE 7.14   Mapping the Structure and Process of Government

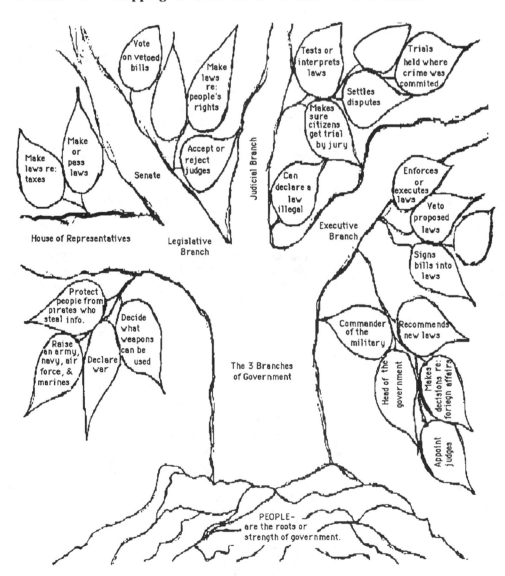

(PAC). Each PAC is given a copy of the articles we have collected. The folders get thicker each year. Students are challenged to prepare a portfolio. They learn that a portfolio usually describes the dilemma in question, identifies potential benefits and disadvantages, compiles the problem(s) and potential problems related to the dilemma, and lists a range of recommendations. In addition, students learn that a portfolio should present information about the position constituents and experts hold relevant to the issue. In essence, this aspect of the "feed them manure" phase constitutes the writing of a research paper.

Stand Back and Watch Them Grow: Proposing Solutions

At the completion of the "feed them manure" phase, students have new insights into processes involved in government and lawmaking, some new information-using strategies, and a new facility with collaborative techniques for wrestling with difficult ethical issues, including researching for information and listening and collaborative ethical decision making. It is time for teachers to get out of their way, to relinquish our central role in the educational process, and to let students use the "manure" to solve problems. It's time for students to write legislation.

Because legislative writing is generally informed by input from constituents, students read the section from their text about public opinion and polling. We help students examine sample questionnaires and discuss how survey questions might be constructed using Likert scales, fixed responses, and open-ended questions. Students write questions about their issues based on insights from the research they used to poll their fellow students. Polls are published, classmates are questioned, and groups tally and interpret the results.

Armed with a sense of the positions their classmates are likely to take on issues, each group sets about crafting a legislative bill. Whenever a group feels they have a passable bill, they call for a meeting of "Congress." Individual students are elected by classmates to serve as President Protem and Sergeant at Arms. These students are responsible for conducting the congressional sessions. Those proposing a bill present it to the class. Debate follows. A vote is held, and each group learns whether their bill will be passed on to their President.

When students flowcharted the process during the "feed them manure" phase, they learned that a bill must be signed by the President before it becomes law. The teacher always serves as the President. Any bill passed by students is referred to the "President." The "President" examines the bill and either signs or vetoes it. Reserving the role of President for teachers, we are able to challenge groups with concerns the class might not have recognized. The dynamic of writing, debating, voting, and seeking the President's signature continues until all bills are written and signed. If one were to visit Denny's classroom during this phase, the observer might wonder where the teacher was. Denny does not appear to be "teaching." Instead, he spends his time ensuring a safe, productive learning environment, monitoring the progress of groups, asking questions, recommending resources whenever necessary, and acting as final provocateur when bills are sent to him for consideration.

Chop Off Their Heads and Ship Them: Connecting to the World

The intent of this phase of the mushroom management strategy is to provide culminating activities that bring the pieces together, to explicitly demonstrate to students the ways in which their learning transfers to real-life applications, and to allow students to assess their own learning. To accomplish these goals, students are asked to choose a partner. With their partner, students read the sections from their textbook on the executive, legislative, and judicial branches and on how laws are made. For each section, students are asked to create a comparison chart listing what was similar and what was different between the simulation and the information in the text. A day is set aside for all the partnerships to come together for a general class discussion, ensuring that students fully understand the relationship between the simulation and the U.S. government. As a final activity, students are individually asked to write a pen pal letter to a student living in a country with either a Communist system or a dictatorship describing how laws are made in the United States and how U.S. citizens can participate in the process. This serves two purposes. The first purpose is to bring the simulation to a close, with students describing what they have learned and how that learning might be used; the second is an evaluative tool. We established a checklist of concepts we hoped each letter would include. We then used the checklist to assess students' letters for what was learned.

The first time Denny implemented the problem-centered simulation, I spent as much time as I could in Denny's classroom. Perhaps my favorite day was the one when a student who had left class the previous day quite frustrated by his classmates' unwillingness to see the viability of his group's bill came barreling into class minutes before the bell. As he approached Denny, he pulled a wadded piece of paper from his pocket. "This," he said, "is a list of all the reasons everybody ought to vote for my bill. My dad and I brainstormed this list at dinner last night. May I please call another legislative session at the beginning of class?" Both Denny and I knew the simulation was having an impact. Not only were students involved in class but that involvement was spilling over into their conversations outside of class. Denny and I had successfully turned the notion of a problem-centered approach to curriculum and mushroom management as a planning strategy into a reality.

1988—To the Problem-Centered Simulation
We Add Learning with Technology

Phase II began one afternoon when Catie arrived at my University office. "I have been struggling for two years to get the social studies people to consider using computers," she said. "Now, one of the government teacher has wandered into the computer lab asking what he can do with computers."

"Boy," I thought quietly to myself, "do I have an idea for you." I reached to a bookshelf behind me and removed the package with all the materials for "The First Intergalactic Congress." We began recreating the simulation to engage students in not only studying about government and about technology but to do it using technology as well.

I had been invited to join the faculty at the University of New Mexico in the fall of 1984. Catie Angell was a student in the first graduate class I taught. She was a high school art teacher at one of the local schools who had started her career as a home economics teacher. When she had taken the district's training course for computers, her imagination had been captured. She had returned to the university to complete a Master's degree in art education. Within two years, Catie had left art education to become her school's computer lab teacher, charged with helping the high school faculty integrate computers into their various programs. We were later selected as the 1989 Christa McAuliffe fellows. One of our adventures had centered on the elaboration of the problem-centered, mushroom management simulation Denny and I designed, first incorporating actual computer experiences into the simulation and then later using it to build a comprehensive, nine-week unit bridging five subject areas for a sophomore-level school-within-a-school.

We called Denny in California and requested copies of all the articles he had collected over the years. We enlisted the assistance of the school librarian to find additional resources. Then, we built a database of all the articles and books, and made six copies of it for other groups to use. Once they identified what they wanted to read using the database, they could go to the resource cabinet and file folders available in the computer lab. We designed a comprehensive protocol for students to use in the construction of the research portfolio during the "feed 'em manure" phase. The protocol we designed that first time included the use of *PrintShop* to construct a cover, a word processor to complete their research paper, and a graphics program to present the results of their survey. Nowadays, it is much more comprehensive. Their graphs must accompany a full proposal (see Figure 7.15).

In addition, all legislative bills were written using a word processor. This facilitated the process of writing and rewriting when either the student body, acting as congressional representatives, or the teacher, acting as President, sent the bill back to committee for revision. Because the legislation could be printed and reprinted in a finished format, we were able to post copies of proposed legislation for students to study before debates and votes. We used the *PFS:File* database program for all surveying and voting. Each team constructed their survey by creating a database form, and students were able to go to a designated computer and enter their responses. Then, the groups who had constructed the survey or proposed legislation could use the database to tally responses quickly and efficiently.

Once Catie and I had compiled research resources and completed the additional materials necessary for the revised computer-using version of "The First Intergalactic Congress," we approached Bob Schultz, the government teacher. Although we were able to convince him that the simulation might work, he felt it was far too divergent from his teaching style and felt he would be unable to implement it. Catie offered to team with him; he was still reluctant. Ultimately, he agreed to turn his classes over to us for six weeks. I cleared my daytime calendar and so did Catie. For six weeks, she and I were the government teachers. Bob was an observer most of the time, but we introduced him as the "President."

That year we used video recordings of news items to introduce the issues outlined in Estabol's journal as well as the dilemma stories. This allowed us to bring television into the classroom. Channel One had not yet been installed at Catie's high school, but we both had VCRs at home as did many of the students. I remember one discussion from that year very clearly. Catie and I had shown a one-minute segment from a report on the previous evening's news to illustrate the dilemma of robots in the workplace. Before we played the recording, we asked:

> "Who saw the news last night?"
>
> "Not me," replied one student. "It's boring."
>
> "Not if you think about what is reported," we countered. "For instance, last night there was a report about McDonald's interest in developing a robotic arm to cook and serve french fries."
>
> "Cool," replied the bored student.
>
> "Yeah, but what happens to the jobs you guys get hired for at McDonald's? Where will you work?"
>
> "Hey, that's not fair," shouted one boy from the back of the room.
>
> "Maybe not for you," we replied. "But shouldn't the owner of McDonald's be allowed to use whatever technology he can to make as much money as he can?"
>
> "Yeah, but . . . Oh, I see the problem." hesitated the "bored" student, not quite as bored as before.

Using technology to augment learning about government and about the impacts of technology was a resounding success. Students were excited about using technology; they were excited about government and the quality of their work was better. The capacity to present professional, finished research portfolios stimulated pride in their work, not only about how it looked but about the quality of its content as well. The ability to publish and distribute drafts of legislation before a congressional session led to more reflective debates. Students were more prepared and aware of ideas under discussion. Students were thinking. One student wrote on an ending evaluation, "It gave me a chance to express some ideas that I've always wanted to. It taught

FIGURE 7.15 **Sample Research Portfolio**

The First Intergalactic Political Action Advisory Panel
5739 Galaxy Way
Capitol City, Earth
Email IN%panel@galaxy.pac.gov
Voice Mail 101550-438-942-6704

Dear Citizen:

We would like to take this opportunity to inform you that your application for recognition as a political action committee has been approved. We applaud you for your dedication to the creation of a better Union and your commitment to guarantee that all citizens have full rights. If you should want to respond to President Estabol's request for legislative action related to the technological issues challenging our Union, the following information should assist you in the preparation of materials.

Political action committees (PAC) desirous of submitting legislation must first submit a portfolio that includes the following:

Description of the Political Action Committee:
A cover sheet presenting the PAC (Use *PrintShop*)
A copy of the logo by which your committee can be recognized (Use *SuperPaint*)
Biographical statements describing all members (Use *MacWrite*)
A statement of purpose (Use *MacWrite*)

Demonstration of Understanding of Political Process:
Presentation of understanding of the nature of governmental organization (Use *SuperPaint*)
Presentation of understanding of the process for passing legislation (Use *Inspiration*)

A Comprehensive Research Analysis:
Using the format described in the attachment, present research using proper referencing and formatting (Use *MacWrite*)
Include research related to at least the following areas:
- a definition of the issue and related terminology
- case study examples of related dilemmas
- expert opinion and recommendations

An Analysis of Public Opinion:
Copies of questionnaire used to complete survey
A description of procedures used to collect data (Use *MacWrite*)
Result of your survey of public opinion on related issues presented as both:
1. summative data (tables with means and percentages of responses)
2. graphic data (bar, line, and circle); data may be presented using *PFS:File, Report,* and *Graph*

Again, we would like to congratulate you on your recognition as an official political action committee. All of the telecommunication resources for research and completion of your portfolio available through the Advisory Panel are at your disposal. Should your portfolio be accepted, you will be contacted to bring legislation before "The First Intergalactic Congress." We look forward to receiving your material. On behalf of the Advisory Panel, I am

Sincerely yours,

Marcus de Fritzburg, Esquire

me to think for myself and not to worry about what other people think of my ideas. It also gave me a sense of responsibility."

Yet students were frustrated because they had to confine their work on the simulation to fifty minutes a day; they still wondered why they had to write reports in government, not English; and we were still frustrated that we could not support their learning about the issues they confronted as completely as we wanted, especially in relation to scientific concepts. The next semester, Bob was willing and able to collaborate with Catie, and the two of them team taught the simulation. The following year, Catie was able to replace the computers in her lab with new Macintoshes, and Bob agreed to take six of the old ones into his classroom. Until recently, he has taught the simulation as part of his government class each semester without assistance. But Bob's and Catie's collaboration had made their traditional attitudes about teaching seem limiting, and they have embarked on yet a new, even more adventurous, collaboration with a team of five.

1992—We Continue to Use the Problem-Centered Simulation to Teach About *Technology with Technology, Only Now, We Collaborate with Three Other Teachers*

Early in the summer of 1993, I received an e-mail message from Bob and Catie. It read simply: "We want to create a technology school-within-a-school. Will you help us?" It was a summons that could not be ignored. I e-mailed them back: "Set up a meeting time with all the players. I'll be there." Things at Catie's and Bob's high school are very different now than they were four years ago. Various faculty have collaborated to form schools-within-schools in an effort to create "family groups" so that freshman do not feel lost in a low socioeconomic, urban school with a student body of nearly 2,000. Using district computer resources, some of the teachers at the high school are now participating in the use of telecommunications resources like e-mail and Internet.

When we gathered the following week, I met Stacy who taught general science, Rick who taught general mathematics, Dick who taught communication skills, and, of course, Catie and Bob. They had been working on this project since Christmas of the previous year. Their plan was quite straightforward. They wanted to build a school-within-a-school with 150 sophomores. These students would be divided into five groups of thirty and rotated through each of their classes, taking a physical education class as their sixth class. These teachers had convinced the administration of the viability of their plan, soliciting agreement to schedule students appropriately, to make necessary room changes so that their classrooms were all in the same wing of the high school, and to make provisions for a common preparation period. The Restructuring Committee had agreed to allow them to bring together many of the technology resources scattered throughout the school and to schedule one of the school's computer labs for classes.

Students in the "Sophomore Circle" would be registered for general science, general math, one semester of government, one semester of New Mexico state history (Bob would teach government in the fall and New Mexico state history in the spring), communication skills (an English credit course), and an elective called Computer Skills. Participating students would be drawn from the regular education student body with the addition of at least five special education students in each cluster of thirty. This supported the school's commitment to full inclusion of special education students. They wanted the project to reflect a curriculum with intellectual cohesiveness as well as social cohesiveness. They also wanted technology, primarily computers, to play a central role.

Before I joined the team, they had explored cooperative learning, using themes, designating one day a week for a common curriculum, and using learning cycles.

With each option, however, they had had trouble finding common ground. A second dilemma faced by the team was determining exactly what role technology might play. Was it a tool, a tutor, a gimmick, or could it be a central component in enhancing the learning experiences of students. At that first meeting, Catie and Bob shared their experiences with "The First Intergalactic Congress" simulation. I talked about my notions of a problem-centered curriculum and the use of mushroom management as an organization strategy. Stacy, Rick, and Dick were a bit unsure about how the model might work for them, and uncertain if they could adjust their teaching style quick enough to make such a project work when school opened.

Would it be possible to build on that simulation and find a way to intersect with communication skills, science, and mathematics? I suggested that we ought to build on the strengths that Catie and Bob had already developed. Perhaps, thought the group. In order to start, we had to spend a long time talking about what the curricular expectations for those classes were. Stacy, Rick, and Dick talked us through their course objectives and contents. Dick's communication skills course was not bound by a textbook but by state-defined competencies in speech and communication. For Rick and Stacy, it was a bit more difficult because they had traditionally used a textbook and planned their curriculum to follow the sequence defined by that text. I asked them if they would be willing to make one change—to use the text in a nonlinear fashion, selecting chapters appropriate to the group's work. They were reassured that they would be able to continue with their familiar strategies of lecture, discussion, demonstration, and individual assignments. They could support the "feed 'em manure" phase of the curriculum. In addition, Rick and Stacy agreed to try at least one cooperative learning activity.

Prior to our third meeting, Bob, Catie, and I expanded the simulation to a nine-week unit. To expand the simulation, we outlined activities and planned intersections between the government class and the computer skills class, making sure we had the technological resources necessary. Expanding the simulation allowed us to spend an entire week discussing technological topics that presented ethical dilemmas. We were able to spend time helping students to see that many questions did not have "right" answers—a notion contrary to many of their educational experiences. Designating Catie's class time for student groups to create an identity as a PAC supported our efforts. It also created small, easily completed, introductory activities for many of the computer applications that were used throughout the simulation.

With the addition of two complete weeks of instruction at the end of the simulation, we were able to use a hypermedia application called, *HyperStudio,* as a context for helping students bring their entire experience together as a whole. Throughout the simulation we asked students to keep a group notebook with all their materials: their PAC application, their copy of Estabol's journal and their mind map and flowchart, their legislative portfolio (like Figure 7.16), their drafts and final legislative bill, and their charts comparing the First Intergalactic government and constitution and the U.S. government and Constitution. During the seventh week, Catie introduced the notion of hypermedia in her Computer Skills class and helped students design the beginning of their government "stack" by creating "screens" and "linkages" that presented their PAC. This strand summarized their purpose, logo, and biographies. For the remaining two weeks, all the Computer Skills and government classes met for almost two hours a day in the computer lab to elaborate on their government stack so that it would include all their learnings during the simulation. Each group designed the organization of their stack and made decisions about what they wanted to include from their experiences.

Figure 7.16 shows the organization pattern for the hypermedia presentation created by one of the groups. This group decided they wanted to make their final legislative bill the centerpiece of the stack. They divided their bill into six sections, placing each section on an individual screen. These six screens were linked in a linear

FIGURE 7.16 Sample Hypermedia Presentation

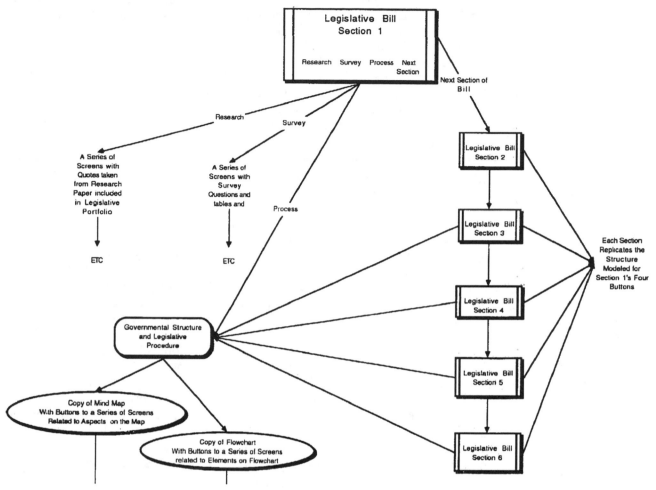

From class work for a Computer Skills course. Used with permission.

fashion. They then developed a set of icons to represent "buttons" or active points to be placed on the bottom of each screen. One icon allowed "readers" to access references and case studies presented in their legislative portfolio created during the "feed 'em manure" stage. One icon or "button" led to tables and/or graphs summarizing relevant results from their survey results. Another icon led the reader to a summary of the structure of the Intergalactic government, the legislative process, and a chart comparing that structure and the structure of the U.S. government and legislative process. A final icon moved the reader forward to the next section of the bill. Mark, one of the students in this group, wrote of the hypermedia stacks: "We took our whole notebook and put it on one little disk. When we put in the buttons, I could see how it all added up."

All that was left for the remainder of the summer was to prepare material, locate resources, collect reference material, and do some self-learning. Dick committed to working on mastering video cameras as well as collecting appropriate stories and videos. Ultimately, Dick chose an article about high-tech spying from *Discover* magazine and the movie *War Games* for the second week; a *Time* magazine article on cloning and a story by Charles Sheffield called "Dancing with Myself" for the third week; Isaac Asimov's *The Bicentennial Man* and a *Star Trek* episode where Mr. Data attempts to create a daughter for the fourth week; and for the fifth and sixth weeks, he used a computer invasion of *Law and Order* and the movie *Sneakers*. Rick worked on mastering LOGO programming. Because Catie was anxious to introduce telecommunications into her computer skills curriculum, she worked to master Internet, online database searching, and found three other computer skills teachers at other high schools who were willing to have their students use e-mail to answer questionnaires designed by students.

Our final curriculum used technology in all the ways we had posed as possibilities. Computers and videos were used as tools for acquiring information through e-mail, online database searches, and video watching. They were also tools for rendering student understandings through preparation of portfolios, video news programs, desktop publishing, graphic designs, turtles dancing in geometric patterns, and hypermedia stacks. Computers were also used as tutors. Tom Synder's *Television: Media Ethics* simulation guided student learning as they set goals and made decisions. Rick used Sunburst's software program on graphing to help students develop their skills in interpreting graphs. Students also learned how to use a variety of technological applications while they completed projects. They learned with computers; they learned about the social and ethical implications of technology in their lives. The lesson for us was: Technology supports the curriculum in many ways, but one should not ask about technology first. Curriculum planning comes first. A well-planned curriculum suggests the ways technology can support learning. In fact, it does so quite naturally when it becomes an integral part of a much larger process.

Realizing technology's possibilities and learning to use "mushroom management" to plan a problem-centered curriculum is a developmental process. Denny and I had started our work ten years earlier; Catie had been experimenting with these ideas for nearly eight years; Bob had accepted the challenge only four years earlier. Stacy, Rick, and Dick have just begun their experimenting. Just as students need to learn and change cooperatively, so do teachers. And you can probably imagine my surprise when Stacy asked midway through "The First Intergalactic Congress" simulation if we could plan the next nine-week period around environmental science, using a range of issues in New Mexico like the Rio Grande River pollution problem and the Golden Mine leaching problem. As I write this, we are in the middle of planning.

References

Bly, R. (1983). *Ronald's dumb computer*. New York: Dell Publishing Co.

Bradbury, R. (1980). There will come soft rains. *The stories of Ray Bradbury*. New York: Knopf.

Galbraith, R. E. and Jones, T. M. (1976). *Moral reasoning: A teaching handbook for adapting Kohlberg to the classroom*. Minneapolis: Greenhaven.

Kidder, T. (1981). *The soul of a machine*. New York: Avon Books.

Norton, P. (1992a). When technology meets the subject matter disciplines in education—Part one: Exploring the computer as metaphor. *Educational Technology*, 22(6):38–46.

Norton, P. (1992b). When technology meets the subject matter disciplines in education—Part two: The computer as discourse. *Educational Technology*, 22(7):36–44.

Norton, P. (1992c). When technology meets the subject matter disciplines in education—Part three: The computer as method. *Educational Technology*, 22(8):35–44.

Norton, P. (1986). The first intergalactic congress: An ethics simulation. *Ethics and excellence in computer education: Choice or mandate*, Sixth Annual Microcomputers in Education Conference. Rockville, MD: Computer Science Press.

PART III

Solving Problems

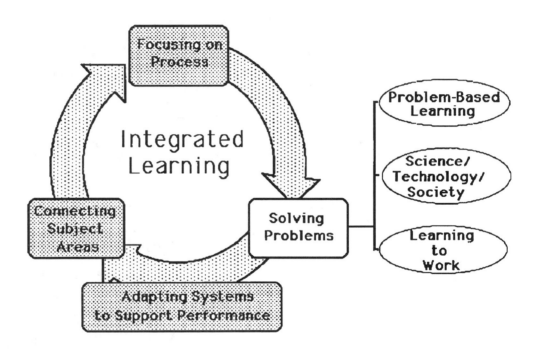

Solving ill-defined problems is our fate. From buying shoes to selecting a career, we struggle with ill-defined problems, multiple options, and contentious judgment criteria. Seldom are we called on to solve a problem with a ready-made answer. Problems are really problems only if there is no ready answer. Consider the steps a real problem forces us to take. As Brooks and Brooks (1993) say, when facing any one of life's problem situations, we have to:

- Size up and define a problem that isn't neatly packaged;
- Determine which facts and formulas stored in memory might be helpful in solving a problem;
- Recognize when more information is needed, and where and how to look for it;
- Deal with uncertainty by brainstorming possible ideas or solutions when the way to proceed isn't apparent;
- Carry out complex analyses or tasks that require planning, management, monitoring, and adjustment;

- Exercise judgment in situations where there are not clear-cut "right" and "wrong" answers, but more or less useful ways of doing things;
- Step outside the routine to deal with an unexpected breakdown or opportunity.

Because ill-defined problems call for so much of what we know and how we know it, high school teachers have begun to explore ways to use problem solving as the organizing process for their teaching. Problems create a context in which knowing something, and knowing how to manage information, clearly are important. Facing an important but ill-defined problem, high school students stretch their skills and knowledge to fashion the best answers they can develop, and still they must recognize the risk and doubt that accompany any such struggle with problems that matter.

Chapter 8, Problem-Based Learning: Meeting Real-World Challenges—We need to do little more than look at the morning paper to see the kinds of problems students will face as adults. In the daily news, problems arise not as abstract issues but as events: "Loggers Protest Spotted Owl," "Salmonella Afflicts Restaurant Patrons," "Unknown Drifter Sustained in Coma." Problem-based learning (PBL) has made its way from medical education to high school teaching. In Chicago, Bill Stepien and his colleagues developed problem-based learning as a way to teach higher-level thinking across content areas. These teachers, and a growing number of teachers in other areas, pose problems that require extensive research, then show students how to propose solutions on the basis of the best evidence available. Proposing clear answers under ambiguous circumstances forces them to weigh evidence carefully and to weigh the risks associated with never knowing everything.

Problem-Based Showcase—Icarus Project: Assessing Water Quality
  Bob Benoit, Tim McClure, and Robert Kuintzle, Paradise High School, Butte County, CA

FIGURE III.1   Questions in the Problem-Solving Cycle

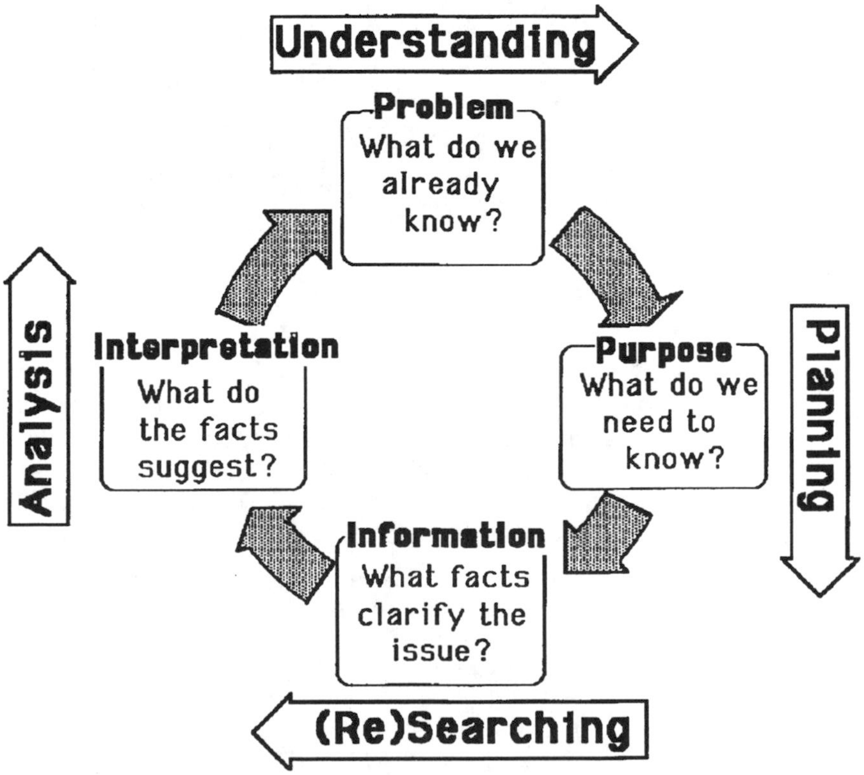

Chapter 9, Science/Technology/Society: Complex Issue Analysis—Science/Technology/Society (STS) has gained a national reputation as a method for integrating science, mathematics, and social studies through student investigation of local and national issues. Using the basic format of the scientific method, students conduct research on questions that affect their own lives and the quality of life in their region. As in problem-based learning, hard science and mathematical analysis have a central place in STS, but social science also serves as a learning tool. In a broad ranging STS study, students would investigate the scientific basis of a problem—in the environment, biology, or physics—but they would also research public opinion and public policy to better understand both problems and their potential solutions. STS students learn to apply the scientific method, but they also experience the political and social challenge of taking new knowledge to the public.

STS Showcase—From Chernobyl to Yucca Flats: A High School Nuclear Chemistry Unit
  Kevin Koepnick, City High School. Iowa City, IA

Chapter 10, Learning to Work: Experiential Learning—The problems that really matter are more often found outside the classroom than in it. If the purpose of high school education is to prepare students to manage the problems they will face in the adult world, helping students gain experience in the adult world and evaluate their participation may prove indispensable to progress. Increasingly, schools and districts are integrating work apprenticeships and service learning with the high school curriculum. Working in a job setting or volunteering to serve in a community setting, students come to recognize the complexity of problems in the real world and begin to hone the skills they will need to succeed in adult roles. Integrating academic learning with real-world experience brings life to subject-area learning.

Curriculum Showcase—REAL Enterprises at Riverside High School
  Cory NeVille, Kendra Austin, and Rick Larson, Riverside High School, Chattaroy, WA

CHAPTER *8*

Problem-Based Learning

Meeting Real-World Challenges

We teach in an interdisciplinary program using an integrated approach. The students need math to do the problems, but on any given day we may not have a math class. In eighth grade yesterday, we used exponential math to predict changes in world population. I know I have had a good day when we come to the end and some kid says, "Well, that was good. Are we coming in later to do math?"

Eric Weiss, Math Teacher,
U32 High School, Montpelier, VT

Problem Solving for the Year 2010

The following problems exist in our town. How might they be solved?

Because so many people have moved into the area, and others may follow, the school building is too crowded to provide the kind of education the community needs to prepare students for life in a complex society. The school board will open hearings on January 8 as a first step in planning that may result in a new bond vote.

When Interstate 99 was build through the center of the city, six residential properties were cut off from the neighborhood of which they had been a part (see map). Two buildings are now vacant. Two more have been condemned. The owners have failed to pay taxes for three consecutive years. Police have raided the area three times in the last six months, making several arrests for crack possession and prostitution.

Big Jumbo Discount Emporium has just bought an old warehouse on the edge of town in the residential area known as Greenville. They plan a half-acre store with parking for 400 cars. You will be assigned to one of three groups: The Downtown Merchant's Association, the Greenville Ad Hoc Planning group, or the Mayor's Task Force on Growth and Taxation. The zoning board will begin permit hearings next week.

Tuberculosis has made a sudden return to the downtown area, with six new cases reported in the last month, largely among homeless people.

Propose a solution to one of these problems based on a thorough analysis of all facts relevant to the case.

For any of these ill-defined problems, the process of investigation and solution might take several days, weeks, or several months. Simply to understand connections between causes and effects, students would have to investigate many realms of knowledge: sociology, epidemiology, economics of taxation, political science, urban planning, geography, and medical diagnosis and treatment. They also would have to manage many different kinds of investigation: library research, database search, interviewing, survey design, statistical analysis, and discussion. To make a case for the solution they create, they would have to develop the strongest possible case by analyzing their data from a clear perspective; creating a logical proposal; preparing charts, graphs, and other illustrations; weighing costs against benefits; and pitching their presentation to a skeptical audience of peers or professionals with confidence and flare. They would have to know enough about alternative solutions to counter potential criticism of their plan. Problem-based learning generates enthusiasm by calling on students to use multiple talents to solve a "real" or authentic problem using all the facts and skills they can muster.

Bill Stepien, former Director of the Center for Problem-Based Learning at the Illinois Science and Mathematics Academy (IMSA), describes problem-based learning as a pair of scissors with process and knowledge as opposing blades (see Figure 8.1). The development of a reasonable database is critical to all problem solving," he pointed out during an interview at the 1993 Summer Conference on Problem-Based Learning. "But I want the kids to have the complete tool, both process and knowledge. With only half of the scissors, all they can do is stab at solutions." Guiding students through a careful investigation of the facts and tutoring them through the process of testing solutions gives them a clear and compelling purpose for learning. "The more authentic the problem—the more closely learning resembles life—the more we respond," Stepien asserts. "We are hardwired to respond to a challenging environment."

Ill-defined problems put pressure on students to develop a deeper knowledge of the subject before they begin to consider solutions. Stepien, Gallagher, and Workman (1993) outline the characteristics of ill-structured problems:

- More knowledge than is initially available will be needed
  a) to understand what is occurring;
  b) to decide what actions are required for resolution.

- Since every problem and problem solver is unique, there is no absolutely right way or fixed formula for conducting an investigation.

- As new information is obtained, the problem changes.

- You can never be sure you have made the right decision because important information is lacking, data or values may be in conflict; but decisions have to be made.

Students working through an ill-defined problem gain respect for the volume of knowledge related to any problem situation and also recognize the element of risk that

FIGURE 8.1   How Real Problems Activate Knowledge and Intellectual Skill

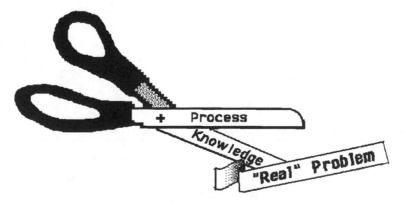

Adapted from the concept of B. Stepien, Center for Problem-Based Learning, ISMA, Aurora, IL. Used with permission.

accompanies any solution. Nevertheless, the "real" character of the problem forces students to propose solutions, recognizing the level of risk embedded in the whole process.

Problem-based curricula engage students in proposing solutions to problems that are as real for the adult community as for any group of high school students. Ross (1991) says:

- Problem-oriented curricula are ones where problems are used as selection criteria for content (and methods);
- Problem-based curricula are ones where students work on problems as (part of) the course;
- Problem-solving curricula are ones where students are given specific training (or development experiences) for solving problems.

Teachers who employ problem-based learning relax their roles as content experts and emphasize their roles as facilitators and guides; they carefully craft the problems, specifying content and process goals clearly in advance and set up criteria by which they and their students will measure success (Marshall, 1993). Teachers may design problem-based learning units that cover virtually all the material in some part of the curriculum or they may "post-hole" problem situations at points in the semester where they want students to synthesize the information they have learned from conventional methods.

Although it is possible for individual students to work independently on an ill-defined problem, the size of the enterprise more often makes group work a practical necessity. If a teacher chooses to pose one problem to a whole class, cooperative groups (working in the jigsaw pattern) might take on different aspects of the investigation then rejoin their peers to develop solutions. On the other hand, students might join competing teams of investigators who work together to propose a solution that will win the vote of a panel of experts at the end of the unit. In problem-based curricula, learning has a clear purpose. It is also a public event in which errors of process or fact may receive instant recognition and clarification. Problem-based learning gives students control over the process of learning new materials and representing what they know (Glasser, 1986).

Like Inquiry Teaching in Chapter 2, Computer-Based Learning in Chapter 6, and Science/Technology/Society in Chapter 9, problem-based learning lets the process of discovery drive the process of assembling and interpreting factual knowledge. Problem-based learning, however, draws as much attention to the process of solution-building as it does to the process of problem analysis. Inquiry teaching leads students to ask, "What really happened and why?" Problem-based learning asks students to propose solutions that fit a complex problem that has many facets. "What solutions best fit the problem?" STS uses the scientific method to unravel the connections in a complex problem situation; problem-based learning asks students to test their proposals against costs and benefits—and against other solutions from other students who have taken a different approach. Teachers in a problem-based classroom list the content and skills objective for the unit they are teaching, as they would in conventional teaching, but they also include the mastery of those objectives in the process of understanding a problem and designing a solution.

Adapting Medical Education for High School Students

Problem-based learning moved into high school teaching from medical education, where it has enlarged its scope to accommodate problems from across subject areas. Medical education is a field in which the volume of information related to any problem is expanding exponentially. To teach the bulk of organized scientific knowledge independent of any related medical problems is to create a profession skilled in memorizing but unpracticed in making knowledge work for patients. More than twenty years ago, McMaster University Medical School began placing small groups of students in a tutorial group with faculty members to begin solving the kind of problems they might face as doctors with real patients. Working cooperatively, students gathered information from library and human sources and then brought their findings together and worked through a process of diagnosis and treatment planning (Aspy, Aspy, & Quinby, 1993). Whereas textbook learning tends to leave knowledge inert in the learner, the case-based approach forces students to search actively and to make connections among the facts they are learning (Brown et al., 1989).

Howard Barrows, a physician who is a pioneer in problem-based medical education, has also developed a laboratory school at Lanphier High School in Springfield, Illinois, where teachers, students, and consultants from the Problem-Based Learning Institute at Southern Illinois University School of Medicine work together designing problems and demonstrating the kind of teaching required for a problem-based curriculum. In problem-based learning, the teacher begins as a designer, creating problems that move students from simple conceptions of a situation to more complex conceptions using information from increasingly various sources (Barrows & Myers, 1993). After designing the problem situation, the teacher adopts the tutorial role, asking clarifying questions, guiding students toward resources, and helping them visualize connections between what they are learning and the problem they face (Barrows, 1988). The tutor does not supply answers to any question, but supports student confidence in being able to locate useful information and provokes them to keep searching until a complete view of the problem situation and its alternative solutions finally come into view.

A simple four-part framework provides the structure for the learning/tutorial process at Lanphier High School. After introductions and an orientation to the idea of solving real problems, the teacher/tutor describes a problem situation and works with the group to "bring it home," activating what they already know of the problem and its implications. At this time, the teacher also describes the presentation the students will have to make, with a deadline, as well as the audience that may be on hand.

For "homework," individuals take responsibility for carrying out different parts of the emerging plan, ensuring that the contribution of each student will have a place as the resolution slowly comes into view. Different kinds of information and shifting perspectives on the problem constantly move deliberation toward greater sophistication and deeper understanding. When a resolution is at hand, with its costs and benefits, students can appreciate the definitions, concepts, and principles they have uncovered. They also can critique the process they used to find a solution, sharing new insights on the process of gathering information to solve problems.

In problem-based learning, students go public with what they have learned at regular intervals, struggling with others who have learned differently. Given the public nature of problem-based learning, students pay as much attention to strategy in their approach as the substance of the problem itself. "Students must acquire through practice, well-developed, metacognitive skills to monitor, critique, and direct the development of their reasoning skills as they work with life's ill-structured problems: to critique the adequacy of their knowledge and direct the process of their own continued learning" (Barrows, 1988, p. 3).

Although problem-based learning does not appear to improve the short-term acquisition of content knowledge compared to conventional curricula (slight negative effects have been reported), notably positive effects occur in student motivation, the acquisition of concepts from problem situations, knowledge retention over the longer term, transfer of concepts to novel situations, and development of self-directed learning skills (Norman & Schmidt, 1992). Few would argue that short-term retention of factual information is the aim of high school learning. To the extent that long-term conceptual understanding, supported by facts and the skills of information management are the purposes of high school education, problem-based learning offers a promising vehicle.

Teaching Problem Solving as a Process

Problem solving can be taught in a number of formats, some of which emphasize rational analysis (Bransford et al., 1987; Nickerson et al., 1985; Schoenfeld, 1979; Beyth-Marom & Dekel, 1985) and others, like synectics, that urge students to be more expansive and creative in their search for solutions. Teaching that asks students to design or invent new products, in fact, can be considered a variant of problem-based learning (Matson, 1993). Most problem-solving protocols define a set of steps students can take to understand the problem thoroughly and, then, to search widely for the solution that fits the best and costs the least. Using process steps as a guide serves to reduce impulsive leaps from perception of a problem to specific proposals. With impulsive flailing subdued, students can bring knowledge of the subject to bear, search out connections among all the facts, develop a general model explaining how problems occur, and propose solutions that can be tested and refined. Experts in a subject area scan problems, model relationships, and propose hypotheses with fluid ease (Schon, 1983; Larkin et al., 1980). Novices in any area, having less knowledge and less complex ways to organize it, tend to apply whatever they have available and fall early to frustration. A managed approach to problem solving lets high school students operate as experts at reduced speed.

Giving students a strategy to follow lets them compensate for what they don't know yet, learn as much as possible, and entertain the widest spectrum of options, each with costs and benefits. Giving students a clear process to manage increases their control over learning. As Barrows (1993, p. 3) states, "metacognitive control" is best represented by questions students can use to guide their own progress: When confronted with a difficult, unexpected, or puzzling situation or problem, the problem solver must ask questions such as:

> What is going on here?
>
> Do I have the entire picture?
>
> Have I thought of all the possibilities?
>
> Do I have all the facts needed?
>
> What does this finding mean?
>
> What is the best way to manage this?
>
> Have I had experiences with situations such as this in the past?
>
> Am I right about this or is there another way of looking at it?
>
> Do I know enough about this kind of thing?
>
> What facts do I need?
>
> Where can I find them?

While an expert might use these questions in any order, a novice needs a workable framework. At Vanderbilt University, developers have videodisc problem situations, creating access to a vast repository of prepackaged information and problem-solving guides (Cognition and Technology Group, 1990). In more conventional classrooms, however, students pursue information from the community in which they are learning.

Problem-Based Learning at Illinois Mathematics and Science Academy

At the Illinois Mathematics and Science Academy (IMSA), teachers are applying and adapting a general format with six basic steps, which Gallagher, Stepien, and Rosenthal (1992) describe:

1. *Fact Finding:* Searching for information that might help organize a "mess";
2. *Problem Finding:* Identifying a specific problem that is central to the mess";
3. *Brainstorming:* Generating a list of possible solutions to the problem;
4. *Solution Finding:* Evaluating the brainstormed list to consider the efficacy of possible solutions; identifying the most viable solutions based on a set of criteria;
5. *Implementation:* Putting into place a solution or solutions on either a permanent or temporary/experimental basis;
6. *Evaluation:* Testing the effectiveness of the implemented solution.

Figure 8.2a includes a variation of these steps, represented as a double cycle of inquiry and invention (Stepien, 1992).

Both cycles in Bill Stepien's problem-solving spiral use the same basic approach to thinking. Before defining a problem or proposing solutions, students look carefully at the facts and gather further information. Then, they try to make sense of the facts they have collected, looking for connections and drawing inferences that will let them identify a central issue. Finally, they present their central problem in a way that clarifies relationships and commits them to a point of view. They use the same facts-based approach to define and test potential solutions. Because this process depends entirely on information gathering, it is a promising tool for high school teaching, where learning new material is a high priority.

Teachers can guide students through each of these steps, questioning and supporting as necessary. The task of the teacher of problem solving is not to provide right

FIGURE 8.2a   Two Turns in a Problem-Solving Cycle

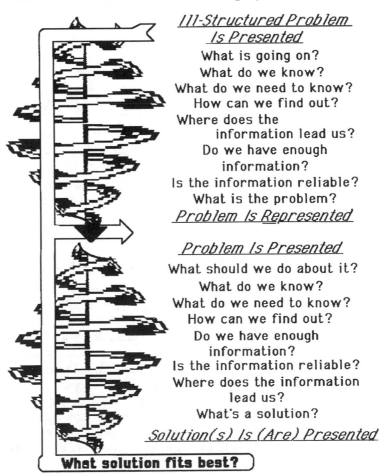

Ill-Structured Problem Is Presented

What is going on?
What do we know?
What do we need to know?
How can we find out?
Where does the information lead us?
Do we have enough information?
Is the information reliable?
What is the problem?

Problem Is Represented

Problem Is Presented

What should we do about it?
What do we know?
What do we need to know?
How can we find out?
Do we have enough information?
Is the information reliable?
Where does the information lead us?
What's a solution?

Solution(s) Is (Are) Presented

What solution fits best?

Adapted from B. Stepien, IMSA, 1992. Used with permission.

answers to the issues that emerge, but to use metacognitive questions to drive inquiry deeper and focus student attention on the process itself, just as much as on the problem and its emerging solution. Each step is accompanied by metacognitive "time out." How is thinking progressing? How confident in the facts are you? Is your method working for you? What else might work better? Barrows (1992) lists these tasks in teaching: (1) keep the learning process moving, (2) probe the student's knowledge deeply, and (3) make sure all students remain involved in the process. Providing right answers does little more than decrease student awareness and control over the process of learning and thinking.

Creating Problem Situations

The first step in problem-based learning is developing problem situations. For better or worse, we are not likely to run short of problems in the foreseeable future. Teachers need only to look at the local newspaper or national news to find problems too complex and ill-defined to give way to easy answers. The best situations fit a number of criteria:

> **Relevance**—the problem is close enough to student experience to feel real and important;

> **Complexity**—the situation requires new information from multiple sources that allows multiple perspectives;

> **Curricular Fit**—investigation of the problem will engage students in gathering information related to curriculum goals;

> **Uncertainty**—the situation will require students to assess both the costs and benefits of their proposed solution under conditions of uncertainty.

The best situations require students to look at a problem from multiple perspectives and to propose solutions that may have multiple effects, both good and bad.

Throughout 1992, Bill Stepien created problem situations from newspaper articles appearing in the Classroom Edition of the *Wall Street Journal* (see Figure 8.2b). Each situation was accompanied by a list of questions for brainstorming, with additional guides for vocabulary development, research process, guides for cooperative groups, and writing assignments or thinking logs. Additional guides and activities could be developed by teachers for their students, as happens during the workshops on problem-based learning at IMSA each summer. To fit a curriculum to a clear purpose for teaching, teachers should develop their own situations with the supports their students might need to work through problem situations.

Guiding Students through Information Overload

What do you already know? What do you need to know? These first steps focus on information gathering. At the IMSA, the teachers have developed a number of ways to make sure students search widely within a problem area. Figure 8.3 shows a problem situation called Jane's Baby, with the guide that a teacher might use to help students question the case and develop a method for gathering information.

The questions in Jane's Baby require access to more knowledge than any student in a class may be expected to have: social studies—legal history, professional standards/medicine, legal process, legal aspects of fetal tissue use; science—brain physiology, medical testing and diagnosis, causes for anencephaly, fetal tissue research; mathematics—probability, prediction from data (math modeling); cost–benefit analysis; and humanities—ethics and philosophy, religions, literature of motherhood, decision making under uncertainty.

FIGURE 8.2b **Problem Situations Developed from Articles in an October 1992 *Wall Street Journal* Classroom Edition**

Article: Tiny T-Shirt Business Made Money until Bud Rolled In

Problem:	Brainstorm:
You are a member of the product review committee for a growing clothing specialty company in a large city. The top designer at your company has a "can't miss" idea. The marketing department also feels the new product could be a clothing sensation. The designer wants to make copies of high school jackets and sweaters based on the biggest high schools in major cities around the country. Names on the jackets would be subtle parodies of the actual school names and designs would mimic their team mascot or school logo. The design department wants to create a line of varsity sports and activity jackets for the clothing that could be bought separately and added to the jackets and sweaters later on. In this way, buyers could relieve their high school days and possibly change history a little by adding the appropriate letter to their new clothing. What should the committee do about the designer's new idea?	1) Is there a problem here? Is there more than one problem? What information will you need to evaluate the situation? 2) Who has the problem or problems? 3) How might these problems affect the clothing company? How might they affect the high schools whose logos and names are parodied? 4) What will happen if the company goes ahead with the designer's program? Do you need more information to determine the impact? 5) Is there a way to approve the designer's basic idea without creating any of the problems identified above? 6) Would the problems change if the situation were reversed and a group of high school students studying fashion wanted to make jackets that mimiced the NFL or NBA team products? 7) You must give the designer an answer. Will you approve the idea?

Article: Timbertown Bitter over Efforts to Save Rare Spotted Owl

Problem:	Brainstorm:
You are a member of the U.S. House of Representatives from the State of Washington. One of the committees on which you sit you must resolve the issue of the Northern Spotted Owl and future lumbering practices in the northwestern United States. Under the terms of the Endangered Species Act of 1993, the owl was declared an endangered species in June 1990. In 1991, a federal judge ruled that logging in the owl's habitat be suspended until a plan to preserve the owl was developed. You have already received countless letters on the issue. Some remind you that being too zealous in protecting the owl could cripple the timber industry. Others claim that once the timber is felled, the owls are gone forever. What are you going to do about the Northern Spotted Owl?	1) What is the relationship of the owls to the forest? 2) Why is the timber industry concerned? 3) How has the judge's action changed the situation? 4) How would you as a legislator be affected by the situation? 5) Cutting down the forest can ruin vital watercourses. Does this change the nature of the problem? At least one logger was so upset by the situation, he committed suicide. Does this change the nature of the problem? 6) What is your solution? Are the consequences fair and desirable for those involved? Do all parties get what they want and are entitled to? Has the solution created any new problems? 7) What does your solution cost? Do the consequences justify the cost?

Adapted from work of B. Stepien, IMSA. Used with permission.

Whether students work independently or cooperatively to gather information in these areas, in the classroom context their findings may have value for all. In fact, the different perspectives they adopt on what they learn may cause vociferous debate.

To make sure students are learning specific kinds of information, steps of the problem-solving process are accompanied by reflective assignments called "thinking logs" (see Figure 8.4). Thinking logs are guided by questions that ask students to look at both the content and the process of problem solving. The answers to these questions may constitute the "content" of the course. With many students completing

FIGURE 8.3   Jane's Baby Problem Situation

Scenario

You are the head of pediatrics in a large city hospital. Jane Barton is one of your patients. Doctor, what will you do in the case of Jane's Baby?

Jane Barton is pregnant. She first came to you about three weeks ago after she and her husband received the results of tests ordered by her family doctor. The tests indicate that Jane and Ralph's baby is anencephalic. The couple is concerned about the fetus and wonder what to do if Jane cannot deliver a normal, healthy infant.

What do we know?	*What do we need to know?*	*What should we do?*
Jane is pregnant.	What is Jane's general health?	Order another test.
Jane is married.	Do they have other children?	Discuss the condition of the fetus with the Bartons before too long.
Medical tests indicate that the fetus is anencephalic.	What are their religious beliefs?	Have technology ready to help the baby at birth.
They have been referred by another doctor.	What was the test? How accurate is it?	
Anencephalic babies do not live very long.	Does anencephaly affect future pregnancies?	
It has something to do with the brain.	Is abortion possible in this case?	
	What is the law on abortion?	
	What is the medical description of anencephaly?	
	What causes the condition?	

Adapted from B. Stepien, S. Gallagher, and D. Workman, ISMA, 1993. Used with permission.

logs in one problem area, the content of any unit may grow large indeed. For individual students, the problem log makes up a record of inquiry, including sudden realizations, misconceptions, new information, and new questions—an inquiry portfolio.

Ill-defined problems lead inquiry in a wide swath. Pamela Samulis, teaching high school in Chicago, developed a problem situation related to lead in city water:

> **Situation:** You are one of a group of experts scheduled to testify before the Blue Ribbon Panel on Water Quality established by the Chicago City Council. The City Council and the public are concerned that children are being exposed to dangerous lead levels in the City's drinking water. There is also concern that the safe maximum concentration levels of lead permitted in drinking water may be set too high. In addition, the Council wonders why the tests coordinated by the City gave results much lower than the tests done by an independent group.
>
> You are to present evidence on Friday, October 30, to which the Panel will respond in writing.

To help them gather information from a wide variety of sources, Samulis created a web diagram to guide students in generating questions for their research (see Figure 8.5). On the day of the hearing, her students would bring different kinds of information to bear on the issue, leading the whole class to work up connections and define one central problem.

In problem-based learning, investigations of the fact may range widely, from the local library to the streets of the city. Basic research skills are essential, whether the research base is library books, professional literature, or the record of news stories in

FIGURE 8.4   Sample Problem Log on Jane's Baby

Log Exercise 1:

Based on your current understanding of Jane's situation, write a statement of the problem you face.

Log Exercise 2:

Provide a medical description of anencephaly. (Provide your own drawing to clarify your verbal description.) Specifically:

a) What causes anencephaly?
b) What is the prognosis for an infant born with anencephaly?
c) Describe the nature of the cranial abnormalities in an anencephalic infant?
d) What brain functions are missing in an anencephalic infant? What functions are present?

Log Exercise 3:

Describe the ethical dilemmas you and the Bartons face in this situation.

Log Exercise 4:

Now that you have investigated the situation, what is your advice to the Bartons?

Adapted from work of B. Stepien, IMSA. Used with permission.

local papers. Beyond the library lie living resources—the people who know something about this problem. Action research includes interviews with political figures, professionals, scientists, engineers, mothers of sick children, and people in the building trades. As different students bring home different facts from multiple sources, the complexity of the situation becomes clear. The students with access to the greatest number of sources may gain greater influence than students with fewer sources, no matter how compelling their ethical stance may be. If students can define the problem from a perspective linked to the facts they have collected, they can exert a great deal of influence over the process of proposing solutions. In a problem-based classroom, facts and their interpretation gain respect for the people who have them.

Figure 8.6 is a cause/effect map that lines up causes of lead-contaminated water with effects of the situation. As students gather facts that allow them to understand the situation more clearly, they also begin to see how long-term and short-term causes lead toward short-term and long-term effects. An originating cause of lead in water may be population density, leading to a centralized water system that concentrates lead in residential neighborhoods. Another might be poverty, restricting the ability of some residents to manage solutions on their own. Short-term effects might include localized instances of neurological damage, accentuating the health-care crisis in the city as well as affecting the educational system. As students tie causes to effects, they gain respect for complexity and also recognize how difficult it will be to propose solutions that fit the problem well. The easiest solution may do little to solve a problem. The best solution may prove impossibly difficult. "Best fit" is the test that counts.

FIGURE 8.5   Lead Poisoning Web Diagram: What Do We Need to Know?

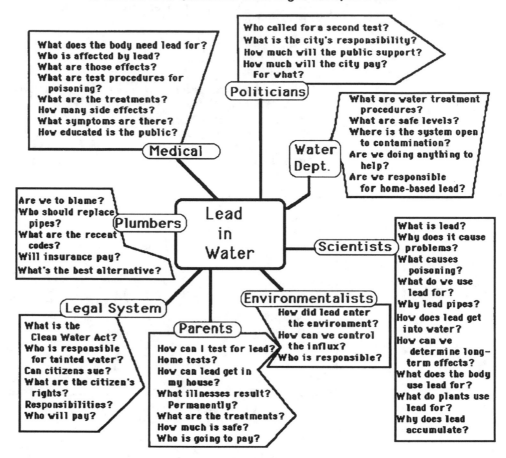

Brainstormed Questions from Eight Perspectives

From work of Pamela Samulis, Saucedo Scholastic Academy, Chicago, IL. Used with permission.

Different students will conceive of the water-borne-lead problem differently. This could be a simple plumbing problem, throwing the cost to the homeowner and the benefit to the plumbing trades. It could be a basic problem of city government, throwing the question into the political process. If there are no ways to remove lead from the water system, this is a medical problem, raising questions of diagnosis and treatment, bound to the city's social service system. As students conduct their research, they gain insight into solutions as well as problems. They begin to recognize feasibility questions, costs, and benefits associated with different perspectives. More important, perhaps, they begin to struggle with the ethical issues that torment society: Who is responsible for individual welfare? How do we balance the rights of individuals with the needs of a larger group? Weighing the evidence is much more than a mechanical exercise when the consequences of one's work reach far into the lives of people one knows.

Guiding Students Toward Solutions

Every definition of a problem implies a different set of solutions. Once a central problem is defined, students have to create one solution that fits better than others. How many options do we have? To find out, they have to conduct further research,

FIGURE 8.6   Chaining Causes and Effects from a Problem Situation

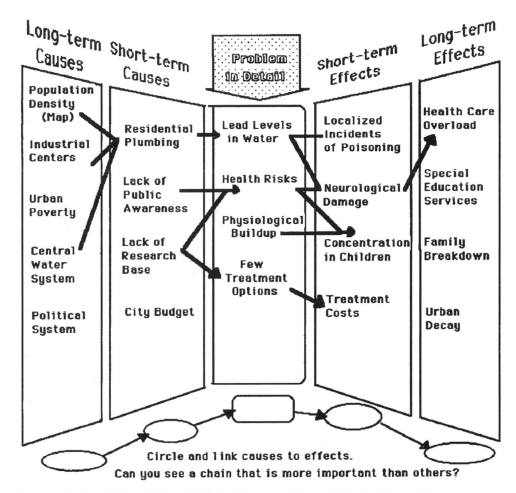

From work of Pamela Samulis, Saucedo Scholastic Academy, Chicago, IL. Used with permission.

using a process to assess a set of options and work toward a solution. In a problem-based classroom, students have to trace the effects of their proposals in the same way they traced causes in the problem situation. The process of examining solutions requires more facts—facts that will illuminate the spin-offs and unintended second effects from the various options: What are the costs of each solution? What are the predictable benefits? What are the risks? How sure are we that the desired benefits will actually occur? Do these solutions fit the problem? How practicable are these solutions in the problem setting? What will sell? What are the implications of the solutions we have proposed? Do they fit with what we believe? In the end, however, facing a panel of experts, the City Council, or simply a jury of fellow students, students have to present one decision and be able to recommend it with persuasive power.

Making a Case in Public

Assembling evidence behind an argument is a skill central to life's work. Students in a problem-based classroom have to use what they learn about the problem setting to sell a solution. They have to assemble the right facts, interpreted from the right perspective, to persuade other people that one road among many is the road worth taking. Passion helps, but facts usually prove more reliable. Conviction reassures an audience, but a well-structured presentation can bring along the skeptical or the timid. They have to express the logic that led them to choose one answer over others. They have to judge their audience, tailoring their argument to what they know about the listeners. They have to describe steps to the outcome they believe in that are feasible given the resources available. When problems are important, they are also public. Standing up in front of others with a sense of confidence takes preparation and practice.

Carol Lacy at Essex Junction High School in Vermont developed the following series of problem statements to organize the study of geology, weather, and architectural design for students in a vocationally oriented science course:

> A large international corporation has announced its plans to build a year-round resort on 300 to 500 thousand acres on one of five designated quadrangles in the United States: Chief Mountain, Montana, Bigelow, Maine, Charlotte, West Virginia, Harrisburg, Pennsylvania, or Mount Shasta, California.
>
> Because the corporation has established agreements with conference planners from around the world, money is not an object at this time. At this preliminary stage, the client will select a site based on the following criteria: (1) a setting of natural beauty, (2) land adaptable to multiple uses, (3) suitability for construction, (4) availability of water, and (5) access to suppliers and a labor market.
>
> As a consultant to one of these five areas, your task is to prepare a portfolio, three-dimensional model, and advertising campaign for a hearing early next month.

With topographic maps in hand, her ninth grade students begin a frenzied month of research and planning.

To support their work, Lacy prepared a series of guides to help students brainstorm the attributes of a successful resort, locate promising building sites, describe the setting, identify problems and benefits in the setting, and propose solutions. She allocates $300.00 (in hypothetical money) to each group and then offers her services, as well as the services of other teachers, for a fixed price. Trips to the site (library) cost the group $100.00. An enlargement of a map section costs $10.00. Consultation with a mathematician (herself) or with a geologist (her intern) costs $10.00 per minute. Her students receive extra points toward their grades if they can complete the presentation and still have money left over. The group that wins the contract gets to have a business lunch with the client, who serves as the school's principal as well. As Figure 8.7 shows, her students built the model, maps, and ad campaign with an eye toward positive impact. Because her students had little experience or confidence in standing up in front of others, Lacy developed a set of guides for them to use in preparing presentations such as this one, two of which are included in Figure 8.7.

Goals, Standards, and Assessment Rubrics

Assessment of problem-based learning follows the goals and objectives set up by the teacher or grade-level curriculum. To the extent that students are expected to engage a specific body of knowledge, conventional tests may be employed to assess content acquisition. To the extent that planning, presentation, and higher-order thinking are included among the goals, however, teachers need to design an assessment process that fits those purposes. Problem-based learning units end with a performance—a demonstration by students that they have learned to solve a problem using both information and intellectual skills. To assess student performances, teachers need to develop and publicize criteria for the standards they will use to measure attainment of a curriculum goal.

FIGURE 8.7 Developing a Presentation

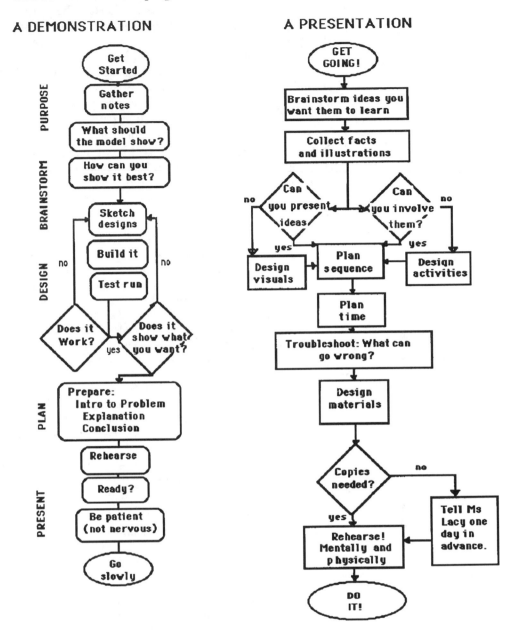

From class material of Carol Lacy, Science Department, Essex Junction High School. Used with permission.

Assessing problem-based learning should include tests that match the authenticity of the problem situation. In the work setting, success is measured through a production or performance that meets criteria set in advance. Grant Wiggins (1989) argues that authentic testing in school courses should have the same features:

> Authentic tests have four basic characteristics in common. First, they are designed to be truly representative of performance in the field; only then are the problems of scoring reliability and logistics of testing considered. Second, far greater attention is paid to the teaching and learning of the *criteria* to be used in the assessment. Third, self-assessment plays a much greater role than in conventional testing. And fourth, the students are often expected to present their work and defend themselves publicly and orally to ensure that their apparent mastery is genuine.

Performance assessment of problem-based learning should set criteria both for the information contained in the presentation and the process of making the presentation work for an audience (see Chapters 9 and 11 for examples).

Problem-based learning does not reduce the need for testing. Instead, it makes testing an aspect of performance, integrated with the process of finding problems and solving them. In a sense, the students who work on a presentation—a proposal, project or public presentation—are always preparing for exams. They are not performing for the teacher as much as they are performing for each other and themselves. With the criteria defined and the presentation public, the onus is on them to perform with power. "Truly effective learning should be situated in a culture of needs and practices that gives the knowledge and skill being learned context texture and motivation" (Perkins, 1992, p. 68). Problem-based learning gives students a reason to learn, and strategies for learning that they can use for a lifetime.

Priscilla Norton (1994) clarified the importance of putting problems at the center of attention as she wrote to us about the "Computer Processing Curriculum Showcase" in the previous chapter.

> The traditional debate between a "student-centered" and "teacher-centered" curriculum is likely asking the wrong question. Rather, I believe an effective strategy for creating a curriculum is to place a "problem" at the center. A problem-centered curriculum is one that is built around the solution to a real-world problem of interest. The phrase "at the center" means that a theme, a unit, or mastery of specific content is replaced as the main focus of the curriculum. Instead, students' abilities to solve the problem, to present their solution, and to revise their solutions in light of additional information become the goals. Placing the problem at the center emphasizes students' *doing* rather than their mastery of discrete pieces of information or skills.
>
> In selecting appropriate problems, educators should pick problems that are contemporary, nontrivial, and real—complex enough to engage students, and amenable to concrete outcomes. In the selection of appropriate problems, one should keep in mind John Dewey's creed, part of which reads, "Education is a process of living and not a preparation for future living." Traditional curricular goals are thus recast in a "problem-centered" curriculum. Curriculum designers select content to be taught not because a textbook, tradition, or curriculum guide specifies its teaching but because it is necessary and related to the problem's solution.

Students working on problems also practice important "life skills" (Drinan, 1991) in the patterns that will be most common when they take on adult responsibility in family and work:

1. Developing the ability to make decisions;
2. Raising awareness of the complexity of real-world issues;
3. Acquisition of or exposure to a body of knowledge;
4. Motivation for learning through use of professionally relevant material;
5. Developing the capacity for self-directed learning;
6. Developing the ability to extend learning beyond the presented situations (problems) to new ones;
7. Generating the desire and ability to think deeply and holistically;
8. Generating enthusiasm for learning from, and using all, life's experiences in personal, professional, and community development;
9. Encouraging a search beyond one's own preconceptions, so becoming ultimately innovative and critical with respect to self and one's profession.

They may come to respect knowledge as an aim in learning, but students also recognize how managing the processes of their own minds makes knowledge valuable.

PROBLEM-BASED LEARNING SHOWCASE

The Icarus Project:
Studying Water Quality from Macrosystems to Molecules

Bob Benoit, Timothy McClure, and Robert Kuintzle
Butte County Instructional Resource Center,
5 Country Center Drive, Oroville, CA;
and Paradise High School, Paradise, CA

When students do not do the work, do not ask
"What's wrong with the student." Ask,
"What's wrong with the work?"
Phil Schlecty, 1994 Speech

ICARUS

A Context for Change

Teachers and administrators from seven high schools and the county office of education in a rural area of rolling foothills, orchards, and rice fields in Northern California gathered in 1991 to determine why so many young people were unchallenged and disengaged in their science classes. The teachers spoke of bright, capable students who simply endured their classes, contributed little, and made few connections between the curriculum taught in the classroom and the application of the theories and ideas in the real world. The teachers expressed concern for these talented under-achievers whose intelligence and creativity remain untapped.

Educators also took a close look at the changing nature of students in California. They determined that in the past five years the range of student abilities and backgrounds in the same classroom had changed considerably to include students who had limited English proficiency (LEP), were economically disadvantaged, under-achieving, gifted and talented, of average ability, and those receiving special education services. These diverse students were bored and distanced from learning because, in the traditional learning approach, students were viewed as recipients of facts and concepts organized in a predetermined sequence. Little organized effort was made to accommodate the students' different developmental stages and learning styles in the typical high school classroom or to appeal to their natural inquisitiveness.

Supported by a planning grant from the California Department of Education, educators from the school districts and the county office joined with professors from California State University in Chico to discuss two key questions: "How do we motivate students? and "How do we prepare our students to succeed in the twenty-first century?" The group began by exploring recent secondary education reform documents and identifying elements that could be changed to revitalize instruction in the classroom. They were influenced by *Learning a Living: A Blueprint for High Performance* issued by the U.S. Department of Labor which identified skills, abilities, and attitudes students need to succeed in the twenty-first century and by *Second to None: A Vision of the New California School* published by the California Department of Education, presenting components of powerful teaching and learning. While exploring the ideas in these and other documents, the county office of education leadership team discovered the efforts of Bill Stepien at the Illinois Mathematics and Science Academy (IMSA) in the realm of "problem-based education." The problem-based units developed by the IMSA are models of units that are interdisciplinary, project-based, relevant, challenging, and excellent preparation for citizens of the twenty-first century.

Project Icarus began with a group of teachers and administrators who wanted to develop this kind of education for their own students. They wanted to change from an approach that featured the teachers as regulators of learning to a student-centered approach where the teacher acts as a coach and facilitator to encourage and support student investigation (see Figure 8.8). They decided to move away from the narrow confines of a single subject to a broad, interdisciplinary approach in which students could apply learning to real problems. As is done in real life, Icarus students would use learning from the natural sciences, mathematics, the social and behavioral sciences, literature, fine arts, and technology to view human problems from multiple perspectives.

The Icarus teachers also wanted to connect students with practicing professionals in the surrounding community so students could understand how the ideas and concepts they were studying in the classroom were actually applied in the world of work. And they decided to center the student investigations in the laboratory, the source of new knowledge and all the social ramifications that follow discovery; once the students understand the scientific principles involved in the laboratory, then their learning extends into the ethics, economic impact, and other aspects of public policy relative to any science problem.

FIGURE 8.8 Icarus Course Outcomes

1. Students will learn and demonstrate critical thinking skills by:
   - Exhibiting a reasoning process which leads to alternative solutions and/or meanings;
   - Drawing inferences, arriving at conclusions, making predictions, solving problems, and making decisions based on sufficient researched evidence as well-organized ideas, maintaining continuity, and showing cohesiveness;
   - Using concept mapping to conceptualize complex or ill-structured problems or issues.

2. Students will study a variety of ethical issues in science, showing:
   - An awareness of the role played by ethics in the life of individuals and societies;
   - Understanding of their own values and application to social, political, and environmental issues.

3. Students will demonstrate communication skills by:
   - Writing and speaking acceptably in English;
   - Differentiating fact from opinion;
   - Supporting statements and hypotheses using well-founded facts, theory, and opinion;
   - Distilling information clearly and succinctly;
   - Effectively organizing ideas in a variety of ways (e.g., written, video, mapping);
   - Demonstrating creativity through style, organization, and development of content;
   - Experiencing and respecting differing viewpoints and recognizing various reading and listening purposes.

4. Students will apply scientific processes by:
   - Observing, communicating, comparing, ordering, categorizing, relating, inferring, and applying information to explain his/her world and suggest improvements for the quality of life;
   - Recognizing the effects of sciences, technologies, and societies on one another and on the environment.

5. Students will show growth in instructor and self-observation by:
   - Demonstrating an awareness of his/her strengths and weaknesses through self-evaluation;
   - Accepting responsibility for his/her actions as controlled by his/her personal values;
   - Understanding the need to set and strive to achieve goals.

Assessment Portfolio Opportunities

video of formal debate and/or oral presentation	interviews
	classroom performances
written summary of current problems	computer research logs
project write-ups	use of electronic online research
written reactions to each major problem	processes

The teachers wanted students to become more active learners, to seek information from print, technology-based, and human resources and to construct their own understanding of a complex problem. In the approach, fact delivery is replaced by online research that produces a bounty of the most current and relevant information. Primary sources might include the latest photos from a NASA mission or the Human Genome Project. Students are able to pursue topics, as professionals do, seeking relevant information from many venues, people, and sources, pursuing new trails as they emerge.

Icarus called for a bold departure from the teacher-centered, single-subject, abstracted curriculum that isolates students from their vibrant communities and forces them to read, disengaged, through the textbook. Icarus students move beyond the classroom confines of instruction to tackle real-world problems that affect their lives in direct and powerful ways. They think critically, use technology as an investigative tool, and understand the connection between science and public policy. Figure 8.9 represents the whole process of solving ill-defined problems.

Students in the project research a variety of topics. In each, they play the role of an "expert" who must provide testimony or advice to a decision-making body preparatory to a key decision. Typical problems might be local (e.g., water quality, town growth issues, air pollution), or be national (e.g., health care, the placement of electromagnetic lines, or genetic engineering of humans or plants). The students work in cooperative groups, develop their facility with technology, and form partnerships with

FIGURE 8.9   Problem-Based Learning: A Flow Chart

Teacher determines content focus or topic
If using a concept, use state or local curriculum guide
(e.g., concept: ecosystems)
Subconcept: "How do organisms interact with ecosystems?"
or "What are the responsibilities of humans toward ecosystems?"

Concept Map Development
Brainstorm a map of potential sub-aspects of a problem.
Perhaps develop a secondary map based on occupations.

Problem scenario presented through "Authentic Correspondence"
(e.g., memos, letters, see "B")
Teachers should identify ways to obtain "real-looking" examples from
actual organizations as indicated below:
letterheads from actual companies, logos, etc.
Correspondence must clearly identify the student's role and task.
The task includes the audience and type of culminating activity. The other
correspondence must identify the stakeholders such as
environmentalists, developers, public, etc.

Problem Determination – Does there seem to be a problem?

If NO ---> Stop

If YES then

Visual Representation
Have students draw the problem as they understand it.
(optional, but useful)

Linguistic Representation
Students list words or phrases below each
picture as they deem appropriate.
Students move on to known elements of the problem
Focus Question: What DO we know?

(Continued)

FIGURE 8.9 *(Continued)*

Information Sifting
Students determine which information they are sure of,
being careful to note assumptions vs. facts or hypotheses
Focus Question: Do we REALLY know this?

Concept Map
Potential aspects of problem:
What does the problem seem to be?
Generate group ideas, generate whole class problem statement.

Information Identification
Refinement of the Problem Statement
Focus Question: WHAT do we need to know?

Resource Identification
Focus Question: WHERE can we find this information?

Resource Search
Students move out into the libraries, community, on-line, etc.
to gather information. Students will also participate in whole class
investigations and experimentation (e.g., water quality testing)

Debriefing
Students meet in small groups and whole class to discuss findings,
discuss areas to pursue, continue researching.

Identification of Solutions/Actions
Small groups begin to make decisions as to
what information will be included in final activity
and how it will be presented.

Selection of Solution/Action
Continuation of above

Culminating Activity/Performance

mentors and other students around the county and the nation. Unlike typical high school situations, our students do not simply recount information once they find it. Facing an ill-defined problem either local or national, the students are guided to gather information not just to get an answer but rather to develop a carefully reasoned approach. When a problem is "real," any answer may prove controversial. Making the whole process of problem solving visible to their audience as well as to themselves can help make the unacceptable more acceptable.

Water Quality Examples of an Ill-Defined Problem

The students are attracted to the situation by means of a scenario, often initiated by a series of memos and reports ("authentic correspondence") which induce them to consider investigation of an ill-structured problem. Scenarios can be presented in a number of forms, including memos, warned public meetings, or invitations to bid on a project. In Paradise, the water quality unit had a long-term focus punctuated with short-term problems of a lesser degree. The larger problem, for which all students were responsible, involved the question of development in the Paradise Lake watershed. On the longer term, students considered a proposal to create a housing development in the Magalia watershed. After receiving a "memo" from local builders stating their intention to create a housing development in the watershed, the students formulated their statement of the problem:

> **Problem Statement:** Given the projected amount of contamination per unit, and the possible economic benefits of the development, under what conditions (density, proximity to the actual water sources, sewage system type) can I as a town engineer recommend to the Water Resources Board that the development be built?
>
> As board members, our problem is to decide whether the Steiffer Road Development should be allowed. In the next four weeks, we must weigh the benefits of development, such as increased jobs and an improved economy, against the possible complications such as water contamination by septic tanks, trash, construction roads, oil, and so forth. We must also consider the impact of possible improvements in our water purification system on the Steiffer Road Development.

Problem-based learning begins with a review of what a class already knows about the situation, based on what they have seen in the scenario.

> *What we know:*
>
> There is danger down slope to other people and communities
>
> Someone wishes to build next to the water reservoir
>
> There are at least two concerned citizens
>
> A government agency must approve the project
>
> The Paradise Irrigation District (PID) is in opposition to excess single-family units
>
> Re-zoning has not yet been approved
>
> There is some question about the environment and the economy in this scenario

As students examine the list of what they know, they realize that there remains more to know.

> *What we need to know:*
>
> If an Environmental Impact Report (EIR) says no, is that the end of the process? Who gets the last word?
>
> Will the present sewage treatment system be upgraded?
>
> What if the units meet current zoning requirements?
>
> What is density to acreage?
>
> Is a consideration the concerns of the poor?
>
> What is the definition of a watershed?

At several different stages, students struggle to define the problem. Is it that there will or will not be a development? Students learn quickly that few issues are so clearly defined.

Because first-hand knowledge can help students imagine a problem and envision its solution, the class traveled to the dam to interview water resource managers for the district. Figure 8.10 is a list of some questions they had developed for their first

FIGURE 8.10   Questions and Answers from the Field Trip to Paradise Lake

---

What We Need to Know

Will the chlorination of the water go down when the water is being 100% filtered?
Answer: Generally, the dosage of chlorine can go down if you're not bypassing.

What chemicals are used in the water besides chlorine?
Answer: Alum and polymers for coagulating and flocculating the water.

Is there any time when water can be unsafe to drink even after filtration?
Answer: If there is a potential problem with contamination, normally there will be a boil order.

What exactly is a boil order?
Answer: You can boil your water for 120 minutes to kill any microorganisms.

How often do you do linology tests?
Answer: Every two years.

Where do water samples have to be taken from?
Answer: It depends on what kind of test you are doing. If possible, it should be taken while on a boat.

Is there a certain depth at which samples should be taken from?
Answer: Different studies use different depths.

Have there been any problems with contamination in the Paradise water before?
Answer: No.

---

interview at the reservoir to gain a perspective on what they did not know about water-quality systems in their local district. Taken to the (supposed) site, students realize that they need to know how to test for turbidity, percolation, porosity, oxygen content, coliform, and chemical contaminants for the long term as well as this short-term problem. This leads to a desire to know, *in context and with meaning,* and an equal desire to figure out how to find answers. The methodology of specific tests is taught in traditional classes, but without a meaningful context for students. More specific scenarios can be used to introduce the need for more specific knowledge in science and the methods of inquiry.

Introducing Basic Science

In addition to problem solving, it is envisioned that students will learn science in this unit. To begin understanding water distribution issues and to integrate chemistry with the Paradise Lake problem, the class focused on a more constrained issue—the effects of chemical contamination in the watershed. As part of the unit, the Magalia Dam Spill scenario began with an emergency:

The Magalia Dam Spill

You are the supervisor on the day shift for the California Highway Patrol. It is 6:00 A.M. on a cold winter morning. You are sleeping when the phone rings. You answer and hear, "Come to the Magalia Dam on the Skyway in Magalia. There has been an accident and you are needed."

Quickly you dress and hurry to the site of the emergency. As you approach the dam, you see an overturned tanker truck that has apparently crashed through the guard rail. It has lost one wheel and is perched on the front axle. You see "CORROSIVE" written on a small sign on the rear of the truck. There is a huge gash in the side of the truck and from the gash a clear liquid is running down onto the road, down the dam, and into the reservoir. Steam is rising from the water. All traffic has been stopped and everyone has been told to remain in their cars. . . .

Although the driver is unconscious, the purchase order in the driver's manifest soon shows that the liquid may be $79,208 worth of HCl (hydrochloric acid) being shipped from Groton, Massachusetts.

This ill-structured problem requires more information than is readily available, is as yet unsolved or has no "right" answer, is relevant and important, and requires research and problem solving to determine an action, though not necessarily a solution. Figure 8.11 is a concept map representing what students already knew as a class, based on their prior understanding of the Magalia Dam Spill.

As with the question of watershed development, a first, and sometimes optional step, is to have students visualize and draw a *visual representation* of the problem. Without discussion, students are asked to actually draw their perceptions of the problem on large sheets of paper hung on classroom walls. This assists those who learn in other than linguistic ways to construct the problem. (Typically, those with linguistic skills will feel most uncomfortable with this stage of the process.) Students then can

FIGURE 8.11   What We Know about the Magalia Dam Spill: Concept Map

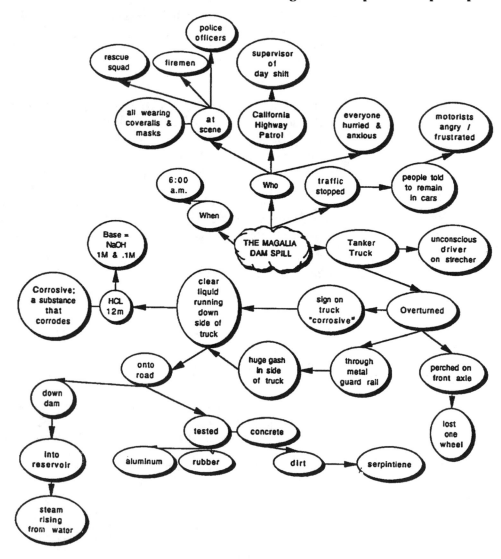

look at all versions and write phrases or sentences below various drawings. These drawings become the stimulus for the next *linguistic phase* in which students in small groups begin to verbalize their reactions to the problem.

Students are first asked to describe what they know. Experience indicates that it is best if small groups do this, then share information as a whole group so that more students have a chance to, and would be willing to, contribute through the small-group process. Each group, in "round-robin" fashion contributes one piece of information at a time until the supply of facts is exhausted. At some point, it is important that the instructor question students as to whether statements are facts, conjectures or assumptions, and so forth. (This is known as *information sifting*.) They may make assumptions that cause them not to investigate new information carefully. Yet the instructor must remain in the role of facilitator and not become, again, one who disseminates "the truth." Students in this methodology must be supported, but allowed to stumble, as adults do in life.

As students examine the list of what they know, they realize that there remains more to know. When students recognize what they still need to know or learn about, they can be guided to use a variety of information sources. Research about water pollution and contaminants might entail use of online databases via modem, information from CD-ROM sources, print sources, visual media, or treatment plant operators in the community or at a local university. More localized issues means reliance on local water boards, engineers, health departments, planning boards, or private individuals ("mentors") for assistance and information. After listing what they need to know, students will naturally identify sources of information that include local expertise and potentially useful scientific investigations they must conduct on their own.

Conventional laboratory experiments play an important role in problem-based learning, but they derive their meaning from their connection to the scenarios being presented. Students maintain a problem log over the course of a unit, keeping track of what they learn and what it might mean to the problem under study. They also develop their own labs to test questions that occur as they study an issue. The lab experiment in Figure 8.12 begins with a fairly standard exercise in determining how acids and bases react but turns quickly to the question of how to neutralize spilled hydrochloric acid. The lab also includes more speculative questions on soil acidity and vegetation. A careful experiment will yield the most reliable results on the question of what it might take to neutralize a huge HCl spill.

Experimentation in problem-based learning also takes on an applied focus. What difference would it make if the HCl were simply allowed to dissipate or to flow down stream toward the town? Is this a problem that needs solving or will it solve itself? Three students in an Icarus lab designed and conducted an experiment with twelve kinds of material and three concentrations of HCl. They concluded that HCl has no effects on the environment. They also noted that there were not absolutely confident in their conclusions because they had run out of time in their work. Did other student teams achieve the same results? What does it mean that a test is reliable? Do results pointing in different directions make problem solving impossible or simply more difficult?

Solving Complex Problems

After the Magalia Dam Spill problem, students returned to the larger but related question: Should the zoning board allow a major development in the Paradise Lake watershed? Development might bring chemical contamination, but it also increases the likelihood of biological contamination and silt formation. At this stage, students still struggle to define the problem. Is it that there will or will not be a development or is the larger arena of risk the issue? As a class of decision makers, they determine that the most logical statement of the problem is:

FIGURE 8.12   Linking the Problem to Text-Based Information

Name _____   Icarus Science

Acids and Bases Problem Log 1
(Get this done NOW!)

1. Using a periodic table found in a chemical or chemistry book, identify the compound as a base or acid, and give its molecular weight (grams/mole).

Molecular Formula	Acid or Base	Molecular Weight
H_2SO_4	_____	_____
HCl	_____	_____
KOH	_____	_____
NaOH	_____	_____
NH_4OH	_____	_____
HNO_2	_____	_____

2. Complete the table. Use: $M_1V_i = M_2V_2$

Initial		Final		Volume of Water Added
Volume	Concentration	Volume	Concentration	
	6 M	100 ml	3.0 M	
	6 M	50 ml	0.1 M	
5.0 ml	6 M		1.0 M	
8.0 ml	6 M		2.0 M	
	6 M	75 ml		

3. How many grams of NaOH pellets would be necessary to neutralize the spilled concentrated HCl acid (12 M)?

Additional information:

   • The loaded truck weighed 33,000 pounds *before* the accident.
   • The truck and the remaining HCl acid in the tank weighed 20,945 pounds *after* the accident.

Hints:

   • Conversions of masses—pounds–kilograms–grams.
   • Mass of one mole of HCl (12 M)
   • Molecular weight of NaOH
   • A balanced chemical equation

4. The hydrangea plant is a popular flowering bush. The pH of the soil affects the color of the flower, from pink to blue. What will the addition of aluminum sulfate do to the color of the flower? Please explain why.

Given the projected amount of contamination per unit, and the possible economic benefits of the development, under what conditions (density, proximity to the actual water sources, sewage system type) can I as a town engineer recommend to the Water Resources Board that the development be built?

In the case of a local development, they realize that the interaction of agencies, concerned citizens, and laws may lead to several possible solutions, each with its own set of conditions. To determine the answer to this question, students must gather information from a variety of resources in print, through community experts, and perhaps online by finding other people in other locales who are facing the same problem. They formed teams to take on aspects of long-term projects supporting their eventual decision:

Team A: Building a working model of the PID watershed

Team B: Constructing posters and models of groundwater concepts

Team C: Constructing a working poster of a water purification process

Team D: Plotting and sharing water issues from the National Geographics Project, using Internet and online data services

Different teams might create different problem representations pointing toward different kinds of solutions. Team C created an interactive model of water purification using HyperCard, a software program that lets the developer link a wide variety of information sources in a wide variety of media (see Figure 8.13).

There are also ethical extensions to the unit, based in the study of literature. Students read "Enemy of the People" by Henrik Ibsen. This play considers the dilemma of a doctor who discovers hazardous contaminants, which have caused several deaths, in the town spas. These spas, however, are a major source of revenue to leading citizens. Ibsen's character must choose whether to expose these health concerns to the public at the risk of offending leading citizens and investors and losing his job and the inheritance of his wife and child. Figure 8.14 is a student's response to a quotation about the willingness of public officials to respond to the ideas of citizens. This student writes from a knowledge of the play, but also from the experience she gained while working with public officials on the Paradise watershed project.

Recommending a Course of Action

Students demonstrate the range and depth of their newly constructed knowledge as they participate in performances, such as board meetings and interviews, that simulate real-life forums for resolving complex problems. During these performances, students are interviewed or questioned. The interactive nature of these sessions discourages recitation of facts by the students because they must reorganize information to respond to questions just as a town engineer, doctor, or FDA officer must do in the course of actual duties. But they will also learn about the political and economic relationship of private individuals, the water resources board, the planning department, the health department, and state agencies. Students will visit a meeting of the water board in preparation for their own "performance" as an expert engineer advising the board. In this "performance-based" assessment, they will make recommendations to a mock board comprised of actual board members, community members, and faculty. Groups of two or three students will meet with each small "board" and be assessed against a predetermined rubric in this *culminating activity*.

Student-generated performances and projects become assessment vehicles for the instructor. In addition to the performances mentioned before, students produce a portfolio consisting of high-quality science reports, short stories, drawings and sketches, multimedia programs, legislation, and other products that chronicle their

FIGURE 8.13 Creating a HyperCard Stack on the Water System

PID Filtration Plant

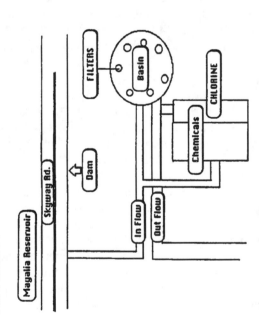

Magalia reservoir dam

This is the earth made dam that holds in the water for the Paradise water shed. Without this dam the people of Paradise would find it hard to to get a clean glass of water! You might find it hard to see but that is because it hides under Skyway Rd.

[BACK TO MAIN]

Out Flow

The "Out Flow" is the name for the water that has been purified and sent down to the citizens of Paradise! Probably most of the water that you drink has been through the water purification process!

[Back to Main]

CHLORINE

The chlorine is used to disinfect and kill all other bacteria that the filter might not catch. The amount of chlorine used in the water is one to one million. Which means that for every one million gallons of water there is one gallon of chlorine to the water.

[BACK TO MAIN]

Chemicals

The chemicals that are used to clean the water are alum, cationic polymer, nonionic polymer and chlorine. The first three   chemicals are coagulants that make the dirt clump together and the clumps are then sucked to the bottom of the filters.

[Back to Main]

Magalia Reservoir

The Magalia Reservoir is a body of water that supplies fresh drinking water to households all over the Paradise area. The water in this area is made up of a molecule called H_2O (see diagram).

[Back to main]   [Diagram]

Filters

The filters are located at the bottom of the basin. The purpose of the filters are to trap any clusters of dirt or debris left in the pipes after being pumped in from the lake.

[Back to Main]

234

FIGURE 8.14   Student Reflection on "Enemy of the People" (Literature)

> "Officials are not generally very ready to act on proposals that come from other people."
>
> I like this quote very much. (Heck, that's why I chose it.) The main reason I like it so much is that it tells the truth. When I first read the quote I had to stop and read it again, for some reason as simple as it is, it really stuck out in my mind. It expresses things that many people think about, but don't necessarily want to believe.
>
> The idea is definitely valid today. As I started to say before, it tells the truth. Sure, we would all like our ideas to be accepted and thought about, but for some reason people in positions of authority think they are god. Not in all cases, but in many. My point is, officials think they are better than anyone else and would hate to think that someone elses ideas could be better than their own.

rigorous investigation and responses to problem-based units of study. These project materials become valuable evidence of their accomplishments as they make the transition to the world of work and higher education.

Problem-based units focus on science, but in the context of substantive problems students will confront in their lives. This relevance is linked to the active role the student must play as inquirer. Students also realize through their struggles that real decisions (how to manage public safety after a contamination event) are rarely black-and-white decisions. Most often, approval of such projects is given, but with conditions. Students learn to define the conditions that solve a problem in a rational and equitable manner. The student as "expert" advisor to the water resources board or Congress must consider both sides of an issue. Conditional approval of the housing development might include requirements regarding lot size, traffic flow, and water connections. Finally, students learn how to become informed and involved citizens of their community. The Icarus Project intent is that students will become engaged by—rather than simply exist in—schools. They will become careful thinkers, not careless citizens. Students will become insightful investigators and active citizens prepared for the twenty-first century.

CHAPTER 9

Science/Technology/Society

Complex Issue Analysis

In many sections of the country, teachers of science and mathematics have led an effort to extend the teaching of science beyond its traditional content boundaries into "real-world" application. Supported by national science education leadership beginning in 1977, this movement is generally described as STS, or Science/Technology/Society. STS applies the principles and the processes of scientific inquiry to problems resulting from technological and scientific development at local, regional, or national levels. This student-oriented approach continues to emphasize the basic facts, skills, and concepts of traditional science, but it does so by embedding that science content into sociotechnical contexts that are meaningful to students (Aikenhead, 1992). Like problem-based learning, STS focuses on current issues. As students in problem-based learning become problem solvers, students in STS classes become scientist/arbitrators of social conflicts (see Chapter 8).

Although problem-based learning favors the process of solution testing to some greater extent, STS relies on problem analysis—systematic research on problems and issues. High school social studies and industrial arts (tech prep) teachers have become enthusiastic participants in such curriculum efforts. Technology educators see STS as an opportunity to integrate their subject area and remove it from isolation in vocational areas (Zuga, 1991). And finally, while the origins of the STS movement may be rooted in the science community, social studies teachers are enthusiastically working with their science teaching colleagues to help students engage the world as it exists (Splitburger, 1991). As an aspect of the movement toward integration, STS can make connections across a large proportion of the existing high school curriculum, creating a context in which learning becomes meaningful through its association with contemporary issues.

The STS movement, perhaps best exemplified by the work of Robert Yager and his associates at The University of Iowa, has become a powerful force in encouraging schools to engage in interdisciplinary teaching. Yager's NSTA-NSF Chautauqua Program, started in Iowa in 1984, has helped thousands of teachers develop and introduce STS models into their science classrooms. STS becomes interdisciplinary by fusing the study of issues (social studies and English) with the practice of scientific research (science and mathematics) (Marser, 1992). In STS learning, groups of students use the methods of science and social studies to investigate issues that arise in the collision of scientific knowledge, technological progress, and social values (S-T-S).

As shown in Figure 9.1, the interactions between science, technology, and society create six basic questions that teachers can use to focus curriculum design (Hickman, Patrick, & Bybee, 1987; Ramsey & Hungerford, 1989). These relationships and their attending questions are not purely abstract and hypothetical. They

FIGURE 9.1   Questions Generated by STS Interactions

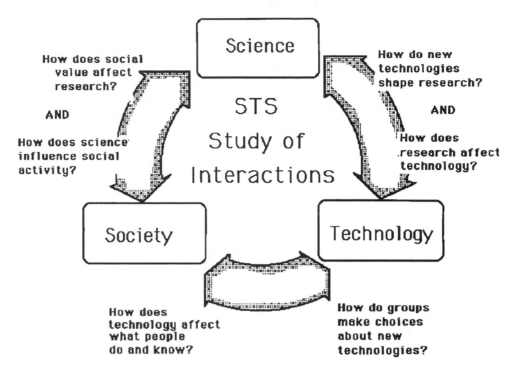

Compiled from ideas in Hickman, Patrick, and Bybee (1987), and Ramsey and Hungerford (1989).

make themselves visible on a daily basis in news headlines about landfills, wetlands, frost-resistant tomatoes, price tags on supercolliders and space stations, coma patients, fish kills, oil spills, and freeze-dried millionaires. With training, students can begin to see the influence of invisible forces in specific events in their experience: forces emanating from progress in science, technology, and society. With training in the scientific method, they can begin to add their own voices to the value questions that we face as a people. STS brings the reasoned approach of science to the "hot" issues that divide our impassioned culture. This chapter provides an overview of the issues that arise when schools move in the STS direction and gives examples of promising projects and applications of STS theory.

Science as a Way of Knowing

Science is *a way of knowing and thinking* about the natural and physical world that results in the creation of an organized body of knowledge. Technology is *applied* science that translates scientific knowledge into applications that benefit humankind. Society supports both science and technology in the belief that research and development should work on behalf of social values. As Collette and Chiappetta (1989, p. 234) point out, many people do not comprehend the relationship between science and technology and often confuse them. Further, they do not understand how science and technology influence society, or conversely, how much of an influence society exerts on science and technology. Students in an STS classroom apply the scientific method to the problem of discovering how technology affects our lives and how we might better manage technological innovations to support social values.

Many years ago, the British writer and scientist, C. P. Snow (1959) pointed out what he saw as an unfortunate dichotomy between the intellectual world of the scientist and that of the humanist. His book, *The Two Cultures and the Scientific Revolution,* brought that contention to prominence and most readers agreed that, yes, conversation at a social gathering of scientists and non-scientists usually winds up being conducted in discipline-based clusters where one group cannot understand what the other is talking about. Vocabulary divides the sciences from the humanities, but so does attitude. Science tends toward *positivism*—the belief that what is important to humanity can be understood and managed if we investigate the issues and apply what we discover. The humanities, focusing on immutable forces in the human condition, tend toward relativism and a conservative estimation of what is possible to achieve through human effort. Today's advocates of STS and indeed, of interdisciplinary teaching, acknowledge the communications barriers across the disciplines and see the need for what might be called "cultural interchange." They seek to solve human problems with scientific methods.

The Promise of Science/Technology/Society

Some educators see STS as a clear opportunity to help make education relevant to students. An obvious way of doing this is to emphasize technological and societal issues in science courses. For example, students in a biology class studying gene structure and replication might learn how the human genome is mapped. More important, they would learn how genetic engineering, a technology, can help discover individuals who may be predisposed to a particular disorder such as diabetes, colon cancer, or sickle-cell anemia.

Increasingly, science educators believe that for science education to be relevant students must examine social problems such as drug and alcohol use, AIDS, overpopulation, abortion, and hazardous waste. The "bottom line" for those who urge science teachers to incorporate STS issues into their teaching is that students should be given the knowledge and skills to make decisions that will affect their lives. Stated somewhat differently, they want students to be able to learn methodically and act responsibly. To do that, students will need to examine social problems and apply scientific principles and processes to them. Perhaps most important, students must be given the opportunity to discuss their beliefs and values and to propose solutions to real-life problems *they* have identified (Collette & Chiappetta, 1989, pp. 236–237).

Robert Yager (1993) called attention to the points of contrast between standard science programs and the experimental STS programs he and his associates developed in Iowa and elsewhere. To obtain the desired benefits from STS, he urges fundamental changes in the science curriculum and how it is taught. In most current science curricula, students try to acquire text-based information and aggregate basic understanding of what is known in the sciences and how knowledge is organized. In STS, students turn to the world around them for the knowledge they seek. Using established knowledge as a starting point, students conduct research and use their research to clarify social and philosophical issues.

Merging science and social issues education radically changes the nature of teaching and learning. Although the objectives of high school science instruction conventionally have aimed toward concepts, processes, and skills, actual instruction in the science classroom overwhelmingly has favored lecture/recitation and text-based learning over "hands-on" activities that more closely support these objectives (Weiss, 1993). In a survey of science texts in biology, chemistry, and physics, Chiang-Soong found that only 1 to 5 percent of the page space was devoted to issues as opposed to factual knowledge. The distinctions between conventional science and STS are evident in the comparison chart in Figure 9.2. Teachers in many disciplines have found effective ways to design STS instruction, and we will highlight them in the stories to follow.

FIGURE 9.2   Comparing Traditional Science and the STS Approach

Standard Science Curriculum	The STS Approach
Survey of major concepts found in standard text-books	Identification of problems with local interest
Use of labs and activities suggested in textbook and accompanying lab manual	Use of local resources (human and material) to locate information that can be used in problem resolution
Passive involvement of students assimilating information provided by teacher and textbook	Active involvement of students in seeking information that can be used
Science being contained in the science class room for a series of periods over the school year	Science teaching going beyond a given series of class sessions, meeting room, or educational structure
A focus on information proclaimed important for students to master	A focus on personal impact that makes use of students' own natural curiosity and concerns
A view that science is the information included and explained in textbooks and teacher lectures	A view that science content is not something that merely exists for student mastery as it is recorded
No attention to career awareness other than an occasional reference to a scientist and his/her discoveries	A focus on career awareness—emphasizing careers in science and technology other than research, medicine, and engineering
Students concentrating on problems provided by teachers and text	Students becoming aware of their responsibilities as citizens
Science occurring only in the science classroom as a part of the school's science department	Students learning what role science can play in a given institution and in a specific community
Science being a study of information where teachers discern the degree to which students acquire it	Science being an experience students are encouraged to enjoy
Science focusing on current explanations and understandings; little or no concern for the use of information beyond classroom and test performance	Science with a focus on the future and what it may be like

Adapted from Robert Yager's work. Reprinted with permission from NSTA Publications, Jan. 1993, from *The Science Teacher,* National Science Teachers Association, 1840 Wilson Blvd., Arlington, VA 22201-3000.

Focusing on Hot Issues

Fortunately for teachers, we are not short of questions to answer coming from the interactions of science, technology, and society. A group of science educators (Hickman, Patrick, & Bybee, 1987, p. 16) has ranked the following issues as getting better, staying the same, or getting worse by the year 2000.

Getting Better	*Staying the Same*	*Getting Worse*
Human health	Nuclear reactors	Population growth
		Water resources
		Hunger and food
		Air quality
		War technology
		Energy shortages
		Land use
		Hazardous substances
		Life extinctions
		Mineral resources

As the millennium draws to a close, high school students may face specific instances of these issues in their own towns as well as in the world community.

STS studies usually take on a local flavor as students and teachers become sensitive to the existence of STS problems in their area. At Easton High School in Easton, Maryland, LeeAnn Hutchinson has managed a number of STS investigations and an equal number of exploratory studies and activities with her tenth grade biology and eleventh and twelfth grade environmental studies students:

Recent Studies	*Exploratory Activities*
Stream restoration	Trash incinerators
Chesapeake Bay monitoring	Aquarium marine mammals
Dune restoration	Wetlands waterfowl
Overpackaging	Rockfish endangerment
Cloning	Bluebird houses
Animal research	

Advocates of STS urge teachers to identify *contemporary* issues for study. Teachers have much to choose from, but need to select STS opportunities wisely. Faith Heald, a teacher at Bellows Free Academy in Fairfax, Vermont, created an instructional sequence around BST, or *b*ovine *soma*tropin hormone. The synthetic version of this hormone, when injected into lactating cows, markedly increases the amount of milk produced. This practice has attracted considerable attention in regions where milk production is a significant contributor to the economy. Faith has her students read articles on the topic from both scientific and health journals, as well as newspapers and magazines. They also interviewed local farmers and milk consumers using interview protocols they developed.

Some of the issues raised include: the effect of BST on small farms, the effect of BST on milk quality and milk prices, marketing value (Ben and Jerry's Homemade Ice Cream refused to use milk with synthetic hormones in it), short- and long-term effects on the dairy industry, chemical composition of BST, and how BST use in Vermont compares with its use in other states. As a science teacher, Faith links this study to the science concept of *cause and effect,* which is a syllabus commitment. The culminating experience for this short "module" was a structured debate on the pros and cons of BST. Such a learning sequence helps students understand the link between science, technology, and society.

Topics that are *timely* and relate to the lives of the students and region are best. BST was "hot" at the time Faith designed her module. She may reuse it in a modified form another year, but it will likely be displaced by something new. Jake McDermott, a science/environmental studies teacher at Brattleboro (VT) Union High School, developed a module derived from an important political issue in his region. He had students investigate social impact factors associated with the development of hydropower dams in Quebec, Canada. The electricity produced there would be sent hundreds of miles by transmission lines to consumers in his community. The engineering that was required would flood thousands of acres of land and displace native peoples. Jake's students invited, and paid for the travel expenses, representatives of the affected Cree Indian nation to come to their school to tell first-hand how they felt about the project. Again, the topic was important to the region and to the lives of the students, and it provided an opportunity to analyze an important technical-social issue.

Another illustration—several years ago one of this book's authors worked with several teachers at Colchester (VT) High School to develop and teach a week-long module on the effect of construction of flood-control dams on the Richelieu River in Quebec. Such a plan, active at the time, would have regulated the water level of Lake Champlain. Teachers of biology, English, French, and social studies met and brainstormed how each would contribute to the conduct of this collaborative effort to help their students see beyond the boundaries of their individual subjects. This resulted in their setting aside parts of their individual classes over a three-day period for students to aggressively study the topic. The biology teacher handled the "content" of ecological effects of such a flood-control practice; the social studies teacher helped students consider the legal, sociological, and legislative dimensions; the English teacher helped students organize formal presentations for a simulated public hearing; and the French teacher's students translated contemporary articles from the French language newspapers that gave prominent coverage to the topic. The entire school was invited to a debate/public hearing in the school auditorium that simulated a meeting of decision makers on whether the dam should be constructed. Roles were created for students to testify pro and con. Student learning was impressively demonstrated by the knowledge-based argumentation presented and the polish of public presentation. A videotape recording was produced for later analysis and sharing with wider audiences.

Although STS instruction may engage most of the concepts of conventional science courses, it does not fit comfortably within the course structure of a conventional science curriculum. Robert Yager points out the dangers of a teacher trying to integrate an STS unit into an existing course, and clearly favors the development of intact modules that are not just the same science found in textbooks with technological and societal dimensions "added on." Yager (1990, p. 53) states the essence of the STS movement when championing the importance of independent student inquiry:

> Real science learning cannot be the result of teachers "presenting" information or "announcing" a new STS module. Students must have a hand in constructing the problem and determining their actions concerning it. STS programs begin with real-world issues and concerns. Hopefully these are (or will become) student issues and not simply information teachers with to present to students.

When students define their own problems and develop their own research procedures, the chance to retrofit student projects to an existing course structure evaporates.

Still, STS units or modules can be integrated within existing courses, perhaps as post holes or quarterly projects, if a teacher is willing to help students make the leap from knowledge-based science to process-based research (Heath, 1992; Kellerman, 1993). STS appears to be not so much inconsistent with conventional science topics, and it is appositional in purpose. Students approaching the topic of ozone in Figure 9.3 from the STS perspective (right side) may not "cover" all the gas laws with the same precision as students in a text-based course (left side). Both groups of students would study ozone and atmospheric gas, but one group would focus on established scientific laws while the other focused on the reliability of atmospheric modeling. They would not emerge with the same information in quantity or quality.

Organizing STS Learning: Decision Making and Research

Two processes—issue analysis and scientific research process—organize most STS curricula. While issue analysis gives structure to the whole STS enterprise, the scientific method usually provides structure for individual or small-group STS projects related to issues. When individual students focus scientific studies on different aspects of an issue, their separate projects can be used to educate other students, as well as policy makers, about specific aspects of an STS issue in more detail than would be possible in a conventional class. In conducting specific studies, students cover a wide range of information from many disciplines. Students in an STS classroom also practice using research skills— using science, social science, and library-based research methods—that are generally useful across subject areas. Because students are using these skills in a meaningful enterprise with a specific audience of students and adults in view, they may take more care in creating research questions, reviewing available information, designing a method of study,

FIGURE 9.3   Connecting a Text to an STS Theme

Grade Level: High School Chemistry
Teaching Length: 25 Days

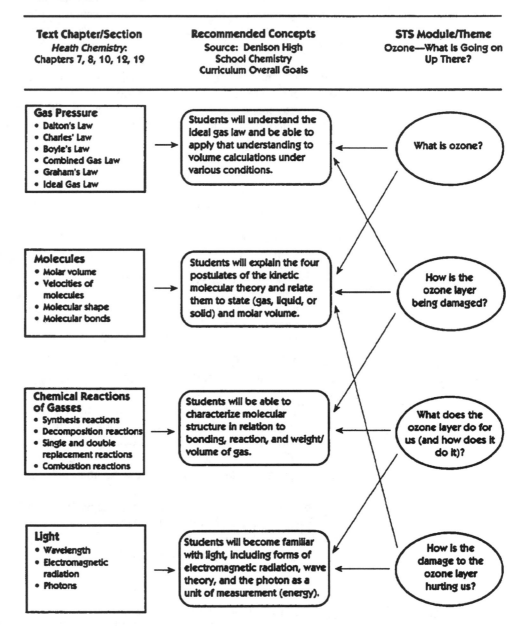

From L. R. Kellerman (1993) in *The science-technology-society movement* (R. Yager, Ed.). Arlington, VA: NSTA, p. 14. Reprinted with permission from NSTA Publications, Jan. 1993, from *The Science Teacher*, National Science Teachers Association, 1840 Wilson Blvd., Arlington, VA 22201-3000.

analyzing what they gather, and presenting their findings than they would if they were practicing any of these skills in isolation from a focusing issue.

Decision-Making Process: Issue Analysis

Teachers can design STS curricula using general decision-making formats, as in problem-based learning in the previous chapter, or the decision-making protocol in Figure 9.4. With two decades of experience, however, a general approach has emerged that

FIGURE 9.4   A Process for Examining STS Issues

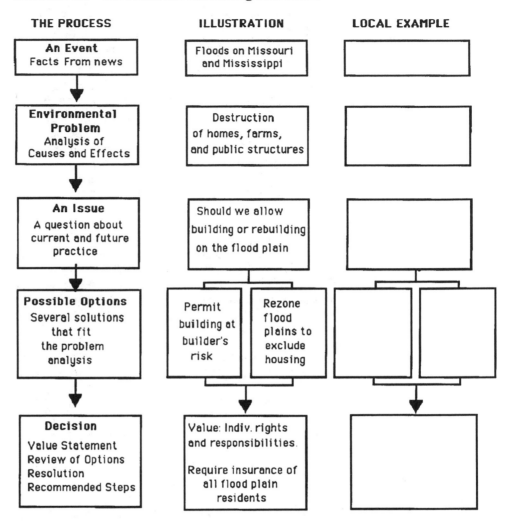

THE PROCESS

An Event
Facts From news

Environmental Problem
Analysis of
Causes and Effects

An Issue
A question about
current and future
practice

Possible Options
Several solutions
that fit
the problem
analysis

Decision
Value Statement
Review of Options
Resolution
Recommended Steps

ILLUSTRATION

Floods on Missouri
and Mississippi

Destruction
of homes, farms,
and public structures

Should we allow
building or rebuilding
on the flood plain

Permit
building at
builder's
risk

Rezone
flood
plains to
exclude
housing

Value: Indiv. rights
and responsibilities.

Require insurance of
all flood plain
residents

LOCAL EXAMPLE

Adapted with permission from Hungerford, H. R., Litherland, R., Peyton, B., Ramsey, J., and Volk, T. (1992). *Investigating and evaluating environmental issues and actions.* Champaign, IL: Stipes Publishing.

mixes elements of scientific inquiry with a systems sequence based on public or "jurisprudential" decision making (Bonstetter & Pederson, 1993). Harold Hungerford and his colleagues (1992) in Illinois have published a comprehensive guide to STS development that many teachers have used successfully to build units. As Figure 9.4 suggests, teachers can use this format to create the over-riding structure for an STS unit. Within this structure, students can practice the skills of data gathering and analysis within a logical structure that has wide applicability. Weighing costs and benefits against the goals of a proposed solution can be carried out using weighting scales or decision trees.

STS issues are usually "hot" because they have inspired impassioned response from people with widely different interests. The issue of whether to refit a closed coal mine as a wetlands habitat or restore it to farmland raises different questions of cost and benefit in the minds of different constituents (see Figure 9.5). Adopting multiple perspectives on any issue is a challenging intellectual exercise that also engages students in estimates of probability that are interdependent. The example of issue analysis in Figure 9.5 illustrates the challenge of assessing options that imply different value positions from multiple perspectives (Ramsey, Hungerford, & Volk, 1990). Complex issues can be investigated from multiple perspectives using a "Futures Wheel" like the one in Figure 9.6.

FIGURE 9.5   Issue Analysis: An Example

Issue

Should 483 acres of land to be strip mined in Perry County be reclaimed for agricultural use or converted to a state-owned wetlands habitat?

The Players/Positions	The Beliefs	Associated Values
Perry County Chairman Reclaim as farmland (Inferred position)	Too much farmland has been lost due to economic dependency on coal mining	Economic
Perry County Farmers Reclaim as farmland	Geese are eating crops and increasing weed populations	Economic
Former SWCD Chairman Reclaim as farmland	Weed control costs will be high	Economic
Wildlife Representatives Reclaim as wetlands habitat	Additional wildlife acreage will help counterbalance the loss of wetlands	Ecological
Sportsman Coalition Reclaim as wetlands	Farmers could make money from operating geese hunting pits; geese will save family farms	Economic
Dept. of Conservation Reclaim as Wetlands	Recreation area will be increased; use will generate $1.2 million	Recreation and economic
Parent "A" Reclaim as farmland	Schools will lose property tax	Economic
Parent "B" Reclaim as wetlands	Family hunting trip is as educational as reading a book	Educational

Questions for Consideration

How valid is the scientific (and other) information used by each player?

What additional information must be obtained in order to make an informed decision concerning the issue?

Do the solutions proposed by the various players address problems that are "real" or simply perceived?

From Ramsey, J., Hungerford, H., and Volk, J. (1990). Analyzing the issues of STS, *The Science Teacher* (March): 63. Reprinted with permission from NSTA Publications, National Science Teachers Association, 1840 Wilson Blvd., Arlington, VA 22201-3000.

Scientific Research Process: Creating Knowledge

Figure 9.7 represents an STS research process that activates skills from a wide variety of disciplines. In selecting a topic and trying to narrow a research question in the library, students practice the kind of text-based research usually required in English and social studies classes. As they collect secondary source information, they are also practicing the skills of writing conventional letters and gathering direct quotations from interviews. As they prepare their own ways to collect primary data, they engage mathematical knowledge (sampling, graphing, and statistical analysis) as well as sci-

FIGURE 9.6   Web Map for Decision Making

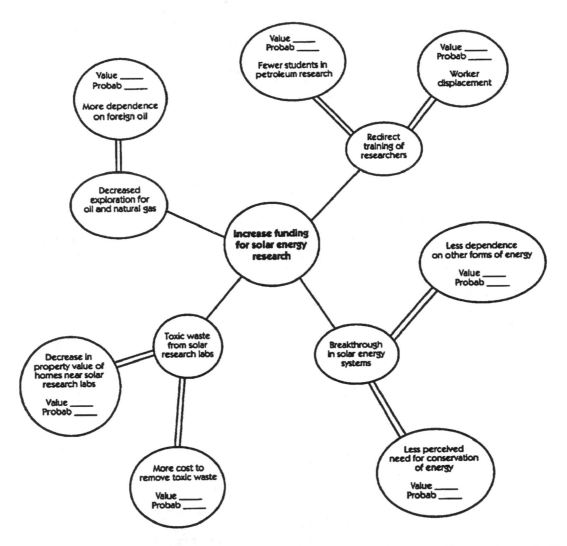

Sample Futures Wheel
(Decision to increase funding for solar research)

From Piel, E. J. (1993). Decision-making: A goal of STS. In R. Yager (Ed.), *The Science, Technology, Society Movement.* Reprinted with permission from NSTA Publications, National Science Teachers Association, 1840 Wilson Blvd., Arlington, VA 22201-3000.

entific process skills (instrument design and interpretation of findings). As they prepare their final reports, they are working as *scientists*—people who may know a great deal, but who must know how to develop and explain new information in order to make a difference in the human community.

The process of teaching library research is not unusual in any high school. Designing scientific research studies and developing social science surveys are more unusual, yet they lie at the heart of STS instruction. Students in an STS classroom are expected to conduct a study that will bring to light new information and help the whole class understand more deeply the issue in question. In STS, hard science and social science may go hand in hand. If the issue is water quality, some students may sample the local river at set intervals to assess contamination levels while other stu-

FIGURE 9.7   Guide for Individual and Group Research

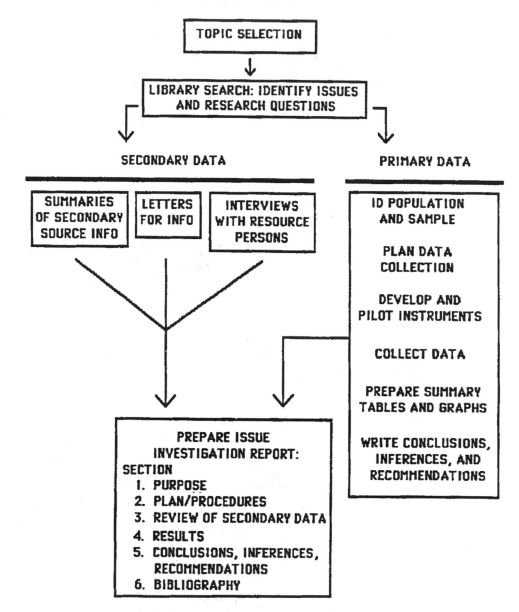

SUGGESTED ISSUE INVESTIGATION: A FLOWCHART

Adapted with permission from Hungerford, H. R., Litherland, R., Peyton, B., Ramsey, J., and Volk, T. (1992). *Investigating and evaluating environmental issues and actions.* Champaign, IL: Stipes Publishing.

dents survey the local population about their use of the river, while other students map septic and central sewer systems in the town. Whether it brings hard scientific facts to bear, or more subtle social science opinions as did the Opinionnaire in Figure 9.8, a well-coordinated STS study brings all this information back to the class, where costs and benefits can be assessed in light of "real" information.

Whether students are assessing contaminants in water or attitudes among citizens, they all learn the basic procedures that bring reliability to scientific study: sampling techniques, statistical analysis, and data representation. Mathematical principles

FIGURE 9.8   A Student-Designated Opinionnaire

Introduction

My name is David Connolly and I am collecting information about the effects the construction of Lyons Farms will have on the Chesapeake Bay and the stream adjacent to the farm. This information will be used for an Environmental Biology project which I am participating in at Easton High School. Your responses to these questions would be greatly appreciated.

Background

Age: __under 18   __18–25   __26–40   __41–65   __66+

How long have you been a resident near Lyons Farm?

    __less than 5 yrs.   __5–10 yrs.   __10–25 yrs.   __25+ yrs.

Item 1: Did you know there was a stream adjacent to the farm that links directly to the Chesapeake Bay?

    __Yes   __No

Item 2: What effects will the construction of Lyons Farms have on the stream?

__erosion of banks

__elimination of aquatic plants due to cloudy water

__elimination of frogs, fish, snails, etc., due to poor oxygen levels

__elimination of buffer strip*

__polluted runoff from cars due to increased traffic

Item 3: Of what benefit is the forest, wetland, and stream adjacent to the farm?

__provides food for animals   __provides homes for animals

__filters and absorbs pollutants   __controls erosion

__provides wind/storm protection   __controls flooding

__influences Chesapeake Bay health   __other _____

__don't know   __don't care

Item 4: To what extent do you believe the construction of Lyons Farms will affect the Chesapeake Bay?

1	2	3	4	5
Not at all	Slight extent	Moderate extent	Considerable extent	Great extent

Item 5: Do you believe there will be more damage done to the stream and Bay during or after construction?

    __during   __after

Item 6: Do you feel the development should be constructed?

    __Yes   __No

Item 7: Do you feel that the development will have a minimal impact on the area?

    __Yes   __No

Item 8: Do you feel the developers and residents can arrive at a compromise to benefit both parties?

    __Yes   __No

Thank you for your time!

Buffer Strip—Strip of trees surrounding a stream or river that filters and protects the water.

Developed by A. LeeAnn Hutchison and David Connolly, Easton High School, Easton, MD. Used with permission.

and procedures attain a certain vibrancy when used to support an emerging belief in the mind of a student. As they look at their data, students practice drawing inferences with different degrees of certainty, proposing general models of complex systems, and making decisions under uncertain conditions. STS science, as opposed to text-based science, makes students respect the lockstep procedures of math as a partial counterbalance to the roiling wash of public decision making. They may take greater care in analyzing numbers on a data sheet because they understand the risk involved in making human sense of any difficult question.

STS is infused with mathematics. Harold Hungerford and his colleagues (1992) in Illinois developed the data sheet in Figure 9.9 to represent the virtues of systematic data collection related to the "hot" question of recycling in different neighborhoods. Let us imagine that three groups of students living in three different neighborhoods were to develop and use this data collection sheet. If the respondents in Neighborhood A were twice as likely as those in Neighborhood B to reuse glass containers, wouldn't the student group in Neighborhood B carefully question the sampling procedures with some personal commitment, looking for sources of bias? Wouldn't they want to investigate the correlation between purchase of glass containers and recycling of glass containers as a ratio, hoping to reduce the perception of differences? Wouldn't they want to account for any differences that might appear between male and female recyclers in all neighborhoods as a source of the disparity? In short, students in all groups might become more interested in statistical procedures based in algebra than they would be in algebra as a construct of rules and procedures alone.

Under the new National Council for the Teaching of Mathematics (NCTM) standards, mathematics is seen as a problem-solving technique as well as a set of discrete skills and concepts. Some mathematics teachers have taken up the challenge and converted part of their efforts to teach math applications related to social issues.

This book prizes the work of teachers that have *created* outstanding interdisciplinary teaching strategies. The advantages of teacher-generated STS units are obvious. A teacher can construct an STS unit based on the interests and abilities of her or his students, aiming inquiry at locally "hot" issues. Teachers can build on elements of content they deem most important based on locally available resources. As designers and teachers, they can modify the plan as student discoveries warrant.

The Showcase for this chapter, for instance, takes us to City High School in Iowa City, Iowa, where Kevin Koepnick describes his STS work in a unit called, "From Minutemen to Star Wars; from Chernobyl to Yucca Flats: A High School Nuclear Chemistry Unit. However, fully developed STS curricula are also available, some of which were developed by teachers whose efforts are made more prominent through national dissemination and/or commercial outlets; so are books and workshops that guide teachers through the process of designing and field testing new STS units. Experience with a packaged unit could lead a teacher to design and develop other STS units, perhaps in association with an STS workshop.

Prepackaged STS Unit Plans

Prepackaged STS-based units are widely available. In addition, units developed by funded projects and development centers can be found in ERIC. Other development centers have received federal or foundation funding to support the development and implementation of new science curricula. For example, federally funded National Diffusion Network (NDN) (1994) centers are located in every state in the country, and make information available on exemplary K–12 curriculum and instructional practices. Driving the information highway (Chapter 7) includes a description of another NDN program—Fish Banks, Ltd. Tapping into existing NDN projects and unit plans is easily done by calling their toll free number (800-659-5004).

FIGURE 9.9   Data Sheet Designed to Support Comparisons

ITEMS	Population of Neighborhood A.		Population of Neighborhood B.		Population of Neighborhood C.		Totals	
Glass and Metal Questionnaire Data Summary Sheet								
Number of Males Responding								
Number of Females Responding								
Average Number of People per Household								
Groceries (Not Beverages) Purchased in Metal Cans	Yes	No	Yes	No	Yes	No	Yes	No
Beverages Purchased in Metal Containers								
Beverages Purchased in Glass Containers								
% of glass reusable =								
% of glass thrown-away =								
% of cans thrown-away =								
% of cans recycled =								
% of throw-away glass thrown away =								
% of throw-away glass recycled =								
Has any family member requested grocers to stock only reusable containers?	Yes	No	Yes	No	Yes	No	Yes	No

Adapted with permission from Hungerford, H. R., Litherland, R., Peyton, B., Ramsey, J., and Volk, T. (1992). *Investigating and evaluating environmental issues and actions*. Champaign, IL: Stipes Publishing.

NDN programs are clearly interdisciplinary, introducing students to the differences and relationships between science, technology, and society. What is especially worth noting is the NDN emphasis on teaching students the *technical skills* needed to investigate issues: information processing, survey design and conduct, data collection and analysis, drawing of inferences and conclusions. Indeed, this program is aptly described as a *skill development curriculum* which is "... designed to teach students how to investigate and evalaute STS-related issues.?

The Engineering Concepts Curriculum Project (ECCP), developed at the Polytechnic Institute of Brooklyn in the early 1970s, introduced scientific concepts in an engineering context. Featuring a text, *Activities Approach to the "Man-Made World,"* it showed high school students how systematic analysis (logic circuit boards, optimization and algorithms, system modeling, game theory) and technology could help solve human problems—population explosion; famines; water, thermo, and air pollution (Polytechnic Institute of Brooklyn, no date). In the ECCP project, science takes a back seat to engineering design. Wasn't it really trying to get high school students interested in becoming engineers? The ECCP program, provided a logically structured and rigorous "tour" of engineering technology, and in many ways was a frontrunner to the large-scale STS projects of today. However, it never found a niche in the high school curriculum because it competed for instructional time with in-place physical science courses and the perception that it was too difficult for many students.

Professional organizations also have had a hand in developing STS curricula. ChemCom, or "Chemistry in the Community," is a chemistry curriculum developed with support from the American Chemical Society. A popular alternative to a traditional chemistry course, it offers what it terms a "balanced" view of chemistry, showing how it interfaces with society and technology, and how it will serve students in the "real world" they live in. Nevertheless, ChemCom suffers from the perception among *some* science educators that it, along with STS programs in general, are for the "less-able" students, while "better" students take *real* science courses. Advertising for ChemCom (Promotional brochure, 1994) focuses on the audience for the course and why it makes sense:

> Are you teaching chemistry to less than 5% of your students? You could be. Most of your students—95% for that matrter—are not planning careers in chemistry or even science. Most chemistry courses are taught as a prerequisite to college chemistry and do not serve the majority of the students taking the course. For them, this is the only chemistry course they will ever take. So, don't miss this opportunity to make them literate, life-long science learners, too.

Clearly, ChemCom aims to produce scientific literates rather than science majors. Whether these choices are mutually exclusive is still a real question.

Although the table of contents for ChemCom's brochure is strikingly different from what most of us remember from traditional high school chemistry, the text covers almost all traditional chemical concepts. It also more accurately reflects the substance of contemporary chemical science, including biochemistry, polymer chemistry, and nuclear science. The curriculum has activity-oriented units entitled: Supplying Our Water Needs; Conserving Chemical Resources; Petroleum: To Build or to Burn?; Understanding Food; Nuclear Chemistry in Our World; Chemistry, Air, and Climate; Chemistry and Health; and The Chemical Industry: Promise and Challenge.

Student activities for the ChemCom curriculum focus on the process of scientific problem solving, the hallmark of all STS teaching. Activities guide students in applying their knowledge of chemistry and ask them to consider the following components (ChemCom, 1994):

- Analyze the issue
- Identify and define questions of concern
- Generate a list of alternatives

- Weigh burdens and benefits
- Seek and process any new information
- Reweigh burdens and benefits
- Commit to a decision
- Implement decision (with contingency plan)

Concerns about the STS Approach

Although STS may be "the hottest game in town" for many within the science teaching community, the movement also has its detractors. Some teachers see the STS approach as great for the average to below average student, but less rigorous and desirable for the college bound student, particularly those oriented toward science and engineering. Some science teachers, trained under National Science Foundation (NSF) stipends to teach science curriculum, such as BSCS, IPS, PSII, ESCP, CHEM Study, still believe that those programs represented the zenith of U.S. science curriculum development. For some of them, STS is seen as "dumbing down" the science our best students will need to function in the twenty-first century. In the absence of agreement on what constitutes reasoned inquiry, STS could become the platform for interests that are anti-science, anti-technology and even anti-social, creating a podium for passionate naysayers and Neo-Luddites (Shamos, 1993). Other educators see STS programs as potentially self-serving and are wary of them for that reason.

Criticism within the science education community has been directed at the need to keep clear the distinctions between *technology* and *science*. Perhaps the most forceful perspective comes from J. Myron Atkin, a respected science educator at Stanford University. He argues that one possible motive for elevating technology to prominence in our schools is an economic one (i.e., to respond to global competitiveness) (Atkin, 1990, p. 32). Before we look at specific approaches to introducing technology into the school, he (Atkin, 1990, p. 34) would have us first decide whether we want to do so:

> One difference between science and technology is that in science one seeks generalizations, the fewer the better. Part of the beauty of science is to comprehend the ubiquitousness and applicability of its fundamental insights. Newton's Three Laws are eminently serviceable in thousands of contexts; therein lies their elegance and power. In technology, on the other hand, there are often dozens of answers to a given problem. There is no one best pull-toy for toddlers, or stage set for a school production, or reading light for the bedroom, or baby's feeding chair, or ventilation for a greenhouse, or method of distributing newspapers.

In this view, "What's true?" is the question that guides science. "What works?" is the question that guides technology (see Chapter 1). Although both may share some interest in the same issues, science and technology are strongly motivated to move in different directions.

Managing Rough Spots in STS

For many teachers, especially those who teach science, an STS approach makes sense as a means of transforming the American secondary school. The intensity with which this approach is pursued can range from a year-long course like ChemCom, one or more units like Kevin Koepnick's during the school year, or selected activities inserted from time to time. Charlotte D. Sherman, a Vermont secondary school teacher who has used an STS approach for many years, offers these suggestions for first-time STS teachers:

1. Never force (instill) your personal views on students.
2. Reach out to colleagues and the community for help in the conduct of STS instruction (i.e., don't be a "loner").
3. Acknowledge, up front, that you may not be informed on a particular issue to be investigated with your students.
4. Whenever possible, "go with the flow" of what students and the community find important—don't resurrect issues that have peaked and are no longer perceived as vital to the community.
5. Spend the time necessary to learn about a topic, and don't rush for coverage when the material dictates greater attention.
6. Switch an instructional plan midstream when the initial direction of inquiry is not working—have alternative activities in mind.
7. Don't give out "inquiry" assignments without providing guidance or play "Guess what's on in my mind?" with your students.

Teaching within an STS framework, like teaching in any integrating context, changes the nature of teaching and increases the demand on teachers for supportive, as opposed to directive, teaching techniques.

Assessing STS Instruction

Assessment in an STS framework may cause some concern. It would be surprising if students in an STS course scored higher than students in text-based courses on text-based examinations. Current evidence does suggest that students and teachers in STS classrooms gain respect for science; become aware of scientific processes, concepts, and applications; and affirm creative skills in asking questions, proposing causes, and predicting consequences as a result of their experience (Yager, Tamir, & Kellerman, 1994).

Aikenhed and Ryan (1993) describe the VOSTS Project *(Views on Science, Technology, and Society)* in Canada that has assembled a complete item pool for assessing changing student conceptions of science, technology and society. Information is available from: VOSTS Project, Curriculum Studies, University of Saskatoon, Saskatoon, Canada S7N OWO. Other research also suggests that STS may help reduce the gender gap that makes science less attractive to female students (Blunck, Giles, & McArthur, 1993).

A varied approach to student assessment appears most promising (Cheek, 1992). Student research reports would clearly have a place in any portfolio-based system, as student presentations could fit assessments based on "performances." Essay tests would appear appropriate if the questions aim at connections between science, technology and social change. Multiple choice tests would appear useful if they were designed as case analysis items. Under the best of conditions, the studies developed in STS student projects and the recommendations developed by students in STS classes can be assessed by a wide audience of adults interested in the issues being raised. Under those conditions, student learning will be assessed using the following adult criteria:

1. Is the event accurately described?
2. Are the issues clear?
3. Do the fact/findings clarify the situation?
4. Are the methods reliable?
5. Are the conclusions valid?
6. Is the recommended decision useful?
7. Is the recommendation politically palatable?

Whether or not a student can make a decision stick, having their work taken seriously is an appropriate welcome into the adult world.

STS SHOWCASE

From Minutemen to Star Wars:
From Chernobyl to Yucca Flats:
A High School Nuclear Chemistry Unit

Kevin Koepnick
City High School, Iowa City, IA

The news came through slowly at first: rumors about elevated levels of radioactive particles in rainfall in eastern Europe; evacuations in central Ukraine; finally, acknowledgment by the Soviet government that an accident had occurred at a nuclear power station near a little-known Ukrainian town called Chernobyl.

The past decade has seen a revolution in science teaching. Historically, science had been seen as a body of facts to be assimilated by students for later regurgitation on standardized multiple choice tests and then promptly forgotten. This long record of futility led to our current population of relative science illiterates, citizens unable to evaluate the plausibility and significance of the many science and technology-oriented issues and stories presented each night on the evening news. The Science/Technology/Society (STS) movement has attempted to revamp science education, moving away from encyclopedic facts and toward the science practiced by scientists, a system of solving problems through careful examination of nature. STS promotes the study of the problems modern science and technology present for society; problems like what to do about nuclear power.

The Chernobyl accident captured students' imaginations and concerns. They came to class with questions about nuclear power plants, weather patterns, health, cancer therapy, and bombs (Figure 9.10 shows an issues worksheet). The time was right to develop an STS unit. Many approaches to opening such a unit have been discussed, but the consensus seems to be that STS units should be centered around students' past experiences, current interests, and future needs as citizens. Three questions seem to be critical.

Each time the nuclear chemistry unit has been taught, students were asked, first, what they already knew about nuclear energy. The responses to this question provide the instructor guidance not only regarding what students already know, but also what misconceptions they need to overcome. Typical responses have been:

- "It comes from atoms."
- "It's dangerous."
- "It was wrong to bomb Hiroshima."
- "$E = mc^2$ . . . whatever that means."
- "You can make electricity with it."
- "The waste is dangerous."
- "It makes really big bombs.

The next question is, "What do you think you ought to know about nuclear energy?" This question is important because it allows students to think as adults and citizens, considering not only what high school science students ought to know, but what responsible voters should understand. Some common responses have been:

Showcase materials used with permission from Kevin Koepnick, kevkoep@chop. isca.uiowa.edu.

FIGURE 9.10   Issues in Nuclear Chemistry—The Nuclear Winter Hypothesis

Use the space provided to respond to the following questions regarding Carl Sagan's article "The Nuclear Winter."

1. According to the World Health Organization, how many people might be expected to suffer death or serious injury as a direct result of a nuclear exchange?

2. Scientists are generally very conservative when making predictions of future events. Why might this practice not be the best approach when predicting the after-effects of a nuclear war?

3. Explain the origin of the "nuclear winter" hypothesis.

4. What would be some of the effects of a "nuclear winter" on living things?

5. What affect does the size of a nuclear exchange have on climatic effects?

6. Many politicians advocating further arms build-up are labeled as "conservatives," while those in favor of arms reduction are called "liberal." In this case, how do the labels fit the facts?

- "What atoms are"
- "How bombs are made"
- "Who has the bomb?"
- "How and when are nuclear weapons used?"
- "Where are nuclear power plants located?"
- "Where is nuclear waste stored?"

The final question opens up room for simple curiosity, asking, "What would you like to know about nuclear energy?" (See Figure 9.11 for a way to review issues.) Responses to this question have included:

- "Is our electricity nuclear?"
- "Are there any nuke plants around here?"
- "What happens to the waste?"
- "Are there any bombs around here?"
- "Is Iowa City a target?"
- "Why did we bomb Japan?"
- "Why is our town a nuclear-free zone?"

The history of the nuclear age is introduced by having the students read an article from *Science 84* on the people involved in the Manhattan Project (Lightman, 1984). We then view the award-winning film *The Day after Trinity*. To bring students up to date, PBS's NOVA program, "Nuclear Strategy for Beginners," takes beginning strategists through the events of the Cold War up to the time of Star Wars and deterrence. Three main activities bring up some of the realities of nuclear war. "Drop the Bomb!" asks students to target a number of cities for destruction, using fifty Minuteman III missiles, each with three warheads (see Figure 9.12). Because the students know little about Soviet cities, we target U.S. cities. "Current Nuclear Armaments" has students refer to sources, such as *The Nuclear Weapons Data Book* (Cochran, 1984), to prepare capsule summaries of weapons systems such as the Poseidon sub, Minuteman III, and Air-Launched Cruise Missile. Finally, the nuclear winter hypothesis (Sagan, 1983) is introduced and explored as a possible deterrent which all countries must respect.

Once students are concerned with the possibilities of nuclear energy, it's time they learned about the nature of the atom and the ways in which energy is released. The second phase of the unit has students doing labs and readings about atomic structure. Lab activities include a shielding experiment in which students use radioactive sources and Geiger counters to determine which forms of radiation can pass through which substances and making inferences about particle size and speed. Rutherford's experiment is simulated using a computer (Rittenhouse, 1988) and again by rolling marbles at a fixed target. The old "Black Box" experiment is performed, asking students to infer the contents of a sealed box by manipulating it from the outside. All of these labs are intended to demonstrate the idea that atomic structure is inferred from evidence rather than observed directly. Finally, some of the applications of special relativity are brought up, notably the energy–matter relationship—$E = mc^2$.

FIGURE 9.11   Sample Activity: Basic Knowledge-Review and Reflection

---

Name _____

Section _____

Basic Chemistry Issues in Nuclear Energy to Cleave an Atom

Use the accompanying article to answer each of the following questions.

1. How was the atom pictured prior to the discovery of the electron? How did the discovery of the electron call the old ideas into question?

2. Describe Rutherford's experiment. Explain the evidence for his conclusions.

3. Describe Bohr's "drop of liquid" analogy for the process of nuclear fission.

4. Why is nuclear energy so much more potent than any form of energy known before?

5. What do you think the author means when he speaks of "abstracting" the danger of nuclear arms away?

FIGURE 9.12   Drop the Bomb!

You are in command of fifty (50) Minuteman III missiles, each equipped with 3-W78 nuclear reentry vehicles with a total yield of 1005 kilotons (or about one megaton). Your total available yield is roughly 50 megatons.

Your objective is to maximize civilian casualties by targeting your missiles to destroy as much of these cities as possible. We will assume the destructive area of a one megaton explosion is 80 km^2.

Target your missiles, but *do not* fill-in the "Deaths" column. When you are done, your teacher will help you complete the activity.

From the work of Jan Wielert, Iowa City West High School. Used with permission.

The third phase of the unit applies the energy-producing aspect of nuclear energy as students explore the risks and benefits of nuclear power. After reading and hearing about the design of nuclear power reactors, students are given the chance to operate their own station via computer simulation. Of the simulations available, Berggren's (1980) is the most useful due to its simplicity and very low (free) cost. Students evaluate their own performance and then read and discuss the problems of high-level waste disposal. The video used with this part of the unit is the NOVA program "Back to Chernobyl."

Students are asked to explore their own opinions on some issue in nuclear energy as they prepare the second trimester position paper. Any nuclear-related issue is fine. In the paper, students are expected to define the issue, discuss opposing points of view, explain the science needed to make a responsible decision, and explain their own position. The position paper takes the place of the exam for this unit.

Many wonderful movies have been made about issues of the nuclear age. Some, like *Fail-Safe,* are tense dramas about nuclear disaster. Others, like *Dr. Strangeglove,* are comic masterpieces. Still others, *Testament* and *Amazing Grace and Chuck* in particular, explore human issues in the nuclear age. We bring these films together in the "Nuclear Film Festival." Students who come in after school to watch one or more of the movies—*China Syndrome, The Hunt for Red October, Search for the Super,* and so on—are awarded extra credit. Typically, a dozen movies are scheduled during the months of January and February.

Each year, the nuclear chemistry unit has been different. Students' interests change as the issues in the news change. Certainly, the basic core activities are still important, but the context within which we operate shifts. During the first year, most discussions and many position papers concerned the problems of nuclear power stations. Another year, intermediate-range ballistic missiles in Europe dominated. During the Gulf War, students were very interested in modern weapons systems, and, after the *Exxon Valdez* oil spill, the emphasis was on pollution and long-term storage of radioactive waste.

The nuclear chemistry unit is just one attempt to address the needs of students who will live, work, and vote in an age of ever-increasing scientific and technological complexity. Many other STS units, designed around the experiences, needs, and interests of students, are also needed to continue the revolution leading to scientific literacy.

References

Berggren, S. R. (1980). Apple nuclear power plant. *Creative Computing,* (December): 130–137.

Cochran, T., Arkin, W., and Hoenig, A. (1984). *The nuclear weapons data book.* Cambridge, MA: Ballinger Publishing.

Department of Energy. (1990). *Annual report to congress.* Washington, DC: Office of Civilian Radioactive Waste Management.

Department of Energy. (1987). *Progress report on the scientific investigation program for the Nevada Yucca Mountain side.* Washington, DC: Office of Civilian Radioactive Waste Management.

Department of Energy. (1987). *Atoms to electricity.* Washington, DC: U.S. DOE Assistant Secretary for Nuclear Energy, Office of Support Programs.

Koepnick, K. (1991). Issues in nuclear chemistry: A high school STS module. In D. W. Cheek (Ed.), *Broadening participation in science, technology, and medicine: Proceedings of the Sixth Annual Technological Literacy Conference.* Washington, DC, February 1–3. Bloomington, IN: ERIC Clearinghouse for Social Studies/Social Science Education.

League of Women Voters. (1985). *The nuclear waste primer.* New York: Nick Lyons Books.

Lightman, A. P. (1984). To cleave an atom. *Science 84,* 5(9):103–108.

Mayers, T. K. (1986). *Understanding nuclear weapons and arms control.* Washington, DC: Pergamon-Brassey's International Defense Publishers.

Rittenhouse, R. C. (1988). "Alpha-Scatter." *JCE: Software,* Vol. 1A:1. Washington, DC: Division of Chemical Education of the American Chemical Society.

Sagan, C. (1983). The nuclear winter. *Parade Magazine,* October 30:4–7.

CHAPTER 10

Learning to Work

Experiential Learning

> *Can I solve the problem I have set? Do I like what I get when I solve this problem? Have I made the situation coherent? Have I made it congruent with my fundamental values and theories? Have I kept inquiry moving?*
> Donald Schon, *The Reflective Practitioner*

Is experience really the best teacher? Not in and of itself. Experience becomes useful in learning in connection with clear purpose, access to new knowledge, interaction with others, and opportunities to reflect with guidance. As Gish (1979) states:

> Learning can be seen as a process in which a person experiences something directly (not vicariously), reflects on the experience as something new or as related to other experiences, develops some concepts by which to name the experience and connect it with other experiences, and uses the concept in subsequent actions as a guide for behavior.

Devoid of an organizing context, experience in the world offers no more intrinsic value than experience in a classroom. Like classroom teaching of the worst sort, it can be random, uninspiring, disjunctive, confusing, and essentially meaningless.

To become meaningful, experience has to be incorporated into a problem-solving framework, in which students take stock of what they know, gather more knowledge and skills, and put both to work on making a difference in the situation they face. Youth apprenticeship and service learning are both forms of experiential learning that achieve form and purpose in a problem-solving framework.

David Kolb's experiential learning cycle has provided a general framework for service learning and apprenticeship learning for several years (Kolb, 1976). In Kolb's cycle, *concrete experience* provides the impetus for learning and the test of its accomplishment, challenging students to respond as adults. Through *reflective observation,* students begin to recognize the skills that are required for success in real settings and adjust their learning to attain that success. Using *abstract conceptualization,* they begin to understand the connection between knowing things and doing well, recognizing rules and general procedures that pertain to real problems. Through *active experimentation,* they adapt their understanding to fit the shifting demands of a job-in-progress, testing and refining the knowledge they have gained. (See Figure 10.1.) Bernice McCarthy adapted Kolb's cycle as a guide to her 4MAT system that is described in the Thinking Strategies Showcase in Chapter 5. In this chapter, the same cycle guides students toward learning on the job or in service to their communities. In Kolb's learning cycle, experience anchors a process of continuous reflection, guiding students to gain knowledge and learn how to use it, whether they are working on their own or within a formal class.

FIGURE 10.1   David Kolb's Experiential Learning Process

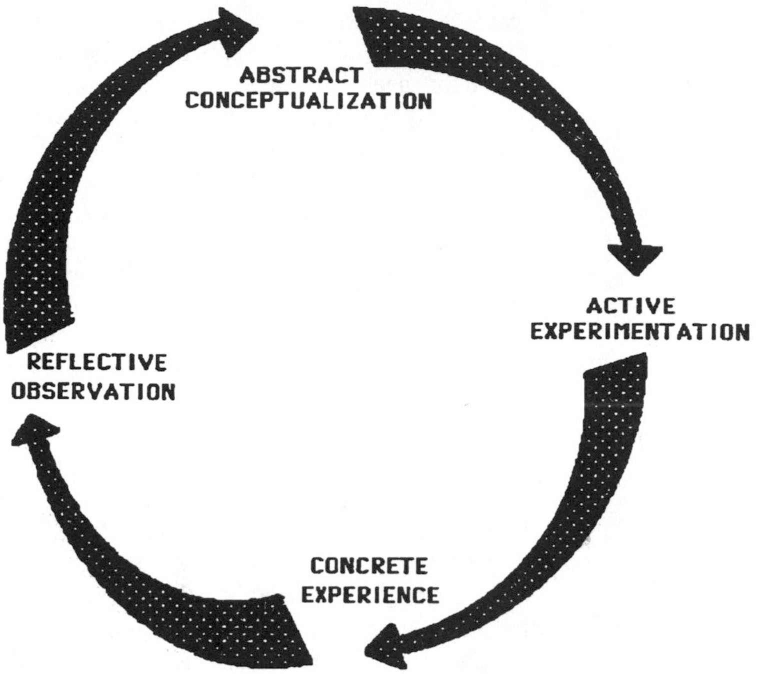

From Gish, G. (1979). The learning cycle. *Synergist,* National Student Volunteer Program (ACTION). Washington, D.C.

Leaving School to Learn

Service learning programs and work apprenticeships are emerging as a response to the perceived isolation of high school students from the challenges of the surrounding community. Whether in work or service, representatives from the world of work or service are creating partnerships with schools that anchor learning to real problems. As young adults, high school students face a developmental imperative to show themselves as competent, not in the narrow confines of school life, but in the society at large. Working in service to their community or learning on the job site, high school students may gain a perspective on their own abilities that no high school classroom can offer.

For nearly one hundred years, a high school education has given young people a chance to suspend their involvement in the community while they assembled enough knowledge and skill to survive as adults. Bolstered by child-labor laws during the last century, high schools have protected young people from the depredations of labor recruiters so that all U.S. citizens would have the same opportunity to develop to their full potential. By mandating school enrollment to the age of sixteen, the states and the nation created a partial sanctuary for young people against exploitation in the adult world and against intrusive requests from the community outside school walls.

With some notable exceptions in vocational education, the high school curriculum became preparatory and preliminary to involvement in the community, without strong connections to that community that would ensure a good fit between initial preparation and later readiness. As an increasing number of young people remained in high school to complete a diploma, the period of their isolation from adult interaction also grew longer. Apart from reducing stress in the labor market, isolation of young people from the adult world has had an unintended secondary effect. Young people themselves have no vantage point from which they can view their academic learning and assess their own trajectory into the adult world. Good grades may be a motivator for some aspiring students, but the quest for grades has little to do with the quest for meaningful learning.

Deprived of meaningful connections with the adult world, many high school students see no meaning in the rituals of their days in school. Without connection to situations in which knowing something really makes a difference, many lose the incentive to know much at all. They may comply with the requirements that have descended on them out of history, course distribution requirements, Carnegie units, college, vocational and general tracks and still see no compelling purpose to their school work. At home, bombarded by reports from the outside world—war, famine, poverty, rebellion—young people may experience a vague, tingling sensation suggesting that something big is going on out there without recognizing how their own lives intersect with world affairs or how their current effort will play out in future opportunity.

Undeniably, big things are going on out there. Problems are legion. The stakes are enormous. If young people grow aware of the problems that surround them without also learning how they can solve complex problems, they are apt to feel both helpless and passionately frustrated. Requiring young people to remain passive when they are most anxious to become engaged deprives them of access to their aspiration, and ours as well, to become self-directed learners capable of recognizing and solving problems wherever they encounter them. Young people have been forced into the spectator section at the very moment in their lives when they need to test their skills against realities. For many, suspending involvement in work and the community until after high school graduation makes the leap from passive learning to active engagement impossible. For high school students whose programs integrate work or service and learning, the transition to adult involvement is more gentle and manageable. Students who learn to apply high school learning to the work setting carry with them a continuing respect for the connection between work and learning as they enter the rapidly changing work force.

Involvement Is the Key

Involvement is the key to learning, whether learning takes place in the classroom or the streets. John Dewey saw engagement in experience as essential to learning and to a democratic way of life. From his perspective, separating a growing human mind from the world where the individual would have to make a place was educationally self-defeating and retrograde to the needs of a society requiring broad participation from all citizens. The following is Robertson's (1992) summary of Dewey's (1929) thoughts:

> The mind is within the world as a part of the latter's own ongoing process. It is marked off as mind by the fact that wherever it is found, changes take place in a directed way. . . . From knowing as an outside beholding to knowing as an active participant in the drama of an ongoing world is the historical transition whose record we have been following.

A spectator is essentially helpless. In action we gain insight and power. When we direct our mental energy toward real situations, we engage all our talents and become capable of creative ingenuity.

Involvement in work or service has long been a feature of extracurricular activities in high schools. School newspapers, drama clubs, and even football teams put students at the center of a planned activity, then ask others to come and view the learning that has occurred. The effects of involvement appear to be long lasting. Participation in noncurricular learning has been associated with a wide variety of positive effects: higher self-esteem, improved race relations, educational aspiration, community involvement, and higher academic achievement, at least among males (Holland & Andre, 1987). The degree and quality of involvement appear to influence the degree to which these effects are obtained. Programs in service learning or work apprenticeship aim to capture the positive effects of active, extracurricular activities and use them to support learning within the existing curriculum.

Service Learning: Making a Difference

In July of 1992, the State of Maryland became the first to mandate service learning as an aspect of the high school curriculum (see Figure 10.2). State codes now require seventy-five hours of service prior to graduation, including reflective seminars and classes. Given the choice of adopting a statewide service curriculum or designing a response to the mandate for themselves, all 24 districts in the state chose to design their own approach to fit the needs of their local communities. As they began to

FIGURE 10.2   Maryland's Required Community Service Program

Some Questions and Answers

1. *What is the community service learning requirement and when does it go into effect?*
   a) Seventy-five hours of community service that includes preparation, action, and reflection components, perhaps beginning in the middle grades, or
   b) A locally designed program in student service that has been approved by the state superintendent of schools.

2. *What will my child get out of fulfilling the service requirement?*
   Service learning will help awaken students to the great potential they have to make a difference in their schools and community. Students involved in service increase their teamwork and problem-solving skills, as well as leadership and initiative. Their self-respect increases as they see that they can tackle tough problems and succeed.

3. *Won't the requirement take class time away from the basics?*
   . . . One of the most exciting aspects of service learning is that it helps students understand how different subjects fit together in the real world and helps them see the significance of their classes. Service learning moves instruction from X's and O's on the chalkboard and puts them in the game.

4. *How will schools deal with liability and transportation problems?*
   . . . In some cases students will be able to fulfill their service requirement without leaving the school—they will serve each other through peer mediation and tutoring programs. In cases where students are permitted to leave school to perform service, the host agency is being asked to provide proof of insurance coverage, supervision of students while on site and training for students.

5. *How will students receiving special education services be affected?*
   Students receiving special education services are expected to fulfill this graduation requirement. A student's ARD committee can, however, decide not to include service learning in a student's individual educational plan.

6. *Who will be responsible to make sure that my child meets the requirement?*
   Ultimately, your child is responsible for meeting the requirement. Each school district, however, will help by providing opportunities to engage in service in the school, by accepting service performed at outside organizations, and by keeping a cumulative record of hours of service.

Selected from the Service Learning Requirement of the Maryland Department of Education.

design service learning components for their curricula, 90 percent of the districts chose to integrate service learning with courses in their existing academic program. Some schools have developed stand-alone courses for service learning, while others have made service a component of the English, social studies, math, or science courses. The Maryland Student Service Alliance is a state Department of Education agency that offers seminars to teachers and promotes the development of programs connected to the state's service needs.

Julie Ayers at the Maryland Student Service Alliance describes service learning both in "stand-alone courses" and in regular courses from the academic curriculum:

Stand-alone: Ida Hines at Douglas High School in Baltimore offers a stand-alone course on peer mediation. Her students take classes in conflict management, and then offer to intervene in disagreements at the school.

Technology: David Brown at Westminster High School has integrated a project on storm drains called "Danger in the Chesapeake" with his regular drafting and architectural drawing course.

Applied Arts: Hope Shannon at Chesapeake High School in Maryland has adapted her home economics course to include a "meals-on-wheels" program for elderly citizens; and Norma Cole at Sayer-Harvard Institute has instituted an "adopt-a-high-rise" program, bringing students in her alternative high school to serve residents of local housing projects.

Sciences: Joan Johns of Northern High School in Baltimore has focused her environmental science course on local initiatives, which now include an urban garden project, an adopt-a-highway project, and a neighborhood recycling program in which her students act as block captains.

English: Joey Hoffman at Middletown School in Maryland has incorporated tutor training with some of her English courses and developed agreements with local elementary and middle schools to tutor in reading and writing.

The impulse to integrate is compelling. Work in a nursing home can support a course on modern history. Work on a neighborhood newspaper can challenge students in a high school journalism course. Environmental cleanup campaigns can provide artifacts for analysis in a anthropology course. Putting high school learning to public use is sometimes as simple as finding an adult audience for the work that high school students have done. Virtually all the curriculum projects described in the chapters on problem-based learning and science/technology/society (STS) have potential value as service to the community.

Over several years, Marie McNamara at Brookline High School in Massachusetts developed a comprehensive program in service learning organized and led by her students. She teaches one or two sections of a course for peer leaders that may subsequently involve more than 400 volunteers working in teams led by her leaders. Her course prepares students to assume responsibility for service activities in any one of the social service agencies in the Boston area. Her students conduct needs assessments, plan activities, recruit volunteers, manage service activities, evaluate progress, and arrange special events for local hospitals, food banks, shelters, and museums. Her class meetings are dedicated to developing the skills students will need to lead any complex endeavor. (See Figures 10.3a and 10.3b.)

Service learning thrusts young people into adult roles under circumstances that would be challenging for any of us. Social problems and social needs remain abstract and distant until one of us steps in to try and make a difference. Problems arise; they need creative solutions. Personalities influence success and failure; differences must be accommodated. Groups of more than two require steady attention to remain vibrant and effective. Factors in the setting may intervene at any time to confuse and divert us from the purpose. In making a difference in the lives of others, high school students also explore their own capabilities and stretch themselves to fit the task at hand. Patience, inquiry, and durable goodwill are not the least of the knowledge generated by hands-on learning that counts in one's own community.

FIGURE 10.3a   A Sampler of Student-Led Service Groups in Brookline, Massachusetts

Kids and Schools

Lincoln Little Brother and Sister Program—Students meet one-on-one with a needy K–3 child, two hours a week, flexible hours

Peer Buddies—Volunteers serve as teacher aids, job coaches, and lunch companions to buddies during the school day

Extended Day Program Homework Centers—Student volunteers mentor and tutor elementary school children at the schools and community centers

Building Friendships—Volunteers work with special buddies on weekends in group settings in a variety of activities

Project Star and Project Kinship—Students volunteer to entertain for one hour a week or do food shopping for HIV-infected kids

The Elderly and Disabled

Spaulding Rehabilitation Hospital—Volunteer service may include patient transport, radiology, physical therapy, and book or craft carts

Nursing Homes—Students pay friendly visits to the elderly

Discovery Shop—Students merchandise new and used goods, sorting, pricing, selling, and creating displays

Samarateens—Trained volunteers answer suicide hotline, managing calls on suicide depression, incest and abuse, drug and alcohol problems, offering support and comfort to teens in crisis

Homelessness and Hunger

American Red Cross Pantry—Volunteers bag food for needy families on Tuesday afternoons and Saturday

Shattuck Shelter—Volunteers bake desserts and visit residents three Tuesdays per month

Boston Food Bank—Volunteers salvage food for pantries and shelters 2:00 to 4:00 on Thursdays

Environment

Recycling—Students recycle paper and cans for the high school, during X block

Live Animal Center—Students clean cages and take wild animals for exercise at the Museum of Science

Each group was coordinated by leaders trained in Marie McNamara's class at Brookline High School, Brookline, MA. Used with permission.

FIGURE 10.3b   Community Service Leadership Seminar

Goals

Peer leaders enrolled in this course will organize a service activity for Brookline High School student volunteers:

- assessing community needs and determining service goals for the year
- experiencing field-based learning while exploring career opportunities
- developing and utilizing leadership skills in team discussion and reflection
- gaining a broad understanding of the complexities and interconnectedness of crucial issues related to our greatest societal needs, preparing to become informed and active citizens

Outline

INTRODUCTION: COURSE EXPECTATIONS
Student self-assessment
Community needs assessment

SERVICE EXPECTATIONS
Agency needs
Student needs

AGENCY INTERVIEWS
Compile agency data
Define orientation, training, evaluation, and volunteer recognition

LEADERSHIP SKILLS
Leader responsibilities
Team-building skills
Group meeting skills
Authority skills
Feedback, problem-solving, and decision-making skills

RECRUITMENT
Informing students
Task overview: Contact with agencies, faculty updates, contracts, and club dues, groups meeting schedules, bulletin boards, and volunteer recognition

PLACEMENT AND ORIENTATION
Interviews, contracts, and expectations (50 hours = .25 credit; 100 hours = .5 credit; 200+ hours = 1 credit)

REFLECTION
Via writing and group discussion (Weekly journals, Quarterly Reflection papers, Portfolio Development, and Agency Issues Discussions)

EVENT PLANNING
Fund-raisers and other events that will benefit an organization of their choice.

Evaluation

Seminar participation (20%); Service and Leadership (40%); Weekly journals (20%); Quarterly Paper and Portfolio (20%)

From class materials for Marie McNamara's class at Brookline High School, Brookline, MA. Used with permission.

Learning on the Job: Youth Apprenticeships

In the expanding global marketplace, the nature of work has changed. Surely, new technologies have reduced the number of jobs in which one worker with one machine made one part of a product. Now, even production workers must accommodate computerized design, manufacturing, and quality-control technologies. As Berryman (1988) states, the change in work, however, is also one of quality:

> Productivity gains are coming as much from changing the way workers work together, their orientation towards their work, and the nature of their responsibility and involvement in the firm's changing strategy and orientation to the market as from applications of new technology.

Learning to become part of a team that works toward a common goal, organizes to recognize and solve problems, and adapts quickly to changing circumstances may best occur on the job site.

Now, high schools across the country are investigating partnerships with local industry, aimed at preparing a work force capable of filling highly skilled/high-paying jobs in business and industry. To succeed, programs in work-based learning must avoid the kind of vocational training aimed at one specific job—a job that is likely to be either dead-end or obsolescent—and find ways to use specific job experiences to teach generalizable work skills linked to emerging fields and emerging technologies. Clearly, to adapt to the information age, workers in any context will need a broad array of higher-level cognitive skills, as well as specific technical knowledge, that they can apply to a shifting panorama of work-based problems. Research suggests that new jobs for high school graduates will require higher levels of problem-solving skill than current jobs. In particular, workers will need to manage various computer-based operations in which they must manipulate symbols in a computerized plan rather than objects on a production bench (Berryman, 1993).

The U.S. secondary school curriculum is too closely tied to the curriculum of higher education (Bailey, 1993a). The purpose, tone, structure, and standards for high school learning all derive from the link to higher education, despite the fact that less than half of the students in our high schools will go on to a four-year degree. For students moving toward work rather than college, the relationship between school learning and the work setting is nonexistent. The college-prep curriculum connects nicely to the college curriculum; high school programs that do not aim toward college connect to nothing in the future. Neither students nor their prospective employers believe that success in high school courses bears some relationship to success on the job. Few employers peruse transcripts as a step in hiring. Few recruit in school settings. Nevertheless, employers complain actively that high school graduates do not enter the work force with even the basic skills needed for success on the job (Byrne, Constant, & Moore, 1993).

Part of the past success of U.S. business can be attributed to a production line model of work that reduces the scope of worker responsibility to a single station on the line, for which little training is necessary and from which little learning is possible. Fast-food chains have "dumbed down" their cash registers to fit the lowest common denominator—a part-time worker who can recognize the image of a hamburger but not read the word. As long as we could compete successfully using turn-of-the-century manufacturing methods and low-skilled workers, vocational training could follow the same path. Vocational students mastered a catalogue of discrete work skills and then applied for positions in factories needing one or two of those skills. If it ever existed at all, the link has been broken between generalized skill training in school and specific skill application on the job. High school students, who recognize that they are preparing for no work in particular except low paying jobs, may be expected to exhibit a profound disinterest in school-based learning that offers little and goes no where.

In 1993, the Secretary's Commission on Achieving Necessary Skills (SCANS) produced a report for the U.S. Department of Labor entitled "What Work Requires of Schools: A SCANS Report for America 2000" (see Figure 10.4). The basic skills described in that report offer nothing new to education. The five competencies necessary for high productivity, however, underscore the need for new workers who can help solve problems in a real-life setting. Some of these flexible competencies can be achieved using problem-based learning or STS techniques (see Chapters 8 and 9). In Fort Worth, for example, a high school science class was asked to find the most effective and environmentally safe fertilizer for the school to use on its grounds. This task challenged students to use the SCANS basic skills and the work-related competencies (Packer, 1992). Putting high school learning to public use is sometimes as simple as finding an adult audience for the work that high school students have done.

For Larry Dean, who teaches physics at Lick-Wilmerding High School in San Francisco, making a connection between physics and the high-tech workplace lets students see how the abstract laws and principles of physics play out in life. Student sculptures, paintings, and designs, representing different aspects of physics, occupy the desk space and cover the classroom walls. In Dean's class, the "ropes and pulleys" force-and-energy unit plays out in rock climbing. During his optics unit, students

FIGURE 10.4 SCANS Objectives

Foundation: Three Skills and Personal Qualities for High-Performance Work

Basic skills: reading, writing, mathematics, speaking, and listening

Thinking skills: creativity, decision making, reasoning, and problem solving

Personal qualities: individual responsibility, self-management, and integrity

Five Competencies Applicable to the Work Setting

The ability to productively use	Objectives	Illustration
Resources	Ability to identify, organize, and allocate resources	Design a small business bottling and marketing potable water within defined quality limits.
Interpersonal skills	Ability to work effectively with clients, customers, and colleagues	Gather residents of low-income housing project to share interests and form interest groups.
Information	Ability to acquire, evaluate, and interpret information	Assess local air quality under different weather conditions and publicize information to local citizens
Technology	Ability to select, apply, and troubleshoot appropriate technology	Run analysis of high school budget and prepare graphics for town meeting.
Systems	Ability to analyze and change complex interrelationships within human economic and technological systems	Conduct feasibility study for a locally based recycling company.

Adapted from "What Work Requires of Schools: A SCANS Report for America 2000," U.S. Department of Labor, 1993.

build their own telescopes. Bending light looks easy on a textbook page; it looks more difficult when students are programming the computerized grinding mill, welding telescope parts, grinding lenses, taking endless measurements, or rewelding to correct a mismeasurement. Students who succeed in Larry Dean's applied physics labs may spend a summer at the Lawrence Berkeley Labs working on one of several high-energy physics projects in which their teacher has an ongoing role.

Youth Apprenticeships and School Learning

If the current movement in school/work collaboration is to succeed, learning the job cannot be the same as learning on the job. As Bailey (1993b) states:

> One of the most widely accepted conclusions about the operation of employment and training programs in the United States is that programs that simply place students on the job to gain "work experience" are not effective. Much more is required than exposing students to the work-place.

Aiming to provide workers to mass production, vocational instruction followed the same path as the Taylor method of task analysis and job specification, breaking meaningful work into meaningless pieces. To develop the generalized skills and attitudes described in the SCANS report, students need much more than exposure to the routines of the workplace.

Despite some controversy over the term *apprenticeship*—a word used for decades to describe a specific industry-based method for learning a trade and earning a license, "youth apprenticeship" has become the popular term for high school programs that link learning and work. Even though there are wide variations in design and practice, youth apprenticeship programs share two characteristics: (1) a pedagogy based on learning by doing and on the progressive mastery of skills by a novice learning on-the-job from masters; and (2) a long-term relationship that yields certification of occupational skills broadly recognized by one's industry (Jobs for the Future,* 1993). Program structure tends to rely on the unique intersection between school and business needs. Basically, a specific group of school and industry leaders need to sit down to set the purpose, the skill standards, the curriculum, the training process, and the financial assumptions that will guide their partnership. In bringing two quite different cultures together in one enterprise, at the outset, both partners need to recognize the time, patience, and understanding that will be required during their collaboration.

Generally, employers in youth apprenticeship programs provide paid work experience and access to skilled trainers on the job site. Schools, on the other hand, adapt their academic programs to support learning on the job. These programs are managed within school/industry partnerships that coordinate the integration of school and work-based learning. Some states offer direct reimbursement to participating businesses, while others provide tax incentives to companies sponsoring a youth apprenticeship program. In some states, agreements with community or technical colleges (often called "2X2" or "dual-system" programs) let students bridge between high school and college-level study while working at a partnership site.

The dual-system training process, having guided German apprenticeship programs for a hundred years, has become the focus of development in the partnership between Siemens Stromberg Carlsen and two high schools in Lake Mary, Florida (Garman, 1993). In this system, high school students receive basic technical training

Note: We would like to thank Jobs for the Future, Cambridge, Massachusetts, for their hospitality and support during the Jobs for the Future Conference in Boston on June 24–27, 1993.

while they are also participating in industry-based training in plastics, metalworking, and electronics. Following their high school graduation, the same students may qualify for a full apprenticeship at Siemens Stromberg Carlsen while enrolled in an Associates Degree program at Seminole Community College. The company pays a stipend to its apprentices, as well as covering college tuition and books. Apprentices finishing the program have both training and experience in assembling, testing, installing, and servicing "high-tech" products, and an inside track to jobs in the sponsoring company.

A Sampler of School/Industry Partnerships

The variety of work-based learning programs is enormous, responding to a large degree to specific opportunities available in different parts of the country.

Industrial Production—metalworking, machine tools, manufacturing technology, engineering technology, assembly, robotics, pre-trades construction, and remodeling;

Services—automobile mechanics, telephone repair, government services, banking and financial services, insurance, food services, health services and hospital management, publishing, printing and graphic design;

Agriculture and Food Industries—animal science, plant and soil science, farm production, food services, nutrition, packaging;

Business Management—administration, accounting, budgeting, marketing, advertising, retailing.

Recent experimentation has included a strong emphasis on applied technology in management information systems, design, production, and communications. Although the movement toward youth apprenticeship is widespread, most state programs are still in the development stage, creating guidelines, support systems, and model programs with an experimental flavor.

Kalamazoo County Health Care Partnerships

Responding to the predicted shortage of health care workers in the year 2000, local health care providers and high schools in Kalamazoo, Michigan, formed a consortium (Health Occupations, Bronson Hospital, c/o Truesdale Hall, 10 Healthcare Plaza, Kalamazoo, MI 49007) through which high school students could prepare for careers in allied health services. Eleven participating high schools offer work-related courses and integrate an "externship" component in graduation requirements. Two local hospitals and other providers offer work experience under the guidance of their own personnel. Kalamazoo Community College then offers courses to graduating students for college credit. As shown in Figure 10.5, two years of job shadowing and externships, supported by high school courses, are followed by a job in health services supported by college courses in the health professions.

Tech Prep in Pickens County

The Pickens County Youth Apprenticeship Initiative (B. J. Skelton Career Center, 1400 Griffin Mill Road, Easley, SC) prepares high school students to work in the electronics industry. The school-based curriculum combines basic and academic courses with classes focused on emerging technologies (see Figure 10.6). Apprenticeships in local industries feature specific applications of technologies that pay students to work while they learn. During the 1993–94 academic year, the program expanded to include specialties in business, electricity, and automotive technology. Students working in apprenticeships are eligible for a job and college tuition when they complete the program.

FIGURE 10.5   Kalamazoo Valley Consortium Health Occupations Career Pathway

HEALTH OCCUPATIONS I (Year One) — 11th and 12th Grade Students

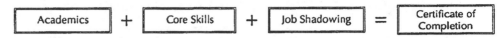

HEALTH OCCUPATIONS II (Year Two) — 12th Grade Students

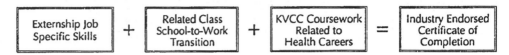

HEALTH OCCUPATIONS III — Post-Secondary

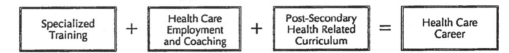

From the Kalamazoo County Education for Employment program, Comstock, MI. Used with permission.

Printing Apprenticeships

At West Bend High School (1305 Decorah Road, West Bend, WI 53095), juniors may take a tech-prep program in printing trades or in banking and finance (see Figure 10.7). Students interested in printing and publication take an introduction to printing in their sophomore year, then as juniors split an eight-period day between morning classes at the high school and afternoon classes offered by a technical college at a West Bend printing company. They also work for pay under a mentor from the printing company. At the end of their apprenticeship and after graduation, they receive an apprenticeship certificate from the state with their diploma. Students may then elect to seek a job in the printing industry, enroll in a technical degree program, or continue toward a four-year college degree.

Oakland Health and Bioscience Academy

The Oakland Health and Bioscience Academy (Patricia Clark, Director, 4351 Broadway, Oakland, CA 94611) began in 1985 in response to the need to increase the number of underrepresented students beginning careers in health medicine and life sciences. Operating as a "magnet school" for the Oakland Unified School District and also a "school-within-a-school" at Oakland Technical High School, the Academy offers a wide variety of internships at area health organizations, including ACME Ambulance Company (for EMT certification), the American Red Cross, the Asian Mental Health Clinic, the Bay Area Black Quality Health Care Consortium, Children's Hospital, the Biology Department at CSU–Hayward, Kaizer Permanente Medical Center, the March of Dimes, Lawrence Berkeley Labs, and the Oakland Zoo.

Students spend up to eighty percent of their day in interrelated academic and lab classes for three or four years. They also participate in work-site learning at various levels of involvement, including career exploration, voluntary work, job shad-

FIGURE 10.6   Plan for Career Preparation

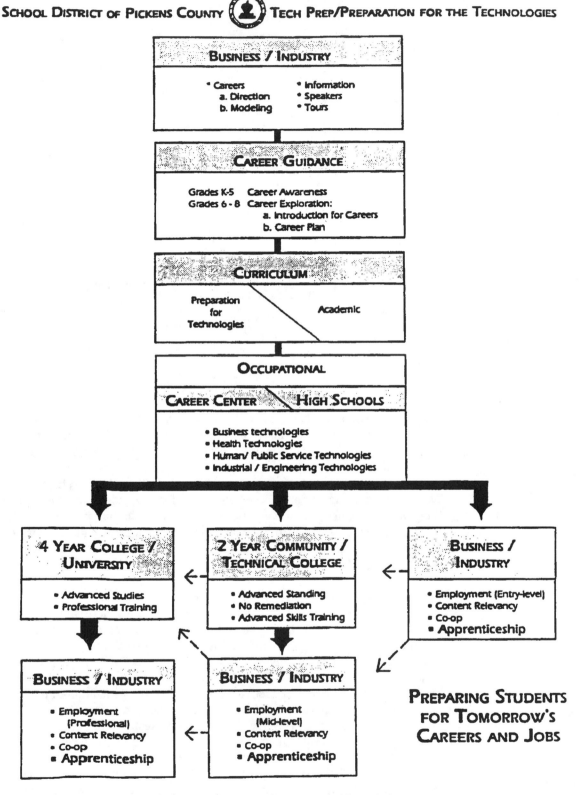

SCHOOL DISTRICT OF PICKENS COUNTY ⬤ TECH PREP/PREPARATION FOR THE TECHNOLOGIES

BUSINESS / INDUSTRY

- Careers
  - a. Direction
  - b. Modeling
- Information
- Speakers
- Tours

CAREER GUIDANCE

Grades K-5   Career Awareness
Grades 6 - 8   Career Exploration:
  a. Introduction for Careers
  b. Career Plan

CURRICULUM

Preparation for Technologies   Academic

OCCUPATIONAL

CAREER CENTER   HIGH SCHOOLS

- Business technologies
- Health Technologies
- Human/ Public Service Technologies
- Industrial / Engineering Technologies

4 YEAR COLLEGE / UNIVERSITY

- Advanced Studies
- Professional Training

2 YEAR COMMUNITY / TECHNICAL COLLEGE

- Advanced Standing
- No Remediation
- Advanced Skills Training

BUSINESS / INDUSTRY

- Employment (Entry-level)
- Content Relevancy
- Co-op
- Apprenticeship

BUSINESS / INDUSTRY

- Employment (Professional)
- Content Relevancy
- Co-op
- Apprenticeship

BUSINESS / INDUSTRY

- Employment (Mid-level)
- Content Relevancy
- Co-op
- Apprenticeship

PREPARING STUDENTS FOR TOMORROW'S CAREERS AND JOBS

From the Pickens County Youth Apprenticeship Initiative program, Easley, SC. Used with permission.

FIGURE 10.7   Banking/Finance Apprenticeships

West Bend High Schools
1305 East Decorah Road
West Bend, Wisconsin 53095

Spartans
West High School

Suns
East High School

Marilynn Orlopp, Youth Apprenticeship Coordinator, 335-5538

YOUTH APPRENTICESHIP IN BANKING/FINANCE

BACKGROUND

The Youth Apprenticeship--Banking/Finance Program OFFERS students, beginning in their junior year, work experience and guided learning opportunities in a financial institution such as a bank, credit union or saving and loan. It is a structural linkage between secondary and post secondary education, and a close integration of academic and work based learning, both in school and at the work place.

HOW THE PROGRAM WORKS

* Student applicants will be sophomores at the time of the application and will begin the program in the fall of their junior year. The applicant will have a career interest in banking and finance, have good math and communication skills, has taken keyboarding, and has some computer experience.

* Students will complete an application form and include references and their academic record. Selection of the youth apprentices will be made by the businesses participating in the program. It is quite possible that there will be more applicants than there are positions.

* The students day will consist of three periods of academic courses, one period of a specialized course in the banking/finance industry and three or more hours of work based learning. Students wages are to be based on the minimum wage scale during the hours of employment.

* Youth apprentices are high school students and we encourage the extracurricular activities when their schedules allow it.

* When the youth apprentice has completed the program he/she will receive a high school diploma, a certificate of occupational proficiency from the Department of Industry, Labor and Human Relations (DILHR). The youth apprentice will also have the opportunity of receiving technical college credit for those courses that have been identified as tech prep. With the above documents the student will be able to go directly to work, pursue an associate degree from a Wisconsin technical college, or apply to a 4-year university.

WEST BEND YOUTH APPRENTICESHIPS--PREPARING OUR STUDENTS TO MEET THE DEMAND OF A HIGHLY SKILLED WORK FORCE.

From the Youth Apprenticeship program, West Bend, WI. Used with permission.

owing, clinical rotations, summer and senior-year internships, and senior projects. Through a technical portfolio, students accumulate demonstrations of mastery in several areas of health care or technology.

Roosevelt Renaissance 2000: A Comprehensive Reform

As the last decade of this century began, staff and students at Roosevelt High School found they could no longer ignore the problems they faced. Twenty percent of the students qualified for special education; 35% of the student body turned over before graduation. Only 20% of the student body went on to a four-year college. In surveys conducted within the student body, 80% could not see any connection between their schooling and employment. Frustrated by their lack of success, teachers began asking why and concluded that "the general track is a pathway to nowhere" (Wernsing, 1993). Teachers, over 90% of them, believed that the curriculum would better meet student needs if it had a technical and vocational thrust. They initiated a three-year development project (James C. Wernsing, Coordinator, Roosevelt High School, 6941 N. Central, Portland, OR 97203) aimed at integrating academic and vocational preparation for all students in the high school.

To prepare the groundwork for curriculum renewal, the school adopted a new mission—to integrate work and learning for all Roosevelt students. The school then assembled three teams of teachers, students, state officials, and representatives from area businesses to:

1. Begin reframing the curriculum to fit a vocational mission;
2. Develop public relations that would explain the new initiative; and
3. Develop summer internships for teachers in businesses or industries, where they could see their subject areas in action.

To further clarify the demands of the work setting, teachers went on field trips to local sites while business people worked as substitutes on faculty development days. At a series of faculty retreats, they designed a new structure for the school day aimed at engaging all the kids in work-related learning.

The school restructuring team developed six pathways for its new curriculum, each associated with an area of economic growth in which several career opportunities could be projected:

Information Systems and Processing—data processing, telecommunications, computer technology, and office jobs;

Manufacturing Technology and Engineering—electronics, construction, and metal fabrication;

Health and Human Services—all health care professions;

Natural Science and Resources—environmental services, resource management, fisheries and wildlife;

Professional, Public, and Commercial Services—banking, retail, and services for government or social services;

Trade and Tourism—import/export, hospitality, tourism and recreation.

Each pathway was to be taught and managed by an interdisciplinary team of teachers and business representatives who would develop a four-year program of integrated work and learning. Each pathway emphasizes general skills for success, as well as job-based skills, allowing students the flexibility to choose throughout their school experience.

During the four years of a Roosevelt education, students shift their study from the basics of learning (while they explore work) to work related education (while they integrate academic knowledge). Work experience begins with an exploration of all the options (see Figure 10.8), supported by job shadowing in several settings, but ends with job experience in a specific setting related to their chosen career pathway.

FIGURE 10.8   Roosevelt High School Job Shadow Program Student Question Sheet

Name: _____

Focus Class Period: _____

The following guidelines should help you to get the most out
of your job shadow experience. You should try to ask
as many of these questions as possible, but feel free
to ask other questions that might also be appropriate.

1. What is the primary mission of this organization? _____
_____

2. What are the responsibilities of your department? _____
_____

3. What are your responsibilities? _____
_____

4. How does your job relate to the overall organization? _____
_____

5. What other people do you work most closely with? _____
_____

6. Are computers used on the job? If so, in what capacity? _____
_____

7. What type of education and/or training does one need to do the job? What type of education/training have
   you had? _____
_____

8. How did you decide to do this type of work? _____
_____

9. What do you see as the demand for jobs like yours in the future? _____
_____

10. What do you like *most* about your job? _____
_____

11. What do you like *least* about your job? _____
_____

12. What is the salary *range* for someone working in this field? (What is a typical starting salary?) _____
_____

From the Roosevelt Renaissance 2000 program, Portland, OR. Used with permission.

Students in the first two years of the Roosevelt program are expected to explore all the possible pathways and qualify for a certificate of initial mastery, a CIM. The CIM can be earned through repeated trials throughout the ninth and tenth grades, showing that the student has demonstrated mastery of basic skills in reading, writing, and math, as well as work-related behaviors such as punctuality, attendance, and responsibility. During the tenth grade, students choose one of the six pathways. During the eleventh- and twelfth-grade levels, students work toward a Certificate of Advanced Mastery (CAM) in their chosen pathway. The CAM for each pathway is designed by the school/industry team associated with that pathway. Each CAM should qualify students for work in that area, and also prepare them to enter postsecondary schools and colleges (see Figure 10.9).

Throughout their high school studies, Roosevelt students are expected to master general work-related skills in addition to basic skills. Skills for success include:

FIGURE 10.9   The Student Experience at Roosevelt High School

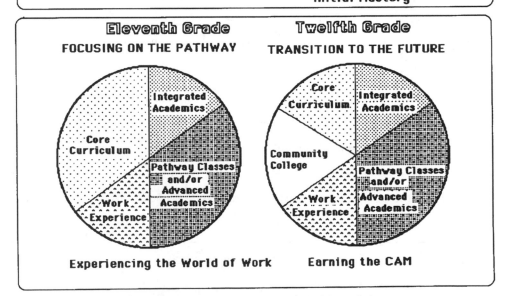

From the Roosevelt Renaissance 2000 program, Portland, OR. Used with permission.

Thinking Skills—how to understand complex relationships, how to acquire and use information, and how to understand new technologies;

Communication and Interpersonal Skills—teamwork, problem solving, decision making, and flexibility.

The focus, or generalizable skills, allows students to change pathways while they are at Roosevelt, and it also combines college-preparatory advanced skills as they work within one pathway.

The existence of pathway teams has forced the school day into new patterns. Faculty are beginning to see their work as a function of their pathway team rather than their core discipline. As the teams have assumed responsibility for planning and implementation, the role of department chairman has diminished accordingly. On Tuesdays, the buses arrive late at school, allowing faculty to meet with their pathway teams or with the advisory boards that have been formed to guide each team. Field experience becomes the subject of most classes, as well as the "glue" that holds them together. Classes may be canceled while freshmen explore careers, guided by a new "job-shadowing" packet. Seniors may take college-level classes on the job site in association with a community college. Multiple pathways, with multiple options for demonstrating mastery in different fields, allow Roosevelt to remain flexible as it creates its new program.

Integrating Academics

How can we use experience in the field to drive more conventional academic learning? One way is to use the issues that arise in a work or service setting to help students develop generalizable skills and knowledge connected to their experience in the work setting. Teachers can use themes from the workplace to organize content from the conventional curriculum, and also assign students to complete investigations of those issues in their own apprenticeship or service setting. For students in six apprenticeship sites, the teachers in the Pittsburgh Youth Apprenticeship program have developed a project-based curriculum supported by study in core subject areas.

In Pittsburgh, issues of the workplace have become themes organizing focused study in English, mathematics, social studies, science, and occupational subjects that support the Pennsylvania Youth Apprenticeship program. Themes include work ethics, problem solving, youth in society, technology and society, and job safety. For each theme, students complete an independent project and bring it back to the classroom for discussion. The theme for each academic quarter also guides teachers in organizing materials and tasks that connect their classes to the workplace.

Figures 10.10 and 10.11 provide an overview of the thematic unit on job safety in Pittsburgh's Youth Apprenticeship program. During the quarter, students write newsletters and create posters that focus on issues of safety in their own work setting. In their academic classes, they read, write, solve problems, and study materials that clarify the causes and effects of safety problems on the job. As students are reading a report of the Triangle Fire of 1911, they are also studying fire dynamics and fluid dynamics in science, area and volume in math, and the poetry of Edgar Lee Masters. As they learn more about the conditions of safety in a work setting, their projects assume increasing sophistication. In effect, their learning also serves to enrich the places where they work.

FIGURE 10.10   Integrating Academics with Work in the Pittsburgh Apprenticeship Program

---

Integration of Content Areas

Theme: Safety on the job
Focusing question: Why is safety important?

Social Studies: Students read *The Great Triangle Fire* (American Heritage Series). Each selects an element of the event and develops a newspaper article focused on that aspect (e.g., floor space and mortality, panic, or immigrant workers).

English: Teacher introduces "Butch Weldy" from Edgar Lee Masters's *Spoon River Anthology* and students write poems about responses to workplace tragedy.

Mathematics: Teacher explains calculation of volume and asks students to measure off the maximum area of floor space meeting requirements for 250 cubic feet of working space.

Science: Teacher illustrates Bernouli's Principle with paper and hair dryer. Students relate principle to both instances of building fire dynamics.
     Teacher asks students to illustrate "lapping in" process with candles and a hair dryer—and explain the connection to fire conditions.

Machine Technology: Teacher shows the film *Shake Hands with Danger* and helps students analyze OSHA guidelines for safety.

Student Project for the Quarter (for Student Portfolios): Students complete a series of posters and newsletters for their own workplace, assembling the whole collection for Workplace Portfolio.

From a presentation by Maggie Holder, Ronnie Eileen Izenson, Dave Pacolay, Glen Reis, Dave Baraday, and Jean Simcic. Boston, MA: Jobs for the Future Conference, 1993. Used with permission.

Creating Cognitive Apprenticeships

In both service learning and youth apprenticeship, students should be guided to use a particular experience as a source of general or "strategic" knowledge about how to solve problems in a real-world context. As an ideal, proponents of youth apprenticeship describe a "cognitive apprenticeship" for high school students, aiming not for replicated skills in one job setting, but for higher-level problem-solving strategies that form the basis of effective work in any setting. Students in a cognitive apprenticeship do not aim to assimilate domain-specific knowledge embedded in a particular task, but to identify the underlying patterns of thought that let us amend procedures, redefine basic knowledge, and invent new ways to do things. They have to look for the strategic skills that define expertise (Berryman & Bailey, 1993). To gain control over internal patterns of thought that define expertise in any realm, students have to stand back from the job at hand, question what they see and do, develop a general plan of attack, and search out new information that will fill the gaps in what they know. Clearly, students cannot learn to "see" and use expert strategies without careful instruction of a type not normally found in standard classrooms.

In a cognitive apprenticeship, students would be guided to observe experts work, try to emulate high performance, create new responses to the problems that emerge from work, and discover new techniques for isolating and solving any problem. Time is an essential ingredient in helping students develop abstract models from concrete processes. Many hours of listening to automobile engines, for example, are required

FIGURE 10.11 Integrating Literature in the Pittsburgh Job Safety Unit

Introduction

The following poem can be used to introduce the project on safety in the work-place. After using it to initiate and focus discussion about job safety, students may wish to read additional selections from *Spoon River Anthology* by Edgar Lee Masters. Butch Weldy is one of many characters who tells his story from the grave. Why is his name appropriate?

"Butch" Weldy

After I got religion and steadied down
They gave me a job in the canning works,
And every morning I had to fill
The tank in the yard with gasoline,
That fed the blowfires in the sheds   5
To heat the soldering irons.
And I mounted a rickety ladder to do it,
Carrying buckets full of the stuff.
One morning, as I stood there pouring,
The air grew still and seemed to heave,   10
And I shot up as the tank exploded,
And down I came with both legs broken,
And my eyes burned crisp as a couple of eggs
For someone left a blowfire going,
And something sucked the flame into the tank.   15
The Circuit Judge said whoever did it
Was a fellow-servant of mine, and so
Old Rhodes' son didn't have to pay me,
And I sat on the witness stand as blind
As Jack the Fiddler, saying over and over,   20
"I didn't know him at all." *

Discussion Questions

1. Describe the accident in your own words.

2. Tell the attitude of the character and the author toward the accident and the judge's decision.

3. Explain the Circuit Judge's decision.

4. Could such an accident happen today? Explain.

5. Can you describe an accident that you or someone you know has experienced?

6. How might the judge's decision differ today from the poem's setting of 1915?

*From *The Spoon River Anthology* by Edgar Lee Masters.

From a presentation by Maggie Holder, Ronnie Eileen Izenson, Dave Pacolay, Glen Reis, Dave Baraday, and Jean Simcic. Boston, MA: Jobs for the Future Conference, 1993. Used with permission.

before a mechanic can convert the sounds heard from a stalling motor to a vision of engine function as a general model in which one kind of problem is leading toward one kind of result, implying only a few possible solutions.

The cognitive apprenticeship, whether in experiential learning or conventional classrooms, requires teaching strategies that support the development of problem solving (Collins, Brown, & Newman, 1989):

Modeling: For students to model expert performance, the learning situation must include an expert performing a task so that students can observe and build a conceptual model of the processes that are required.

Coaching: Observing students as they carry out a task and offering hints, support, feedback, modeling, reminders, and new tasks to bring their performance closer to expert performance.

Scaffolding and Fading: Scaffolding refers to supports that a teacher provides to help a student carry out a task. Supports can take the form of either suggestions or help or actual physical supports such as the short skis used to teach downhill skiing. *Fading* is the gradual removal of supports until students are on their own.

Articulation: Any method that gets students to articulate their knowledge, reasoning, or problem-solving processes. It makes visible otherwise invisible cognitive processes and guiding assumptions.

Reflection: Any technique that allows students to compare their own problem-solving processes with those of an expert, another student, or ultimately an internalized model of expertise in the field.

Exploration: Any device that pushes students into a mode of problem solving on their own. Forcing them to explore is critical if they are to learn how to frame questions or problems they can solve.

Reflective time may be more rare on the job than it is in school. Yet mindless or rote performance does as little good on the job as it does in class. By focusing student attention on the process of improving the way they attack problems, experiential learning may serve students and sponsoring agencies simultaneously.

EXPERIENTIAL LEARNING SHOWCASE

**School-Based Businesses:
REAL Enterprises at Riverside High School**

Cory NeVille, Facilitator
*Riverside School District #416, Riverside High School,
E. 4120 Deer Park/Milan Road, Chattaroy, WA*

Kendra Austin, Student
Johnson & Wales University, Providence, RI

Rick Larson, Associate Director
REAL Enterprises, Chapel Hill, NC

REAL Enterprises (Rural Entrepreneurship through Action Learning) uses a curriculum guide for small business development to help students develop a business plan as well as important life skills. Some students complete their plan and then begin to put their business in place, sometimes using a high school as a temporary home base. In North Carolina, students planned and developed businesses in their high schools that include a restaurant, a bakery, a shaved ice/snow cone stand, clothing design studio, upholstery shop, small engine repair, furniture making, weaving, pottery, poultry farming, shoe repair, office supplies recycling, an elderly shut-in shopping service, screenprinting, lingerie, formal wear, and a used book and comic book store. In North Carolina, thirty businesses have been started since 1992. Six of those received start-up loans from REAL's Revolving Loan Fund. Other students use their work with REAL Enterprises as an exercise in the logic of personal planning, an essential part of their high school experience without the additional challenge of beginning a business of their own. The REAL Business Planning Program is composed of Microsoft® Works word processing and spreadsheet templates for writing the business plan and managing the necessary financial data. Whether students actually begin a business or not, they use the process to think through the question of what they want to do outside of school and to develop skills they will need to thrive in any context.

One essential key to REAL Enterprises and its success is the application of the experiential learning cycle. What is so unique about experiences designed to guide participants through the difficult process of researching, planning, and running small businesses? What is meant by experiential learning? The experiential learning cycle summarized in Figure 10.12 describes the process by which people learn experientially. Using experience as a source of learning, the REAL Enterprises program has two fundamental goals: The first is to give students the opportunity to research, plan and operate economically viable small enterprises that meet a need in their community; the second, and equally important, goal is to give students the opportunity to develop critical thinking and life skills they will need regardless of their ultimate career choices. REAL's professional development process stresses the need to use the cycle over and over to reach all students, regardless of their learning style.

FIGURE 10.12   The Experiential Learning Cycle

The cycle begins* with a concrete experience—an event or exercise in which the learner actively participates.

Next, the learner reflects on the experience, focusing on what happened, how he/she felt about it, and why the experience was (or was not) valuable and educational.

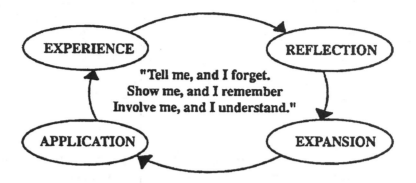

"Tell me, and I forget.
Show me, and I remember
Involve me, and I understand."

The learner completes* the cycle by transferring his/her newly acquired knowledge and skills to situations in the "real world." This stage involves application and active experimentation.

After reflecting, the learner expands on the original experience by identifying the abstract ideas, theories, and principles behind it. This step may include research, lecture, reading on related topics, analysis, and hypothetical application.

*The steps in the cycle are arranged in a sequence for sake of discussion, but technically a cycle has no beginning or end.

The development of a business plan, the central project of the REAL Enterprises course, is the primary vehicle for achieving both of these goals. Skills, knowledge, and actual enterprises are all desired outcomes of the REAL program (see Figure 10.13). First, the business plan is an end in itself, a detailed "road map": for an enterprise the student may eventually open and operate, depending on its feasibility. It may include elements of a "life plan" describing steps the student will take to achieve his or her career goals. Second, the plan is a means for learning problem solving, decision making, communication, and cooperation and for helping students assess their entrepreneurial capabilities. By developing a business plan, students develop entrepreneurial skills and determine the feasibility of their business ideas. The process by which the REAL Enterprises course is taught is critical to the success of the program.

The Riverside REAL Story

Riverside School District and, in particular, Riverside High School started testing the effectiveness of school-based businesses in the fall of 1988 when it was awarded a grant by the state of Washington. Under the direction of district vocational director,

FIGURE 10.13 Desired Outcomes

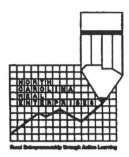

What Does Getting REAL Mean?

The REAL Entrepreneurship course is designed to help participants develop skills, expand their knowledge, and create tangible products, including new enterprises. A summary of these three areas follows:

SKILLS

- LIFE SKILLS: skills which equip participants for life and the world of work, regardless of their ultimate career choices:

    a. effective thinking
    b. getting along with others
    c. communication
    d. understanding the world
    e. operating effectively within organizations
    f. personal empowerment and effectiveness
    g. utilizing technology
    h. business effectiveness

- OPPORTUNITY IDENTIFICATION: the ability to recognize favorable circumstances in one's personal life and community

- OPPORTUNITY EVALUATION: the ability to measure and analyze opportunities for their feasibility and practicality, including:

    a. community analysis
    b. industry analysis
    c. market analysis
    d. financial analysis

- OPPORTUNITY REALIZATION: the skills required to seize opportunities which have been recognized and evaluated, including:

    a. start-up procedures
    b. operations
    c. personnel management
    d. bookkeeping

KNOWLEDGE

- OF ENTREPRENEURSHIP, including:

    a. the vocabulary of small business
    b. characteristics and behaviors of successful entrepreneurs

- OF THE PLANNING PROCESS

- OF THE LEGAL REQUIREMENTS OF OPERATING A SMALL BUSINESS, including:

    a. structure
    b. taxes
    c. licenses
    d. permits
    e. bookkeeping

- OF SELF

    a. ability and aptitude as an entrepreneur
    b. strengths and weaknesses
    c. feasibility of accomplishing entrepreneurial goals

(Continued)

FIGURE 10.13   *(Continued)*

PRODUCTS

- STUDENT JOURNAL: a documentation and evaluation tool that includes:

    a. assessment of personal attributes, skills, goals, and needs
    b. personal budget
    c. drafts of sections of the (business) plan
    d. chronicle of the planning process

- ORAL PRESENTATION: a presentation to an audience beyond the class itself that describes the venture detailed in the written business plan

- BUSINESS PLAN: a comprehensive and substantive document based on real research of the local community, written for a significant enterprise, economic in nature, such as:

    a. a for-profit or nonprofit venture
    b. a project that addresses a real business or community need

- VIABLE VENTURES: businesses, community services, or projects, which students may implement themselves or offer (in the form of completed business plans) to other entrepreneurs, agencies, or organizations for implementation

---

Used with permission.

Galen Hansen, the start-up funds were used to create the Riverside Vocational Center and convert a row of unused portable classrooms into student-operated, district-owned business incubators. Using the REAL Enterprises business plan outline, Riverside students develop a complete business plan for a product or service in which they are interested. Students may implement viable ventures themselves—businesses, community services, or projects—or offer their completed business plans to other entrepreneurs, agencies, or organizations for implementation. Figure 10.14 is a basic outline for a business plan.

The first incubation site was the district Printshop. This renovated portable classroom houses a myriad of copying machines, off-set printers, and other binding and collating machines designed to meet the entire district's printing needs. Since the program's beginning in 1988, several other incubators have sprung up in the district. These business incubators include a computer repair shop, a thrift and gift shop, a landscape business, a day-care center, a student employment center, and a screen-printing shop. Students are also assigned to food services and custodial services where they learn the skills necessary for success in those areas.

Students from Riverside High School enroll in a program called Diversified Occupations which introduces them to the world of work in the relatively safe and secure environment of the business incubators. The incubators make up for the school's inability to place its vocational education students with private businesses, which are scarce to the area. The Vocational Center makes it possible for interested students to develop basic employment skills necessary for a successful venture into the real world of work.

The goals set for Riverside School District and its small business incubators, coupled with REAL are to:

- Provide on-site training in various occupational endeavors
- Act as a feeder program for industry and business
- Provide students with skills and incentives to succeed in today's work force
- Act as a median for school-to-work transition
- Explore opportunities for business ownership

FIGURE 10.14   REAL Enterprises Business Plan Outline

Executive Summary

One-page summary of the plan: purpose, who prepared it, brief description of the business, its products and owners, form of organization. If you seeking a loan, include the amount requested, over what period you wish to repay it, the use of the loan proceeds, collateral you are prepared to offer, and your equity investment.

Product or Service

Detailed description of the product or service (include an example or photo if possible)

- If you are selling a product: key suppliers and your terms and arrangements with them
- If you are selling a service: which services will be provided at the business location and which will be delivered "in the field"

Marketing

- Target market/customer profile: specify age, gender, income, preferences, location, etc.
- Industry analysis: what the trends are in your industry
- Market analysis: total market size and the share you will capture, seasonality, unique aspects
- Describe the "five P's" for your business
  - **Product:** how will you design and package your product/service
  - **Price:** how will you price your product/service
  - **Place:** where your customers will learn about your product/service
  - **Promotion:** what media and marketing methods you will use to generate awareness and interest about your product/service; include examples of your promotional materials (brochures, print ads, copy for radio ads, calendar of events for special/regular promotions)
  - **People:** who will be responsible for marketing your product/service
- Competition: list of competitors by name, location, and their strengths and weaknesses; how you will succeed against them; how they will react to your entry into the market

Operations

- Legal structure and why you chose it; include legal/governing documents (Articles of Incorporation and By-laws for corporation, partnership agreement for partnership)
- Management and personnel
  - who the key managers/owners are and what relevant experience and background they bring to the business (include resumes)
  - describe non-management positions, responsibilities/qualifications, personnel policies
- Customer service: procedures and policies regarding your work and how you will treat customers
- Location and operations
  - your facility, including a store layout, description of business image, hours of operation
  - operations plan: how you will deliver your product/service to the customer, from start to finish (who does what tasks, how long it takes, etc.)
  - renovations and equipment list (including prices and condition—new or used)
  - taxes to be paid, licenses required, and insurance needed
- Key people: who will provide accounting and legal services, technical assistance and support

(Continued)

FIGURE 10.14   *(Continued)*

Financials

- Cash flow projections for three years
  - loan amortization schedule
  - detailed assumptions for each line item
- Breakeven analysis
- Personal financial statement for all owners, co-signers
- Risk factors: identify major risks and describe how business will overcome them

Used with permission.

Individual students are allowed a continuum of choices concerning job training as well as their education. This innovative approach has been an excellent method in assisting youth to receive "top-notch" training in several work opportunities and to help prepare them to own and operate their own businesses. The training program is assisted by trained paraprofessionals in their respective areas of expertise. Students and aides receive additional support and assistance through the high school's Diversified Occupations Coordinator. Students not only receive on-the-job training, but also receive training relative to every job survival skill they will need to possess as a productive employee or successful employer.

The Riverside REAL program has established articulation, cooperation, and partnerships between business, labor, industry, and education. The program also serves as a catalyst for rural community economic development, strengthens school/community bonds, and helps individual students develop a more positive attitude toward themselves and their abilities. REAL dovetails with the incubators by providing entrepreneurial training in an exciting and special way. One of the most beneficial outcomes of the entire program is the incentive it provides for students to stay in school and further develop necessary job and life-survival skills. One additional goal is for each incubator to become financially self-sustaining. Starting a tee-shirt company, as Toni did (see Figure 10.15), provides hard skills within a highly creative process. The "culminating experience" represented in the figure serves to pull together a student's work in most sections of the REAL curriculum guide.

Kendra Austin, a graduate of Riverside High School, provides one specific example of how the program works. Kendra is currently a freshman at Johnson & Wales University in Providence, Rhode Island. Through her efforts in regular academics and in the development of her own business, Kendra qualified for over $26,000 worth of scholarships toward her education at Johnson & Wales. The following is her story.

From Pizza to Office Products: Kendra's Story

If someone had told me five years ago that I would own my own business by the time I was sixteen years old, I would have thought them crazy. It's not that I didn't think I wasn't capable, I just never would have thought it possible for a person my age to own and operate their own business. The fact that I also lived in a rural area with no town and no business district didn't seem to help either. All these notions in my head were changed at the beginning of my sophomore year of high school, the day I walked into Cory NeVille's REAL Entrepreneurship class.

From "day one" the class was a learning experience. The first thing I learned was that there was no textbook in the course, just a resource library with most of the answers to the "why's" and "how's" of running a business. Secondly, Mr. NeVille was to be a facilitator, not a teacher in the strict sense of the word. He was not there to give answers, but to help students find them. Suddenly, through the REAL program, my eyes were opened to other

FIGURE 10.15

 **TONI'S T-SHIRTS**

PURPOSE:

- to learn how to perform breakeven analysis
- to understand how fixed and variable costs affect the breakeven point
- to perform breakeven analysis on proposed business idea

READY?

Participants are ready for this Culminating Experience when they have collected "ball park" cost figures for operating expenses and costs of goods sold for their proposed business.

MATERIALS:

- flipchart or chalkboard
- copies of "Are Toni's T-Shirts Greeeaaat?" worksheets (1 per participant)
- at least one calculator for each group
- optional: computer with REAL Breakeven Analysis (Microsoft® Works) program

TIME:

60 to 90 minutes

PROCEDURE:

1. Divide the class into groups of 3 to 5 members each. Hand out the first page of "Are Toni's T-Shirts Greeeaaat?" Ask each group to choose a spokesperson.

2. Allow about 5 minutes for the groups to reach consensus concerning which costs are overhead and which are costs of goods sold in part A.

3. Ask one group to write their suggested division on the board. Ask the other groups to share their decisions. Check those that agree and record differences. For example the first and second groups both say phone is an overhead cost, but the third group says it is cost of goods sold. Write telephone under Overhead with a check by it, and write telephone under Cost of Goods Sold.
   NOTE: It is critical that students understand that there is not one right answer to this division of costs. However, they must be able to justify why a particular cost belongs in one category or another. A good rule of thumb is that an overhead cost is usually described as dollars per unit of time (month, year, etc.), while cost of goods sold is usually described as dollars per item sold.

TIP: This is an excellent time to review the definitions of overhead (fixed costs), cost of goods sold (variable costs), contribution margin (gross profit), and breakeven.

(Continued)

FIGURE 10.15 *(Continued)*

4. Have groups complete part B and report out. Discuss any differences in the answers. Be sure they understand the concept of contribution margin - the dollar amount contributed to overhead and gross profit.

5. Have participants complete part C. Be sure that they understand, if their division of overhead vs. cost of goods sold is different for that listed in part C, that this is simply one of several ways to divide the costs. For the sake of this exercise, they need to accept this division.

6. Groups complete parts D-I and report their answers. Discuss any differences.

REFLECTION:

Allow 15–30 minutes for discussion and debrief, based on questions such as:

- Why is computing the breakeven point important to Toni? Will her breakeven point change as her business changes?
- As overhead costs increase, what happens to the breakeven point?
- As the cost of goods sold rises, what happens to the breakeven point?
- Does the breakeven point of sales cover the cost of starting Toni's business?
- Are you comfortable with the concept of breakeven? Could you determine the breakeven point for other ventures? For your own business?

BRIDGES:

- Use this activity to prepare students for performing breakeven analysis for their own business ideas, and for using the REAL Breakeven Analysis (Microsoft® Works) program to calculate the breakeven point.
- Breakeven at this stage is used to test the feasibility of an idea by determining sales revenue and the number of customers required to reach the breakeven point. In the Market Feasibility section, participants determine whether there are enough customers for the business to be a success.

Used with permission.

students throughout the country. Students who were successful owners and operators of their own businesses. If they could do it, why couldn't I?

My first attempt at opening a business was a joint effort between myself and several other students as we planned to open a pizza parlor. This venture was probably one of the most eye-opening events of my entire classroom experience. I very quickly learned that it took a lot more than just moving into a building and putting up a sign to start a business. Zoning codes, raising capital, and this thing called a "business plan" were just a few of the numerous items we quickly found necessary to start our business. Though we worked most of the schoolyear to try to get our pizza parlor up and running, the end of the school year found us with nothing but experience to show for our efforts. It was a business that just wasn't feasible at the time being.

After going through the entire pizza deal my first year, I must admit I had doubts going into my junior year about starting a business. This all quickly changed, however, when Mr. Barton Cook approached the class with an offer none of us could refuse. Mr. Cook, a graduate of Riverside, was an employee of a company called Eldon/Rubbermaid that had a lot of products unusable for certain markets. He offered us a shipment of office products for fifteen cents on the dollar. The products he had to offer were in no way damaged, but were selling poorly in their respective markets. Two other students, Aftan Buchanan and Thad Dormaier, and I quickly seized the offer. We would soon be the proud owners of approximately $28,000 worth of office products. I didn't really grasp the reality of what was going on until one day when a truck drove up with our first shipment of products. It was then that it hit me—I was a business owner with all the responsibilities that go with being one.

Being based in a mostly lower-income area forced us to decide to market our products in the schools and assorted social service offices located in the region. Our main source of advertising was a catalog of our product line that we put together with the help of Mr. NeVille, the class computer, and Aldus PageMaker. Even though we were now up and running, the classroom was still a very important element in running our own business. Most of our calls for orders came there, and we had easy access to the computer, fax machine, and telephone. Mr. NeVille even took our business calls and delivered messages to us.

As expected, we were at first met with much skepticism by the adult world because of our age. However, most of the time, once we were able to demonstrate and show our product line, any doubt was erased from the minds of our customers. Suddenly we were no longer high school students but legitimate business owners with a quality product for a great price. My mother loves to tell the story of how she used to have to force me to enter a grocery store to buy a loaf of bread so I could learn to get over my shyness. Now I was making sales presentations to business owners several years older and supposedly wiser.

Fighting our way through the hectic spring schedules, we continued to operate our business as a trio. This continued until the end of our junior year of high school. At this point in time, due to many reasons, we decided to split our remaining inventory three ways and set out for our own business opportunities. It's called business liquidation, something we were pretty naive about. I continued to sell my portion of the inventory throughout my junior summer and senior year of school. During my senior year I decided to compete for a scholarship opportunity at Johnson & Wales University in Providence, Rhode Island. The fact that I might qualify for financial assistance and actually move clear across the country became both an incentive to liquidate my remaining inventory and to find employment sufficient for my new-found college needs. I successfully accomplished both and left for Providence in August of 1993.

Looking back on the entire experience, I know that owning and operating my own business during high school changed my life more than I'll probably ever know. I do, however, know for sure that it definitely renewed my interest in learning. There was suddenly a good reason for me to attend school every day. It gave me confidence and poise that will be with me always. But most of all, through hands-on experience, I was able to learn about the business world. This knowledge didn't come from a book or from some lecture. It came from my participation in life. From me actually having become a part of something much bigger and more powerful than myself. Today, when people find out that I am an entrepreneurship major at Johnson & Wales, they often ask me if I ever hope to own my own business. I simply reply, "I already have, thank you!"

Learning to Plan Experience

Kendra Austin's story is just one that could be told of how students from Riverside have been changed by participating in the REAL Enterprises program. Many other students have emerged from the program with new goals, future plans, and critical thinking skills necessary for success in the real world. For the business plan to be both a useful document and an effective vehicle for the acquisition of critical skills, we believe the following principles are essential:

1. The work, which teachers and students do together, must reflect student needs, desires, and concerns. The program must be infused from the beginning with student choice, design, revision, execution, reflection, and evaluation.

2. The role of the teacher must be that of facilitator, coach, team leader, and guide rather than boss.

3. The instructor ensures the academic integrity of the program by creating opportunities for students to master certain basic competencies during the preparation and execution of the business plan.

4. Work in the REAL program is characterized by student action rather than passive receipt of processed information. The process emphasizes peer teaching, cooperative learning, and teamwork.

5. Connections between classroom work and the communities beyond the classroom are clear. The class goes to the community, and vice versa.

6. There must be an audience for student work beyond the teacher. The audience may include individuals, small groups, or the community at large, but it must be an audience the students want to serve, engage, or impress.

7. The content and competencies addressed in the course should build progressively toward established goals, allowing students to apply and benefit from past experience as they acquire new knowledge and skills.

8. We must acknowledge the value of entrepreneurial experience, model entrepreneurial attitudes in our interactions with students, and resist the use of policies and practices that deprive students of the chance to think and work creatively.

9. Opportunities for conscious, thoughtful reflection (e.g., in journals) on the work being undertaken must be provided throughout the program (see Figure 10.16).

10. The program must include constructive, ongoing evaluation of skills, content, and changes in student attitudes.

What sort of students does REAL attract? Because budding entrepreneurs are to be found throughout the student body, the REAL class typically mixes students from college-prep, vocational and "at-risk" populations. A student entering REAL may have a specific skill or idea he or she wishes to turn into a money-making venture, or

FIGURE 10.16   Business Planning Journal

MARKETING: Competition

- Who are your five strongest competitors, either direct or indirect? Where are they located? What do they sell?

- Is their business growing, holding its own, or declining? Why?

- How will your business be like your competitors' businesses?

- How will your business be different from your competitors' businesses?

- How will your business compete successfully against your competitors?

- How do you anticipate your competitors will react to your entry into the market?

- How will your answers to the above questions affect your financial projections?

---

may simply wish to explore the option of going into business for themselves. Research indicates that entrepreneurs often are not academically oriented, not because they are not "smart," but because they learn in ways different from those addressed by traditional teaching methods. For this reason, experiential learning is a critical component of REAL, for it provides opportunities to reach students with a variety of "learning styles." This diversity is a challenge for teachers and an important asset for students who benefit from the range of skills, experience, and knowledge present in a heterogeneous group. It also begins to clarify the issue of ethics in all business activities, as suggested by the Activity Card in Figure 10.17.

FIGURE 10.17   Ethics Activity Card

Good or Bad in *Whose* Eyes?

Imagine yourself walking into one of the small auditoriums on the university campus. It's your first class for *Philosophy 22: Introduction to Ethics.* The room feels warm—a combination of the lingering humidity of early autumn in the South and the body heat generated by a hundred students wondering what will happen in this class. Most of you are strangers to each other, as well as to the subject of ethics.

Like you, the other students are not philosophy majors. They've signed up for *Philosophy 22* for a variety of reasons: wanting to be with their best friend, needing to fulfill some university requirement, having the suspicion that a lack of ethics is behind many societal problems, or hearing that this class is taught by an entertaining professor. One of the things all of you share is the belief that you have a pretty clear sense of right and wrong, good and bad.

At the front of the class is Professor Geoff Sayre-McCord, whose appearance and behavior signal students that he is relatively young, smart, energetic and approachable. Instead of launching into the long, boring lecture you and the other students had been fearing, Professor Sayre-McCord starts by passing out a 3x5 index card to everyone in the room. He assures you that your answers to the questions he's about to ask will be completely anonymous. You are instructed *not* to write your names on the cards, and he reminds all of you that he couldn't possibly identify anyone by their handwriting. In return, he requests you to be completely honest in your answers. He jokingly says that any saints in the room are exempt from this assignment.

[Using a 3x5 card, or a sheet of paper, please do as Professor Sayre-McCord asks. You will *not* have to turn this part of the assignment into your REAL teacher(s). In fact, you are welcome to *destroy* this bit of writing once you've completed the entire REAL lesson/activity card.]

First, Professor Sayre-McCord requests that you write down one thing you *actually have done* in the past two or three years that **you absolutely would not want the police to know.** Second, he asks all of you to write down the thing you actually have done in the same period that **you would be most reluctant to tell to your parents.** Third, he urges you to write

down the thing you actually have done in recent years about which **you, personally, are most ashamed.**

As you can imagine, there's a fair amount of nervous laughter across the classroom as you and the other students confront some uncomfortable truths about your imperfections. Nevertheless, while making sure no one is peeking at what is being written, everyone answers these questions pretty thoughtfully and honestly.

The cards then are passed to the front, shuffled well, and samples from each of the three categories are read aloud to the whole class. The students discover that *it is unusual for students to name the same action in more than one category.* In other words, what they want to keep from the police, what they want to hide from their parents, and what they are least proud of about themselves turn out to be *different* things. Professor Sayre-McCord indicates that this pattern has been the same for all the years he has posed these questions.

Professor Sayre-McCord created a clever way of helping his students realize that there are different levels of ethical/moral judgments. The first level involves the distinction between **legal** and **illegal.** Society's most obvious way of indicating that it judges an action to be "wrong" or "bad" is to make that action or behavior *illegal.*

However, there are numerous examples of laws that are broken without the people involved feeling unethical, immoral, or ashamed. For example, during the time when the federal government made it illegal to drive at more than 55 miles per hour, a majority of citizens violated this law without any particular regret—and without harming their sense of themselves as good people. They would not have been afraid to tell their parents about driving over 55 m.p.h. (often because their parents were doing the very same thing, too!). Moreover, they didn't feel personally ashamed about this behavior.

At the same time, there are actions that are legal, but which society as a whole views as "unethical," "wrong," or "bad." These are the things that you might be reluctant to tell your parents. For instance, while it is perfectly legal for you to treat your teachers very rudely for no good reason, it probably

(Continued)

FIGURE 10.17 *(Continued)*

is *not* the kind of behavior you would choose to reveal to your parents. Thus, the ethical distinction here is between **socially approved** and **socially disapproved** behavior.

The final level of ethical judgments involves those actions of your that **you** genuinely believe to be "bad" or "wrong"—and about which you feel ashamed. They may be legal or illegal. Similarly, they may be socially approved or frowned on. They may reflect your religious beliefs, or there may be another source for these self-judgments. What's important about them is that *they violate your own personal values.* For instance, your best friend may have called and pleaded for help with a personal crisis on the same evening you were cramming for a really important exam. Rejecting your friend in order to study doesn't violate any law, and neither your parents nor society will condemn you for being such a dedicated student. Nevertheless, you may feel ashamed and judge your own behavior harshly.

The first part of your assignment is to answer Professor Sayre-McCord's three questions about yourself. The second part is to have a discussion with a group of other REAL students, with your REAL teacher(s) and/or with one of your REAL mentors about the ethical standards that apply to your personal behavior, and those that apply to the actions of an enterprise you own. Do you believe the ethical standards are the same for you and for your enter-

prise? Why or why not? Is it enough for your business to act legally? Why or why not? Must your enterprise "do the right thing" in the eyes of the law, *and* in the eyes of society (e.g., your parents and community), *and* in your own eyes? Why or why not? Please turn in a *brief* paper summarizing your opinions.

Activities

1. Answering, confidentially, a series of questions about your own ethical behavior.
2. Analyzing three ways in which actions are judged to be right or wrong, good or bad.
3. Discussing whether you and your enterprise should be held to the same ethical standards, and writing a paper that explains your beliefs.

What's the Point?

1. Determining what is "ethical" is not a simple matter, but it is a very important one.
2. Society, your parents/community, and you (personally) may use different standards for judging whether certain actions are right or wrong, good or bad.
3. Exploring whether your personal actions and the actions of your enterprise could (and should) be held to the same ethical standards is a fundamental task of this whole box.

© REAL Enterprises, 1991. Used with permission.

Teachers need practice and continual feedback to master the use of experiential learning techniques. Consequently, REAL has developed support and evaluation functions that are required of any teacher entering the program. Backing up the curriculum guide are national and state-level organizations providing support and assistance to teachers implementing REAL in their schools. New teachers attend a two-week teacher institute for two summers in a row, along with other educators from the twelve states implementing the program. In their states, teachers attend in-service seminars and receive on-site and phone support from staff trained in experiential learning and business development. REAL also provides an evaluation process that measures student achievement in acquiring skills and creating businesses.

PART *IV*

Adapting Systems to Support Performance

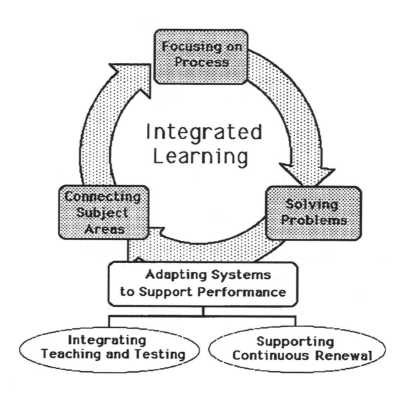

High school learning is suffering, not from lack of effort, but from diffusion of effort. On behalf of innumerable special (and important) interests, high school programs have continuously expanded their services. In place of one clear goal—educating young people to use their minds to manage their world—high schools have adopted scores of goals and purposes that change with each ringing of the bell and that differ for each student. The ideas behind these last chapters, and those that precede it, are quite simple indeed:

- Transforming high school teaching depends on making exhibitions of student learning the main purpose of all school activity.
- With student exhibitions of learning at the center of activity, virtually all other school functions must be called into question and adapted so they support student performance.

Only by simplifying the purpose of high school learning can we achieve the value we need from the high school experience.

FIGURE IV.1   Performance Assessment: Aligning Authentic Tasks to Clear Standards

Math and Technology

By collaborating with others in your group and by gathering locally available data, estimate the number of bricks in the cart and the approximate weight of the load. Then demonstrate the most efficient way to move the cart and the bricks to the job site.

From Casey Murrow's Teachers Workshop, Brattleboro, VT. Drawing © Janusz Kapusha. Used with permission.

Chapter 11, Integrating Teaching and Testing: Authentic Assessment—Teach-test-teach-test. The pattern seems as firmly established as the Friday quiz. The examples of assessment in this chapter integrate the functions of testing with the process of student learning (see Figure IV.1). As students complete learning tasks, they use established goals and standards to assess their accomplishment. Authentic learning tasks, portfolios, exhibitions or performances, standards for performance, rubrics for measuring achievement, and continual reflection on progress toward clearly stated purposes constitute an approach to measurement distinct from externally based, comparative tests of knowledge and skills acquisition. Against clearly stated purposes, students can produce work of high quality and also learn to manage the processes of thought that result in quality productions. Whether these methods produce a competitive work force, they do support the development of individuals who have learned how to achieve results from their own effort.

Assessment Showcase: Student Trek: Assessment at University Heights High School Nancy Mohr and Paul Allison, East Harlem, New York City, a guide to portfolio development written by teachers, students and administrators.

Chapter 12, Supporting Continuous Renewal: Systems Adaptation—Change is our destiny in a changing world. Adapting to continuous change forces high school teachers to design more flexible systems for learning. The shape of the school day, conceptions of the teacher role, conceptions of leadership, and school management all must be rebuilt for greater adaptability. For change to occur, time within the school day must be allocated to the process of change. This concluding chapter features alternative schedules for "learning-centered" high school programs, with notes on further changes that should occur when quality becomes the guiding principle in learning.

CHAPTER 11

Integrating Teaching and Testing

Authentic Assessment

The Promise of Assessment

A friend of ours was trying to counsel one of his students against dropping out of high school. The student was flunking math, among other subjects, and was impatient to leave a situation in which failure had been his hallmark.

"What will you do for work?" the teacher asked.

"I think I will cruise timber for the logging mill," the student replied.

"What do you mean, 'cruise timber'? " the teacher inquired.

"Cruising is trying to find out how much marketable lumber is standing in a forest, so you can figure whether to cut or not."

"And how would you find that out?" our friend inquired.

"Oh, you just measure the bore of any tree at chest height, stand back to estimate the number of log lengths in the tree, then convert that to board feet using a formula or conversion sheet. If you do that honestly for several trees in a section and the section is pretty much like the rest of the forest, you can get close to figuring how many board feet are ready for cutting without having to measure the whole area. If you can estimate the amount of hardwood and softwood, you can get pretty close to the dollar amount the whole thing is worth."

"And what if you're wrong? " the teacher inquired.

"You can look for an easier line of work," the student replied.

How can it be that a high school dropout, flunking math, can qualify for a job requiring complex math skills? Quite possibly, the tests used to measure school math do not measure working-world math. Apparently, they do not reflect the math skills this student had worked to his level of proficiency; out in a timber stand, he is able to do things tests say he is unable to do. The same hyperachievement phenomenon can be noted among low-achieving students calculating baseball averages, weight gain and loss, or the relative price advantage of fixing up an old Ford junker versus an old Chevy junker. Standardized testing, decontextualized from meaningful activity, may not measure the knowledge we use quite adequately in daily affairs. The assessment of atomized skills and knowledge, like the teaching of atomized skills and knowledge, deprives students of a context that lets them value what they are learning.

Portfolios of student work and other demonstrations or performances, assessed through scoring rubrics based on school standards or simply presented as valid evidence in its own right, have created some answers and some further challenges for teachers who are working toward integrated teaching (Mabry, 1992). At the national, state, and local levels, teachers are developing methods of assessment that integrate teaching and testing and that link directly to the goals they have set for student learning. Some schools and some teachers have decided to let student performance stand for itself in public exhibitions of what high school students have learned. Others are developing elaborate scoring systems that let teachers and students compare student work to an established standard. Still, the energetic proliferation of new assessment models testifies to the importance of assessment reform and also to the early stage of our development in this area.

Problems in Assessment Strategy

No aspect of high school teaching causes quite as much consternation as does assessment. The world itself inspires anxiety, though different people experience discomfort for different reasons. Students see assessment as testing, a procedure that will play out directly in their prospects for the future. Parents often see report cards as assessment, though the report card itself is just a reporting instrument that may obscure as much of the school experience as it reveals. Teachers may see assessment as a source of threat—to students who may not put in the effort required for success and to themselves if their class scores on standardized measures fall below the scores of other teachers. School administrators, often lacking deeper knowledge of their own schools, are apt to see assessment as a source of control. "Since teachers teach to the test," they say, "use the test scores as leverage to change teaching." The general public responds the same to all assessment results—from districtwide SAT scores to commission reports; people see it as evidence of spreading mediocrity and reason to believe that the nation is plunging headlong into third-rate status on the globe.

To the extent that testing stands distant from teaching and learning, teachers will continue to regard assessment with suspicion. Most large-scale testing simply fails to account for the various kinds of learning taking place in different classrooms. Like curriculum itself, assessment of high school learning has fallen into place without the guidance of a broad purpose or general plan. Local, state, and national tests meet a collection of narrow concerns without reflecting a general consensus about the results we want a high school education to achieve. According to Resnick et al. (1992, p. 187):

> The United States has no national curriculum to guide our thousands of separate jurisdictions and no system of board examinations to set standards. Postsecondary admission is controlled by tests (The Scholastic Aptitude Test and the ACT tests) linked to no particular program of study. Textbooks have a kind of default curriculum control; in each subject matter, three or four textbook series dominate the market. And a system of commercially provided standardized tests, although not imposed by any centralized authority, has substantial impact on day-to-day instruction.

By failing to connect testing practices with a clear sense of educational purpose, we create confusion at every level of educational practice.

As assessment moves to center stage in the drama of educational reform, teachers will bear an increasing responsibility for explaining its complexity to others—students, parents, administrators, and public officials. Generally, teachers have not been well prepared to explain assessment to others. Teachers put their energy into classroom teaching, an activity that assessment has seldom been used to improve. Teachers, however, are for better or worse, uniquely positioned to understand and explain assessment to those most concerned—students, parents, administrators, and their colleagues. "Old forms of testing can limit how far and how fast the movement for change will proceed. Newer assessments can be proactive tools of reform, pressing toward new forms of teaching and learning (Resnick et al., 1992, p. 186). As assessment becomes a more central part of teaching, teachers will need to refine their understanding of the options and present the choices to others. If assessment is to be integrated with classroom learning, as several propose, teachers will need to convey the kind of reasoning that makes assessment meaningful.

The Primacy of Purpose

Why bother? This simple question is central to understanding how both conventional and new forms of assessment may contribute to the transformation of high school teaching. At the heart of it, purpose determines the validity of a testing process: "How are the results to be used?" The question itself has an enormous number of possible answers:

1. To help students understand what they have learned and what they need to learn.
2. To let parents know how their children are doing.
3. To help teachers compare achievement among students.
4. To establish a basis for tracking.
5. To measure teacher performance.
6. To set budget priorities.

In light of all these different purposes and others, validity does not reside in any test. Validity occurs when an assessment procedure produces results that serve a given purpose well. To ask any test to serve multiple and unrelated purposes is to ask too much. As the number of purposes for assessment has increased, the idea of validity has shifted away from psychometric characteristics toward ideas of validity based on consequences, fairness, complexity, quality, and meaningfulness (Moss, 1992).

The vast and disparate machinery of national testing has obliterated the question of purpose in assessment, particularly avoiding the issues of relevance, value implications, and social consequences that connect to purpose (Shepard, 1992). Commercially available standardized tests are used to measure student ability, teacher effectiveness, program strength, and educational quality in a district, whether or not the tests fit the goals of those entities. Moreover, the mechanization of testing may undercut its most basic purposes. Do tests impel students to perform at their highest level, producing an accurate measure of achievement? Probably not. "American standardized tests actively discourage effort. Patterned on intelligence tests, they compare students with one another rather than with publicly established standards of achievement" (Resnick et al., 1992, p. 189). Do tests allow students from many backgrounds to display valuable skills and knowledge? "With fifteen million children at risk, schools must shift their focus from sorting and selecting to teaching and learning (Canady & Hotchkiss, 1989). As George Madeus points out, "When important things like promotion, graduation from grade to grade, teacher evaluation, school district certification and financial support . . . depend on test scores, [testing] corrupts the process you're trying to improve" (Brandt, 1989).

Conventional assessment is painful. On a given day, students assemble in gym or cafeteria, waiting for instructions that tell them when to start bubbling in the bubbles and when to stop. In the worst of circumstances, assessment imposed from outside the classroom to meet a narrow purpose becomes the standard by which students, parents, and teachers judge individual worthiness. Though the standardized tests may bear no relationship to the existing curriculum, the needs of the students or the plans a school has created for its own development, standardized tests are used broadly to assess individual students, teacher effectiveness, a school program, or even a state curriculum. Standardized tests, such as the SATs or any of the commercially available testing systems, may be administered each year, whether or not a school has discussed their purpose and limitations. The fact that one test may serve none of the many possible purposes particularly well has initiated an era of reform in assessment practice.

Examining Purpose: K–12

Understanding purpose is the key to understanding assessment. Linking a set of assessment practices to a clear purpose is the key to making assessment meaningful. In the Rutland Northeast Supervisory District in Vermont, the district assessment committee set out to align its assessment practices with the purposes to be served by tests of different types. Through several months of exhaustive analysis, the committee identified four general areas of purposeful assessment and nine specific reasons for sampling student performance so the results would prove both useful and reliable (see Figure 11.1). That assessment methods aimed at one purpose would have limited use in other areas pointed to the need for a carefully delineated assessment strategy.

Figure 11.1 arranges the nine purposes for assessment in ascending order from purposes related to individual students to purposes related to public understanding and public policy:

1. *To focus student learning:* The central reason for assessment is to guide student effort. Students need assessment results that will show them (and their supporting parents) what they have learned, and also suggest what they need to learn so they can adequately manage the direction of their own work.

2. *To focus teaching:* Teachers need assessment results that will let them adjust daily plans to meet student needs and to evaluate the effectiveness of the strategies they use in the classroom.

3. *To improve supporting systems:* School administrators and program managers need assessment results that will let them allocate special services, evaluate the systems that run the school, and suggest adjustments in the curriculum.

FIGURE 11.1   Why Test? Nine Purposes for Assessment

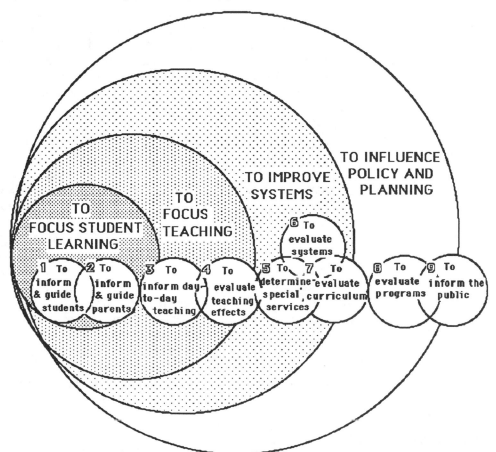

From materials used by Nancy Cornell, Curriculum and Staff Development Director, Rutland Northeast Supervisory District, Brandon, VT. Used with permission.

4. *To influence policy and planning:* Board members, with all the teaching community, need assessment results that will help them evaluate whole programs and inform the public about the quality of education in their schools.

Clearly, no single instrument will serve all these purposes equally well. In addition, no school or district has the money to support each purpose to the same degree. Developing a comprehensive strategy means setting priorities and making it clear how one assessment effort connects to larger purposes.

Relating one kind of assessment result to a purpose it ill-serves causes misunderstanding and anxiety. The Rutland Northeast Assessment Committee decided to survey all its assessment practices for each of the nine purposes to clarify the current situation and provide a basis for decisions. For each of the nine purposes in the district, they asked the following eight questions:

1. What tools are we already using?
2. How are we using the results?
3. How are we reporting the results?
4. To whom are we reporting?
5. What school proficiencies (goals) are being measured by the results?
6. What are the relative strengths of the process?
7. What are the weaknesses?
8. What should we do to better achieve our purposes?

Figure 11.2 includes the results of the committee's deliberations for one assessment purpose—improving day-to-day instruction.

When redirecting daily instruction is the purpose, teachers employ a mass of different strategies, some of which test student knowledge in conventional ways and others that test student learning as a process. Teachers were using conventional quizzes, unit tests, running records, writing and reading conferences, as well as a districtwide social studies tests, for periodic reports of achievement. They were using observation, science logs, reading journals, and general student portfolios to gain an understanding of how the students were learning. They were using the Vermont Portfolio Process to assess both achievement and learning and for reporting scores to students' parents, teachers, and the state. Quite predictably, district teachers were not using standardized or nationally normed tests to improve their daily teaching, though public acclaim (and budgets) might rise and fall on those results. They were not using general portfolio results to inform administrators about student learning, though administrators held program planning in the balance. In Vermont, a four-point drop in English SAT scores matched with a rise in math, was front-page news in the state's largest paper, quickly consuming public interest in the question of assessment. Conventional tests, despite their limitations, have enormous evocative power in public debate.

When assessment specifically aims to improve daily teaching, what are the strengths and limitations of different techniques? In Rutland Northeast, the existing assessment techniques were all limited by similar weaknesses. They consumed time, were subjectively based, required training to be useful, or yielded unreliable results. Despite these limitations, many forms of assessment proved useful and valuable in guiding instruction, particularly reading and writing conferences, informal observation, running records, portfolios, science logs, and journals. The Assessment Committee could see in its table that the most useful assessment techniques for improving teaching occurred within the classroom as teachers used student work to assess their own direction and technique. They concluded that the costs in time and effort were most justified when the assessment contributed directly to student learning. "Student-centered" testing served both students and teachers with prompt feedback, helping them adjust their efforts to learn or teach more effectively.

FIGURE 11.2   Assessment to Improve Instruction

Purpose	Assessment Tools	How are we using results?	How are we reporting results?	To whom are results reported?
Improve day-to-day instruction	teacher-made quiz	Inst. planning; evaluating skills and proficiencies	Letter or number grade; verbal report	Students; parents (possibly)
	reading conferences	Inst. planning; evaluating skills and proficiencies; setting individual student goals	Narratives; continuums; grades verbal report	Students; parents' support staff
	informal observation	Inst. planning; evaluating skills and proficiencies; setting individual student goals	Narratives; grades; verbal report	Student; parents; support staff
	writing conferences	Inst. planning; evaluating skills and proficiencies; setting individual student goals	Narratives; continuums; verbal report	Students; parents; support staff
	running records	Inst. planning; determining readability	Written record; verbal report	Other professionals; parents (possibly)
	portfolios—general	Evaluating skills and proficiencies; evaluating student's progress; setting individual student goals	Narrative; verbal report	Students; parents
	teacher-made unit tests	Evaluating skills and proficiencies; determining grades	Grades; verbal report	Students; parents
	pretest/interview	Instructional planning	Written questions/answers; verbal report	Students
	textbook tests	Evaluating skills and proficiencies	Grades; verbal report	Students; parents
	science logs	Checking for understanding; checking for science process skills	Written questions and answers; verbal report	Students; parents
	reading journals	Checking for understanding, engagement, and reflection	Written questions and answers; verbal report	Students; parents
	Vermont math portfolio and uniform test	Inst. planning based on student progress in meeting statewide standards	Written statewide and RNE summaries; school summaries of uniform tests; individual student results on uniform tests	Students; parents; RNE boards; state; receiving teachers
	Vermont writing portfolio and uniform test	Inst. planning based on student progress in meeting statewide standards	Written statewide and RNE summaries; school summaries of uniform tests	Students; parents; RNE boards; state; receiving teachers
	social studies assessment	Inst. planning; promoting self-assessment	Written RNE summary; verbal report	Students; parents; central office; 3rd grade teachers
	U.S. history assessment	Inst. planning; promoting self-assessment	Written RNE summary; verbal report	Students; central office; U.S. history teachers

From materials used by Nancy Cornell, Curriculum and Staff Development Director, Rutland Northeast Supervisory District, Brandon, VT. Used with permission.

Integrating Tests with Learning Tasks

As in other realms of human endeavor, efficiency and effectiveness in assessment seem to ride the see-saw in school testing programs. Highly efficient tests do not seem to measure what really matters. Highly effective tests seem to eat up a huge amount of instructional time. When efficiency goes up, effectiveness drops. Conventional testing, using multiple choice or similar measures, uses a brief sampling of factual knowledge and basic skills to efficiently measure student learning. Authentic testing, using portfolios of student work and problems requiring applications of basic knowledge to novel and open-ended problems, seeks out evidence of thoughtfulness and strategic skill in the work students complete as they learn. Conventional testing offers real advantages in efficiency. How much of the basic material are students learning? Quickly and uniformly applied, conventional tests let teachers compare students against each other and against national or local norms. They interrupt teaching to the least possible degree. Authentic testing offers a clear view of effectiveness. How well are students learning the things that really matter? If we were to pursue both efficient and effective tests equally, testing would soon take more instructional time than teaching and learning.

The only solution to the efficiency/effectiveness paradox that supports development of effective assessment strategies is to integrate testing and teaching. We must test as we teach, using common standards to judge the development of learning over time. If we sample performance in daily learning activity, we are sampling learning as an ongoing process rather than as an end point. Assessment from this perspective becomes one more occasion for learning, a chance for students and teachers to look at what is being accomplished, celebrate progress, and set new directions with new challenges. "The road to reform is a straight but steep one: test those capacities and habits we think are essential and test them in context" (Wiggins, 1989b). Using integrated or authentic testing to evaluate curriculum or school effectiveness, however, is not a challenge we will easily manage.

New Tests for New Purposes

The flurry of activity supporting development of authentic tests is matched by the simultaneous effort to reform norm-referenced tests so they appear both valid and reliable (O'Neil, 1993b). Redevelopment of norm-referenced tests is largely a centralized exercise, developed through collaboration between the government and private testing corporations. The development of authentic tests, in contrast, is taking place at every conceivable level of the educational enterprise. Classroom teachers are developing and field-testing "exhibitions" and "performances" to replace text-based tests in their own courses. Schools across the United States have begun experimenting with standards for graduation that will provide teachers with a framework for widespread authentic testing. Vermont and other states have instituted portfolio assessment as a practice leading toward development of a statewide core curriculum (Mabry, 1992). Regional centers, such as the Far West Laboratory, have developed assessment guidelines that nicely reflect the whole concept of learning-centered schooling and integration of learning with life (Koelsch, 1994). Lauren Resnick and her colleagues in Pittsburgh have been developing assessment instruments in ten content areas for use on a national basis. Despite a notable lack of coordination, these efforts share a governing logic that attempts to fuse testing with learning skills and knowledge applicable in real-life situations. As the methods converge, we may expect the gradual formation of some consensus on the purpose and process of authentic testing.

Portfolios form the centerpiece of most efforts to reform assessment at the high school level; a portfolio is a collection of student work arranged to reflect the goals of a school community. Some schools, particularly many in the Essential Schools Coalition, prefer to let student portfolios stand for themselves. Students collect their best work over time, arrange it in categories that reflect school goals, and exhibit it publicly to demonstrate their competence. Such portfolios rely on the idea of "face validity," allowing the student or adult viewer to draw conclusions about what the work represents.

Arts PROPEL in the Pittsburgh public schools is an example of an open portfolio approach in which students generate the standards for good writing and then assess their own work on the basis of criteria a class establishes for itself (Howard, 1993). On the other hand, Pittsburgh is also home to the New Standards Project (NSP) in which teachers and professional organizations set the standards, develop performance tasks to test student learning, and devise highly specific grading rubrics teachers use to judge student products, aiming for high reliability among different people grading different student work (Simmons & Resnick, 1992). While Arts PROPEL sees the student as the first audience and uses the portfolio to celebrate personal learning, the New Standards Project sees teachers and administrators as the first audience and the portfolio as a way to measure educational effectiveness and to drive school reform. Different purposes create different assessment tactics.

Whether the purpose is to celebrate individual student learning or to compare a large group of students against one standard, authentic tests use rubrics or grading criteria to assess student work (portfolios of products, performances, or exhibitions) that represent standards or learning goals a school or district determines essential to its educational mission. Figure 11.3 reflects the logic behind developing authentic assessment strategies.

Educational Mission: A mission statement describes the purposes a school will serve for all its graduates, including social, vocational, intellectual, and personal development.

Graduation (or Grade-Level) Standards: Standards describe the outcomes that will be measured to determine whether the mission has been accomplished by a student or group.

Assessment Plan: The plan specifies the instructional goals, learning activities, and performances (products or exhibitions) that will be used to judge whether students have met graduation or grade-level standards.

Grading Rubrics: Grading rubrics define the criteria by which student performances will be assessed—by students, teachers, parents, and administrators alike.

Benchmarks: Scales developed for each criterion that mark the extent to which a student has met established expectations.

Different purposes have convinced different educators to develop these five elements to different degrees. A rubric for a "celebratory" assessment might include simple "benchmarks": excellent, good, fair, poor. Rubrics and benchmarks for comparative assessment may run to several pages for a single task. To be useful, authentic testing requires consistency or coherence between the rubrics used to judge student performances and the purposes a community has set for assessment.

Communities differ in size and complexity. A classroom, a school, a district, a state, a nation—each is a community in its own right. Who may claim the right to define the governing educational mission, and thus assume control over assessment? Teachers have clear claim, by virtue of professional training and experience, to adapt their teaching and testing to serve the many individuals who fill the seats in their classes. Schools may formulate a mission on the basis of local educational priorities, particularly among the taxpayers who support school budgets. A state educational bureaucracy may use its association with elected government to fashion a mission for all its public schools, bolstered by state-aid formulas that feed state taxes back to local schools and an established regulatory system. The federal government has its

FIGURE 11.3   Assessing Integrated Units

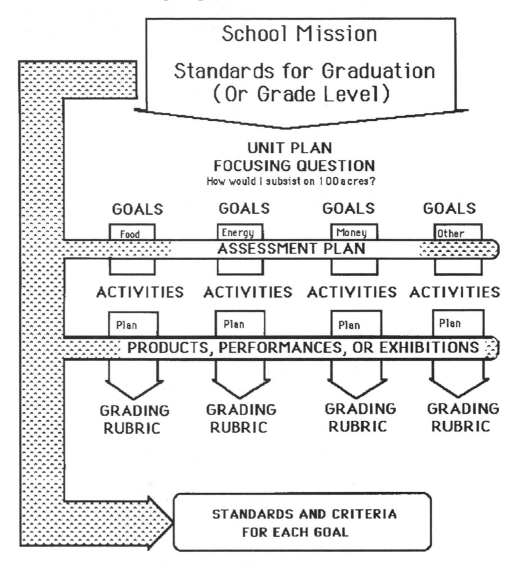

From materials used by Nancy Cornell, Curriculum and Staff Development Director, Rutland Northeast Supervisory District, Brandon, VT. Used with permission.

own sense of mission, based on international economics, industrial competitiveness, national security, and national welfare interests—all backed by federal grants going to the schools. At the present time, none of these communities has the power to unilaterally assert a set of standards, performances, and criteria for teachers and students to use as a guide to learning. The race is on to formulate assessment practices that will guide the reform of high school teaching.

National Scope: The New Standards Project

Setting a national mission for schools and their reform may be a larger undertaking than mere politics can perform. When President Bush called for national tests in 1990, he did so without referring to any greater purpose than "accountability"—to make schools more responsible for the achievements of their students. Lacking a clear national mission for high schools, redevelopment of existing tests has proceeded from the status quo. Critics expect the National Assessment of Educational Progress (NAEP) to look very much like the norm-referenced tests that have preceeded it and to suffer from the same limitations. Professional organizations linked to the subject areas, following the example set by mathematics, have begun developing assessment strategies for their areas. In light of political complexities, assessment reform at the national level has begun without a clear declaration of mission. Debate at the national level is clarifying the issues in assessment and, if nothing else, helping local educators narrow the purposes of their own assessment programs.

By far the most ambitious and promising national effort is led by Lauren Resnick, Director of the New Standards Project in Pittsburgh, aiming to "design and implement a system of performance standards, authentic assessments and professional development intended to change the way the American school system works" (Simmons & Resnick, 1992). The New Standards Project is committed to an assessment system with six major features (Resnick, et al., 1992):

1. Assessment linked to content standards;
2. High standards, the same for all groups of students;
3. Direct assessment of valued outcomes (scheduled performance examinations and portfolios);
4. Performance standards set publicly and widely known;
5. Internalized standards embedded in educational practice;
6. Assessment reform linked to other elements of systemic reform.

Bowing to conventional practice, the NSP strategy is based on established subject area divisions rather than a more practical estimation of "essential skills" related to an overall statement of mission. The NSP aims to develop an assessment guide for each of ten academic areas, tested at the fourth-, eighth- and tenth-grade levels. Content-specific standards will organize the entire examination system. Currently, guides for language arts and mathematics are being tested in seventeen states but only at the fourth- and eighth-grade levels.

The primary goal of the New Standards Project is "to use a new system of standards and assessments as the cornerstone strategy to greatly improve the performance of all students, particularly those who score least well now" (NSP, 1993). Setting the same standards for all students, despite manifold differences in background, motivation, prior learning, and disposition toward learning, flies in the face of established practice and provides the Project with a clear challenge. The comprehensive NSP plan calls for portfolios with three kinds of work: (1) work chosen by the district school or student, (2) work prescribed in NSP projects and extended learning activities, and (3) student performances responding to NSP "matrix-examination tasks." The matrix examination is a preset task for which NSP has developed a scoring rubric that has been matched to its standards for a subject area. Figure 11.4 is a matrix examination problem for mathematics, asking students to create a table guiding shoelace length, a rule customers can use to figure out what to buy, and an explanation of what the student has developed. How can a national test with a distinctive interest in equity "provide the opportunities all students need to prepare themselves well?" (Simmons & Resnick, 1992, p. 12).

Reliability is the short-term problem NSP has set out to solve. Enormous bulk may limit the widespread use of the NSP system. As more tasks are developed for each standard and as more subject areas yield performance-based assessments, the size of the system could prevent most teachers from understanding it all. If six days of preparatory work and scaffolding precede each matrix examination, a total of sixty days would be devoted to matrix exams in the fourth, eighth and tenth grades, eclipsing other opportunities as well as eating time that might be spent on individual port-

FIGURE 11.4   Sample Task from the New Standards Project

How Long Should a Shoelace Be?

Suppose you work for a shoelace company. You receive the following assignment from your boss.

Sports Laces

ASSIGNMENT

We have decided to sell laces for sports shoes. We will sell different lengths for shoes with different numbers of eyelets. We will offer lengths for sport shoes that have 4 eyelets all the way up to 18 eyelets (no odd numbers, of course). No one has ever sold so many different lengths for sports shoes before. You have to figure out what lengths to make and which lengths go with which shoes, based on the number of eyelets.

We collected some data from store customers last week. It is confusing because there haven't been very many lengths available. That means that sometimes the customers have had to use lengths that are too short or too long. That's not what we want! We want a unique length for each number of eyelets.

DATA FROM STORE CUSTOMERS WITH SPORTS SHOES

Customer I.D.	Lace Length (inches)	Eyelets (numbers)	Customer I.D.	Lace Length (inches)	Eyelets (numbers)
A	45	8	G	54	12
B	54	10	H	24	4
C	26	4	I	72	14
D	63	14	J	54	12
E	63	12	K	72	16
F	36	8	L	72	18

Write your decisions about lace length so the advertising people making the sign can understand it. They want a table, so customers can look up the number of eyelets and find out the length of lace. They also want a rule, so customers who don't like tables can use the rule to figure out the lengths. Don't worry about making it pretty, they will do that, just make sure the mathematics is right. You better explain how your decisions make sense, so the advertising people will understand.

Thanks.

YOUR BOSS,

Angela

folios and extended projects. Still Resnick and her Project have managed to integrate teaching and testing around authentic tasks for the subject areas. If a national curriculum is to emerge from the movement toward nationally based performance testing, the NSP tasks and rubrics would not be a bad place to start.

State Performance Testing: Vermont's Core and Portfolio Projects

Discouraged by the failure of fit between state goals and norm-referenced testing, several states have joined the quest for a results-oriented assessment system. Oregon and Arizona are working with the Far West Laboratory to develop portfolio systems based on defined state outcomes. In Kentucky, fourth-, eighth- and twelfth-grade students keep writing portfolios and work through performance events in science math and social studies (O'Neil, 1992). With McGraw-Hill, Maryland has developed a reading/writing assessment that asks students to read through a variety of sources and then write a response to a realistic situation related to the reading (Mitchell, 1992). These states aim to use performance-based testing both to improve teaching and to satisfy public demand for accountability in the schools, a double motive that will require delicate balance.

In Vermont, three years of experimentation with writing and math portfolios, including both student-selected, "best-piece" assessment and "on-demand" tasks under test conditions, are leading toward a core curriculum combining process and skills development with content learning. This new portfolio system has had more of an impact on instruction than on accountability, and more impact on grade K–8 students than on the high school students. Still, the excitement of performance-based assessment has begun to moderate the fear of standardized tests felt among high school students and shift teacher focus toward new ways of teaching at all levels. At the very least, the Vermont assessment rubrics have created a vocabulary for teachers, students, and citizens to use in talking about the purpose of school learning.

In both mathematics and English, the Vermont portfolio rubrics emphasize a few clearly stated performance standards. In the writing portfolio, teachers used five criteria for writing effectiveness to judge both a "best piece" submission from daily work and a "uniform test" for which the conditions of testing were held constant for all students. Teachers used a four-point scale—extensively, frequently, sometimes, rarely—to judge (1) purpose, (2) organization, (3) use of detail, (4) voice/tone, and (5) grammar/usage/mechanics. In the 1992–93 schoolyear, inter-rater reliability was not high enough to permit comparison of students, schools, or districts. The mathematics portfolio assessment, linked to a sample of questions from the NAEP, yielded more reliable results. Figure 11.5 shows Vermont's eighth grade math results, emphasizing change in achievement by some criteria over the two years and underscoring the need for further effort in others.

During the schoolyear, students practice using the seven criteria for assessment on their in-school work, then, they completed an "on-demand" problem in a testing situation. As Figure 11.5 suggests, portfolio assessment in mathematics creates a great deal of useful information in relation to the seven criteria for the seven achievement standards in mathematics. Comparison with the previous year's scores allows teachers and students to recognize improvement in five of seven areas:

- How students solved the problem.
- Why they made certain decisions along the way.
- Whether they generalized from the problem they solved (so what?).
- How they used mathematical language.
- How they presented the problem.

FIGURE 11.5 Eighth Grade Mathematics Portfolio Scores—1992 versus 1993

MATHEMATICS PORTFOLIO—GRADE 8

		Level 1	Level 2	Level 3	Level 4
PROBLEM SOLVING CRITERIA	**PS1** Understanding the Problem	...didn't understand enough to get started or make progress.	...understood enough to solve part of the problem or to get part of a solution.	...understood the problem.	...identified special factors that influenced the approach before starting the problem.
	1993 / 1992			MEAN SCORE: 2.8	
	PS2 How Student Solved Problem	...approach didn't work.	...approach would only lead to solving part of the problem.	...approach would work for the problem.	...approach was efficient or sophisticated.
	1993 / 1992			MEAN SCORE: 2.8	
	PS3 Why - Decisions Along the Way	...no reasoning is evident from the work or reasoning is incorrect.	...only partly correct reasoning, or correct reasoning used for only part of the problem.	...didn't clearly explain the reasons for decisions, but work suggests correct reasoning was used throughout the problem.	...clearly explained the reasons for the correct decisions made throughout the problem.
	1993 / 1992			MEAN SCORE: 2.9	
	PS4 So What - Outcomes of Activities	...solved the problem and stopped.	...solved the problem and made comments about something in the solution.	...solved the problem and connected the solution to other math OR described a use for what was learned in the "real world."	...solved the problem and made a general rule about the solution or extended the solution to a more complicated situation.
	1993 / 1992	MEAN SCORE: 1.2			
COMMUNICATION CRITERIA	**C1** Mathematical Language	...didn't use any math vocabulary, equations, or notations or used them incorrectly.	...used basic math words or basic notation accurately.	...went beyond occasional use of basic math language and used the language correctly.	...relied heavily on sophisticated math language to communicate the solution.
	1993 / 1992		MEAN SCORE: 1.9		
	C2 Mathematical Representation	...didn't use any graphs, tables, charts, models, diagrams or drawings to communicate the solution.	...attempted to use appropriate representation.	...used appropriate math representation accurately and appropriately.	...used sophisticated graphs, tables, charts, models, diagrams, or drawings to communicate the solution.
	1993 / 1992		MEAN SCORE: 2.0		
	C3 Presentation	...response is unclear.	...response contains some clear parts.	...if others read this response, they would have to fill in some details to understand the solution.	...response is well organized and detailed.
	1993 / 1992			MEAN SCORE: 3.1	

From the Vermont Assessment Program, Vermont Department of Education, Montpelier, VT. Used with permission.

With a state standard set, teachers and students could see that Vermont students were achieving acceptable levels in presentation of the problem. They could also see that progress would be most desirable in connecting the problem to the real world (so what?).

Vermont has begun work on a common core of learning, an effort that may lend structure and purpose to the high school assessment projects flourishing around the state. To define a common core, Vermont gathered a random selection of community members into "focus forums" that met in cafeteria and gyms across the state. Facilitators asked participants to answer four basic questions (Mathis, 1994):

1. What do we want all our graduates to know and do?
2. What are we doing now that reflects these goals?
3. What could we do that would take us further toward our goals?
4. How will we know when we are making progress?

Compiled and condensed, the focus forums revealed four common goals, called "vital results," that could link teaching in all the subject areas and provide the basis for a coordinated high school assessment process.

As Figure 11.6 suggests, Vermont's Common Core would focus instruction on four "vital results" in four content areas. It would also create a basic structure to

FIGURE 11.6   Teaching Unit Analysis Matrix: Vermont Common Core

Guided Reflection—Teaching Core Knowledge and Skills

The Vermont Common Core of Learning asks teachers to recognize and emphasize knowledge and skills that are basic to good teaching. Consider a unit, theme, or topic you taught with satisfaction over the last four months. The matrix below can guide you to recognize aspects of the Common Core in what you already do—and to consider additional aspects that might add further power to your teaching.

Unit Topic: _____   Grade: _____

Within this unit, what activities or content helped students develop skills and knowledge connected to the Common Core.

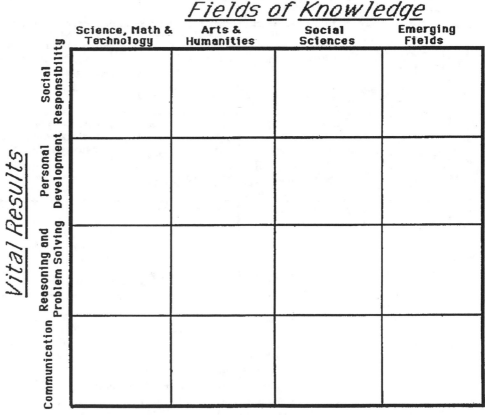

What activities or content might you add in any empty box to further extend the power of this unit?

From the Vermont Assessment Program, Vermont Department of Education, Montpelier, VT. Used with permission.

guide the development of further assessment projects based on "authentic" tasks. In Vermont, Ray Henderson at Missisquoi Valley High School in Swanton has taken a leadership role in developing meaningful tasks for his students and for the Vermont mathematics portfolio. The "pasture" problem in Figure 11.7 asks students to determine the maximum grazing area available to a tethered Vermont cow. Tasks like this fit both the core curriculum matrix and the Vermont mathematics portfolio, giving local teachers and students a way to explore the application of mathematics to problem solving in a local context.

District Assessment Projects: Gwinnett County, Georgia

Because a test should be meaningful in its own context, locally developed standards, goals, tasks, and rubrics are being developed in many high school settings. Recognizing the independence of high school teachers and the need to fuse authentic assessment with the teaching and learning that actually takes place in a school, Grant Wiggins has been active in promoting the idea of an assessment toolbox that local schools could use to tailor assessment to their own curricula (Wiggins, 1989b, 1992). By developing a districtwide tool-kit linked to established standards at the local level, schools can ensure some coherence in the K–12 curriculum while teachers go on to invent tasks and rubrics that fit their own teaching and inspire their own students.

In Gwinnett County, Georgia, local teachers and instructional designers began by creating a simple mission statement and six outcomes of significance that would represent achievement of that mission. Through significant work in the schools, a student would become: (1) a complex thinker, (2) a collaborative contributor, (3) an innovative producer, (4) a self-directed achiever, (5) an involved citizen, and (6) an effective communicator (Kirby et al., 1993). As Figure 11.8 shows, the assessment process asks teachers to develop "Personalized Learning Experiences" for students at each grade level, an age-appropriate challenge representing specified "Adult Role Performances." Figure 11.9 shows the standard and rubric for the adult role "Complex Thinker." Each standard is benchmarked to adult roles and responsibilities in the community. Still, the schools of the county can define assessment tasks that are also appropriate to all grade levels. As students learn through the grades, they measure their success against the same basic standards. Over time, the purpose of assessment clarifies the purpose for learning.

School-Based Assessment: Cabot School K–12

In a school setting, an assessment process can be developed that fits the stated mission of the school. To make such assessment possible, parents, teachers, and students have had to develop and publish a simple set of goals for all school learning, set standards or expectations for each goal area at each grade level, and then ask teachers to develop "rubrics" that define criteria for assessment and "benchmarks" that define different levels of achievement, often using a point system that determines student grades. At Cabot School in northern Vermont, the school community created the following twelve goals to guide all learning in each of the twelve grades:

Cabot High School Graduation Requirements

1. Be able to appreciate the arts and the value of competent craftsmanship.
2. Be able to read for comprehension and enjoyment.
3. Be able to read and speak clearly and effectively.
4. Be able to read, write, speak, and comprehend another language.

FIGURE 11.7   Authentic Task on Rural Mathematics

THE TASK:

A cow is tethered to a barn which is 20 feet wide by 40 feet long.   A rope, 50 feet in length, is attached to a ring on the barn, thus tethering the cow.   The barn has twelve rings to which the cow's rope may be attached.   They are evenly spaced every ten feet around the barn, including the four corners. To which ring should the cow be tethered to give her a maximum grazing area?   What is that area?

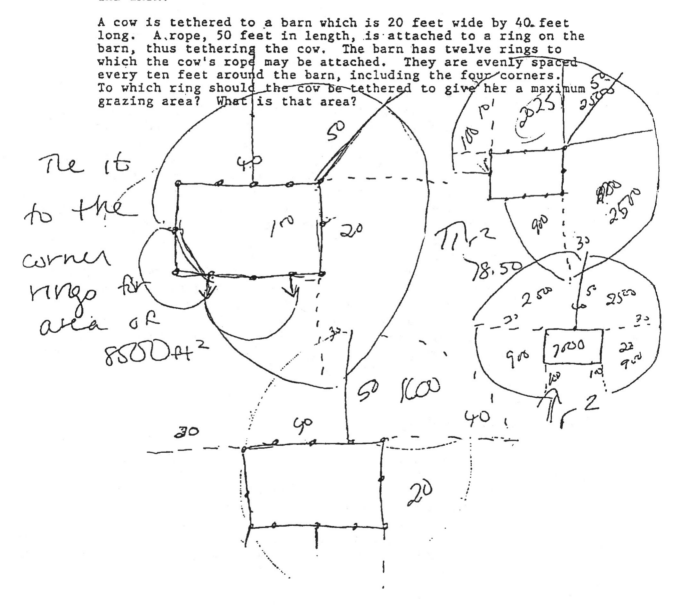

From Ray Henderson's math class at Missisquoi Valley Union High School, Swanton, VT. Used with permission.

FIGURE 11.8   Instructional Framework for Successful Learning

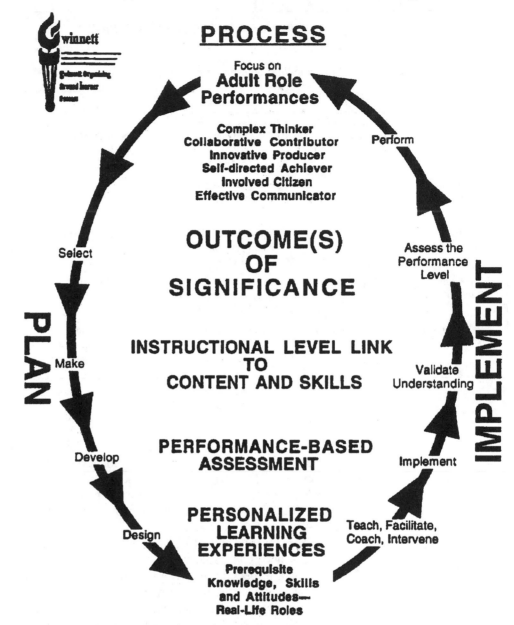

PROCESS

Focus on
Adult Role Performances

**Complex Thinker
Collaborative Contributor
Innovative Producer
Self-directed Achiever
Involved Citizen
Effective Communicator**

OUTCOME(S) OF SIGNIFICANCE

INSTRUCTIONAL LEVEL LINK TO CONTENT AND SKILLS

PERFORMANCE-BASED ASSESSMENT

PERSONALIZED LEARNING EXPERIENCES

**Prerequisite
Knowledge, Skills
and Attitudes—
Real-Life Roles**

PLAN — Select, Make, Develop, Design

IMPLEMENT — Perform, Assess the Performance Level, Validate Understanding, Implement, Teach, Facilitate, Coach, Intervene

"Our Mission Is to Guarantee Individual Student Success"

From materials used at the Gwinnett County Public Schools, Lawrenceville, GA. Used with permission.

5. Be able to compute and interpret numbers.
6. Be able to formulate concepts, gather and interpret data, apply problem-solving skills, and reach reasoned conclusions.
7. Be aware of scientific discovery and advances and their social impact.
8. Be able to use a variety of current technology.
9. Be aware of the interrelatedness of all disciplines (science, math, social science, literature, language, and the arts).
10. Be prepared to function as an informed and interested citizen.
11. Be able to manage himself or herself in the American economic system.
12. Be prepared to function as a socially responsible, healthy, physically fit, and independent individual.

FIGURE 11.9   Assessment Rubric for Adult Role as a Complex Thinker

ADULT ROLE: COMPLEX THINKER

Outcome 1:

Recognizes problems and opportunities; devises, implements, evaluates, and revises a plan of action.

Criteria	Not Yet	Nears Goal	Meets Goal	Exceeds Goal
Recognizes problem	Does not recognize problem which needs attention	Identifies problem, but does not respond	Identifies and chooses a problem for further investigation	Identifies several problems; selects more than one to solve, or prioritizes problems to choose most crucial
Recognizes opportunities	Does not recognize opportunity to be proactive	Recognizes opportunity, but does not respond	Identifies opportunities to be proactive	Identifies multiple opportunities
Devises a plan of action	No plan developed	Plan developed but incomplete or unrealistic	Develops a plausible plan	Develops systematic, detailed plan including time and activities
Implements plan of action	No implementation	Implementation does not follow plan or is unsuccessful	Follows plan successfully	Implements plan systematically and successfully; revises in process, if appropriate
Evaluates plan of action	No evaluation of plan	Limited evaluation, little evidence	Uses appropriate criteria or evidence to evaluate plan	Detailed evaluation of plan using student established criteria

From materials used at the Gwinnett County Public Schools, Lawrenceville, GA. Used with permission.

At each grade level, teachers then defined the standards that students would have to meet to move on to the next grade. Student records were adapted to allow teachers to monitor student progress toward each goal and then to move the record with the student to the next grade and set of expectations. Finally, teachers created grading rubrics for the tasks they presented to their students, linking specific criteria to the standards they set. The Salt Marsh Food Web problem in Figure 11.10 sets the criteria for information and presentation, linked to the tenth grade-level standards for science and the school goal. Students, parents, and other teachers can look at the grading rubrics as a project unfolds, refining the product to meet the established standards. Teachers record student achievement against each standard in a student's record that describes the project or performance (Sable & Clarke, 1994). Cabot has dispensed with Carnegie Units in favor of performance-based assessment.

Student as Subject and Audience: Racine's R.O.P.E.

In spite of the needs we have for valid and reliable measures of student performance, the student is still the most important consumer of assessment information. Surely, national competitiveness, state mandates, and the desire for accountability are all active interests of the educational system. To the extent that the main interest of education is the individual learner, however, the primary audience for assessment information should remain the high school student who is trying to guide his or her own development in a clear direction. If the mechanics of assessment—standards, criteria, performances, and rubrics—obscure the meaning of assessment results to the individual learner and deprive him or her of control, all the portfolios on earth could not compensate for the loss. To control the process of their development, high school

FIGURE 11.10   Assessment Based on Standards and Rubrics

Salt Marsh Food Web

The cards represent some of the organisms that live in a salt marsh. The cards contain the name of the organism and some of the food that they eat. **Your job is to complete the following:**

   a) Complete the construction of the Salt Marsh Food Web;
   b) Using your map as a guide, answer all the questions in complete sentences.

The following Rubric will be used to assess your project:

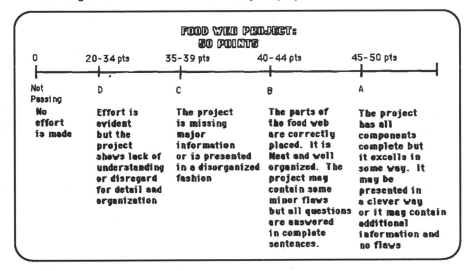

1. What are the producers in the community?
2. What is the source of their energy?
3. Name three organisms that are herbivores.
4. Name two organisms that are carnivores.
5. Name three organisms that are omnivores.

From Cabot School materials, Cabot, VT. Used with permission.

students need to collect evidence of high performance that they regard as authentic and meaningful in light of their own growing sense of purpose.

At Walden III in Racine, Wisconsin, student self-assessment is the cornerstone of a long-standing portfolio assessment system. As Figure 11.11 shows, the Right of Passage Experience (R.O.P.E.) requires all high school students to assess their own performance in sixteen areas as they proceed through the high school years, including a portfolio of quality work assessed by the student, a project related to human culture, and a demonstration of competence in skills and knowledge.

In their senior year, a year-long R.O.P.E. course and adult committee helps them gather up portfolio components, develop an independent project in self-expression, and design special demonstrations of mastery in five areas of competency. The portfolios include letters of recommendation that connect student achievements to the school's main goals. Students make their presentations before their committee, which includes another student, a faculty member, and an outside adult. For seniors, spring semester focuses on the development of these presentations. Quite unpredictably, R.O.P.E. assessments achieved high reliability. "Of 42 external rater scores, half were identical to the committee's agreed-upon grades. Of the other half, all but one was a single measurement point away from the committee's grades" (Mabry, 1992).

FIGURE 11.11   Racine's R.O.P.E. Areas in Portfolios, Projects, and Demonstrations

---

Distribution and Coverage of the R.O.P.E. Areas

A frequent source of confusion for R.O.P.E. students is the relationship of Portfolio, Project, and Demonstrations to the specific R.O.P.E. areas. The "model" below is intended as a general guide as to how the R.O.P.E. areas may be covered. Specific cases can and will differ, however, so students are advised to consult with the R.O.P.E. instructor and, especially, with the individual R.O.P.E. committee on the final approach to their own personal R.O.P.E.

Portfolio	*Project*	*Demonstrations*
(2) Reading	(11) U.S. history	(3) Mathematics
(1) English	English	(4) Government
(5) Self-expression	Self-expression	Self-expression
(13) Multicultural	Multicultural*	(14) World geography
(6) Personal growth		(16) Physical challenge**
(7) Ethics		(15) Proficiency areas
(8) Fine arts		
(9) Mass media		
(10) Human relations		
(12) Science		

---

* Multicultural option
** Check-off by P.E. instructor
__ District competency area
O R.O.P.E. area

From R.O.P.E. project, Walden III Alternative School, Racine, WI. Used with permission.

Student self-assessment in Racine's R.O.P.E. is represented in part by the Science Course Work History in Figure 11.12. Students complete a more comprehensive self-assessment in the autobiography that is required as part of each senior portfolio and presentation. The autobiography asks students to reconstruct their high school experience in light of larger questions: "Who am I?" "What is it to be human?" "Where am I going?" "Am I ready?" The autobiography makes students view their high school experience from some reflective distance, distinguishing between trivial and important events, establishing a values position on their growth, and developing a "yardstick for determining what is important in a person's life (Walden III, 1993).

Validity of Self-Assessment

For any learning to become permanent and transferrable, it must be recognized as valid by the individual learner (Preece, 1994). If students remain unaware of the

FIGURE 11.12   Senior Student's Self-Assessment of Learning in Science

---

Science Course Work History

Tenth Grade
Physics: First semester—B Second semester—A
I liked what I learned in physics. It was the most interesting part of science I have studied. What I really
liked studying was light and sound. Especially since the
developments of sound have such an impact on my guitar
playing.

Eleventh Grade
Biology: First three quarters—A Fourth quarter—B
I didn't like biology. The only part of biology I liked
was genetics. I really doubt I'll use biology in the
future, except possibly the environmental part of it.

Twelfth Grade
Chemistry: Grades pending
I haven't had enough experience with it yet.
   I don't really like science. It is very hard for me to
understand. Although I can appreciate science because I
know how much I use it every day, especially in music.

From R.O.P.E. project, Walden III Alternative School, Racine, WI. Used with permission.

purposes of authentic tasks and their use in assessment, the projects they complete in high school may be no more memorable than answers to standardized items in norm-referenced assessment tests. At the least, students should be able to understand the meaning of the standards that will be applied to their projects and performances and use assessment criteria to measure their progress. They should also be able to reflect on the meaning of assessment results and use them to redirect their own learning. If an assessment task is authentic, students should understand how well they did, how they achieved their results, how to achieve better results, and how the task reflects the need for high performance in the world that waits for them outside the school.

Bena Kallick advocates devoting class time to reflective activity in which students assess the strategies they used to think through a problem and make connections to other parts of what they have learned (Kallick, 1989). Journal entries directed at reflection can initiate an "internal conversation" in which students represent and critique their own strategies and "external conversations" during which students share their observations and develop a collective model of how learning takes place and how it can be improved.

In Kallick's view, assessment standards and criteria exert the greatest influence on student learning when students and teachers collaborate in their development. At the beginning of a project, setting up the guidelines for assessment clarifies the purpose and creates a common language students can use to assess and guide their work. When students collaborate in developing standards and criteria for several projects in succession, the criteria become generalized guides for use in other classes, in a whole school, or in a school district, forming the framework for a learning community in which expectations are developed and shared by all (Kallick, 1991).

In the Communications Academy at Drake High School, Tamalpais Union High School District in Larkspur, California, students assess their own work and also receive teacher feedback on the connection between their work and school goals. Figure 11.13 is a self-assessment guide for students to use in connecting various projects to their educational purpose. Figure 11.14 is a reflection guide that asks them to connect their own efforts to scoring criteria for the standards set for a performance. In both cases, students review the product or performance they completed, look for

FIGURE 11.13   Student Reflection on a Learning Project

Student Reflections*

1. Using a complete sentence, describe the assignment.

   _____

   _____

   _____

2. Check all of the scoring criteria (see rubric) you believe the selection demonstrates:

   ___ self-esteem   ___ creativity
   ___ responsibility   ___ technology
   ___ cooperation/   ___ accessing and utilization
        mutual respect   of information
   ___ problem solving   ___ communication skills
   ___ complex thinking   ___ content mastery
   ___ motivation

3. Which of the criteria that you checked are you **most proud** of? Explain why.

   _____

   _____

4. Explain the **steps you took** in completing this assignment.

   _____

   _____

5. What do you feel was the **hardest part** of this activity? _____

   _____

6. What did you **learn** from completing this assignment? _____

   _____

7. What **improvements** could you make if you were to revise your work?

   _____

   _____

---

*Student completes a REFLECTION sheet for each portfolio selection

Prepared by Bena Kallick who is now a consultant in Westport, CT. Used with permission.

FIGURE 11.14   Outcomes Verification by Faculty and Parents

Outcomes Verification Sheet: Critical Thinking

Student: _____   Year: _____

Through the projects listed below, this student has met the required
outcomes in a satisfactory (S) or excellent (E) manner.

OUTCOME:	1	2	3	4	5	6
acquire information						
analyze information						
apply information to make decisions						
self-assessment through portfolio						
self-assessment through performance						
self-assessment through exhibition						
practice artistic self-discipline						
practice intellectual self-discipline						
take responsibility for own education						
understand and apply learning processes						

PROJECTS   (see key below)

PROJECT KEY:

Project #1: _____

Project #2: _____

Project #3: _____

Project #4: _____

Project #5: _____

Project #6: _____

From class materials at the Communications Academy at Drake High School, Tamalpes Union High
School District, San Anselmo, CA. Used with permission.

evidence of having met the standards, and then look carefully at the process of completing the task—for skills, knowledge, and dispositions that play an important part
in all such tasks. As students complete a sequence of tasks, reflective guides help
them recognize progress and respond to new challenges. To the extent that students
participate in their own assessment, they may be expected to understand its purpose
and take some greater responsibility for their own development.

Graduating with Demonstrated Quality

Despite obvious measurement difficulties, "quality" in learning is the goal we seek. Quality is not visible in goals, criteria, and rubrics. It becomes visible in the collected work of students who recognize in authentic tasks a chance to create something new and express something in themselves that has never been expressed before. Its foremost characteristic is uniqueness, reflecting personal experience, values, and responsibility. Quality work communicates its value to an audience, because students have attended to how it is perceived as much as how it was conceived. Quality work expresses connectedness among all the disciplines and all the modes of expression. Most important, it represents work at the edge of established learning, where risk is palpable and where the challenge is new. Quality is not an abstract value that lies far beyond the reach of high school students. Quality becomes possible when any of us try to reformulate what we have learned in a unique expression that aims to make a positive impact on other people. In expressions of quality, we recognize the potential of the human spirit.

The logical extension of quality learning in a high school setting is graduation by exhibition—a final demonstration in the senior year by individuals who have met standards set by their school, know they have met those standards, and make their last learning experience the expression of what they have learned. At Boston's English High School, an exhibition includes a written position paper by every graduate. At Chicago's Sullivan High School, it includes an argumentative essay. At Walbrook High School in Baltimore, a final exhibition is constructed in multimedia. The project proposal in Figure 11.15 initiates the final project at the School Without Walls in Rochester, New York.

As technology continues to move into high schools, particularly through development of software such as IBM's Linkways and Apple's Hypercard, students will be able to fashion an expression of what they have learned using text, photographs, video, music, dance, art, and mathematics—virtually all of their intelligences—and fit it on a 3.5-inch disk. Such measures will prove both valid and reliable only to the extent that an interested audience is willing to carefully look at them for evidence of achievement and capability that really matters.

The Assessment Showcase that follows was written by students, teachers, administrators, and parents at University Heights High School in New York City. It shows how assessment can become the organizing framework for a high school education. "Student Trek" represents the collective effort of a high school community to define their mission, set their goals, adjust teaching and learning to support performance, and locate students at the center of the assessment process; it is a publication of the entire school. A "Roundtable" at University Heights is both a time of testing and a time of celebration in which the entire community gathers to look at what students have accomplished and to reassess its entire program. Making assessment the connecting thread puts students at the center of the learning process.

FIGURE 11.15 Graduation Project Proposal Form

Date: _____

Name: _____   Extended Class: _____

A. What I want to learn _____
   [What the project is about]

B. How I will go about learning these things _____
   [Who will be the advisor, library resources, etc.]

C. What the product will be _____
   [What I will produce]

D. Timeline
   _____
   [Work and conference dates]

E. The Committee _____
   [Members]

Staff	1.	2.
Community	1.	2.
Student	1.	2.
New student	1.	2.

Student	Advisor	Independent Advisor	Program Administrator

From the Senior Handbook, page 6 of 12, School Without Walls, Rochester, NY. Used with permission.

ASSESSMENT SHOWCASE

Student Trek: Assessment at University Heights High School

Principal: Nancy Mohr; Teachers: Paul Allison, Phil Farnham,
Wendy Fields, Gene Harding, Augusta Andres, Irene Zola, Nellie Simmons,
Janitzia Corrales-O'Neil, Kiran Chandhuri, Billy Gully;
Students: Mercedes Vargas, Tyrone Jones, Shakera Ausion, Gloria Chiarriez,
Tyson Jones, Alexandra Lozano; Parents: Martha Ortiz, Lorna Thomas
University Heights High School, Bronx Community College, Bronx, NY

Table of Contents

Introduction

This booklet is an abridged compilation of four publications written and produced by staff, students, and parents at the University Heights High School Summer Assessment Seminars in July 1993. We wanted to produce assessment guidebooks that would be informative and dynamic. We wanted to paint an organized picture while resisting the pressure to neaten it all up. We wanted to present assessment in a way that made sense to all of us.

The U.H.H.S. Summer Assessment Seminars were three weeks of valuable struggle and learning for a lot of different members of our school community: eight 1993 portfolio graduates, ten returning students (with parents), five parents, our principal, our neighborhood worker, our social worker, our college advisor, and twenty-two teachers (including four who had just been hired for the coming semester). These numbers can only suggest the wonderful difficulties and opportunities for learning that we experienced together.

The workshops were designed by and for the staff, students, and parents of U.H.H.S. The theme of the first week was "Describing Work and Standards." In the second week we focused on "Describing Learners" and we worked to revise our "Domains and Outcomes." Finally in the third week, we turned to "Systems," considering everything "From Report Cards to Creating a Public Archive."

To organize our work together, we drew on our experiences with the New York City Writing Project, the Bard Institute for Writing and Thinking, and with the Prospect School's documentary processes. In addition, we built community and learned how to listen to each other better by depending on many initiatives and activities that we have learned in our involvement with Project Adventure. We organized the final week as if it were a workshop in the Foxfire approach to a project-based curriculum; our project was to produce useful and engaging guidebooks for specific audiences.

As you will see from this compilation, we used many different forms to explore assessment. You will find a television interview, a dialogue between an older student and a new student, a list of quotations about assessment, a diagram or two, more traditional "explanations," a journal entry, letters, and a quiz to test your assessment wits. These pieces of writing were drawn from four booklets, each intended for a different audience. We created one book for entering students, one for parents, one for returning students who are caught between two different assessment systems, and one for this year's seniors.

Curriculum and Assessment

In order to graduate from University Heights High School, students must demonstrate mastery in our seven domains of learning, each of which are found in all disciplines. We use a portfolio system including public presentation and evaluation. Students create their portfolios from the work they do in their seminars, and graduate only when they prove they are ready.

Seminars

U.H.H.S. is divided into three academic teams. In each team one group of students and teachers work together for the entire school day and for a number of years to create portfolios that show the students' abilities within the domains.

Cover Letters

Students write cover letters to accompany each item in their portfolios. Cover letters are attached to the work so that one not only sees the product of the students' efforts, but also their self-assessment of what they learned and accomplished.

In cover letters, students refer to the list of outcomes under each domain to describe what they have learned by completing the work. Therefore the cover letter is as important as the work itself because without it we cannot know just how much was accomplished.

Exhibitions

On completion of a unit of study in a seminar, students present their work to others. Sometimes these presentations are informal peer groups, and other times they are formal presentations to an outside audience. When exhibiting their work, students demonstrate what they have done and what they know, and answer questions about the topic studied or the experiences they had.

Graduation Portfolios and Senior Roundtables

During the students' last year at U.H.H.S., they prepare graduation portfolios for each domain. In each, they put work from earlier seminars and additional work completed during the final year. Students present each portfolio at a senior roundtable. The roundtables include the voices of other students, teachers, parents, and critical friends from the community and the university. These multiple perspectives help determine standards for graduation. Students must be prepared to answer questions about their work, and even revise it if it is determined that the portfolio is not graduation-ready. Only when students have successfully presented seven graduation portfolios will they receive their diplomas.

Domains and Outcomes

Effective Expression and Communication

Embedded Disciplines: English, math, foreign language, economics, art, physical education, music, science, media . . . .

- Students read, write, talk, listen, and do mathematics to understand themselves, to increase knowledge, and to develop and communicate their ideas.
- Students create visual art, music, and performance art to express their thoughts and feelings.
- Students demonstrate their ability to use and understand mathematics in life.
- Students read, write, and speak a second language.
- Students use technology to communicate their ideas.

Self-Awareness and Self-Esteem

Embedded Disciplines: English, foreign language, American history, citizenship, health, physical education, psychology . . .

- Students show that they appreciate their individuality, family background, community history, and cultural heritage.
- Students develop their physical potential and demonstrate habits of health and safety.
- Students show pride in themselves, demonstrate respect for others, and develop self-discipline.
- Students recognize their strengths and improve in areas of weakness.

Taking Responsibility and Preparing for the Future

Embedded Disciplines: Math, global studies, citizenship, health, science, career studies, occupational education . . .

- Students demonstrate that they know what it takes to succeed in college and in the world of work.
- Students show that they know about a variety of lifestyles and that people can make choices about how they live their lives.

- Students develop personal plans for what they are going to do after graduation, and they do what is necessary to put their plans into action.
- Students show that they understand the responsibilities of being sexually active and the importance of developing safe habits.
- Students independently investigate what interests and concerns them.

Social Interaction and Effective Citizenship
Embedded Disciplines: English, math, American history, global studies, citizenship, physical education, sociology, politics . . .

- Students demonstrate a commitment to the community by doing community service projects.
- Students make informed decisions about and develop responsible habits toward the environment.
- Students work cooperatively with other people to accomplish tasks.
- Students show that they understand how political and economic processes work.
- Students show that they understand a variety of ways in which individuals participate in political and economic processes.
- Students demonstrate an understanding of the roots, character, and goals of various social and political movements in the past and present.

Critical Thinking and Problem Solving
Embedded Disciplines: English, math, American history, economics, art, physical education, music, science, media . . .

- Students question, analyze, evaluate, and synthesize information.
- Students identify different views people have about complex problems and examine possible solutions.
- Students learn how and when to use scientific methods.
- Students use problem-solving strategies to demonstrate their ability to reason mathematically.
- Students demonstrate that they understand the different ways statistical information is collected and presented.
- Students set up and solve mathematical expressions and explain mathematical theories.

Cultural and Historical Involvement
Embedded Disciplines: Foreign language, American history, global studies, art, music, geography, literature, anthropology . . .

- Students develop a sense of time and place within geographic and historical frameworks.
- Students demonstrate that they understand cultural differences and common experiences among people in and out of school.
- Students show that they understand the role of art, music, culture, science, math, and technology in society.
- Students relate present situations to history and make informed predictions about the future.
- Students demonstrate that they understand their roles in creating and shaping culture and history.
- Students use literature to gain insight into their own lives and areas of academic inquiry.

Valuing and Ethical Decision Making
Embedded Disciplines: English, American history, global studies, citizenship, health, science, philosophy, law . . .

- Students demonstrate that they value honesty, justice, fairness, equality, self-discipline, and cooperation.
- Students show that they appropriately respect, consider, or question the values of others.
- Students evaluate ethical dilemmas in their lives or in the world and take stands that reflect their value systems.

- Students explain and defend personal values and decisions.
- Students use moral reasoning to make choices about their involvement in the school community.

Quotations about Learning and Assessment

In the beginning, when I looked at the papers my daughter brought home, I was confused—it looked like a lot to fulfill. Now, having seen my daughter work and now that I am working with assessment in the summer, I am convinced. I was shocked at the work my daughter did. I think it's a better way of learning. It looks hard, it sounds hard, it *is* hard. But it's better.

Mary Brown, Parent

I take back with me a deep appreciation for the pioneering work you and your colleagues have accomplished and the incredible energies you and they continue to invest in refining your program and progressively increasing the fit between your collective vision of an essential school and the day-to-day realities of school life. I also come away from my visit with some tangible rewards: a better understanding of the means by which schools can keep people focused on the vision, new insights into issues of student commitment, communication among teachers, curriculum, teaching and assessment, and practical ideas for structuring students' reflection on their learning process.

Steven C. Lorch, Head, Harman High School, Jerusalem, Israel

It's a new system and it allowed me to express my knowledge better to myself and to others. There is a lot of writing in the portfolio system and through this writing I got to tell my teachers what I learned, how I learned it. Through credits I would not have been allowed to express myself as clearly. Self-assessment allows me to have better self-esteem because I am talking about what I can do. It makes me feel great about myself—I get to learn more positive things about myself all the time.

Alexandra Lozano, Senior

When I hear the word—standards—I think of goals I have set for myself. Sometimes I set them too high and I fall before I reach the top, but with a good push from a loved one I get back up. For example, when I got in this school three years ago I said it would take me only one year to graduate. It took me three, but I did it.

Cindy Bush, Graduate

I am not quite sure yet how I feel about portfolios. All of her work may be in a portfolio, but how do other people see the portfolio? Do they accept it? Do they understand it? I like the idea and I'm hoping that when she graduates she will have learned everything she needs for college and I hope it is not a setback. I want her to graduate from here having to take only college courses when she enters college. I would be disappointed if she had to take remedial courses. I feel my daughter's progress is still not enough. She is still confused about her project work; she doesn't always understand what is asked of her. If she gets projects, I want her to understand what she is doing. If she can explain her project to me without a problem, then I feel she will have learned, accomplished her goal.

Martha Ortiz, Parent

For the Student Entering into the World of Assessment at U.H.H.S.

I can tell you personally I think the portfolio is all right. I'll explain it to you like this: If I take a test and it has ten questions and I get two wrong and eight right then I'll get an 80 or a a75 or a 60 just like I did when I was in the other school. An "80" isn't anything. But I can write you a cover letter and tell you what I didn't understand about the two I got wrong and how I went about finding the answers to the eight I got right. That is what I learned from this semester. An 80 is nothing because I could have cheated off of the person next to me. In a portfolio I'm showing you exactly what I did to get the 80 and that makes my 80 original. I don't know if you understand exactly what I'm trying to say but that's how I feel. . . .

From a reflection on portfolios by a U.H.H.S. graduate
taking part in the summer assessment workshop

How Portfolios Work in Outcome-Based Assessment—
Questions and Answers about Portfolio-Based Assessment

Characters

Eric, a new student at UHHS with no prior credit.

Melissa, is a senior and a peer counselor at U.H.H.S. She is showing Eric around the school and trying to answer any questions he may have about U.H.H.S.

Setting

It is lunch time. Melissa and Eric are touring the Hall of Fame and talking about U.H.H.S.

MELISSA: So how do you like the school so far, Eric?

ERIC: It's aw'ight.

MELISSA: That's all you have say!! It's aw'ight?!? Don't you have any deeper comments than that? I mean you've just spent half a day here . . . What's going through your mind? Don't you have some questions or comments to make about the school that need clearing up?

ERIC: Why the classes gotta be so different? Why does everybody have to work together? Don't people get to do work by themselves? I ain't into that group thing.

MELISSA: We work in groups for a few different reasons. One being that we learn to fill an outcome called group dynamics, another is so that we learn responsibility for our individual roles, as well as learning how to socialize with others better.

ERIC: What do you mean . . . A outcome? What's that?

MELISSA: In order to graduate we have to master seven domains, each domain has five outcomes. . . .

ERIC: Hold up, hold up, hold up, English please!

MELISSA: Wait, let me finish.

ERIC: Aw'ight.

MELISSA: To fulfill an outcome you have to complete a project. The projects have to be completed by the end of a certain cycle, depending on which seminar you're in and the project you're doing. The domain is like the main subject heading.

ERIC: Outcomes, cycles, domains, seminars all that talks make me wanna to leave, what do I gotta do to graduate?

MELISSA: Well, that depends on how serious you are about your work. If you don't fool around you might be able to finish faster than someone who is not serious. But, you must master all seven domains!

ERIC: Master? What is this Karate school or something? How uhm supposed to master something in school? What happened to learning and #!@?!! like that?

MELISSA: Mastery is when the teachers have looked at your work and decided that it is better than average work. . . . Like when they believe you have done the best that you can do.

ERIC: A Yo, why don't they just give you a 90 or 100 on your report card instead of this master *@&#!

MELISSA: 'Cause, a 90 doesn't show what you can do, whereas, when a teacher looks at your portfolio, they can see that you have not only done all of your work, but you've learned from it, improved on it and did it really well.

ERIC: Portfolio?!? What the hell, is this a modeling school or something? I ain't no model!

MELISSA: Calm down! It's not that much of a big deal really. A portfolio is a folder that holds all of your work from the time you arrive until the time you leave.

ERIC: All of it!!! How could a folder hold all my work from the time I get here as a freshman, up 'til I leave as a senior? That gotta be a big ass folder!

MELISSA: Easy. There are different kinds of portfolios. One kind contains your work in progress, showing different stages of development. Another is your finished portfolio, which holds your best work, which is the same as your graduation portfolio.

ERIC: That's a lot of sh___ !

MELISSA: Yeah. And, next year you'll start an archival portfolio that contains this year's work.

ERIC: A what???

MELISSA: An archival portfolio, which means that your work is stored in a file at the school for future assessment by yourself and the teachers . . . That way you'll see how much you have improved over the years.

ERIC: So what about tests . . . Like the RCTs, SATs, and sh___ like that.

MELISSA: You're required to take the pass six RCTs. You have to take the SATs if the college you want to go to wants you to take it. But, we don't get in class tests because of the portfolios.

ERIC: What's up with this school, no tests? Archivals, Domains, Mastery, it sounds like a damn video game!

MELISSA: Well you have to do something that's like taking a test, which is presenting your work at exhibitions where teachers and students evaluate your progress and let you know what you should do to improve your work and what is great about your work through warm and cool feedback. Then there's roundtables where you present your work to students, teachers, and invited guests, and they basically do the same thing that's done at exhibitions, but you don't normally do roundtables until you're a senior.

ERIC: What! Exhibitions! I thought that was only for like museums and sh___ like that, you know what uhnm saying'.

MELISSA: I know what you're saying Eric, but you have to understand that U.H.H.S. is not a traditional high school. We operate very differently here because we are more interested in what the student can do as opposed to whether or not he/she can pass an examination.

ERIC: Cool. But how long will I have to stay here before I can get out. It seems all this will take forever to finish.

MELISSA: It may seem like forever, but you can reach the senior institute before you know it if you work hard, and listen to all of the feedback students and teachers offer.

ERIC: Senior Institute!?! What the hell is that?

MELISSA: The Senior Institute is a group of students who have reached a certain level in their work, where, like me, you're ready to graduate and move on to the next level of your life. Teachers help students in the Senior Institute focus on things we need to do for college, like filling out financial aid forms, writing cover letters, taking SATs, and all that. Seniors have to do projects aimed toward graduation.

ERIC: Oh! That's the best thing I've heard about so far! If I ever get there.

MELISSA: You'll get there as long as you're willing to concentrate on your work. It's not impossible! I'm in it.

ERIC: True. All right, MELISSA. Lunch is almost over and I need to do a few things so like I'll see you around and maybe we can talk some more.

MELISSA: All right Eric. Good luck.

ERIC: Peace out . . . Uhm, I mean, thanks, same to you. (Eric walks away feeling a little confused about the amount of information he just heard but enlightened by MELISSA's confidence.)

The Road to Graduation

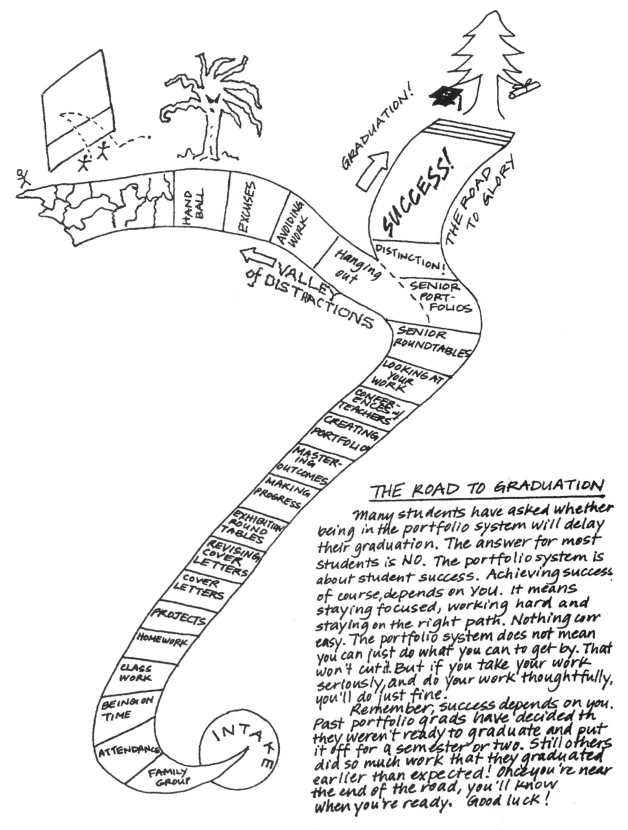

THE ROAD TO GRADUATION

Many students have asked whether being in the portfolio system will delay their graduation. The answer for most students is NO. The portfolio system is about student success. Achieving success of course, depends on YOU. It means staying focused, working hard and staying on the right path. Nothing comes easy. The portfolio system does not mean you can just do what you can to get by. That won't cut it. But if you take your work seriously, and do your work thoughtfully, you'll do just fine.

Remember, success depends on you. Past portfolio grads have decided th they weren't ready to graduate and put it off for a semester or two. Still others did so much work that they graduated earlier than expected! Once you're near the end of the road, you'll know when you're ready. Good luck!

By Tyrone Jones, Student, and Augusto Andres, Teacher. Used with permission.

Field of Dreams

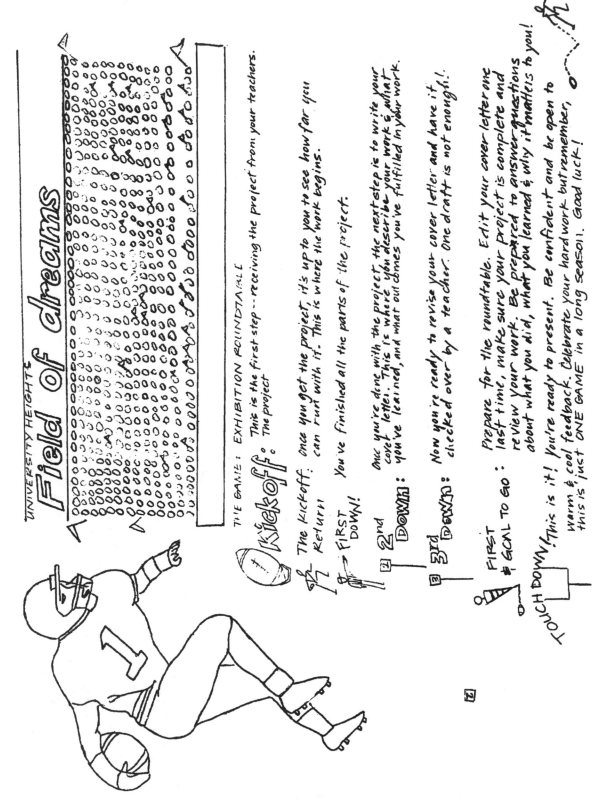

UNIVERSITY HEIGHTS
Field of dreams

THE GAME: EXHIBITION ROUNDTABLE

Kickoff: This is the first step -- receiving the project from your teachers.
The project

The Kickoff: Once you get the project, it's up to you to see how far you
Return: can run with it. This is where the work begins.

FIRST DOWN! You've finished all the parts of the project.

2nd DOWN: Once you're done with the project, the next step is to write your cover letter. This is where you describe your work & what you've learned, and what outcomes you've fulfilled in your work.

3rd DOWN: Now you're ready to revise your cover letter and have it checked over by a teacher. One draft is not enough!.

FIRST & GOAL TO GO: Prepare for the roundtable. Edit your cover letter one last time, make sure your project is complete and review your work. Be prepared to answer questions about what you did, what you learned & why it matters to you!

TOUCH DOWN! This is it! You're ready to present. Be confident and be open to warm & cool feedback. Celebrate your hard work but remember, this is just ONE GAME in a long season. Good luck!

Work of Tyrone Jones, student. Used with permission.

Explanation of "Domains" and "Outcomes"

At University Heights High School, we have developed seven areas of work which we think are important for students to master in order to graduate high school with the skills they will need in the world of college and/or work. These seven areas (domains) are:

- Effective expression and communication
- Self-awareness and self-esteem
- Taking responsibility and preparing for the future
- Social interaction and effective citizenship
- Critical thinking and problem solving
- Cultural and historical involvement
- Valuing and ethical decision making

Within each of these domains students will learn traditional subjects (such as math, social studies, English, science, art, music, language arts, and citizenship). But they will also learn other skills (for example: Students show pride in themselves, demonstrate respect for others and develop self-discipline) which we believe are important for students as they develop into adults.

Under each domain (*domains* in simple terms are titles), we have developed several outcomes (*outcomes* can be seen as goals which are associated with the particular domain). Outcomes are demonstrated accomplishments which students must achieve in order to graduate. If a student reaches mastery level in all of the outcomes under all of the domains, he or she is ready to graduate. While a student attends U.H.H.S., he or she will be working toward achieving mastery level in all outcomes; however, it is not expected that an entering or mid-level student will achieve mastery in all of his/her work.

At the beginning or each "cycle" (*unit* that may last several weeks), students are assigned a project (*projects* are specific work that are related to the outcomes). When a project is explained to students, outcomes which the project will address are also explained. For example, if students are assigned the project of writing a letter to the Mayor of New York City with proposals for what to do about the homeless (including a statistical graph), outcomes which they might be expected to accomplish are:

- Students read, write, talk, listen and do mathematics to understand themselves, to increase knowledge and to develop and communicate their ideas;
- Students show that they understand how local, national and international political processes work and that there are a variety of ways in which individuals can participate;
- Students demonstrate that they understand the different ways statistical information is collected and presented;
- Students demonstrate that they understand their own roles in shaping culture and history;
- Students question, analyze and evaluate information, interpretations and conclusions as presented in a variety of media;
- Students evaluate ethical dilemmas ("doing the right thing") in their lives or in the world and take stands which reflect their value systems.

Teachers design projects that are aimed at addressing all of the thirty-five outcomes during the course of the schoolyear. Through a variety of lessons, workshops, trips and group meetings, students are instructed in how to accomplish tasks. For example, in creating the proposal letter to the Mayor of New York City, complete with statistical charts, students may be taught how to change a percent into a fraction. In this way, students are helped to fulfill outcomes.

What Is a Project

Dear Charles,

When you asked me about that "new project-based curriculum," and how it affected our portfolio assessment a pang of fear struck my heart. I said, "Oh no, something else new has come out and I don't know anything about it." Then it hit me that you were not as up to date as I had first feared. Please forgive me if I sound as though I am talking down to you and your knowledge but I don't know how much you know.

To teach a curriculum thorough a project requires much planning. It is almost a requirement to have students present at these planning sessions. They add a valuable insight. I will describe a project that we just completed.

Listening to the latest studies, it has been reported that our students (Americans) don't know where major cities and countries are, and the math and science skills/knowledge is also low. So the first thing that we decided was that we wanted the students to know geography, math, and science. The project that we designed contained the subjects of history, math (algebra, geometry), science (biology), art, literature, and foreign language (Spanish).

We started by focusing on the life of Don Juan in the seventeenth century using the book *The Roque of Seville* by Tirso De Molina. This took place mainly in Spain and Italy. The students had to compare life in the seventeenth century with the twentieth century. They had to include the opinion of a famous person or a community figure such as a priest, doctor, etc. The students were given materials from the health department, classes in microbiology including lab work where the students were able to identify some of the disease-causing organisms. They were also given activities in which they learned the benefits of various herbs, and home remedies that were available both then (seventeenth century) and now. They were required to make a journey to another part of the world. They had to give reasons why they were leaving (i.e., seeking riches, freedom to practice their religion, etc.). They had to tell who they were traveling with and why. They had to build a ship. They had to first draw the ship to scale, find the water line, tell where it was and its length, determine the hull speed of the ship, how long it would take to get to their destination. Their destination has been determined by finding specific coordinates on a map. They had to use triangulation, geometry, and the Pythagorean theorem whereby they had to hone up on their algebraic skills. Those that needed help were, of course, helped in classes and in one-to-one groups.

They also had to determine where they would make pit stops. These pit stops were also determined in the same way that their destination were determined (i.e., triangulation, geometry, etc.). They would also tell what they would do at these pit stops (i.e., take on water, drop off bodies, get fruits, etc.). They would have to construct a budget depending on the amount of people they had on their boats, making sure they could be fed or paid a salary.

They had to keep a journal (captain's log). Each day's entry included the weather, the health of the passengers, the scenery, and the mood of ship. They also had to tell their location and what stars they saw. Yes they had a class on the constellations and the seasons. At each pit stop they discussed the area they were in, such as the climate, how the people lived, were they farmers, etc. Once they reached their destination they had to construct a house. They had to draw their houses to scale. They had to tell the area and the perimeter of their houses. They also had to describe how they would construct their house and their budget for doing so . . . some had to use their ships as materials. Within their journals there was a time that they had to use their foreign language skills. They, of course, had lessons to learn this language. They always have the option of going to the library for more information. In fact, it is encouraged, so.

I hope that this was a little helpful. I know you will have some questions so I look forward to chatting on the phone and even better going to lunch on your gold Wing.

Later,

Nellie

Ways of Keeping Parents Informed—How will we learn about
our son's/daughter's progress?

You may have a lot of questions about assessment at U.H.H.S., since we are pioneering different methods of evaluating students' progress. We have come up with exciting new ways to understand how much students learn. There are many opportunities for you to get to know how your child is doing.

Your participation in your child's assessment is important to us. First, you will get an invitation to take part in:

Student Exhibitions
Students will be performing their own writing in formal poetry readings, demonstrating their self-defense skills in Karate belt tests, showing their knowledge of world history and conflicts in debate contests. Students demonstrate their understanding of statistics by displaying the results of surveys they have designed.

Roundtables
Join teachers, professional experts and your child's peers in assessing his or her work. Your child will present the portfolio, walking you step-by-step through what has been accomplished.

Report Card Feedback
You will receive two kinds of report cards. One kind will have a long page of comments from the student's teachers, and a long page of comments from the students. Its last page will be a letter inviting you to write us back with your valuable comments. The second kind of report card will be shorter, showing the level of your child's performance; it will also show what areas of expertise your child has been focusing on.

Calls from Teachers
You can expect calls from the student's family group teacher. He or she will be keeping you informed about the student's achievements and difficulties.

> At the end of my son's first week of school, I got a call at nine at night. It was his teacher calling to say that he is doing very good work and that he fits himself right into the group. He has no problems expressing himself. I was surprised because most teachers don't call you when it's good news. Only when it's bad.
> *Margie Richardson, Parent*

> When my son was not feeling too well on Friday, his family group teacher called on Sunday. That was nice. She was concerned. You need all the help you can get. We need more teachers like her.
> *Lorna Thomas, Parent*

Parent–Teacher Conferences
You are strongly urged to attend your child's conferences twice a year, in October and April. It's an important opportunity to meet the teachers and to share with them your concerns.

Orientation
All new parents are expected to come to the orientation for incoming students the week before school starts. This will enlighten you about how the student will be assessed as well as other aspects of the school. It's an opportunity for you to get to know our mixed-age grouping of students, our grading system, etc.

Family Group Breakfast
You'll get an invitation twice a year to come visit your child's family group class, between 9 and 10 A.M. You'll get to meet other parents as well as your child's friends. You'll get to know how the group interacts, and to ask any questions you have. At 10 A.M., you'll be invited to join your child in his or her seminar.

> My husband and I attended my daughter's Family Group Breakfast. We all got to know each other. Everybody got to say something about issues that were brought up. The students were not phony. They acted natural and were respectful. For the first I got to see my daughter speak in public and also I saw what she has learned. The students served breakfast to the adults. It was like having breakfast in bed. All the food was donated by the students. We had donuts, bagels, coffee and juice.
> *Mary Brown, Parent*

Heights of the Roundtable

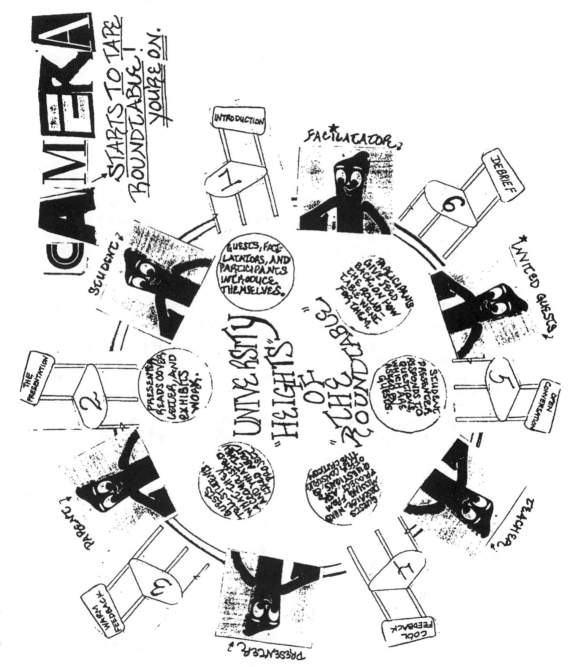

Compiled by Shakera Austion, Graduate, and Billy Gully, Teacher. Used with permission.

A Letter from the College Office

Dear Students and Parents,

Many students who are getting ready to graduate from University Heights have a great deal of anxiety about how the portfolio system will be viewed by a college admission committee. Students worry that they will not be accepted into a college because we do not have ranks or grade point averages. Let me say it loud, and proud: "No student has ever been rejected from their ideal college because we have the portfolio system!"

It has been my observation that the more prestigious colleges are impressed by our system. College admission officers from Brown University, Columbia University, Mount Holyoke College, Sarah Lawrence College, Vassar College and Iona College have all told me how impressed they are with our portfolio system. They feel they can better evaluate a student with our system.

I thought you might find it interesting to see where some of our graduates go on to college. I've also included a list of colleges that have accepted people from Central Park East Secondary School because they also use the portfolio system. This is a list of the colleges the graduates from June 1993 were accepted into. All of these colleges have accepted students on the basis of a portfolio (that means without a rank or GPA):

Allen University
American International College
Bard College
Berkle College of Music
Boston College
Brown University
CUNY-Baruch
CUNY-Borough of Manhattan C.C.
CUNY-Bronx Comm. C.
CUNY-Brooklyn
CUNY-City
CUNY-Hostos
CUNY-Hutner
CUNY-John Jay
CUNY-LaGuardia
CUNY-Lehman
Clark, Atlanta
Columbia University
Cornell University
Hampshire College
Howard University
Iona College
Johnson C. Smith
Johnson & Wales
Knoxville College
Lang College
Lincoln
Manhattanville

New York University
Northeastern University
Northfield Academy
Pace University
Pratt Institute
Saint Thomas Aquinas
Savanna State
School of Visual Arts
Shaw University
Siena College
Smith College
Sorbonne
Spelman College
SUNY-Albany
SUNY-Brockport
SUNY-Buffalo
SUNY-Cortland
SUNY-Farmingdale
SUNY-Hudson Valley
SUNY-Mohawk Valley
SUNY-Old Westbury
SUNY-Plattsburgh
SUNY-Purchase
SUNY-Stony Brook
SUNY-County
Vassar College
Virginia Union

If the college of your dreams is not on this list, most admission committees are impressed with the following fact: The National Association of College Admissions Counselors Approved the Endorsement of Coalition of Essential Schools Work on March 8, 1992.

Seeds of Change: Roundtable

Dear Students, Teachers, Parents, and Invited Guests:

The work that I am about to present fits under the domain of "Taking Responsibility and Preparing for the Future." I'm going to show that I know what it takes to succeed in college and in the world of work. I will present the following pieces of evidence:

1. Student aid report
2. E.O.P. Information Form
3. Letter from S.U.N.Y.–Farmingdale
4. Application for C.U.N.Y.
5. Senior Survival Essay
6. Acceptance Letter to Johnson & Wales

Beginning this past February, I started filling out applications for colleges. I didn't really have any specific colleges in mind. So I went to the college counselor and he helped me choose some colleges. During the process of applying to college I also applied for financial aid and grants. Filling out the financial aid form was hard because it was complicated. It asked a lot of questions but got it done. The easiest thing to do while applying to college was waiting for a response. The colleges that I applied to were S.U.N.Y.–Farmingdale, Johnson & Wales University, and Cazenovia. The reason that I applied to these particular colleges was because they offer me the courses that I want. The course that I applied for was accounting. The reason I applied for accounting was because I like math and I like working with money.

I was sent a letter from Farmingdale saying that I couldn't be accepted for the major I wanted so they had offered me the chance to take the Pathways test that they offered to students who have problems picking a major. So I went and took the test, but I haven't received my results yet.

I haven't heard from Cazenovia, so I called them recently to check on my application and if it had been processed or not, and they told me that I should be receiving a letter within the next week.

I wrote an essay in a class that I had called "senior survival." In this class we talked about our fears about graduating, growing up, and going to college. I will read my "senior Survival Essay." I think you can see from this that I am ready to graduate. I have grown into a responsible young adult and I know what it means to plan for the future.

Last but not least my first acceptance letter to a college. I received a letter on 6/4/93 from Johnson & Wales University. When I opened the letter, the first word that I saw was "pleased." When I saw that word I knew that the letter had brought good news and to my surprise I was accepted. I felt so happy when I got that letter I showed my grandmother and she gave me a big hug and congratulated me. Being accepted to a university is a wonderful feeling. I called my mother and told her and she was excited. I never thought that I could get accepted to a university. But it goes to show that You can do anything if you put your mind to it.

Now that I have been accepted to college I will make the most of it. I'm looking forward to being on my own and making my own decisions. I'm looking forward to those long study sessions and staying up all night reviewing notes for a final. I just have one fear about going to college—will I make the right decisions for myself? I'm going to miss my family and my friends but I guess that's what growing up is all about, leaving and proving to yourself that you're ready to be an adult.

Dear Journal

Recently I had presented some of my work that I did during this past semester in a roundtable. I had my grandfather come in to listen and observe in the roundtable I was presenting so I could graduate.

After my presentation I would receive warm and cool feedback from the observers that were there such as my grandfather. Warm feedback is comments made on the things that people liked or what they heard. Cool feedback is comments or questions that people might have about your work. The work that I had represented went under the domain of "Cultural and Historical Involvement." The outcome was "Students develop a time and place in geographical and historical frameworks." Some of my work that I presented was my seeds of change project that dealt with Christopher Columbus, the autobiography of Malcolm X, a math project, and some dialectical notes also. Another domain that I had to represent was "Taking Responsibility and Preparing for the Future." The outcome was "Students demonstrate that they know what it takes to succeed in college and the world of work." (Here are the cover letters of before and after.)

While I was receiving some cool feedback I heard my grandfather say that he was not pleased with my presentation and that I could have done better, as well as my teacher. Paul he said the same thing also. After I heard that I was upset because I thought that I presented my work to the best of my ability. But after I listened to my grandfather and my teacher tell me why they were not pleased I decided hey, maybe their right. They told me that I could have talked about what I presented a little more and that I could have explained my work a little more clearer. So I took their advice.

So after the roundtables were over I received another chance to present my work over. So I took advantage of this opportunity. I went and did some more work on the work that I presented and got into my work in depth. I put my work in as much detail as I could. The time came for me to represent my work, and I would have to say that my grandfather along with my teacher and the rest of the people that were there were impressed with my work and how I represented it.

A student can learn not to rush their work especially when it means not graduating. Also to always take your time presenting work. Make sure you know exactly what you're talking about and never ever get frustrated.

This has shown me that if you put your mind to it, you can accomplish anything.

The End.

The Great Expectations Quiz

Directions: After answering all ten questions, add up 1 point for each a, 2 points for each b, and 3 points for each c.*

1. If a student has problems understanding their level of achievement, he or she should:
   a) ask a friend
   b) speak to the principal
   c) conference with Family Group Teacher and Seminar Teacher

2. If a student loses portfolio work and doesn't want this to happen again, he or she should:
   a) let the teacher be responsible
   b) make a list of work done and keep it in a safe place
   c) keep a record of work done and make copies of everything (a "just in case" portfolio)

3. If parents want to know what and how their son or daughter is doing in school, they should:
   a) spy on them and look through their personal stuff
   b) speak to the school Guidance Counselor
   c) conference with student, Family Group Teacher and Seminar Teacher

4. The best description of a portfolio is:
   a) a folder with a lot of work in it
   b) a collection of work used to document learning over time and show achievement
   c) a way of maintaining work so they can learn to assess their own progress as learners and so that teachers can get new views of their accomplishment and teaching

5. Cover letters are necessary because:
   a) they make students write
   b) they help you understand what the project is about
   c) they are for students to describe their work and relate it to one or more of the U.H.H.S. Domains and Outcomes and make a self-assessment about the level or quality of their work

6. The best portfolio for a student to create is:
   a) a Benchmark Portfolio
   b) a Seminar Portfolio
   c) both Benchmark and Seminar Portfolios

7. As a parent, I understand my role in the Roundtable process:
   a) a little
   b) a little more
   c) a lot

8. As a student, what I get out of a Roundtable is:
   a) nervous and frustrated by the pressure of being a presenter
   b) the opportunity to prove to others my abilities
   c) a time to reflect on my achievement, help others recognize my strengths and weaknesses, and learn more through their suggestions

9. As a student, I can prove I have met all the requirements for graduation by:
   a) telling everybody I feel I am ready
   b) having a portfolio for proof
   c) having a presentable portfolio; completed Domains and Outcomes; and the agreement of my family, my teachers, and outside guests

10. Using our system, getting into college is:
    a) a bit difficult
    c) no more difficult than any other system
    c) being in a new environment and a new educational system with more responsibilities—all this change is difficult. But other than that it will be just fine because you are meeting new challenges, and being better prepared for the real world.

Scoring

10–15 points: You'd better get involved in the school community
16–25 points: You're pretty involved in the school community, but should come to next years' summer institute!
26–30 points: Wow, I'm proud of you—you basically understand our school system, but that still doesn't mean you can't be more involved!

*This quiz is recommended for both students and parents.

CHAPTER *12*

Supporting Continuous Renewal
Systems Adaptation

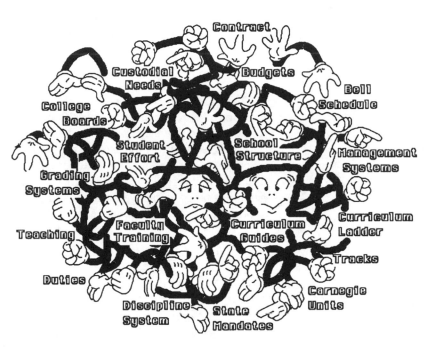

As most teachers experienced in school change will attest, the modern high school is a standing monument to predictable order. The curriculum sequence, departments, academic and administrative roles, and bell and bus schedules all conspire to make changing the system a dispiriting enterprise. Over the years, the conventions of high school management have tied a Gordian knot around teachers, administrators, and students alike. Introducing interdisciplinary teaching would seem a simple adaptation at the outset, but as soon as an idea moves from vision to plan, the stable system throws up its defenses. A well-entrenched tracking system, ten students who want French 5, scheduling the vocational program, assembling Carnegie units required for graduation, the tripartite structure of fifth-period lunch, an immutable bus schedule, SAT prep for college bound students, the duty roster (cafeteria and hall patrols), teacher licensing requirements, honors programs, and spaces built for exactly thirty students at a time all form an interlocking shield-wall around the status quo. To this point, changing high schools has most often amounted to adding new courses and requirements simply because changing what exists is such a formidable task. Those who try to introduce a new system often find that they are running two systems at once, because the old one holds fast while the new one struggles into being.

The modern high school has a politically balanced management system made up of school boards, superintendents, principals, department chairs, and faculty, moderated by a professional ethic that reserves most curricular and instructional decisions for the faculty. Because the faculty is not well organized to make schoolwide decisions and because others have little influence on teaching, most teaching follows the whims of particular teachers in particular classrooms. Students navigate their way from class to class on autopilot, numb to the grinding machinery surrounding them. (From a student perspective: the purpose of a high school schedule is to produce four-minute breaks between class periods in which serious questions can be investigated.) As pressures on teacher time have mounted, the unions have exerted increasing influence over questions of scheduling and workload, making role adaptation an excruciating exercise. Unfortunately, the line of least resistance in school management usually lets teachers retreat to their classrooms and close the doors—to each other and the world changing rapidly around them. The best ideas and the best intentions whither without institutional support.

Changing a school is as difficult and as necessary as changing any one of the smokestack industries on which high schools are modeled. Like aging industries from the nineteenth century, schools have dedicated most of their staff time to direct service to students, leaving very little to be allocated to school development activities. Change, particularly organized change, has not become a part of professional training or of school culture. High school teachers as a profession have not developed the expectation that they can initiate change in the school where they teach. Consequently, few have tried to exert systematic influence over the transformation of high school learning. For the ongoing transformation of teaching to succeed in creating a high school in which learning is the focus, teachers need to develop an expanded vision of what it takes to change a school and practice with leadership in a loosely organized, professional organization.

Organizing for Adaptability

Moving from one organizational paradigm to another requires a long-term commitment. Replacing a system dedicated to predictable order with a system supporting continuous change increases the challenge. Linda Darling-Hammond and her colleagues (1992) at the National Center for Restructuring Education, Schools and Teaching have set out policy guidelines to help schools hold steady during an extended period of improvement. "To help individual schools be accountable to students, parents and the community, Darling-Hammond (1992) writes, "at least three components are necessary:

> 1) A set of policies and procedures that encourage and support good teaching and valuable learning. (These include structures and incentives designed to ensure that the desired practices can and do occur.)
> 2) Methods for regularly eliciting information that shows how the school is functioning for all students and that pinpoint what areas of the school context may be influencing the school's success or failure with individual students and various groups of students.
> 3) Mechanisms for rethinking and changing practices—in individual cases or in cases involving overall school functions—if students are not being well serviced.

Only by making student learning the central focus of all decision-making and flexing systems continuously to support learning can schools set and maintain a steady course toward improvement.

When the Coalition of Essential Schools began in 1984, it aimed to develop specific ways to respond to five "imperatives" that an earlier report, "A Study of High Schools" (Coalition of Essential Schools, Brown University, 1993), showed to be necessary to support high school development:

- Give room to teachers and students to work and learn in their own appropriate ways;
- Insist that students clearly exhibit mastery of their school work;
- Get the incentives right, for students and teachers;
- Focus the students' work on the use of their minds;
- Keep the structure simple and flexible.

These guidelines helped form the basis of the nine "common principles" that now focus the work of more than 700 high schools, several of which contributed examples to this book (look ahead to Figure 12.11).

Integrating Top-Down Empowerment and Bottom-Up Experimentation

As the reports and showcases in this book illustrate, the formidable constraints to change do not make renewing a high school an impossible task; they simply make it a highly complex task, too difficult for any single individual or small group to manage either from the classroom or from a central position of authority. School change requires organizing an entire school community to the extent that all develop a common mission, share some sense of common direction, use a similar vocabulary to describe their common work, and use similar scales to measure progress or success. With a common vision and sense of direction, individuals can pursue their individual interests in light of a collective sense of purpose, and teams of professionals can fashion specific solutions that fit a common sense of the problem to be addressed. Forging a common sense of purpose and direction in a culture committed to specialization and "turf" is the exacting task of high school leadership—whether those leaders are teachers, administrators, or professional teams dedicated to school development. Engaging teachers in school development (bottom-up) and providing a supportive structure for change (top-down) must occur simultaneously for change to occur (see Figure 12-1).

In reviewing research related to school change, Carl Glickman (1993, pp. 17–18) identifies the following five findings that describe successful schools:

1) Faculty in successful schools are less satisfied with regard to their teaching than are faculty in the less successful schools;

2) Successful schools are schools where faculty members supervise and guide one another, plan courses together and work in coordination;

3) In successful schools, faculty are not treated as subordinates, but instead are regarded as colleagues of administration and others involved in decisions and actions;

4) Faculty members, administrators and others in successful schools have established norms of collegiality for discussing and debating the big questions about how to constantly renew and improve the educational environment for all students;

5) Successful schools seek, produce and consume information and they see educational renewal as a continuing process, not as an event

Though these findings seem counterintuitive, they underscore a conception of change that works simultaneously from the top-down and from the bottom-up. Top administrators aim to empower teachers to solve the problems they face; teachers join together to fashion new ways to meet commonly held goals.

Michael Fullen (1993) has pointed out two major reasons why reform efforts fail. One is that the problems we face are, in fact, intractible and complex, making solutions hard to conceive and harder to put into practice. The second reason is that the strategies we use "do not focus on things that will really make a difference. They fail to address fundamental instructional reform and associated development of new collaborative cultures among educators" (Fullen, 1993, p. 46). In short, successful change depends on bringing teachers together to devise more effective ways to teach. In Vermont, school change efforts are aimed at changing four aspects of school life:

FIGURE 12.1   A Cycle of Continuous Renewal—Bottom-Up Development Empowered by Top-Down Coordination

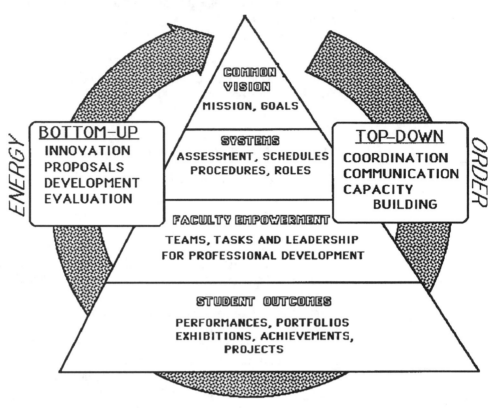

Used with permission.

1. *Developing Common Vision:* Defining the goals and values that will lend direction to school development efforts;
2. *Revising Systems:* Redesigning school management (planning, budgeting, scheduling, and rewards to support change rather than the status quo);
3. *Organizing Faculty Development:* Focusing professional development activity on team-based work in behalf of common goals;
4. *Supporting Student Achievement:* Focusing student work on performances that represent attainment of the common vision.

Because ongoing practice exerts such a strong influence on school life, high schools must attend to these four areas simultaneously, reducing fragmentation and avoiding conflict between the old and the new.

Creating Common Vision

Effective school change depends on the existence of a widely held sense of purpose and a few clear change goals that are endorsed energetically by most members of the school community. To influence a wide array of practice over an extended period of time, a vision statement must represent the values held in common by a whole school community, not a potpouri of values assembled through political wheeling and dealing or a uniform standard imposed from the top. In Vermont, achieving consensus on school goals usually begins with a focus forum, followed by surveys, committee work, community meetings, and publications that clarify the meaning of the goals. A focus forum is a gathering of randomly selected community members, students, and teachers who meet in a gym or cafeteria to create a mission for a school or district. From individual statements of priority, small groups assemble a preliminary vision for their school that the larger group then fuses into a single set of propositions. A focus forum creates consensus around school goals based on a few simple questions: (1) How do we want our school to be? (2) What will we do to make it happen? (3) How will we know when we have succeeded? and (4) How will we ensure the outcome? While the form of the questions has varied in different districts around Vermont, the simplicity of those questions invites response from virtually any member of the school community. They serve to create alignment between community values, school procedures, professional roles, and student expectations (Clarke, Willey, & Maynard, 1994). Alignment creates momentum in the change process.

A general statement of vision or mission provides the rationale for a discrete list of school goals or outcome statements for all students. "What should our students know and be able to do when they graduate from this school?" When the whole school community comes up with a generally accepted answer to this question, that collective answer may empower teams of faculty, students, community members, and school administrators to put their individual energy into making real things happen in student learning. The mission statement should guide policy development, budget preparation, scheduling, staffing, grading, and most important, curriculum. If developing a mission statement involves a whole school community, its application to the decisions that make up the change process appears both natural and useful rather than capricious or arbitrary. The mission becomes an anchoring point throughout the tumultuous process of change.

With different missions in view, different schools develop different learning goals. Littleton, Colorado, is reorganizing to meet nineteen goals. Other members of the Coalition for Essential Schools put different emphases on different kinds of goals. The Cabot School in Vermont organized to achieve nine (Sable & Clarke, 1994). The high school in Cabot used the mission and nine goals shown in Figure 12.2 to achieve thorough school redevelopment: basing the curriculum on outcomes for all students; revising the schedule to support student projects, tutorials, field-based experience in work, and service learning; bringing parents and social services into the school; and infusing technology in virtually all aspects of school life.

Having a single mission prevents the kind of diffusion that occurs when decisions are made on a purely political basis. A clear mission simplifies complex choices. The simplifying effect is powerful as long as the number of goals is discrete and internally consistent.

Among all the common beliefs that support change in a public high school, a belief in change itself is foremost in importance. A school mission should endorse the idea of continuous self-renewal. To move successfully toward new kinds of teaching and learning, a faculty and administration must come to believe that change itself is necessary, desirable, and permanent in the daily life of a school simply because the school is nested in a changing culture. As Joyce et al. (1993, p. 23) stated:

> If the organization recreates itself into a healthy learning community, where working together, studying together, and growing together has been planned into the system as a way of life, working in school becomes synonymous with lifelong learning.

Shifting priority from stability to change will initiate a revolution in the conception of the public high school. It will also require an enlargement of professional education to include change management on an ongoing basis.

FIGURE 12.2   Summary: Mission and Goals for the Cabot School Plan

---

Mission

The mission of the Cabot School is to provide all of its students, including adults, with the skills and knowledge necessary for them to become and remain informed, productive, self-sufficient, and responsible citizens who will contribute to their communities and possess the self-esteem and motivation necessary to continue learning throughout their lives.

Goal 1: Curriculum

The K–12 curriculum will be revised so students move toward completion of graduation proficiences based on high standards rather than Carnegie Units. (Students will complete these requirements by tenth grade.)

Goals 2: Student Performance

New graduation standards based on demonstrated proficiency will be developed and student progress toward those proficiencies will be measured at two-year intervals.

Goal 3: Student Assistance

Student assistance and intervention strategies will be created to ensure that each student excels to the best of his or her ability.

Goal 4: Parent Involvement

Parental involvement will be actively solicited and encouraged through a variety of programs and community service will be emphasized.

Goal 5: Teacher Performance

A new evaluation plan for teachers will directly link assessment of teacher performance to student performance

Goal 6: Teacher Assistance

Ongoing training will ensure that Cabot staff have the necessary skills to develop excellence in all students.

Goal 7: Vocational Opportunities

Business partnerships and career opportunities will be developed, creating access to the widest spectrum of vocational choice.

Goal 8: Continuing Education

Educational opportunities will be designed for all Cabot citizens.

Goal 9: Human and Social Services

A human and social service family center will be established to meet the needs of the community at large.

Used with permission.

Designing New Systems

As modern industry has discovered, a hierarchic, control-oriented management system, featuring clearly defined authority systems and rigid specialization in teaching and service roles, does not easily support change. High schools are learning to distribute control to the people who face a specific problem needing solution—teams of teachers, parents, and administrators working with students. As in "Japanese" management, teams of high school people who are given a problem to solve and resources to apply can produce solutions that they themselves then want to carry out. As Figure 12.3 suggests, moving from a bureaucratic organization, one that favors stability, to a

FIGURE 12.3 Bureaucratic and Professional Systems—Comparison of Two Models

	Bureaucratic Models	*Professional Model*
Program Purpose	Derives program *purpose* from perceived needs of the *school system.*	Derives *purpose* from perceived needs of the *student-client.*
Knowledge Source	Analyzes *national trends* for locally applicable information.	Analyzes *professional knowledge* in light of client needs.
Planning Process	Moves *"top-down"* from program planners to program participants.	Involves *collaborative planning* within whole professional community.
Program Process	Brings *external expertise* to bear on local problems.	Extends *local expertise* into the larger community.
Program Parts	Applies *ad hoc* solutions to atomistic array of problems.	Applies systematic process to develop *interconnected* solutions.
Program Effects	Achieves uneven pattern of *effects scattered* across professional community.	Achieves *incremental change* within increasingly capable community of professionals.

Used with permission.

professionally organized structure, one that supports continuous adaptation, requires a major shift in how high schools think about organization.

In a developing school, a common vision of purpose and outcome gives all participants a sense of what is valid and what is not, creating a common basis for judgments about priorities and a way to prioritize experimental initiatives. Administrative processes are organized to support teacher or community-led development. Teachers join task groups with students and community members to solve problems beyond those of the conventional classroom. Students recognize their responsibility for learning and make their own contribution to the vitality of school-based experimentation. In a changing school, administrative structures support collaborative initiatives that aim to guide students toward the highest development and expression of their capabilities.

At Otter Valley High School in Brandon, Vermont, with 720 students, the faculty, school board, and administration tried to develop a model for school organization (see Figure 12.4) that empowers teachers and students to direct their own development and asks administrators to help them coordinate their work to ensure the success of new ideas. In this conception, empowerment of a changing school is the purpose of the school board and superintendents' office. In the school itself, a principal's team provides support for daily activity and helps coordinate a 7–9 group of faculty and a 10–12 group of faculty. Three instructional leaders coordinate teaching teams in the sciences, humanities, and applied arts at each of the two levels. The six instructional leaders constitute a planning group for school-based change initiatives, developing plans and proposals for ongoing change. The School Development Council, including the instructional leaders, parents, school board representatives, and community members, proposes plans and budgets for those plans to the board and superintendent each year. This conception of school structure aims to balance the need for stable and predictable systems with the need for ongoing experimentation among students and faculty.

FIGURE 12.4   Leadership Cycle (Draft)—Management and Development at Otter Valley High School

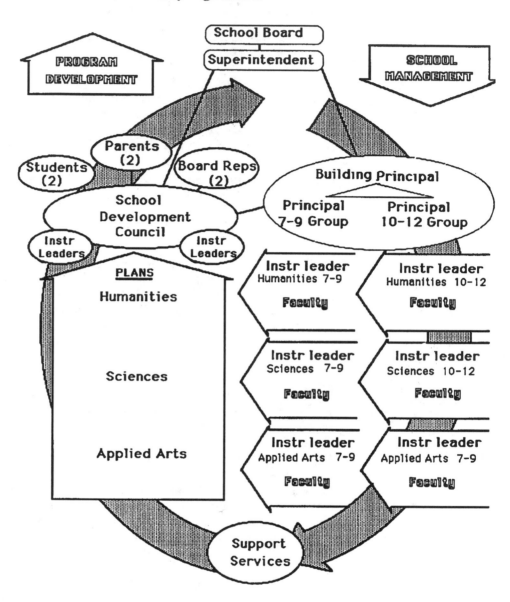

Carpe Diem: Seize the Time for School Development

Ask any teacher what makes change so hard to consider. The answer is invariable: "We don't have the time." The embedded systems—grading systems, report cards, graduation requirements, departmental organizations, and teacher contracts, for example—that frustrate change are trivial in contrast to the limits of time that keep teachers and administrators from focusing energy on new ways of teaching and learning. Bells ring, buses roll, halls swell with kids and fall silent again, juniors become seniors as seniors file into graduation and out again. In the name of efficiency (to please taxpayers) and in the name of student safety (to please parents), schools have scheduled every available minute in the day, allocating all time to direct service, ensuring no "slack" in the faculty workday, and setting aside no time for instructional development. Under current scheduling conditions, for teachers to consider investing in change is to accept frustration and inadequacy that naturally accompanies doing two difficult jobs at once. To make change happen, a school must dedicate time to the task of school development.

Time on task is a necessary precondition to school learning—and to school development. Thus, scheduling in the emerging high school should have two purposes: (1) to create blocks of *learning time* in which teachers help students meet the vision and goals a school has set for its own development; and (2) to create blocks of *development time* for teaching teams to use in planning new curriculum.

The time for change is available in the current schoolyear, but teacher-time must be wrestled away from direct service and dedicated to the task of planning and assessing change. At the same time, student-time must be wrestled away from class hours and dedicated to individual and group initiatives that play out in high performance—inquiry, exhibitions, and learning from work or service. Changing the structure of time in school requires diminishing the time teachers spend on "policing" students and increasing the time they spend on instructional development.

Rebuilding the Schedule

We cannot improve the quality of teaching and learning without changing the schedule of the school day. The conventional high school schedule was built to support a curriculum that covered the core content areas (math, science, English, and social studies) and also allowed for electives in the arts, languages, vocational subjects, personal development, and physical education. Four or five core subjects and three or four electives, coupled to the requirement that all students be supervised by teachers at all times, has created the conventional lock-step seven- or eight-period day. Because different students learn at different rates, the conventional day also forced teachers to limit their experimentation with time-consuming but potentially more effective instruction—cooperative learning, project-based learning, and virtually every other innovation this book describes. By limiting instructional technique, the seven- to eight-period day also reinforced tracking by putting similar students in one room where the pace of instruction could be managed. Changing the schedule has emerged as a quick way to cut the Gordian knot that welds tracking practices, one-size-fits-all-teaching, and subject-based curriculum into an intractable ball. It should be noted, however, that schedule adjustments do not prepare a faculty to individualize, respond to differences, design inquiry projects, or focus on problems. Block scheduling simply makes new techniques more desirable by making conventional teaching almost impossible. Homework checks, chalk-talks, and worksheets simply do not fill an 80- to 140-minute period.

The examples that follow illustrate the enormous variability in high school scheduling rather than an established trajectory toward some generalizable right answer for all high schools. In each schedule, class time is expanded into blocks that teachers and students can use to develop knowledge in depth, making connections among the disciplines and exploring issues that evade capture in a 40-minute class period. The schedule that divides time into small bits to "cover the subject areas" disappears. Time for teachers to meet and coach students has a defined place. Time for teachers and school change-teams to evaluate progress and devise new plans is built into the day, the week, and the year, in the same way that research and development is planned into the budget of any successful business. The process of school change is too important to leave to chance.

The Copernican Plan is an early model of interdisciplinary teaching and learning that created a new way to look at a school day (Carroll, 1989a,b; Munroe, 1987). This Plan relies on two possible schedules that can be selected to fit the plans teachers and students develop for their work. Figure 12.5 shows both plans, with Plan A allowing

FIGURE 12.5   Two Schedules from the Copernican Plan

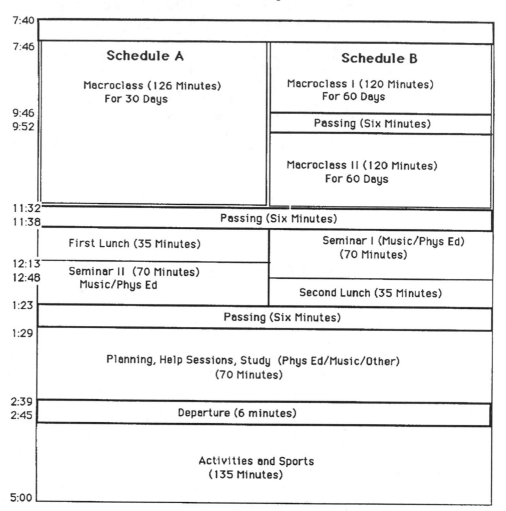

Reprinted with permission of The Regional Laboratory for Educational Improvement of the Northeast and Islands from *The Copernican Plan: Restructuring the American High School* by Joseph M. Carroll. Copyright 1989. Used with permission.

six 30-day courses per year and Plan B allowing six macroclasses in three trimesters. Increased efficiency in both plans, or in combinations, allows a high school to offer integrated seminars, tutorials, and faculty planning time. Both plans "cost" the continuing segregation of phys ed and music, subjects that could be reintegrated with other subjects that are moved into the afternoon periods.

A limited block schedule has proven useful in Vermont, where a transitional schedule is needed to allow teachers to experiment with larger blocks of time and new instructional techniques. Linked consecutive blocks allow team teaching, with greater numbers of students in a scheduled block. Limited block schedules increase the size of the periods teachers have for planning and teaching, thus supporting experimentation with instruction that requires more than forty minutes. If a faculty decides to try doubling the length of its conventional periods, it can extend the time available for trying new kinds of teaching and also allows teams of teachers to link consecutive blocks to create full half-days for team teaching and projects. As Figure 12.6 shows, a modified block schedule allows a school to move slowly toward integrated teaching without violating the scheduling assumptions that create an eight-period day. A tran-

FIGURE 12.6   Converting an Eight-Period Day to a Block Schedule in Two Steps

Transitional Schedule: For Experimentation

	Monday	Tuesday	Wednesday	Thursday	Friday
	Period 1			Period 1	Period 1
	Period 2			Period 2	Period 2
	Period 3			Period 3	Period 3
	Period 4			Period 4	Period 4
Three Group Lunch	Period 5			Period 5	Period 5
	Period 6			Period 6	Period 6
	Period 7			Period 7	Period 7
	Period 8			Period 8	Period 8

40-Minute Seminars   80-Minute Blocks

BLOCK SCHEDULE WITH ONE DAY OF SEMINARS

Period 1	Period 1	Period 5	Period 1	Period 5
Period 2				
Period 3	Period 2	Period 6	Period 2	Period 6
Period 4				
Period 5	Period 3	Period 7	Period 3	Period 7
Period 6				
Period 7	Period 4	Period 8	Period 4	Period 8
Period 8				

(Three Group Lunch shown at left margin)

Used with permission.

sitional year creates two days for experimentation that may become a full block schedule, with one day of seminars, when sufficient adaptation in teaching has occurred.

Canady and Reitig (1993) carry the logic of schedule revision all the way from revision of a seven- or eight-period day to a flexible schedule adaptable to virtually any high school program (see Figure 12.7). Using 25-minute segments as a basic time unit, they created blocks of time that support effective teaching and also fit the tasks that come up in school restructuring. A 200-minute block could allow a full credit course to fill only forty-five days. Or it could give all students a chance to

FIGURE 12.7   Building Multiple Schedules from Sixteen 25-Minute Time Periods

	A	B	C	D	E	F	G
1	50	75	100	200	75	50	75
2							
3	50					50	
4		75			100		75
5	50		100			50	
6							
7	L	50		50		L	L
8	50		L	L	L	A	A
9		L	L		A		
10	50						
11		100	100	L	100		100
12	50			50		200	
13							
14	A	A	A	A	A		
15	50	50	50	50	50		100
16							

50-minute periods: Can schedule a traditional 7-period schedule; may be necessary to accommodate transfer students.

75-minute periods: May be appropriate for subjects such as PE, art, industrial arts, home economics, and lab-type classes.

100-minute periods: Can complete a full credit course each 90-day semester.

200-minute periods: Can complete a full credit course each 45-day quarter.

Plan F may be good for students who have programs in two buildings such as academic and vocational.

Plan G would help a program high in performing arts and labs.

Designed by Robert Lynn Canady, Professor, Department of Educational Leadership & Policy Studies, School of Education, University of Virginia, Charlottesville, VA 22903-2495. Used with permission.

work or serve while the faculty plans curriculum revisions. A 25-minute block could create a medium for tutorials, seminars, or student activities. Still, building a flexible master schedule from such a flexible base would require full mastery of group communication and political skills.

Rebuilding the School Calendar

The yearly calendar of schooling, instituted to provide a consistent standard for a diploma, has now become another constraint to high school development. The 180-day schoolyear, marching on from August to July, with breathing space inserted roughly at eight-week intervals, reinforces the drudgery of an eight-period day, distributed across subject-based classes, activities, and study halls. The conventional calendar freezes in place the idea that learning occurs through regular exposure to a content area rather than through engagement in a focused learning activity. Within a few weeks of September 1, students and teacher alike come to view their time in school as an endurance test. "Can I make it to Thanksgiving?" becomes the question organizing faculty and student effort. By February, the long march has become mindless plodding toward an unsure and distant destination somewhere deep in June. Why not arrange the required number of days to serve clearly defined educational purposes, carried out in units of study built to fit defined periods of time? Why not let differing purposes direct the allocation of calendar days? We need to align the schedule of time to the purposes implied by our mission and goals.

Rettig and Canady also propose different constructions of a 75-75-30 plan, a modest calendar that leaves most of the curriculum intact (see 1993 article). Both the fall and winter terms could be dedicated to interdisciplinary units and work activities in block schedules, followed by a 30-day short term dedicated to acceleration, in-depth study, work experience, or electives. The 30-day spring term could also be designed to allow teaching teams the time they need to design new units and replan their curriculum. The 75-75-30 plan leaves the summer intact, allowing teachers to pursue professional development plans, students to work or play, and parents to plan vacations.

Others have mounted a direct assault on the ten- to twelve-week summer vacation. In one of Vermont's most agrarian counties, some have argued that the summer vacation remains as an atavism from an early agrarian era in which summer term was just long enough to allow sons to plant corn and daughters to can it before returning to school. Now, male students and female students alike see summer as a time to escape thralldom to the relentless 180-day march and forget everything they have learned. Summer vacation has achieved the sanctity of a major religious holiday. Extending the schoolyear will prove possible only after schools have gone far enough toward the common goals they have set to persuade parents and teachers that more school time will prove worthwhile.

To support school development, school boards and superintendents must revise their personnel policies to support faculty groups empowered to pursue a school development goal and important tasks to complete. In school development, whole-faculty retreats, curriculum planning institutes, daily team-time, and budgetary support for groups with a common goal often prove more productive than in-service days for workshops, tuition vouchers, and travel support for individuals seeking renewal (Clarke, Tarule, & Hood, 1994; Clarke, Willey, & Maynard, 1994). Helping a faculty adopt change as part of its professional responsibility may take much time and effort.

Faculty development remains the single most important ingredient in high school redevelopment. Virtually all high school teachers have been licensed to teach in one or two subject-based disciplines using methods largely derived from lecture/recitation techniques. Their first allegiance is to a single discipline and to a department organized around subject areas. Because faculty development plans—graduate courses, conferences, and workshops—are currently designed for individual development, these too reinforce content specialization rather than larger issues in curricular coherence and school effectiveness. To refocus the curriculum on commonly held goals, a faculty has to work in small groups or teams, take on problems of general concern in their high school, and propose those solutions to the whole community. Teamwork on behalf of school change goals forces teachers to adopt a perspective larger than that of their own discipline. When a faculty begins to organize itself to meet a single set of school-change goals rather than the separate subject areas that divide them, they may generate from collective support enormous and enduring influence.

Focusing on Student Learning

To change a school, teachers and administrators must put the highest priority on improved learning for high school students (see Figure 12.8). Once student learning is held as central, other issues can be addressed as they detract or contribute to learning. The following questions begin with a focus on learning:

What are we doing well?

What events best reflect our achievement?

What aspects remain that could be improved?

What kinds of activities would move us forward again?

What goals do we hold for all students?

What would we seek as evidence of quality in learning?

What productions, exhibits, or performances represent our highest hopes?

In any faculty, the examples of desirable outcomes for analysis already exist. From a focus on learning, a faculty team can begin to look at teaching and curriculum: How have we helped students achieve this level of performance? What kind of teaching should we develop that would let more students reach the highest level of achievement? Finally, a faculty may look at the curriculum itself. To support this kind of teaching, what adjustments should we make in the schedule, the requirements, and the content? What adjustments will allow us to meet our expectations? (Clarke & Cornell, 1994).

The purpose of all this—the unequivocal end point for all instructional and systems adaptation—is a high school graduate who can manage the work of his or her mind in a way that increases control over the context in which she or he will live as an adult. A clear vision statement, supportive systems, and teamed faculty come to nothing if students remain outside of the process. At the School Without Walls in Rochester, New York, when they begin school, students and their parents read and sign an agree-

FIGURE 12.8   Questions Guiding Classroom-Based Curriculum Design

---

Focus on Learning

Vision for Learning: What goals do we hold for all students at all grade levels?

Quality Indicators for Schoolwork: For goals such as these, what do we seek in student work as evidence of high quality?

Exemplars of Quality Schoolwork: What student productions best represent the attainment of our goals?

Focus on Teaching

Examples of Powerful Instruction: What unit plans and instructional approaches produce student work of this quality?

Need for Further Examples: In light of our goals and accomplishments, what unit plans or types of instruction do we need now to move us closer to our goals?

Emerging Models of Powerful Instruction: Based on the examples we have gathered, what kinds of teaching appear to have the greatest potential?

Focus on Curriculum

Curriculum Coherence: As we gather examples of teaching that produces learning of the highest quality, what content gaps and overlaps should we repair?

Curriculum Management: What incentives and resources can we apply to the support of existing and emerging models of high quality?

Curriculum Governance: What organizational structure and systems will best support the continuous evolution of high-quality teaching and learning?

---

ment that explains the school's mission and describes the responsibilities students assume when they begin a curriculum based on freedom to pursue goals rather than thralldom to scheduled class periods. They may reconfirm their agreement on five subsequent occasions. Students who have not experienced freedom in their earlier learning need to learn how to manage their own progress, perhaps the highest goal to which a school may aspire. If the purpose of high school learning is to allow students to control their minds and influence the world in which they live, the curriculum must include supports toward that end.

As Figure 12.9 implies, the most important participant in a school-change initiative is the individual student. Students need to subscribe to the vision adopted for their school. They need to understand the system well enough to use it to support

FIGURE 12.9   Agreement of Understanding Summary

Between _____ and School Without Walls

At the School Without Walls, students have rights and responsibilities which you may not have had before. We want you to understand them so you can have a successful career here. If you use your rights and fulfill your responsibilities, you will be able to meet the goals of the school and graduate.

1) You will have a significant relationship with an advisor:

- You must keep a journal about the things you do each day and share it with your advisor.
- You will have conferences every two weeks to discuss your progress and things that are on your mind.
- You will have your own schedule. You must go to class on time and use your time constructively.
- You will help write progress reports with your advisor and teachers, but you will receive no grade.

2) You will have to fulfill a number of academic requirements in order to graduate:

- You must attend class, participate and complete assignments to earn credits.
- You must earn at least five quarters of credit each ten weeks to stay in good standing at SWW.
- You have the opportunity to write proposals to study independently on a contract.
- You must do at least two-and-one-half hours of volunteer work per week during the schoolyear.
- You will make a portfolio so you can see your progress and reflect on what you have learned.
- You must complete a SENIOR PROJECT that shows you have learned how to learn and shows others what you have done to earn a diploma so they can decide if you are ready to graduate.

3) You will make decisions about the activities and plans for your classes and the school:

- You must use the student handbook to understand policies and procedures.
- You will discuss and vote on proposals for school improvements or activities.
- You will help decide the program and direct the school, including class topics and school budget.

4) You will be part of a very special community:

- Our school values civil behavior. You must treat others with respect and work together to solve conflicts.
- We value and care about each other. We do not tolerate theft or put each other down.
- Our community values learning from involvement. Showing up is not enough.

THIS IS WHAT WE EXPECT FROM YOU.

The School Without Walls Agreement ends with a signature line for both students and parents, with five additional lines for reconfirmation at later dates.

From the School Without Walls, Rochester, NY. Used with permission of Andrew Nagel.

their work. They must see the faculty as their primary resource in pursuing their own learning. Most important, they must see learning as the purpose of the whole, and the guiding motive for their involvement. In a changing school, students take increasing responsibility for their own performance. Virtually all the innovations this book describes imply that learning is not done *to* students. It is done *by* students. Students need to understand the purpose and processes of their schools in order to take responsibility for their fulfillment. Helping them learn how to take responsibility for learning is surely the most important purpose a school can serve. School Without Walls, Cabot School, University Heights High School, and virtually all others who have made headway in transforming the high school experience have made student awareness and involvement their first priority.

The purpose of high school teaching is to help students use learning to take control of their own mental work, and thus to better control the world in which they live. Making connections in information, defining ways to think through situations, and solving problems in the work or community setting are way stations in the process of gaining control. They are part of the platform on which performances or exhibitions can be carried out. The purpose of a vision statement is to focus on student learning, setting clear direction for teachers, parents, and community leaders so that all can support the individual who is working on learning. School development activities should work backward from that sense of purpose. As McDonald et al. (1993, p. 5) state:

> The purpose of the vision is to orient the school's first moves and then guide all subsequent ones. Schools that are planning backwards must also dare to compare their new visions of the ideal graduate to the real kids they will graduate this year. In the metaphorical lingo of planning backwards, this is called building a platform. On the school's platform, erected at first atop the same old curriculum, the same isolated teaching cells, the same hierarchic information systems, current candidates for graduation are asked to exhibit in light of the vision.

According to one RAND study, the difference between a school with character and a school without it is that the school with character concentrates on student outcomes to the virtual exclusion of all other matters, while the school without character concentrates on managing its programs and following procedures (Hill, Foster, & Gendler, 1990, p. 35).

Distributed Leadership

Change of this magnitude requires leadership from all constituencies: government, higher education, foundations, parent organizations, and community-service providers. External agents should support, not direct or coerce, locally based change efforts. Although change in a high school depends on empowering teachers as leaders, the role of the state and federal governments is not to be diminished by a focus on local control and school-based development. State and federal efforts are essential in the process of capacity building, funneling resources to areas that need support and communication, and conveying good ideas from one place to the next so they can be analyzed and adapted for new uses. College and university teachers need to leave the sanctity of their academic enclaves to join the rest of their profession in improving student learning. As Peter Senge (1990) points out, the growing school is like a learning individual in many respects and learning in any setting is a process of enhancing capacity. In creating a high school organized for continuous change, we will also be rebuilding the mental models of how organizations work (Kim, 1990). In a learning community, continuous adaptation is not the sign of failure, it is the sign of health. External agents need to see that growth is the purpose of school development, not ossification around any "standard." We need to agree on the direction of change and avoid specifying end points for the process in order to develop self-renewing schools.

For a large-scale change initiative to succeed, school leaders—teachers and administrators alike—need to spend time on change (Purnell & Hill, 1992). Effective leadership is shared leadership, not solely as power sharing or democratic process, but as an endless process of connecting individual effort to collective movement based on the school mission. Wide involvement is the key. Communication and coordination between far-flung school initiatives becomes the problem. Marge Sable, Principal of the Cabot School during its years of accelerated change, built nine local teams to carry out development of the nine change goals in her school. Her own role changed from director to mediator-connector-fixer-facilitator-communicator as the teams developed proposals and plans separate from one another. As Figure 12.10 suggests, her days and nights became a whirlwind effort to get proposals from individuals and groups into a written form the faculty could look at as a whole and not as a blizzard of pieces. Size is not a lethal impediment to change. Setting clear goals and putting resources behind them is the simplest recipe for school change.

The change process heats up the high school context. To avoid overheating, the best guidelines are simple guidelines. Perhaps the best expression of the principles guiding change is the nine common principles of the Coalition of Essential Schools shown in Figure 12.11. Though the members of the coalition now number more than 700, each member is developing ways to put student performance at the center of school learning, aiming for a short list of outcomes that will qualify young people to survive and thrive in the next century. "Less is more," Dean Sizer reminds us. To achieve the vision of learning we desire for high school students, we need to join efforts to achieve those ends and abandon efforts that only diffuse our energies. High school teachers and administrators, working as one profession with a single mission, are building schools that help students manage the work of their minds and prepare to manage the rapidly changing world around them.

FIGURE 12.10   Guidelines for Managing Change Discovered in Cabot, Vermont

Common Values—Focus on student learning! What's going to improve learning is the question that drives all good decisions, in curriculum, teaching, professional development, budgeting and school leadership.

Common Language—Set clear and simple goals! Goal statements developed by a whole school community create a common language for all to use in teaching, curriculum design, and decision making.

Irreverance—Hold no cow sacred! No aspect of school life should be held aside as immutable or beyond questioning.

Team Responsibility—Empower others! Teams with a task can control their own direction and their own resources.

Community Involvement—Open the door! The school must become a known resource to all members of the community. Access reduces tension and increases responsible action.

Leadership Stability—Hold steady! Leaders will remain in place if they are not held accountable for every problem in the life of a school, but become responsive to the processes that bring schools to life.

Commitment to Action—Just do it! Putting something on the ground gives everyone a chance to learn, and to try to do it better next time around.

Coordination Not Coersion—Link achievement to new challenges! School leadership is a matter of connecting people to teams, teams to problems, problems to solutions, and proven solutions to school goals.

From Marge Sable and John Clarke, in W. Mathis (Ed.), *Field Guide to School Renewal*. Brandon, VT: Holistic Education Press. Used with permission.

FIGURE 12.11   The Common Principles

1. The school should focus on helping adolescents learn to use their minds well. Schools should not attempt to be "comprehensive" if such a claim is made at the expense of the school's central intellectual purpose.

2. The school's goals should be simple: that each student master a limited number of essential skills and areas of knowledge. While these skills and areas will, to varying degrees, reflect the traditional academic disciplines, the program's design should be shaped by the intellectual and imaginative powers and competencies that students need rather than necessarily by "subjects" as conventionally defined. The aphorism "Less Is More" should dominate: curricular decisions should be guided by the aim of thorough student mastery and achievement rather than by an effort merely to cover content.

3. The school's goals should apply to all students, while the means to these goals will vary as those students themselves vary. School practice should be tailor-made to meet the needs of every group or class of adolescents.

4. Teaching and learning should be personalized to the maximum feasible extent. Efforts should be directed toward a goal that no teacher have direct responsibility for more than 80 students. To capitalize on this personalization, decisions about the details of the course of study, the use of students' and teachers' time and the choice of teaching materials and specific pedagogies must be unreservedly placed in the hands of the principal and staff.

5. The governing practical metaphor of the school should be student-as-worker rather than the more familiar metaphor of teacher-as-deliverer-of-instructional-services. Accordingly, a prominent pedagogy will be coaching, to provoke students to learn how to learn and thus to teach themselves.

6. Students entering secondary school studies are those who can show competence in language and elementary mathematics. Students of traditional high school age but not yet at appropriate levels of competence to enter secondary school studies will be provided intensive remedial work to assist them quickly to meet these standards. The diploma should be awarded on a successful final demonstration of mastery for graduation—an "Exhibition." This Exhibition by the student of his or her grasp of the central skills and knowledge of the school's program may be jointly administered by the faculty and by higher authorities. As the diploma is awarded when earned, the school's program proceeds with no strict age grading and with no system of "credits earned" by "time spent" in class. The emphasis is on the students' demonstration that they can do important things.

7. The tone of the school should explicitly and self-consciously stress values of unanxious expectation ("I won't threaten you but I expect much of you"), of trust (until abused) and of decency (the values of fairness, generosity, and tolerance). Incentives appropriate to the school's particular students and teachers should be emphasized, and parents should be treated as essential collaborators.

8. The principal and teachers should perceive themselves as generalists first (teachers and scholars in general education) and specialists second (experts in but one particular discipline). Staff should expect multiple obligations (teacher-counselor-manager) and a sense of commitment to the entire school.

9. Ultimate administrative and budget targets should include, in addition to total student loads per teacher of eighty or fewer pupils, substantial time for collective planning by teachers, competitive salaries for staff, and an ultimate per pupil cost not to exceed that at traditional schools by more than 10 percent. To accomplish this, administrative plans may have to show the phased reduction or elimination of some services now provided students in many traditional comprehensive secondary schools.

References

Abramson, G. W. (1993). Technology and the teacher education accreditation process, *Ed-Tech Review, 2*(1):27–29.

Aikenhead, G. (1992). The integration of STS into science education. *Theory into Practice, 31*(1):26–32.

Aikenhead, G., and Ryan, A. (1993). Evaluation of views of high school graduates on STS topics. In R. Yager (Ed.), *The Science, Technology, Society Movement,* vol. 7: *What research says to the science teacher.* Washington, DC: National Science Teachers Association.

Alabama Department of Education. (1983). The Alabama course of study: Humanities K–12. Bulletin #16: ERIC ED 245982.

American Association for the Advancement of Science. (1989). *Science for all Americans.* Washington, DC: AAAS.

American Chemical Society. (1994). *ChemCom: Chemistry in the community* (promotional brochure). Dubuque, IA: Kendall/Hunt Publishing Company.

Ansbacher, P. R. (1991). Humanitas: A thematic curriculum. *Educational Leadership, 49*(2):16–20.

Apple Corporation. (1993). Why CD-ROM is an important addition to your Apple Macintosh computer. Cupertino, CA: Apple Corporation.

Arkansas International Center. (1992). ATLAS: Advanced teaching and learning in Arkansas schools. Little Rock: University of Arkansas.

Asante, M. K. (1991). Afrocentric curriculum. *Educational Leadership, 49*(1):28–31.

ASCD. (1992). *Curriculum Update, 34*(9):2.

Aspy, D. N., Aspy, C. B., and Quinby, P. M. (1993). What doctors can teach teachers about problem-based learning. *Educational Leadership, 50*(7):22–25.

Atkin, J. M. (1990). Teach science for science's sake: For global competitiveness, try technology. *Education Week, 26* (September): 32–34.

Ausubel, D. (1968). *Educational psychology: A cognitive view.* New York: Holt, Reinhart & Winston.

Bailey, T. (1993a). Can youth apprenticeship thrive in the United States? *Educational Researcher, 22*(3):4–10.

Bailey, T. (1993b). Youth apprenticeship in the context of broad educational reform. *Educational Researcher, 22*(3):16–17.

Baldwin, J. W. (1971). *The scholastic culture of the middle ages.* Lexington, MA: D. C. Heath.

Barrows, H. S. (1992). *The tutorial process.* Springfield, IL: Southern Illinois School of Medicine.

Barrows, H. S. (1994). Problem-based learning in secondary schools. Presentation at the Sixth International Conference on Thinking, Cambridge, MA.

Barrows, H. S., and Myers, A. C. (1993). Problem-based learning in secondary schools. Monograph #1. Springfield, IL: Problem-based Learning Institute, Ventures in Education, Inc., Southern Illinois School of Medicine and Springfield School District #186.

Beane, J. (1994). Keynote Presentation at the Second Annual National Conference on Curriculum Integration, Scottsdale, AZ, January 14.

Bergstrom, K., and Carr, J. (1994). Motivators and inhibitors: To teach or not to teach that integrated study. Presentation at Conference on Integrated Teaching. Scottsdale, AZ (available from the author at Goddard College, Plainfield, VT).

Berryman, S. E. (1993). Learning for the workplace. *Review of Research in Education, 19:*343–401.

Berryman, S. E. (1988). *Education and the economy: What should we teach? When? How? To whom?* Occasional Paper #4, National Center on Education and Employment. New York: Teachers College, Columbia University.

Berryman, S. E., and Bailey, T. (1993). *The double helix of education and the economy.* New York: National Center on Education and Employment, Teachers College, Columbia University.

Beyth-Marom, R., and Dekel, S. (1985). *An elementary approach to thinking under uncertainty* (translated from the Hebrew by Darah Lichtenstein, Benny Marom, and Ruth Beyth-Marom). Hillsdale, NJ: Erlbaum.

Bloom, B. (1981). *All our children learning: A primer for parents teachers and other educators.* New York: McGraw-Hill.

Bloom, B. (1992). Chip Bruce's Taxonomy of Educational Technology Applications. In *The Holmes Group Forum,* Winter, Volume VI, Number 2. Lansing, MI: Michigan State University.

Blunck, S., Giles, C., and McArthur, J. (1993). Gender differences in the science classroom: Bridging the gap. In R. Yager (Ed.), *The Science, Technology, Society Movement,* vol. 7: *What research says to the science teacher.* Washington, DC: National Science Teachers Association.

Bonstedder, R., and Pederson, J. (1993). The jurisprudential inquiry model for STS. In R. Yager (Ed.), *The Science, Technology, Society Movement,* vol. 7: *What research says to the science teacher.* Washington, DC: National Science Teachers Association.

Boyer, E. (1983). *High school: A report on secondary education in America.* New York: Harper & Row.

Boyer, E. (1993). Making the connections. Carnegie Foundation for the Advancement of Teaching. Presentation at the ASCD Annual Convention, Washington, DC.

Brandt, R. (1989). On misuse of testing: A conversation with George Madeus. *Educational Leadership, 46*(7):26–30.

Brandt, R. (1991). On interdisciplinary curriculum: A conversation with Heidi Hayes Jacobs. *Educational Leadership, 49*(2):4–26.

Brandt, R. (1994). On crating an environment where all students learn: A conversation with Al Mamary. *Educational Leadership, 51*(6):26.

Bransford, J. D., Sherwood, R. D., and Sturdevant, T. (1987). Teaching thinking and problem solving. In J. B. Baron and R. Sternberg (Eds.), *Teaching thinking skills: Theory and practice,* pp. 163–181. New York: W. H. Freeman.

Brooks, J. G., and Brooks, M. G. (1993). *In search of understanding: The case for constructivist classrooms.* Alexandria, VA: ASCD.

Brown, J. S., Collins, A., and Duguid, P. (1989). Situated cognition and the culture of learning. *Educational Researcher, 18*(1):32–41.

Bruner, J. (1961). Act of discovery. *Harvard Educational Review, 31*(1):22.

Bybee, R. (1991). Science-technology-society in science curriculum: The policy–practice gap. *Theory into Practice, 30*(4):294–300.

Byrne, S., Constant, A., and Moore, G. (1992). Making transitions from school to work. *Educational Leadership, 49*(6):23–26.

Cakmak, S. (1990). Multidisciplinary perspectives on cross-cultural education. ERIC ED 323565.

Campbell, L., Campbell, B., and Dickenson, L. (1992). *Teaching and learning through multiple intelligences.* Seattle: New Horizons Learning.

Canady, R. L. (1990). Parallel block scheduling: A better way to organize a school. *Principal,* (January): 34–36.

Canady, R., and Hotchkiss, P. (1989). It's a good score! Just a bad grade. *Phi Delta Kappan,* (September): 26–29.

Canady, R., and Rettig, M. (1993). Unlocking the lock step high school schedule. In *Getting off the track, National Staff Development Institute Handouts,* March 13.

Carroll, J. (1989a). *The Copernican Plan: Restructuring the American high school.* Andover, MA: The Regional Laboratory for Educational Improvement of the Northeast and Islands.

Carroll, J. (1989b). The Copernican Plan: A concept paper for restructuring high schools. Paper presented at the American Association of School Principals, New Orleans, February.

Casterson, D., McKowen, C., and Willis, T. (1993). "I" search at Soquel High School. *Educational Leadership, 50*(7): 73–76.

Casterson, D., McKowen, C., and Willis, T. (1993). Criteria for assessing authentic learning. Soquel, CA: Soquel High School.

Cheek, D. W. (1992). Evaluating learning in STS education. *Theory into Practice, 31*(1):65–71.

Claremont Graduate School. (1993). *Voices from the inside: A report on schooling from inside the classroom.* Claremont, CA: The Institute for Education in Transformation.

Clarke, J. (1990). *Patterns of thinking: Integrating learning skills with content teaching.* Boston: Allyn and Bacon.

Clarke, J. (1991). Using visual organizers to focus on thinking. *Journal of Reading, 34*(7):526–534.

Clarke, J. (1992). Graphic organizers: Frames for teaching patterns of thinking. In A. Costa (Ed.), *Developing minds: A resource book for teaching thinking,* 2d ed. Alexandria, VA: ASCD.

Clarke, J. (1994). Writing about thinking: How grade school students describe the work of their minds. *Think, 4*(2):12–22.

Clarke, J., and Biddle, A. (1992). Writing on the inquiry cycle. Conference Paper for National Council of Teachers of English, Atlanta.

Clarke, J., and Biddle, A. (1993). *Teaching critical thinking: Reports from across the curriculum.* Englewood Cliffs, NJ: Prentice-Hall.

Clarke, J., and Cornell, N. (1992). *Designer's guide: Developing cross-disciplinary units.* Brandon, VT: Otter Valley High School.

Clarke, J., and Cornell, N. (1994). Building curriculum on examples of quality. In W. Mathis (Ed.), *Field guide to educational renewal: Reports from the field.* Brandon, VT: Holistic Education Press.

Clarke, J., Gilbert, G., and Raths, J. (1990). Inductive towers: Helping students see how they think. *Journal of Reading, 33*(3):7–12.

Clarke, J., Martell, K., and Willey, C. (1994). Sequencing graphic organizers to guide historical research. *Social Studies, 85*(2):70–75.

Clarke, J., Tarule, J., and Hood, K. (1994). University support for school development. In W. Mathis (Ed.), *Field guide to educational renewal: Reports from the field.* Brandon, VT: Holistic Education Press.

Clarke, J., Willey, J., and Maynard, J. (1994). Involving a community in school development. In W. Mathis (Ed.), *Field guide to educational renewal: Reports from the field.* Brandon, VT: Holistic Education Press.

Coalition of Essential Schools. (1994). *Coalition of Essential Schools.* Providence, RI: Brown University.

Coalition of Essential Schools. (1994). Nine principles of the coalition. Providence, RI: Brown University.

Cognition and Technology Group of Vanderbilt University. (1990). Anchored instruction and its relationship to situated cognition. *Educational Researcher, 19*(6):2–6.

Collette, A. T., and Chiappetta, E. L. (1989). *Science instruction in the middle and secondary schools,* 2d ed. Columbus, OH: Merrill Publishing.

Collins, A., Brown, J. S., and Newman, S. (1989). Cognitive apprenticeships: Teaching the craft of writing, reading and mathematics. In L. B. Resnick (Ed.), *Knowing, learning and instruction.* Hillsdale, NJ: Erlbaum.

Cooper, B. L. (1981). Popular music in the social studies classroom. Audio resources for teachers: How to do it series. National Council for the Social Studies. ERIC ED 209163.

Costa, A. (1992). *Developing minds: A resource book for teaching thinking,* 2d ed. Alexandria, VA: ASCD.

Culbertson, J. (1993). Pharaoh's dream . . . and ours. In R. Jennings (Ed.), *Fire in the eyes of youth.* St. Paul: Occasional Press.

Darling-Hammond, L. (1992). *Standards of practice for learning-centered schools.* New York: Teachers College Press.

Deal, T. E. (1994). Keynote Presentation at the Second Annual National Conference on Curriculum Integration, Scottsdale, AZ, January 15.

Denbo, D., Feigenbaum, B., and Morehouse, W. (1984). Global education at the grass roots: Profiles of school-based programs. Washington, DC: Council on International and Public Affairs.

Dewey, J. (1965). *Experience and education.* New York: Collier.

Drake, S. M. (1991). How our team dissolved the boundaries. *Educational Leadership, 49*(2):20–22.

Drinan, J. (1991). The limits of problem-based learning. In D. Boud and G. Feletti (Eds.), *The challenge of problem-based learning.* New York: St. Martin's Press.

Far West Laboratory. (1992). Using portfolios to assess student performance. *Knowledge Brief, 9:*1–7.

Fennelly, S., and Paskiewicz, C. (1993). Graphical analysis of body physics, Wethersfield (CT) High School.

Fogarty, R. (1992). *The mindful school: How to integrate the curricula.* Palatine, IL: Skylight Publishing.

Fogarty, R. (1991). The thinking log: Inking of our thinking. In A. Costa (Ed.), *Developing minds: A resource book for teaching thinking,* vol. 1, pp. 232–242. Alexandria, VA: ASCD.

Fosnot, C. T. (1989). *Enquiring teachers, enquiring learners: A constructivist approach for teaching.* New York: Teachers College, Columbia University.

Freeman, S. L. (1981). Consider Canada: A handbook for teachers. Canadian/Franco American Studies Project. ERIC ED 282782.

Fredericks, A. D., Meinbach, A. M., and Rothlein, L. (1993). *Thematic Units: An Integrated Approach to Teaching Science and Social Studies,* New York: HarperCollins.

Fuentes, K., and Weinberg, P. (1993). New York and the world. In R. Jennings (Ed.), *Fire in the eyes of youth: The humanities in American education.* St. Paul: Occasional Press.

Fullen, M. (1993). *Change forces: Probing the depths of educational reform.* London: Falber Press.

Fulwiler, T. (1987). *Teaching with writing.* Upper Montclair, NJ: Boynton/Cook.

Gall, M. (1984). Synthesis of research on questioning. *Educational Leadership, 42*(3):40–47.

Gallagher, S. A., Stepien, W. J., and Rosenthal, H. (1992). The effects of problem-based learning on problem solving. *Gifted Child Quarterly, 36*(4):195–200.

Gamoran, A. (1992). Is ability grouping equitable? *Educational Leadership, 50*(2):11–15.

Gardner, H. (1985). *Frames of mind: The theory of multiple intelligences.* New York: Basic Books.

Gardner, H. (1993). *Multiple intelligences: The theory in practice.* New York: Basic Books.

Garman, G. (1993). Learning German style. *Telecom Report International, 16:*25–27.

Gilliam, C. (1994). S.A.G.E., Science, Algebra (or Geometry), Geography, English and Human Connections. Presentation at the Second Annual National Conference on Curriculum Integration, Scottsdale, AZ, January 15.

Gish, G. L. (1979). The learning cycle. *Synergist* (Spring), pp. 2–6. Washington, DC: ACTION, U.S. Government Printing Office.

Glasser, W. (1986). *Control theory in the classroom.* New York: Harper & Row.

Glickman, C. D. (1993). *Renewing American schools: A guide for school-based action.* San Francisco: Jossey-Bass.

Goswami, D. (1993). Comment on "Inhabiting other lives." In R. Jennings (Ed.), *Fire in the eyes of youth: The humanities in American education.* St. Paul: Occasional Press.

Gould, S. J. (1981). *The mismeasure of man.* New York: W. W. Norton.

Guilford, J., and Hoepfner, R. (1971). *The analysis of intelligence.* New York: McGraw-Hill.

Gross, S., and Wang, J. (1991). The China project. *Educational Leadership. 49*(4):73–78.

Hamilton, S. F. (1993). Prospects for an American style youth apprenticeship system. *Educational Researcher, 22*(3):11–15.

Heath, P. A. (1992). Organizing for STS teaching and learning: The doing of STS. *Theory into Practice, 31*(1):52–58.

Hellenbrand, H. (1988). American history and literature: An essential dialogue. *Social Studies Review, 28:*64–70.

Hickman, F., Patrick, J., and Bybee, R. (1987). *Science/Technology/Society: A framework for curriculum reform in secondary school science and social studies.* Boulder, CO: Social Science Education Consortium.

Hill, P. T., Foster, G. E., and Gendler, T. (1990). High schools with character. Santa Monica, CA: RAND Corporation.

Hirschy, D., Lopez, H., Rugger, K., and Krull, A. (1993). *The Motion Program.* International High School, New York City.

Hirschy, D., Lopez, H., Stevenson, J., Rugger, K., Weiner, R., and Krull, A. (1993). *Visibility/Invisibility.* International High School, New York City.

Hoffman, E., and Young, M. (1985). From grave rubbings to Maximillian's journey. ERIC ED 262647.

Holland, A., and Andre, T. (1987). Participation in extracurricular activities in secondary school: What is known? What needs to be known? *Review of Educational Research, 57*(4):437–466.

Howard, K. (1993). Portfolio culture in Pittsburgh. In R. Jennings (Ed.), *Fire in the eyes of youth.* St. Paul: Occasional Press.

Hungerford, H., Litherland, R., Peyton, B., Ramsey, J., and Volk, T. (1992). *Investigating and evaluating environmental issues and actions: Skill development modules* (A curriculum development project designed to teach students how to investigate and evaluate science-related social issues). Carbondale, IL: Southern Illinois University (Stipes Publishing).

Hyerle, D. (1990). *Designs for thinking connectively.* Cary, NC: Innovative Sciences, Inc.

Hyerle, D. (1992). *Thinking Maps for transferring thinking skills to content learning.* Cary, NC: Innovative Sciences, Inc.

Hyerle, D. (1994). *Thinking Maps as tools for multiple modes of understanding* (dissertation). University of California at Berkeley.

Hyerle, D., and Lipton, M. (1993). *I see what you mean: Graphic organizers for assessing student thinking.* Cary, NC: Innovative Sciences, Inc.

Jacobs, H. H. (1989). Design options for an integrated curriculum. In H. H. Jacobs (Ed.), *Interdisciplinary curriculum: Design and implementation.* Alexandria, VA: ASCD.

Jacobs, H. H. (1991). On interdisciplinary curriculum: A conversation with Heidi Hayes Jacobs. *Educational Leadership, 49*(6):26.

Jacobs, H. H. (1991). Planning for curriculum integration. *Educational Leadership, 49*(2):27–28.

Jennings, R. (1993). *Fire in the eyes of youth: The humanities in American education.* St. Paul: Occasional Press.

Jobs for the Future. (1993). What's in a name? On the term "Youth Apprenticeship." *Student Apprenticeship News, 1*(5):3.

Jobs for the Future. (1993). Assessments and youth apprenticeships: A fact sheet by Jobs for the Future National Youth Apprenticeship Program. Boston: Jobs for the Future.

Joyce, B., Wolf, J., and Calhoun, E. (1993). *The self-renewing school.* Alexandria, VA: ASCD.

Joyce, W. W. (1985). Canada in the classroom: Content and strategies for the social studies. Washington, DC: National Council for the Social Studies. ERIC ED 278580.

Kallick, B. (1989). Changing school into communities for thinking. Center for Teaching and Learning. Grand Forks, ND: University of North Dakota.

Kallick, B. (1991). Evaluation: A challenge to our critical thinking. In A. Costa (Ed.), *Developing minds: A resource book for teaching thinking,* vol. 1. Alexandria, VA: ASCD.

Kellerman, L. (1993). An issue as an organizer: A case study. In R. Yager (Ed.), *The Science/Technology/Society Movement,* vol. 7. Washington, DC: National Science Teachers Association.

Kim, C. L. (1990). *The fifth discipline: The art and practice of the learning organization* (A conversation with Peter Senge). Framingham, MA: Innovation Associates.

Kirby, K., Bullock, S., Lyle, N., West, M., and O'Neal, J. (1993). *Reinventing ourselves: A large school system takes a journey into redesigning learning and assessment.* Lawrenceville, GA: Gwinnett County Public Schools.

Klein, J. T. (1990). *Interdisciplinarity: History, theory and practice.* Detroit: Wayne State University Press.

Koelsch, N. (1994). *Integrating teaching, learning and assessment.* San Francisco: Far West Laboratory for Educational Research and Development.

Kovalik, S. (1994). Keynote Presentation at the Second Annual Conference on Curriculum Integration, Scottsdale, AZ, January 13.

Kolb, D. (1976). Learning style inventory (manual). Cambridge, MA: McBer and Associates.

Kuhn, T. S. (1970). *The structure of scientific revolutions,* 2d ed. Chicago: The University of Chicago Press.

Kranzburg, M. (1991). Science-Technology-Society: It's as simple as XYZ. *Theory into Practice, 30*(4):230–234.

Levine, T. (1981). *Jumpstreet humanities project learning package.* Washington, DC: NEH. ERIC ED 211442.

Lipson, M. Y., Valencia, S., Wixson, K. K., and Peters, C. (1994). Integration to improve teaching and learning. *Language Arts, 70:*(April).

Mabry, L. (1992). Expanding program assessment methodology: Performance assessment and subjectively evaluated student outcomes. Presentation at the American Evaluation Association Conference, Seattle.

Marger, G. (1992). Integrating science-technology-society into social studies education. *Theory into Practice, 31*(1):20–26.

Marshall, S. (1993). Wingspread Conference Report: Problem-based learning. Aurora, IL: Center for Problem-Based Learning.

Martin, J. A. (1994). Top 10 CD-ROM's. *Macworld, the Macintosh Magazine, 2*(3):91–95.

Marzano, R. J. (1992). *A different kind of classroom: Teaching with dimensions of learning.* Alexandria, VA: ASCD.

Marzano, R., Pickering, D., and McTighe, J. (1993). *Assessing student outcomes: Performance assessment using the Dimensions of Learning Model.* Alexandria, VA: ASCD.

Mathis, W. (1994). *Field guide for educational renewal.* Brandon, VT: Holistic Education Press.

Matson, J. (1993). Designing for failure. In J. Clarke and A. Biddle (Eds.), *Teaching critical thinking: Reports from across the curriculum.* Englewood Cliffs, NJ: Prentice-Hall.

May, M. (1986). Raider of the latest art: American treasure trove. *English Journal, 75*(4):54–56.

Mayer, R. (1989). Models for understanding. *Review of Educational Research, 59*(1):43–64.

McBride, M. (1984). China curriculum for secondary schools. Connecticut Council for Social Studies. ERIC ED 243803.

McCarthy, B. (1990). Using the 4MAT system to bring learning styles to schools. *Educational Leadership, 48*(2):31–37.

McDonald, J., Smith, S., Turner, D., Finney, M., and Barton, E. (1993). *Graduation by exhibition. Assessing genuine achievement.* Alexandria, VA: ASCD.

McKeachie, W. (1984). Spatial strategies: Critique and educa-

tional implications. In C. F. Holley and D. F. Dansereau (Eds.), *Spatial learning strategies: Techniques applications and related issues.* Orlando, FL: Academic Press.

McTighe, J. (1992). Graphic organizers. In J. McTighe (Ed.), *Enhancing learning through cooperative learning.* New York: Teachers College Press.

McTighe, J., and Lyman, F. T. (1988). Cueing thinking: the promise of theory embedded tools. *Educational Leadership, 45*(7):18–22.

Meadows, D. L. (1991). Fish Banks Ltd., National Diffusion Network program. Distributed by The University of New Hampshire, Durham, NH.

Millette, P., and Woodsum, K. (1993). Answering the question, "When Are We Ever Going to Use This?" by integrating high school math and earth science curricula. Presented at the Northeast Regional Meeting of the Geological Society of America, Burlington, VT, March.

Mitchell, R. (1992). *Testing for learning: New approaches to evaluation can improve American schools.* New York: Free Press.

Moffett, J. (1992). *Harmonic learning: Keynoting school reform.* Portsmouth, NH: Boynton/Cook.

Moore, J. (1988). Considerations in getting underway with thematic teaching (unpublished paper). University of Vermont, Burlington.

Moses, Y. (1981). *Anthropology and multicultural education.* Athens, GA: Anthropology Curriculum Project. ERIC ED 231690.

Moss, P. A. (1992). Shifting conceptions of validity in educational measurement: Implications for performance assessment. *Review of Educational Research, 62*(3):229–258.

Munroe, M. J. (1987). BLOCK: Successful alternative format addressing learner needs. Presentation at the Annual Conference of the Association of Teacher Educators, St. Louis, February.

National Center for Improving Science Education. (1989). *Getting started in science: A blueprint.* Andover, MA.

New Standards Project (NSP). (1993). *Using new standards: New work for students,* First Training Volumes 1–4.

Newmann, F. M., and Wehlage, G. G. (1993). Five standards for authentic instruction. *Educational Leadership, 50*(7): 8–12.

Nickerson, R. S., Perkins, D. N., and Smith, E. E. (1985). *The teaching of thinking.* Hillsdale, NJ: Erlbaum.

Norman, G. R., and Schmidt, H. G. (1992). The psychological basis of problem-based learning: A review of the evidence. *Academic Medicine, 67*(9):557–565.

Olcott, M., and Lear, D. (1981). The Civil War letters of Lewis Bissell: A history and literature curriculum. Field School Educational Foundation Press. ERIC ED 247206.

Olsen, C. B. (1991). The thinking/writing connection. In A. Costa (Ed.), *Developing minds: A resource book for teaching thinking,* vol. 1, pp. 232–242 (Rev. ed of vol. 1). Alexandria, VA: ASCD.

O'Neil, J. (1992). Putting performance assessment to the test. *Educational Leadership, 49*(8):14–19.

O'Neil, J. (1993). On the new standards project: Interview with Lauren Resnick and Warren Simmons. *Educational Leadership, 50*(5):9–12.

O'Neil, J. (1994). Aiming for new outcomes: The promise and the reality. *Educational Leadership, 51*(6):6–10.

Ozturk, M. (1991). Education for cross-cultural communication. *Educational Leadership, 49*(4):79–81.

Packer, A. H. (1992). Taking action on the SCANS Report. *Educational Leadership, 49*(2):27–31.

Parisi, L. (1982). China, past and present. A supplemental activity unit on Chinese culture for grades 7–12. ERIC ED 241411.

Perkins, D. N. (1987). Thinking frames: An integrating perspective on teaching cognitive skills. In J. Baron and R. Sternberg (Eds.), *Teaching thinking skills: Theory and research.* New York: W. H. Freeman.

Perkins, D. N. (1988). Thinking frames. *Educational Leadership, 43*(8):4–11.

Perkins, D. N. (1992). *Smart schools: From training memories to educating minds.* New York: Free Press.

Perkins, D. N., and Salomon, G. (1989). Are cognitive skills context bound? *Educational Researcher, 18*(1):16–26.

Peters, R. (1986). The world in perspective: From John Dewey to global perspectives. Plaistow, NH: Center for Applied Ecosocial Studies. ERIC ED 267008.

Petrie, H. G. (1992). Interdisciplinary education: Are we faced with insurmountable opportunities? *Review of Educational Research,* vol. 18, ch. 7.

Piel, E. (1993). Decision-making: A goal of STS. In R. Yager (Ed.), *The Science, Technology, Society Movement,* vol. 7: *What research says to the science teacher.* Washington, DC: National Science Teachers Association.

Polytechnic Institute of Brooklyn (No date). A look into the future. In *Activities approach to the "Man-Made" world.* New York: Polytechnic Institute of Brooklyn.

Postman, N., and Weingartner, C. (1968). *Teaching as a subversive activity.* New York: Dell.

Preece, A. (1994). Self-evaluation: Making it matter. In A. Costa and B. Kallick (Eds.), *Systems thinking for learning organizations.* Alexandria, VA: ASCD.

Presseisen, B. (1988). Avoiding battle at curriculum gulch: Teaching thinking and content. *Educational Leadership, 45*(7):7–10.

Project Zero. (1993). Project Zero: An interdisciplinary research group. Cambridge, MA: Harvard Graduate School of Education.

Purnell, S., and Hill, P. (1992). *Time for reform.* Santa Monica, CA: RAND Corporation.

Ramsey, J., and Hungerford, H. (1989). So . . . you want to teach issues? *Contemporary Education, 60*(3):137–142.

Ramsey, J., Hungerford, H., and Volk, T. (1990). Analyzing the issues of STS. *Science Teacher, 57*(3):63.

Randall, R. E. (1990). *Global education: Educating for our common future.* ERIC ED 354206.

Ravitch, D. (1983). *The troubled crusade: American education, 1945–1980.* New York: Basic Books.

REAL Enterprises. (1993). *REAL Curriculum Guide.* Chapel Hill, NC.

Relan, A., and Kimpson, R. (1991). Curriculum integration: A critical analysis of practical and conceptual issues. Paper presented at the AERA Annual Meeting, Chicago. ERIC ED 334677.

Resnick, L. B. (1987). *Education and learning to think.* Washington, DC: National Academy Press.

Resnick, L. B. (1989). Learning in school and out: The 1987 presidential address. *Educational Researcher, 19*(9):13–20.

Resnick, L., Briars, D., and Lesgold, S. (1992). Certifying accomplishments in mathematics: The New Standards examining system. In I. Wirsup and R. Streit (Eds.), *Proceedings of the University of Chicago School Mathematics Project International Conference on Mathematics Education, vol. 3—Developments in school mathematics around the globe* (pp. 186–207). Reston, VA: National Council of Teachers of Mathematics.

Rettig, M. D., and Canady, R. L. (1993). Scheduling middle schools to reduce school-structured inequality: A transitional plan. Harrisonburg, VA: James Madison University.

Roberts, A. D., and Cawelti, G. (1984). *Redefining general education.* Alexandria, VA: ASCD.

Robertson, E. (1992). Is Dewey's educational vision still viable? *Review of Research in Education,* vol. 18, pp. 335–381.

Rosenfelt, D. (1982). Cross-cultural perspectives in the curriculum: Resources for change. ERIC ED 237392.

Rosenholtz, S., and Simpson, C. (1984). The formation of ability conceptions: Developmental trend or social construction. *Review of Educational Research, 54*(1):31–63.

Ross, B. (1991). Towards a framework for problem-based curricula. In D. Boud and G. Feletti (Eds.), *The challenge of problem-based learning.* New York: St. Martin's Press.

Sable, M. H. (1983). Latin American research resources. ERIC ED 251377.

Sable, M. H., and Clarke, J. (1994). Restructuring a rural school: Cabot rebuilds on higher standards. In W. Mathis (Ed.), *Field guide to educational renewal.* Brandon, VT: Psychological Press.

Saccente, F. (1994). The real world meets the technical drawing curriculum. *Technical Horizons in Education, 21*(8): 72–74.

S.A.G.E. (1994). Science, Algebra (or Geometry), Geography, English and Human Connections. Presentation at Second Annual National Conference on Curriculum Integration, Scottsdale, AZ, January 15.

Sanchez, G. (1993). This hard rock. In R. Jennings (Ed.), *Fire in the eyes of youth: The humanities in American education.* St. Paul: Occasional Press.

Schlechty, P. (1991). *Schools for the 21st century.* San Francisco: Jossey-Bass.

Schon, D. A. (1983). *The reflective practitioner: How professionals think in action.* New York: Basic Books.

School District of Philadelphia. (1993). *World History Project: Teacher resources,* (vols. 1–3).

Schwab, J. J. (1963). *Biology teachers' handbook.* New York: John Wiley.

Senge, P. (1990). *The fifth discipline: The art and practice of the learning organization.* New York: Doubleday.

Shanos, R. (1993). STS: A time for caution. In R. Yager (Ed.), The Science Technology, Society Movement, vol. 7 (pp. 65–72). Washington, DC: National Science Teachers Association.

Shepard, L. (1992). Evaluating test validity. *Review of Research in Education,* vol. 19, pp. 405–450.

Shoemaker, B., and Lewin, L (1993). Curriculum and assessment: Two sides of the same coin. *Educational Leadership, 50*(8):55–59.

Sigel, I. E. (1984). A constructivist perspective for teaching thinking. *Educational Leadership, 42*(3):18–21.

Simmons, W., and Resnick, L. (1992). Assessment as the catalyst of school reform. *Educational Leadership, 49*(February):11–15.

Sizer, T. (1992). *Horace's school: Redesigning the American high school.* Boston: Houghton Mifflin.

Slavin, R. (1990). Ability grouping in secondary schools: A best evidence synthesis. *Review of Educational Research, 60:*471–499.

Snow, C. P. (1959). *The two cultures and the scientific revolution.* New York: Cambridge University Press.

Social Studies Development Center. (1983). The immigrant experience: A Polish-American Model. Bloomington, IN. ERIC ED 258854.

Spady, W. G. (1994). Choosing outcomes of significance. *Educational Leadership, 51*(6):18–23.

Spicer, W. (1986). A core program for the nineties: Changing patterns for instruction, Final report. ERIC ED 298115.

Splitburger, F. (1991). Science-Technology-Society themes in social studies. *Theory into Practice, 30*(4):242–247.

Stepien, W. (1992). Overview of problem-based learning: Materials presented at the Harris Institute on Problem-based Learning. Aurora, IL: Illinois Mathematics and Science Academy.

Stepien, W., and Gallagher, S. (1993). Problem-based learning: As authentic as it gets. *Educational Leadership, 50*(7):25–28.

Stepien, W., Gallagher, S., and Workman, D. (1993). Problem-based learning for traditional and interdisciplinary classrooms (draft manuscript from authors). Aurora, IL: Illinois Mathematics and Science Academy, 1500 W. Sullivan Road.

Tucker, M. (1993). *Designing the new American high school.* Washington, DC: National Alliance for Restructuring Education.

Vars, G. F. (1993). Handout describing the National Association for Core Curriculum, Inc. Kent, OH: Kent State University.

Vermont Institute of Science, Mathematics, and Technology (VISMT). (1994). Curriculum integration and the vital results. Montpelier, VT: Commission Dialogue Paper, January.

Vermont State Technology Council. (1990). Information technology and Vermont education goals (pp. 4–6). Montpelier, VT.

Wajngurt, C. (1993). Problem solving through math journals. In J. H. Clarke and A. W. Biddle (Eds.), *Teaching critical thinking: Reports from across the curriculum.* Englewood Cliffs, NJ: Prentice-Hall.

Walden III: Alternative High School. (1993). Right of Passage Experience (R.O.P.E.) Handbook. Racine, WI: Walden III Alternative High School, 1012 Center St.

Webb, M. (1990). Multicultural education in elementary and secondary schools. ERIC Digest #67: ED 32613.

Weiss, I. (1993). Science teachers rely on the textbook. In R. Yager (Ed.), *The Science, Technology, Society Movement,* vol. 7. Washington, DC: National Science Teachers Association.

Wernsing, J. (1993). Roosevelt Renaissance 2000. Presentation at Second Annual Conference on Work-Based Learning. Cambridge, MA: Jobs for the Future.

Wiggins, G. (1989). Teaching to the (authentic) test. *Educational Leadership, 46*(7):41–47.

Wiggins, G. (1992). Creating tests worth taking. *Educational Leadership, 49*(8):26–33.

Wigginton, E. (1991). Culture begins at home. *Educational Leadership, 48*(14):60–65.

Wisconsin Department of Public Instruction. (1989). *Strategic learning in the content areas.* Madison, WI.

Women's Support Network. (1983). Women's history lesson plan sets. Santa Rosa, CA. ERIC ED 233918.

Workman, B. (1982). How do you visualize a curriculum? *NASSP Bulletin, 66*(54):1–4.

Yager, R. E. (1990). STS: Thinking over the years—An overview of the past decade. *The Science Teacher, 57*(3):52–55.

Yager, R. E. (1993). Science (STS) and critical thinking. In J. Clarke and A. Biddle (Eds.), *Teaching critical thinking: Reports from across the curriculum.* Englewood Cliffs, NJ: Prentice-Hall.

Yager, R., and Roy, R. (1993). STS: Most pervasive and most

radical of reform approaches to science education. In R. Yager (Ed.), *The Science, Technology, Society Movement,* vol. 7: *What research says to the science teacher.* Washington, DC: National Science Teachers Association.

Yager, R., Tamir, P. T., and Kellerman, L. (1994). Success with STS in life sciences, grades 4–12. *The American Biology Teacher, 56*(5):268–275.

Zuga, K. (1991). The technology education experience and what it can contribute to STS. *Theory into Practice, 30*(4):260–266.

Further Reading

Adler, M. (1984). *The Paedeia Program: An educational syllabus.* New York: Macmillan.

Alexander, P. A., and Judy, J. E. (1988). The interaction of domain specific and strategic knowledge in academic performance. *Review of Educational Research, 58*(4):375–404.

Applebee, A. N. (1984). Writing and reasoning. *Review of Educational Research, 54*(4):577–593.

Armstrong, T. (1994). Multiple intelligences in the classroom. Alexandria, VA: ASCD.

Banks, J. A. (1991). Multicultural education: For freedom's sake. *Educational Leadership, 49*(4):32–36.

Blair, D., and Judah, S. (1990). Need a strong foundation for interdisciplinary program? Try 4MAT. *Educational Leadership, 48*(2):37–38.

Boud, D., and Feletti, G. (1991). *The challenge of problem-based learning.* New York: St. Martin's Press.

Duffy, T. M., Kremer, H., and Savery, J. (1994). *Constructivism: Theory and practice.* Bloomington, IN: School of Education, Indiana University.

Durst, R. K., and Newell, G. E. (1989). The uses of function: James Britton's category system and research on writing. *Review of Educational Research, 59*(4):375–394.

Elison, L. (1992). Using multiple intelligences to set goals. *Educational Leadership, 50*(2):69–71.

Fine, M. (1991). Facing history and ourselves: Portrait of a classroom. *Educational Leadership, 49*(14):44–46.

Flower, L., and Hayes, J. (1980). The cognition of discovery: Defining a rhetorical problem. *College Composition and Communication, 31*:21–32.

Fullen, M. (1992). Visions that blind. *Educational Leadership, 49*(5):19–21.

Fullen, M., Bennett, B., and Rolheiser-Bennett, C. (1990). Linking classroom and school improvement. *Educational Leadership, 47*(8):13–19.

Fulwiler, T. (1987). *Writing to learn.* Upper Montclair, NJ: Boynton/Cook.

Gagne, R. M. (1980). Learnable aspects of problem solving. *American Psychologist, 15*(2):84–92.

Gallo, D., and Barksdale, E. (1983). Using fiction in American history. *Social Education, 47*(4):286–289.

George, P. S., Stevenson, C., Thomason, J., and Beane, J. (1992). *The middle school and beyond.* Alexandria, VA: ASCD.

Glaser, R. (1984). Education and thinking: The role of knowledge. *American Psychologist, 39*(2):93–104.

Hoerr, T. R. (1992). How our school applied multiple intelligences theory. *Educational Leadership, 50*(2):62–66.

Honebein, P. C., Duffy, T. M., and Fishman, B. J. (1992). Constructivism and the design of learning environments:

Context and authentic activities for learning. In T. M. Duffy, J. Lowyck, and D. H. Jonassen (Eds.), *Designing environments for constructive learning.* New York: Springer-Verlag.

Hyerle, D. (1991). *Integrating content and process using Thinking Maps.* Cary, NC: Innovative Sciences, Inc.

Kallick, B. (1992). Evaluation: A Collaborative Process in *If Minds Matter,* vol. 2, ch. 26. Palatine, IL: Skyline Publications.

Kallick, B. (1993). Putting it all together. Presentation at the ASCD Conference: *The Curriculum/Assessment Connection: A Miniconference.* Atlanta, November 18–20.

Kiester, E., Jr. (1993). Germany prepares kids for good jobs. *Smithsonian,* (March):44–55.

Larkin, J., McDermott, J., Simon, D. P., and Simon, H. A. (1980). Expert and novice performance in solving physics problems. *Science, 208:*1335–1342.

Lee, V. E., Sryk, A. S., and Smith, J. B. (1993). Organization of effective secondary schools. In L. Darling-Hammond (Ed.), *Review of research in education,* vol. 19, ch. 5, pp. 171–253.

Leshowitz, B. (1993). Teaching students to think critically through problem-based learning. Presented at the Workshop on Problem-Based Learning, Chicago: Illinois Science and Mathematics Academy.

Lohman, D. F. (1989). Human intelligence: An introduction to advances in theory and research. *Review of Educational Research, 59*(4):333–373.

Marzano, R. J., Brandt, R., Hughes, C., Fly-Jones, B., Presseissen, B., Rankin, S., and Suhor, C. (1988). *Dimensions of thinking.* Alexandria, VA: ASCD.

Melendez, A. G., Love, R., and Gonzales, J. (1993). *New Mexico currents: Approaches and resources for teaching New Mexico.* Albuquerque, NM: Hispanic Culture Foundation.

Mitchell, A. R. (1993). *Interdisciplinary instruction in reading comprehension and written communication.* Springfield, IL: Charles C Thomas.

Newell, A., and Simon, H. A. (1972). *Human problem solving.* Englewood Cliffs, NJ: Prentice-Hall.

Olsen, C. B. (1984). Fostering critical thinking through writing. *Educational Leadership, 42*(3):28–39.

Olsen, L. (1994). Bridging the gap: The nations haphazard school-to-work link is getting an overhaul. *Education Week,* (January):26.

O'Neil, J. (1993). Can national standards make a difference? *Educational Leadership, 50*(5):4–8.

Paul, R. (1990). *Critical thinking.* Rohnert Park, CA: Center for Critical Thinking and Moral Critique.

Perkins, D. N. (1986). *Knowledge as design.* Hillsdale, NJ: Erlbaum.

Perrone, V. (1991). *Expanding student assessment.* Alexandria, VA: ASCD.

Petit, M. (1992). *Learning how to show your best: An eighth grader's guide to Vermont's mathematics portfolio.* Cabot, VT: Cabot School.

Rosenstock, G. (1991). The walls come down: The overdue reunification of vocational and academic education. *Phi Delta Kappan,* (February):434–436.

Royer, J. M., Cisero, C., and Carlom, M. (1993). Techniques and procedures for assessing cognitive skills. *Review of Educational Research, 63*(2):201–243.

Schoenfeld, A. H. (1979). Can heuristics be taught? In J. Lochhead and J. Clemmons (Eds.), *Cognitive process instruction* (pp. 315–338). Philadelphia: Franklin Institute Press.

Snyder, K., and Paley, C. (1982). Team English and social studies: An American civilization experience. *History Teacher, 15*(2):197–206.

Stasz, C., Ramsey, K., Eden, R., DaVanzo, J., Farris, H., and Lewis, M. (1993). Classrooms that work: Teaching generic skills in academic and vocational settings. Santa Monica, CA: RAND.

Sternberg, R. M. (1987). Teaching intelligence: The application of cognitive psychology to the improvement of intellectual skills. In J. B. Baron and R. Sternberg (Eds.), *Teaching thinking skills: Theory and practice.* New York: W. H. Freeman.

Vygotsky, L. (1986). *Thought and language* (A. Kozulin, trans.). Cambridge, MA: MIT Press. (Original work published in 1926.)

Voss, J. F., Greene, T. R., Post, T. A., and Penner, B. (1983). Problem-solving skill in the social sciences. In *The psychology of learning,* vol. 17. New York: Academic Press.

Wiggins, G. (1989). Standards, not standardization: Evoking quality student work. *Educational Leadership, 48*(5): 18–21.

Wiggins, G. (1992). The futility of trying to teach everything of importance. *Educational Leadership, 49*(4):44–49.

Willis, S. (1993). Learning through service. *ASCD Update,* August. Alexandria, VA: ASCD.

Wolf, D., Bixby, R., Glenn, J., and Gardner, H. (1991). To use their minds well: New forms of student assessment. *Review of Research in Education,* vol. 17, pp. 31–74.

INDEX